D1514852

DAVID BATHRICK

THE POWERS
OF SPEECH
THE POLITICS
OF CULTURE
IN THE
GDR

▼

University of Nebraska Press: Lincoln & London

Publication of this book
was assisted by a grant from The Andrew
W. Mellon Foundation. Acknowledgments for the use of
previously published material appear on page ix. © copyright 1995 by
the University of Nebraska Press. All rights reserved. Manufactured in the
United States of America. The paper in this book meets the minimum require-
ments of American National Standard for Information Sciences – Permanence of
Paper for Printed Library Materials, ANSI Z39.48-1984
Library of Congress Cataloging in Publication Data   Bathrick, David. The powers of
speech: the politics of culture in the GDR / David Bathrick. p.   cm. – Modern German
culture and literature) Includes bibliographical references and index. ISBN 0-8032-1258-5
(alkaline paper)   1. German literature – Political aspects – Germany (East) 2. German
literature – Germany (East) – History and criticism. 3. Literature and state –
Germany (East) 4. German literature – 20th century – History and criticism. 5. Germany (East) – Cultural policy. I. Title. II. Series.
PT3707.B38 1995 306.2-dc20
95-2354 CIP

for Therese and Frank

CONTENTS

Acknowledgments ix

Introduction: The Powers of Speech 1

PART 1: THE POLITICS OF CULTURE

1. The Writer and the Public Sphere 27

2. Voices from Within: Rudolf Bahro and
Intellectual Opposition in the GDR 57

PART 2: THE POLITICS OF MODERNISM: A
THEATER OF REVOLUTION?

3. Affirmative and Negative Culture: The
Struggle for a Tradition 87

4. From Weimar to Berlin: Reperforming
the Historical Avant-Garde 109

5. History against Itself: Heiner Müller's
Theater of Revolution 129

6. Patricide or Regeneration?: Brecht vs.
Brecht in the 1980s 151

PART 3: THE POLITICS OF THE IRRATIONAL

7. Little Red Riding Hood in the GDR:
Folklore, Mass Culture, and the Avant-
Garde 167

8. The Destruction or the Promotion of
Reason?: Nietzsche in the GDR 193

Epilogue: The Stasi and the Poets 219

Notes 243

Selected Bibliography 269

Index 289

ACKNOWLEDGMENTS

The prolegomena for this book consist of a series of essays written in the 1970s and 1980s in which I sought to analyze the role of critical cultural intellectuals in the process of social change in the GDR. An earlier version of chapter 2 was published as 'The Politics of Culture: Rudolf Bahro and Opposition in the GDR' in *New German Critique* 15 (fall 1978): 3–24. A large section of chapter 3 first appeared in *Social Research* (spring 1980): 166–87 under the title 'Affirmative or Negative Culture: The Avant-Garde under "Actually Existing Socialism" – The Case of the GDR' and is reprinted here with the kind permission of that journal. Chapter 4 represents a revised translation of my essay 'Agitprop-theater in der DDR. Auseinandersetzung mit einer Tradition,' which appeared in *Dramatik der DDR*, ed. Ulrich Profitlich (Frankfurt am Main: Suhrkamp, 1987), 128–49. Chapter 6 first appeared as 'Patricide or Regeneration: Brecht's *Baal* and *Roundheads* in the GDR,' *Theatre Journal* 39, no.4 (December 1987): 434–47 and is reprinted with the kind permission of Johns Hopkins University Press. The initial section of Chapter 5 is based on an earlier version of 'Producing Revolution: Heiner Müller's *Mauser* as Learning Play,' coauthored with Andreas Huyssen and appearing in *New German Critique* 8 (spring 1976): 110–21.

In addition to the above, I should also like to acknowledge the permission to print the following poems: Bertolt Brecht, 'The Solution,' trans. Derek Bowman, in *Poems 1913–1956*, ed. John Willett and Ralph Mannheim, with the cooperation of Erich Fried (London: Methuen, 1976), 440, reprinted with the kind permission of Routledge Press; Günter Kunert, 'Verkündigung des Wetters,' in *Verkündigung des Wetters* (München: Hanser Verlag, 1966), 86, reprinted with the kind permission of the Hanser Verlag; Günter Kunert, 'Als unnötigen Luxus,' in *Der ungebetene Gast* (Berlin: Aufbau Verlag, 1965), 75, reprinted with the kind permission of the Aufbau Verlag.

Acknowledgments

Whenever possible, I have cited from published English translations of original German texts. In those cases in which such translations were not available or deemed inadequate, I have provided my own translations.

Much of the research and even more of the learning for this book began in earnest with my stay in East Germany as a visiting professor at the Humboldt University on an International Research and Exchanges Board (IREX) Fellowship in 1982–83. I owe an enormous debt of gratitude to Allen Kassof, Vivian Abbott, and the entire IREX staff for their continued support of my work in and on the GDR during my tenure on the IREX program committee and as the head of an IREX subcommission on literature and culture from 1984 to 1989. I also wish to acknowledge the support of my colleagues, in particular the faculty and students at the University of Wisconsin from 1970 to 1987, who taught me more than they could ever know or even want to acknowledge and without whom this book could never have happened.

The readers of part or all of this study have been many over the years. For their critical comments and unbending support I am particularly indebted to Andy Rabinbach, Frank Hörnigk, Therese Hörnigk, Jack Zipes, Biddy Martin, Walter Süss, Serafina Bathrick, Helen Fehervary, Allen Hunter, Marc Silberman, Henry Pachter, Peter Hohendahl, Patricia Herminghouse, and Russell Berman. A special word of gratitude is due my unwaveringly rigorous critic Andreas Huyssen, who sometimes seems to know more about what I want to say than I do.

I also wish to offer thanks to my many friends in the GDR who opened their lives and challenged my views so that I might further understand, especially Karlheinz Barck, Simone Barck, Klaus Erforth, Klaus Hermsdorf, Heiner Müller, Michael Opitz, Irene Runge, Dieter Schlenstedt, Silvia Schlenstedt, Adi Stillmark, Sascha Stillmark, and Carola Wiemers.

Finally, I dedicate this book to Therese and Frank Hörnigk, who fed and fought and gave beyond what seemed humanly reasonable at times and whose courageous daily life under socialism taught me much about what it means to be a critical intellectual.

INTRODUCTION:

THE POWERS OF

SPEECH

The 4 November demonstration on the Alexanderplatz in East Berlin was the crowning event in East Germany's October Revolution of 1989. It also marked a moment of unprecedented unity between GDR intellectuals and their people. Summoned into the streets by the official artists union (VBK, Verband bildender Künstler, or Union for Fine Arts/Artists), 500,000 cheering citizens listened to their leading writers pay tribute to the breathtaking events of the previous four weeks.[1] Christa Wolf's concluding words drew on the motto of the 'heroic' Leipzig demonstrations to sum up what some hoped would be a new day in the political life of this beleaguered republic: 'And for me this is the most important sentence of these last weeks: "We are the people!" A simple statement and let us not forget it.'[2]

But many were indeed to 'forget' it almost immediately. The fall of the Wall five days after the demonstration irrevocably reconfigured the direction of political events. Within hours tens of thousands of East Germans were streaming into the West, symbolically never to return again. The 'people's' provocative claim to sovereignty in the face of an oppressive dictatorship, itself a political reversal of Stalinist parlance, quickly metamorphosed under post-Wall, socioeconomic reality into a cry for national unification: 'We are *one* people.' For many of the critical intelligentsia, this meant an end to their utopian dream for a unified movement to build a new, truly democratic socialist order. Their euphoric calls for a 'socialism that does not turn this word into a caricature' (Christoph Hein) or a 'socialism where nobody runs away' (Wolf) were soon rendered politically obsolete and rhetorically hollow by the accelerating push for an-

1

nexation with the Federal Republic. Viewed from the perspective of a population fed up with socialist experimentation, it is not surprising that a manifesto of 26 November entitled 'Für unser Land' (For our country), signed by Christa Wolf, Stefan Heym, Volker Braun, and other intellectuals and calling for the people of the GDR to stop the 'sellout of our material and moral values' and 'develop a socialist alternative to the Federal Republic,' was met with ridicule and even anger in the East and the West.[3] Once portrayed as the harbingers of the revolution, leading dissidents would soon be accused of having defended the 'socialist' status quo, even of having helped sustain the longevity of the dictatorship by staying and publishing there.[4]

Had these critical GDR intellectuals always been pawns of the system despite their efforts to change it? Was the very notion of 'reform from above' effectively a ruse by which the ruling elite had consolidated its power? Were people like Christa Wolf, Christoph Hein, Stefan Heym, Heiner Müller, and Volker Braun ultimately only *Staatsdichter* [poets of the state] with a human face? Or, even worse, had these avowedly antifascist intellectuals unwittingly reenacted the role of political fellow traveler, so familiar from the annals of the Third Reich? Had, finally, the whole notion of an oppositional literary culture in the GDR simply been rendered apocryphal when viewed from a post-Wall, postmodern, even posthistorical perspective?

These are just a few of the queries that fueled the debates during the year preceding German unification.[5] This book represents a response to these questions. While I shall indeed argue, in contrast to some West German journalists and East German exile writers,[6] that the activities of the literary intelligentsia over the years contributed to the process of peaceful social change, even 'revolution,' in the GDR, I am not concerned with establishing the guilt or innocence of individual authors vis-à-vis their involvement with the ruling regime. Rather, I focus upon the evolving institutional and discursive framework of literary and cultural life within East Germany and its relation to the struggles on the part of a number of literary and cultural intellectuals to open up alternative spaces for public speech *from within that framework.* The ultimate goals, political views, and behaviors of individual writers, while important for understanding their own relationship to the power elite at any given time, must also be evaluated in light of what they were or were not actually accomplishing as advocates for change within the broader framework of postwar Eastern European politics.

My choice of this or that individual writer as critical, dissident, or oppositional was dictated in large measure by evolving responses to them on *both* sides of the Wall: all, at one time or another, were denigrated in the East and celebrated in the West for their nonconformity to the official cultural policy of the Socialist Unity Party, or Sozialistische Einheitspartei Deutschlands (SED). In characterizing their political positions, it should also be emphasized that many were convinced Marxists who were or had been members of the Communist Party. Most saw themselves working for a more democratic, humane socialism. None sought to overthrow the existing system as a whole or to replace it with capitalism; nor did they advocate the kinds of market reform and structures of civil society that were such a central part of other Eastern European civil rights movements. As Peter Schneider has pointed out, 'They never questioned the legitimacy of the socialist one-party state . . . [T]heir demands for more democracy were meant not to secure free elections and a multiparty system, but to eliminate censorship and build a plurality of opinion within the socialist power structure.'[7]

Certainly their position 'within the socialist power structure' was one of the factors motivating the massive criticism of GDR writers by Western journalists in the summer of 1990. The debate itself was occasioned by the publication of a fictional story by Christa Wolf entitled *Was bleibt* (*What Remains*), in which she depicted the harassment of a female writer at the hands of the state security (Stasi) in the late 1970s. While the scathing reviews of this book in several leading West German newspapers (*Die Zeit, Frankfurter Allgemeine Zeitung*)[8] focused initially on what was seen to be Wolf's belated attempt to stylize her victim status in order to exonerate herself from any complicity with the cultural and political policies of the SED, the implications of the attack touched on key questions concerning the role of the writer in a socialist public sphere. Wolf, and with Wolf other so-called dissident intellectuals such as Volker Braun, Stefan Heym, Heiner Müller, Christoph Hein, and Helga Königsdorf, were criticized for having mystified and thereby legitimized the real power structures in East Germany by their willingness to publish there and their unwillingness to

3

speak out against the major political transgressions of the day: the building of the Wall in 1961, the invasion of Czechoslovakia in 1968, and, indeed, the activities of the Stasi. Because Wolf focused in her fictional writings on the private and the subjective (Ulrich Greiner spoke of 'that oh so pleasant Christa-Wolf-Sound . . . that doesn't commit you to anything'), she and other writers were accused of having inadvertently perpetuated that very legacy of fascism they claimed to contest, 'that unhappy relationship, long thought a closed book, of the German intellectual with power' (Schirrmacher).

The attacks by Greiner and Schirrmacher prompted immediate responses from every segment of the political spectrum. Moreover, what started as a row about Christa Wolf and literary opposition in the GDR soon developed into an even more fundamental debate about the role of intellectuals and the relation of art to politics in the entire postwar period in East and West Germany.[9] Since much of the discussion touched upon issues and arguments central to the present study, I utilize this first groping, post-Wall attempt at *Vergangenheitsbewältigung* [coming to terms with the past] in order to foreground methodological concerns that will be key to my treatment of intellectual dissent in the GDR.

THE CULTURE OF DISSIDENCE AND THE COLD WAR

A major issue to emerge at the very outset of the debate was the role of Western critics vis-à-vis cultural dissidence in the GDR. Greiner's and Schirrmacher's denunciations of Christa Wolf were not only provocative in terms of their explicit charges. This unequivocating voice of Western accusation also obfuscated the history of its own investment in the very legends it so righteously sought to deflate, conveniently forgetting that the emergence of the GDR dissident writer in the late 1960s was not simply the creation of an Eastern *Kulturpolitik* [cultural policy]. It was also promoted by a Western GDR industry: *Kulturpolitik* and *Kulturindustrie* [culture industry], sometimes hand in hand, two sides of a very complicated system by which writers were elevated to international acclaim – or morally relegated to the dustbin of orthodoxy. Here was a process by which dissidents were celebrated, moral superiority was certified, historical narratives were organized and challenged, and binary systems of value were accepted and utilized.

Thus, in assessing the culture of GDR dissidence historically, we must remember to do so in conjunction with the changing political climates of the *entire* postwar period: in relation to the severities of initially cold and occasionally hot war standoffs; as a part of the shift to economic and cultural competition rather than threats of military annihilation; in the light of *Ostpolitik* [policy toward the East], détente, disarmament, and, finally, the acceptance on both sides of German two-state status. Whatever the crimes of the GDR ruling caste or its obvious lack of legitimacy among the populace at large, what emerged as a central covenant of postwar political culture in East *and* West Germany was a move toward a modus vivendi founded upon the proposition that a liberalizing of the systems on both sides of the Wall would open up relations between the two, would get us beyond war and economic destruction via armaments – maybe even beyond the Wall itself.

But let us return to the realm of literature. The question as to whether the decision of Christa Wolf and others to remain within the system in order to reform it resulted, finally, in 'repressive tolerance' (i.e., a means by which a coercive system only apparently 'liberalizes' itself in order to extend its domination) is an absolutely vital one, and I shall return to this problem often in subsequent chapters.[10] But for Western critics to characterize efforts by GDR writers to establish a voice from within simply as an act of moral capitulation, without the slightest consideration of the role that oppositional discourse played in the West, is nothing short of denial. Given the evolving structures of ideological détente, it should be clear that if there had not been a Christa Wolf, Stefan Heym, Heiner Müller, Wolf Biermann, or, on the other side of the moral ledger, such Party acolytes as Hermann Kant, Wolfgang Harich, Kurt Hager, or Alfred Kurella, we would have had to invent them! This is not to argue that individual intellectuals had no responsibility for the role they played. Nor do I wish to trivialize or underestimate the severity of repression on the part of the ruling apparatus. We must include in the process of evaluation questions concerning Western or, even more precisely, anticommunist as well as liberal and left-wing *investments* in the emergence of a dissident culture in the GDR.

What is this investment in greater detail? In terms of a politics of anticommunism, the matter is clear. The increasing presence of dissidence throughout the East bloc beginning in the mid-1960s and its enormous significance in the West must be viewed in the light of *failed* revolutions within the East bloc during the decade before. The 1953 workers uprising in the GDR as well as the Polish and Hungarian revolts of 1956 helped establish the ground rules for a cold war politics over the next twenty-five years. Basic to these rules were two interlocking propositions: first, efforts to change the existing system, whether through spontaneous strikes (GDR in 1953 and Poland in 1956), planned revolt from below (Hungary in 1956), or reform from above (Czechoslovakia in 1968) would be met with armed intervention if they were deemed a threat to the political hegemony of the Soviet Union; second, the Western powers would respect the geopolitical integrity of the two-bloc system by not intervening militarily in any conflicts within the Soviet area of influence. The acceptance of this latter territorial imperative was most strikingly demonstrated when John F. Kennedy refused to send in troops in order to prevent the building of the Berlin Wall in 1961, even though on the basis of the four power agreements the Western allies had every right to do so. Rather than simply an idealistic affirmation of political bravery on the part of a beleaguered city, Kennedy's 'Ich bin ein Berliner' speech of 1962 can now be seen more realistically as a return salvo in what in retrospect had become a mutually accepted displacement from a potential battle of tanks to a 'war of words' in the struggle to defeat communism.

The culture of dissidence was to become increasingly significant in this displaced battle of the blocs. On one level, the emergence of critical voices even from within the ranks of the Party was greeted in the West as a propaganda triumph of the first order. The struggle for civil rights in the Soviet Union, brought to the surface around issues of freedom of speech, was seen to confirm a central component of the Western totalitarianism argument dating back to its very inception. Key to this Western position of the 1950s and 1960s was the notion that the totalitarian systems of Stalinism and fascism were comparable on the grounds that they both lacked institutional forms protecting free expression, due process, the development of civil society, and democratic rights. The emergence of a democratic opposition in the East demanding greater pluralism in the mid-1960s was depicted as a strong indicator of failure on the part of the entire Soviet system.

In addition to its importance as a weapon in the propaganda struggle, signs of opposition and dissent also pointed to the possibility of change from within, to a peaceful transformation of the socialist system that would lead to both a democratizing of the Soviet Union and a dissolution of tension between the two world powers. Certainly the Soviet scientist and dissident Andrei Sakharov's linking of détente to democratization sought in fact to underline the necessity of *not* sacrificing in the long run the internal civil rights struggle to other economic and political imperatives of two-bloc harmony. In so doing, Sakharov stood against the extreme positions of mutual nonrecognition, on the one hand, and the 'suspected devil's pact' among the superpowers at the expense of their democratic opponents at home, on the other.[11] As I. F. Stone argued, Sakharov was 'no enemy of détente. . . . On the contrary, complete and genuine détente, ideological as well as political coexistence, has been one of the two objectives of the extraordinary campaign that he has been waging since 1968. The other is the democratization of the Soviet Union.'[12]

There is a third important aspect of the dissidence question that is unique to the German situation. The emergence of critical East German intellectuals, with their roots in a German literary and philosophical tradition and speaking to ever larger numbers on the Western side of the Wall, contributed significantly to challenging the legitimacy of official claims (on both sides) to be the sole representative of a German national culture. Günter de Bruyn addressed just this issue in a 1990 article entitled 'On the German Cultural Nation' when he wrote:

> In view of the state's usurpatory omnipotence, the concept of the cultural nation has become important for me in the last two decades, because it was an expression of the fact that culture in the widest sense (from the Ninth Symphony to the way we celebrate Christmas) still connected the inhabitants of the two German states. I had relatives, friends, and readers in both parts of Germany; my life-long interest in German history and literature constantly showed me the artificiality of the border line drawn in 1945.[13]

While these views were increasingly shared (and contested!) by intellectuals in the East and the West beginning in the 1970s,[14] it was the emergence of dissident GDR writers speaking out across the Wall to members of a like-minded generation in the West (Heinrich Böll, Günter Grass, Martin Walser, Hans Werner Richter, Hans Magnus Enzensberger) that perhaps most graphically illustrated an erosion in the notion of two separate cultural German states, with qualitatively opposing traditions.[15]

The growing publication figures and increasing notoriety in the West of such GDR writers as Heiner Müller, Stefan Heym, Christa Wolf, Ulrich Plenzdorf, Christoph Hein, Irmtraud Morgner, and Helga Königsdorf helped break taboos and revise ideological shibboleths on both sides of the German divide. In the East, the notion of an all-German Heiner Müller or Christa Wolf, while lending the system much-needed cultural legitimacy because of the respect for their work internationally, at the same time threatened the supposedly unique identity of this first German socialist national literature 'on German soil.' In addition, the intense dialogue between East and West German writers, assuming as it did shared values about peace, ecology, feminism, and, in many cases, democratic socialism, signalled the blurring of clearly defined cultural and political differences between the two systems – the raison d'être for the existence of the GDR in the first place.[16]

In the West there was also an ideological double bind that emanated from the response of Western critics to literary opposition in the GDR, although of a different nature. Here East German dissidents were initially marketed as oppressed intellectuals whose fate under communism corroborated the superiority of the capitalist system. Yet the fact that these avowedly Marxist and socially committed writers, many of whom continued to publish within East Germany, were being celebrated by mainstream and even conservative critics in the West as great artists helped further undermine a basic aesthetic binarism according to which 'good' art had nothing whatsoever to do with politics. Both Christa Wolf and Heiner Müller won major West German literary prizes and have even been described, in Germany and abroad, as among the greatest living *German* writers. Günter de Bruyn, Ulrich Plenzdorf, Christa Wolf, Heiner Müller, Jurek Becker, Franz Fühmann, Rolf Schneider, Irmtraud Morgner, and even Hermann Kant have all been touted by Western critics as conservative as Marcel Reich-Ranicki for producing a literature that could hold its own with West German standards.[17] It was precisely this increasingly 'liberal' reception of GDR literature in the 1970s and 1980s that critics such as Greiner, Schirrmacher, and Karl Heinz Bohrer sought to challenge in their attacks upon Christa Wolf beginning in the summer of 1990.

But what about the investment of liberal and left-wing critics in the political culture of the GDR? Reflecting upon the disarray among West German socialist intellectuals following 'the departure of real existing socialism,' Helmut Dubiel called for a 'linke Trauerarbeit,' a left-wing mourning of the momentous historical events in Eastern Europe. Significant in Dubiel's discussion was the emphasis upon what he saw as having been repressed in the political culture of postwar West Germany: the intellectual paralysis emanating from the confrontation between a conservative anticommunism, on the one side, and a 'helpless anti-anticommunism,' on the left. 'The critique of one's own political system was neutralized by one's apology for the other,' Dubiel writes of the leftist intellectual, 'with everything ending up at point Zero.'[18] To mourn now the demise of this world would mean for Dubiel to think beyond the either/or; to come to terms intellectually, politically, and morally with socialism's *and* Marxism's historically inadequate answers to questions about cultural pluralism, civil society, freedom of speech, the significance of gender, the role of science and technological/industrial progress, and the notion of violent rupture as the only model for social change.[19]

Dubiel's recasting of postwar/cold war intellectual politics around questions of repression and mourning is helpful for an understanding of left-wing and liberal critics in their relation to the literature and culture of the GDR. The longing for what he called 'an ersatz candidate for a comprehensive alternative socialist politics,' whether in the form of a reputed 'third way' or simply as the search for a more humanist socialism, could be seen as one possible reason for the underlying attachment of Western scholars and critics to the culture of dissidence in the GDR. One could keep alive the utopian dream for a genuine Marxism or a credible socialism while at the same time rejecting (but not really critiquing) its 'real existing' concretization. Conversely, the failure of Western intellectuals to 'mourn,' that is, to work through [*Trauerarbeit*], the 'loss' of that attachment also represents a form of denial. At the very least it would help explain the vindictiveness with which in the summer of 1990 leading liberal West German publications (*Die Zeit* and *Der Spiegel*) and critics, some of whom had helped promote a culture of opposition in East Germany, suddenly discovered a long dormant critical perspective toward the GDR and its dissident poets. Certainly the rhetoric of arrogance helped them efface their own involvement, enabled them to exclude themselves from the death of a project.[20]

To sum up: the collapse of the GDR brought with it a challenge to identity structures basic to how many intellectuals critically conceived and sought to improve the world. This was as valid for East German dissidents as it was for many Western intellectuals.

THE GENERATIONAL QUESTION AND THE LEGACY OF FASCISM

While many of the leading writers in the GDR, like their counterparts throughout the East bloc, played an important and imaginative role in the push toward an alternative society and within the political tumult of the 1980s, their situation was unique – particularly among the first and second generations – in ways that separated them from intellectuals like Czech writer Václav Havel or Adam Michnik of Solidarnösc. Most post-1968 East bloc intellectuals did not view their oppositional struggle as an effort to reform socialism. Rather, theirs was first and foremost a national insurrection against a perceived 'foreign power,' articulated as a struggle to establish constitutionally guaranteed forms of civil society and parliamentary democracy. These differences became particularly evident in the weeks following the demolition of the Wall. As much as GDR dissidents had been at odds with the status quo in their struggle for freedom of speech and more democratic forms of social life, as Marxists and socialists committed to an alternative to the Federal Republic they emerged as spokespeople for a project that put them at odds with the population at large. Thus it was very much a profound misreading on both sides of the national divide – by GDR writers of the broader needs of their own people and on the part of some Western journalists concerning the real intentions of the writers – that led to the anger and confusion in the period following November 1989.

To understand the unique role of GDR writers within the socialist bloc, it is especially important to consider their differing generational experiences. Clearly the GDR intellectuals who were socialized in the 1950s and

1960s (those born between 1929 and 1945) had a relationship to the system that was different from their Eastern colleagues as well as from those GDR writers more recently *hineingeboren* [born into].[21] In this regard, the widespread habit of Western scholars to construct a clearly articulated bifurcation between the Stalinist hierarchy, on the one hand, and the opposition (sometimes underground), on the other, does not apply to the development of a critical discourse by many of the East German dissidents.

Viewed from the perspective of the socialist public sphere, GDR writers were at once the creators of a new audience and a variant of the official voice. As spokespeople and representatives for a struggle to enlarge and enhance the freedoms of speech, their very existence was enabled by, indebted to, and an expression of power. The fact that some of them had been censored, hunted, questioned, and ridiculed does not belie the fact that they were also – and sometimes even simultaneously – privileged, nurtured, courted, and coddled. In a very fundamental, if complicated, way, those writers who continued to publish and speak within the official socialist public sphere ended up functioning, perhaps oxymoronically, as reform-dedicated *Staatsdichter*. In an interview in *Der Spiegel* subsequent to the fall of the Wall, Heiner Müller replied to the question as to where he stood in relation to 'the people' in the GDR with the curt response, 'I was always on both sides.'[22] Indeed, it was precisely their function on both sides of the power divide, as official and nonofficial voices within the whole, that defined a particular kind of intellectual in the GDR.

One can, of course, fault them for this at the level of personal intentions and behaviors: for not speaking out on this or that issue, for losing a sense of the society at large, for failing to grasp the real issues of power and freedom, for chasing a utopian dream. But one can also understand them historically. Here we have a generation of intellectuals who were socialized within the highly dichotomized cold war culture and who found in the mutilated forms of a Stalinist antifascism what they saw as the only chance to start something new in a postwar Germany. Asked in an interview about his relationship to the 'empty' slogans of an 'officially prescribed antifascism [*verordneter Antifaschismus*]' in the GDR, the once dissident and later exiled writer Günter Kunert (b. 1929) spoke for an entire generation when he told how he had internalized those values and what they meant for oppositional writing:

This prescribed antifascism: yes, well I lived through all that and for me it wasn't at all prescribed. I believe that this is a very vital point that is too often misunderstood. The late emergence of any kind of oppositional stand by people in the GDR, also on the part of writers and artists; this somewhat retarded critique of the system is related to the fact that this socialism, unlike the one in other socialist countries, came directly out of fascism. That means that there was a movement here, this socialist-communist movement, which constantly invoked for itself the aura of antifascism by citing the past, the crimes of the Nazis. In so doing, this movement, in which there were many victims and resistance fighters, earned for themselves a special bonus which took a long time to disappear.[23]

This antifascism 'bonus' was certainly a key means by which the SED legitimated itself among intellectuals, as Christa Wolf also acknowledges when she asserts that 'we felt a strong reluctance to organize resistance against people who had been in concentration camps during the Nazi period. We did resist intellectually – for me that became the obvious thing to do starting in the early 1960s – but any massive or even political opposition movement worth mentioning was not formed.'[24] Her clear separation of intellectual resistance and political opposition says much about what that bonus continued to mean right up until the end of the GDR in terms of a basic underlying identity with the project of the Party and the existence of the state, regardless of individual transgressions or even institutional deformations on the part of this or that leader or ruling regime. In a similar vein, Franz Fühmann's much-quoted statement, 'I came by way of Auschwitz into the new social order,'[25] expresses a link that was to serve as an important exculpatory function, particularly during the initial postwar years: the coupling of the GDR state with 'objective' antifascism as a way of guaranteeing a collective moral atonement.

Thus official antifascism, defined in Marxist terms socioeconomically and associated politically with the victims of communist resistance, became an important social imaginary for the absolution of guilt – the separation from the 'bad fathers' – for many living in the GDR. At a psychosocial level, the Marxist-Leninist master narrative about the rise and fall of Nazism functioned to enable a kind of substitute mourning in lieu of a more far-reaching 'working through' of the crimes of the Third Reich.

For instance, as a story of genesis, the SED history of the period 1933 to 1949 was structured to associate the heritage, if not the very existence, of the GDR with a (vastly mythologized) working-class resistance to fascism. For those not in the resistance (i.e., most of the population), there was also a saving grace. Given that fascism was seen as the highest stage of capitalism, and given that the elimination of capitalist property relations ('on the bayonets of the glorious Red Army') in the Soviet Zone had supposedly removed the material and hence the political grounds for fascism, the building of socialism in the GDR came to represent de facto a form of overcoming the past. GDR writer Stephan Hermlin has written astutely of how a discourse founded upon surrogate victory functioned within the larger body politic as a means to compensate and thereby pacify an entire generation of citizens humiliated in defeat: 'One could simply anoint oneself the victor of history. This formula expanded like the ripples in a pond: every citizen of the GDR could suddenly feel him/herself to be on the winning side of history. Flattering and thereby exculpating people this way also makes it easier to rule them. It is difficult to rule people over a long period of time who are feeling guilty about things.'[26]

Certainly the link between the existence of the GDR and the fight against fascism serves in part to explain why so many of the leading writers, despite their repudiation of existing policies, remained almost to the end on both sides; why they, unlike the dissidents from the rest of the Eastern bloc, sought to fashion a voice of resistance out of the discourse of a socialist tradition; and why, finally, the subject of Stalinism was to remain taboo in the GDR for such a long time. 'One would have had to fight antifascists,' Wolfgang Kohlhaase explains, 'in order to fight Stalinism.'[27]

THE POWERS OF SPEECH?

I am supposing that in every society the production of discourse is at once controlled, selected, organized and redistributed according to a certain number of procedures, whose role is to avert its powers and its dangers, to cope with chance events, to evade its ponderous, awesome materiality.
Michel Foucault, 'The Discourse of Language'

But what, in fact, does it mean to be on both sides? Did participation within officially orchestrated public representation constitute a priori a forfeiture of any real resistance, opposition, or even criticism of the system? Or was it possible to contest power relations as a participating member of the literary status quo? And if it was, what would be the framework for realizing, or even evaluating, such a strategy? What then are the powers of speech in a system devoid of formal legal protections for freedoms of expression?

In recent years, attempts to answer these questions have led to a shift in methodological focus in GDR studies toward the premise that 'the comprehension of language allows new insights into the history, society, and behavioral structures of a particular time.'[28] Drawing on the work of Foucault, Lyotard, Barthes, Adorno, Habermas, Bakhtin, and Eliade, some scholars of GDR as well as Soviet culture have sought to reground the study of literature and literary opposition with a paradigm based on competing voices within a 'semiotics of culture'[29] and in relation to the rules of socialist discourse.[30] In so doing, they have sought to challenge the reading of texts simply as discrete, intentional documents that reflect the consciousness or political agenda of this or that social subject or grouping within the larger body politic. Whereas more ideologically or historically critical approaches have often looked at individual writings as being either in conformity with or fundamentally subversive of official cultural policy, analyses oriented toward intertextuality have attempted to reconfigure questions of dissent, opposition, and critical subversion by focusing on the more complex interplay between institutions of power and the various modes of expression within the socialist public sphere.

In most cases, such an approach was *not* intended to depoliticize or dehistoricize the treatment of literary texts by examining exclusively their generic status as linguistic, literary, or aesthetic phenomena. Nor did it deny the importance of earlier studies that sought to trace this literature in relation to the historical phases of cultural policy or sociopolitical history,[31] within the context of Marxist aesthetics and the traditions of socialist literature,[32] in light of the 'function and self-understanding' of individual GDR authors,[33] vis-à-vis the institutionally organized production and consumption of a literary book market,[34] or as an expression of political, social, or 'everyday' consciousness.[35]

However, what such an emphasis upon discourse did seek to establish was how the writing of a text itself is implicated in the process of encoding and decoding history and ideology; how the problems of language and representation force one to rethink the traditional dualisms of text and context, ideology and reality, dominant and subversive works of literature as a network of textual relationships. Writing about the inattentiveness on the part of many historians to problems of reading and interpreting significant texts, Dominick LaCapra has argued that a shift in focus to language and discourse necessarily 'undercuts the dichotomy between text and context and underscores their sometimes ambivalent interaction': '"Text" derives from *texere*, to weave or compose, and in its expanded usage it designates a texture or network of relations interwoven with the problem of language. Its critical role is to problematize conventional distinctions and hierarchies, such as that which presents the text as a simple document or index of a more basic, if not absolute, ground, reality, context.'[36]

My decision to focus on language and discourse has been helpful for unraveling the complex problem of GDR opposition in three interlocking ways: for defining the dominant institutions of official power within the GDR as they are represented and practiced discursively; for understanding how texts and discourses are involved in the complicated process of challenge and transformation within a changing social order; for assessing, finally, the ways that subjects who write and speak publicly may be at one and the same time agents and objects of a power relationship.

In order to delineate how the production of official Marxist-Leninist discourse in the GDR is 'at once controlled, selected, organized and re-distributed' (Foucault), it is important to focus less on explicit ideological pronouncements than on what that ideology does or does not say by virtue of its structural arrangements and procedural operations. Two rhetorical strategies have emerged as important for defining the framework of such a discourse, how it is organized linguistically as well as how it is distributed.

The first concerns the function of discourse as a system of 'exclusion' and 'prohibition,' organized around a dualistic structure by which judgments concerning cultural and societal norms are coded evaluatively – judgments about what is 'true' or 'false,' 'progressive' or 'reactionary,' acceptable or not to be tolerated. Here we are not simply talking about censorship as an institutional practice but rather about the manner in which restrictive aesthetic codes, communicated normatively through the discourses of 'socialist realism' and official *Kulturpolitik*, functioned to legislate value and social identity as a total discursive system.

Key to enacting socialist norms officially was a system of binarisms articulated within a framework that juxtaposed 'enlightenment' and 'antienlightenment' values. Antienlightenment modes of thinking were considered the negative side of the equation and coded variously as 'irrational,' 'bourgeois-individualist,' 'antisocialist,' 'antihumanist,' 'objectively reactionary,' or even 'fascist' in political orientation. To cite one example that will be important for this book: in accordance with such schemata, the writings of Friedrich Nietzsche as an exemplar of 'nineteenth-century irrationalism' and 'bourgeois subjectivism' came to represent one link in a negative chain of ideological deviance to be traced from late-eighteenth-century Romanticism (Schelling, Fichte, et al.) up through the Third Reich into post–World War II forms of existentialism.[37]

As an articulation of power, the 'will to truth' basic to the official Marxist-Leninist binarisms sought above all to prohibit any form of equivocation. Readings of cultural traditions and aesthetic objects had to adhere to a 'singleness' of textual meaning based on a hermeneutical either/or. Works of art that explicitly or implicitly encouraged or enabled ambiguity were, *by that very fact alone,* lacking a clearly articulated sense of *Parteilichkeit* [political commitment]. Peter Zima has labeled such an exclusion of textual ambiguity in the name of a 'unity of cognitive meaning' the 'myth of monosemia.'[38] As I shall argue below, literary dissidence in the GDR often began *not* as a philosophical or political challenge to the ideological principles of Marxist-Leninism but as a sometimes unintended fall into 'polysemic' modes of address that, by virtue of their multiplicity of meaning, were perforce understood and evaluated as negative, that is, as subversive of the official, 'monosemic' mode of discourse.

A second important dimension of the official discourse may be delineated by the major stories it tells.[39] The ideological instantiation of power in the GDR was articulated most coherently in foundational narratives about the genesis of the German socialist state, the struggle to defeat fascism, the liberation of women, the evolution of socialist modes of production, the historical encoding of German cultural heritages, and the function of class in the new society. We are not simply talking about the

Party line on this or that issue but precisely the way abstract historiographical and theoretical conceptualizations were translated into the lingua franca – the speech networks and mythic data – of everyday ethical and political life. Hayden White provides a theoretical model for an analysis of such translations in his effort to undermine the categorial distinctions between literature and history in order to reveal how 'modes of emplotment' inform *all* coherent narratives and how tropes served to construct the linguistic field.[40]

For a writer in the GDR, the problem of ideological or political orientation was not merely a question concerning one's belief in part or all of a philosophical system. Rather, it was a matter of whether one wished to speak publicly or not and *how* one chose to situate oneself in doing so. For to 'speak' meant to function within the paradigms of a carefully delineated and heavily encoded linguistic network and to have internalized the dominant narrative patterns that ensured meaning as part of the lifeworld. One might choose to parody, critique, destabilize, or even attempt to transform them, as many writers did, but in order even to mock one had to partake in the paradigm.

One foundational narrative of vast importance at the level of national discourse concerned one's historical relationship to the Third Reich.[41] While the discourses of class, gender, and production inherited from 'real existing' Soviet socialism were central to the formulation of East German public policy, the narrative of a German socialist 'antifascism' – with its originary conflict in the Weimar Republic of the 1920s and its denouement and closure in the realization of socialism in the GDR – provided a prism through which other languages and narratives were to cohere as expressions of national (or statist) identity.

This national story about fascism was officially inaugurated by the generation of communists returning from exile or domestic imprisonment after 1945 and included the following ingredients: the hagiography of that very generation's struggle and sacrifice in the effort to defeat Hitler and rebuild a society where fascism would never happen again;[42] a prescription for political atonement on the basis of which nonresisters, nonvictims, fellow travelers, and even active Nazis could be anointed 'the victors of history' by virtue of their active participation in the new society (see above); the effacing of specific victims of the Holocaust (Jews, gays, Gypsies) by absorbing and 'commemorating' them under the more generic category of 'the persecuted of fascism [*Die Verfolgten des Faschismus*]'; the construction of a national Other embodied in the existence of the 'imperialist' Federal Republic of West Germany, which was often depicted as having restored capitalist/fascist socioeconomic institutions and having degraded classical, Enlightenment, and humanist cultural values through forms of modernism or commercialized mass culture.

As noted above, the foundational narrative of antifascism was to serve as a national imaginary for many GDR writers of several generations, one within which they would reinscribe the trope of initial fall (into exile from or service to the Third Reich) and attempted renewal/redemption (in the GDR). For members of the exile generation, like Anna Seghers (*The Seventh Cross; Die Toten bleiben jung* [The dead remain young]), Willi Bredel (*Die Prüfung* [The test]; *Die Väter* [The fathers]; *Die Söhne* [The sons]), and Bodo Uhse (*Die Patrioten* [The patriots]), it became a tale of resistance during the Weimar period, banishment into exile, and ultimate return to a newly constituted fold. In the writings of former Wehrmacht soldiers Dieter Noll (*Die Abenteuer des Werner Holt* [The adventures of Werner Holt]), Hermann Kant (*Der Aufenthalt* [The residence]), and Franz Fühmann ('Die Fahrt nach Stalingrad' [The journey to Stalingrad]) we find a ballad of political conversion from brutalizing warrior to good socialist citizen. With the more critical writers of a younger generation, such as Heiner Müller (*Germania Tod in Berlin* [Germania death in Berlin]), Jurek Becker (*Der Boxer* [The boxer]), and Christa Wolf (*Kindheitsmuster* [Patterns of childhood]), there emerges an increasingly problematized view of a German past that continues to haunt the present and that refuses to be overcome by one's simply becoming a citizen of the GDR.

The retelling of the GDR's birth story represents one important terrain upon which the antifascist 'master plot' itself was broadened and inverted to encompass an ever-changing reality.[43] The rewriting of this narrative challenged the models of the status quo that emerged from within the prevailing discourse. Citing Foucault, Wolfgang Emmerich has sought to situate the emergence of a literary 'counterdiscourse' in the GDR historically: 'Beginning in the middle 1960s, significant parts of GDR literature separate themselves . . . from the function of affirming the official discourse and sketch out a notion of literature as "countertext," as a subversion of the prevailing discourse.'[44] Emmerich's criteria for such subversion point to the significance of modernist and Romantic traditions for authors seeking to undermine *and* reinscribe official speech networks at the level of formal technique as well as genre. In the case of the novel, the use of self-reflexive narration, montage, and discontinuity borrowed from the experimental European novel of the 1920s (Joyce, Döblin, Musil) as well as the employment of Romantic narrative traditions of the fantastic and the grotesque[45] destabilized notions of 'realism' that had served as the foundations of aesthetic control in the GDR. Similarly, lyric poets such as Adolf Endler, Karl Mickel, Sarah Kirsch, and Volker Braun engaged in an 'intertextuality' and a 'dialogicity' that 'loosen' the monosemic controls of what one critic, referring to Roland Barthes, has called the 'encrastic language' of the status quo.[46]

While the discourse models employed by Zima, Emmerich, and Berendse help reconfigure the issue of dissent in the GDR within a framework of language and power, they, too, come to rely on forms of binarism. The facile juxtaposition of master discourse (*Leitdiskurs,* monosemia, or encrastic language) to counterdiscourse (countertext, polysemia, etc.) suggests a discreteness of separation that denies the truly contextual and historical nature of the problem we are addressing. The struggle to rewrite and reinscribe the master plot is precisely a process by which one as writer is textually engaged in stretching or realigning cultural political mappings. For example, Christa Wolf continually invokes and at the same time violates a set of formal and ideological codes and in so doing renders those very boundaries historically transfigured. Is she inside or out? On one side or the other? Are the very metaphors of border and boundary even adequate for understanding the fluidity of such a linguistic evolution?

The forms of opposition I treat in this book emerge in every instance from a rewriting of some master code from within the code itself. This is as true for writers of fictional literature as it is for intellectuals within the ideological apparatus or the scientific communities. For instance, the physicist Robert Havemann's critique of the theory and practice of Soviet anti-Einsteinian science in the 1950s generates a reading of that *Urtext* of dialectical materialism [*Diamat*], Friedrich Engels's *Dialectics of Nature,* in order to derive an appropriately Marxist salvation of the theory of relativity. Similarly, Rudolf Bahro's devastating critique of real existing socialism in the GDR entailed readings 'against the grain' of historical materialist [*Histomat*] orthodoxy from within a broadened range of Marxist, pre-Marxist, and neo-Marxist thought running from Hegel through August Wittfogel, Antonio Gramsci, Isaac Deutscher, and Ernest Mandel. Common to both the literary artists as well as other members of the oppositional intelligentsia was a commitment to socialism, not as the real existing system in which they lived but as a rhetorical terrain within which they could generate a position of critique and change.[47] With the exception of the epilogue, this book is concerned with those intellectuals and generations of intellectuals who shared such a view.

But what about the upstart intellectuals who absolutely refused dialogue with the status quo – those more recently *hineingeboren?* Among the youngest generation of oppositional GDR poets to emerge in the 1980s, a commitment to reform socialism was no longer felt to be a viable alternative. Indeed, for the so-called Prenzlauer Berg poets, the language of the official system was absolutely devoid of any potential transformation. Not surprisingly, they came to view the intellectuals of the older generation such as Wolf, Hein, Müller, and above all Volker Braun as being *inside,* not outside or in any way subversive, of official discourse in the GDR. Moreover, unlike their forebears, these intellectuals looked to the theories of French poststructuralism, *not* to a revisionist Marxism, to critique an official language they felt was unable to grasp the 'value of things.'[48] Michael Thulin, a young poet and spokesperson for this group, describes this 'linguistic' crisis in terms very reminiscent of Hugo von Hofmannsthal's famous *Letter to Lord Chandos:*

> That the all-prevailing linguistic order no longer made sense was not
> only the experience of the 1980s; it was a general dilemma. One's very
> words were occupied [*be-setzt*], their meanings at the same time disenfranchised [*ent-setzt*]. And in being bound to a handful of encompassable paradigms of meaning [*Bedeutungsmuster*], language itself
> appeared to have sacrificed part of its power to name and create.[49]

For the poets of the Prenzlauer Berg, the only way out of such a dilemma was to move to the margins of the social order. Their places of abode were often the bohemian slum sections of major cities like Berlin, Leipzig, and

Dresden; their source of employment, the handicraft world of preindustrial artisans; their mode of survival, an effort to recapture a genuine language above and beyond: 'An authentic communication can only be opened if one consciously distances oneself from the conventions of power and its language and places oneself on the edges of society.'[50] For these outcast writers of the 1980s, authentic communication was not something that could be realized within the public domain. Reiner Schedlinski's meditation on the impossibility of public speech is at the same time an indictment of those who sought to generate change from within the prevailing discursive order: 'I thought about forbidden language, . . . about the distance of public rhetoric, about the impossibility of speaking with public officials and functionaries, . . . about the general speechlessness.'[51]

In the epilogue I stage a debate (one that never took place) between two generations of GDR intellectuals – those who worked institutionally from within and those who dropped out – around questions concerning what is political opposition or a genuine public voice, around issues of outside and inside. It is perhaps ironic that the critique of Christa Wolf's generation launched by the Prenzlauer Berg poets from within the GDR in the final years leading up to fall of the Wall in many ways anticipated, almost to the letter, the attack of the West German journalists in the summer of 1990. Both argued that any notion of a genuine opposition in the GDR was, in the words of GDR poet Uwe Kolbe, a 'phantom';[52] both suggested that the culture of dissidence played into the strategies of control and manipulation by the ruling elite. The younger generation poets went the extra step and linked the failure of opposition to the inability to find 'another language.'[53] The power of speech in their paradigm was a one-way street – the prevailing discourse disempowered *any* effort to challenge the status quo.

THE RESPONSIBILITY OF PUBLIC INTELLECTUALS

Given the growing pre- and post-Wall public image of the Prenzlauer Connection as 'the most significant, highly independent literary movement to emerge from the terrain of the GDR,'[54] one can imagine the shock, in November 1991, when it was revealed that two of their most important and visible leaders, Sascha Anderson and Reiner Schedlinski, had been serving as unofficial informants for the East German security system, Anderson since the mid-1970s. Yet these allegations were ultimately to pale in the light of subsequent revelations in January 1993 that the two doyen figures of GDR literature, Heiner Müller and Christa Wolf, were also known to have spoken if not worked with the Stasi.[55]

The questions that emerged from all these disclosures reopened fundamental issues concerning the role of GDR intellectuals that had first emerged in the Christa Wolf debate in the summer of 1990. Was the whole literary opposition itself simply the cynical creation of the East German Stasi as a means to control and manipulate social transition in the GDR? Even more condemnatory, don't such revelations lay to rest once and for all *any* 'belief in a genuine, uncontaminated GDR art,' as suggested by Frank Schirrmacher?[56] And does not the case of the East German intellectual in toto confirm Ulrich Greiner's assertion that 'no other system opened up for intellectuals such possibilities for political power and at the same time demanded such sacrifice as did communism'?[57]

The concerns that have emerged concerning GDR intellectuals under socialism take us to the inner dilemma of the Foucaultian paradigm. If the world of socialist power weaves for itself a closed web through the power of its language, how do we justify *any* efforts to work from within the discursive system? Is not any negative articulation of resistance simply the recapitulation of the system itself in another form? My efforts to answer these and similar questions have led to three emphases that it would be important to signal, if not develop, at this point.

The first is that the linguistic system itself undergoes constant historical change. The process of creative reinscription, even within a highly codified system of cultural norms, is never simply a replication of what was found at hand. A simple study of the modes of what was understood as socialist realism or the socialist canon in the 1950s reveals little in common with the literary paradigms and textual practices prevailing in the 1980s.[58] The breakthrough of modernism (and a critical discourse about 'modernization') in the 1960s brought with it a fragmenting and pluralizing of cultural expression, thematically as well as aesthetically.[59] The emergence of women's literature, ecology literature, literature dealing with alienation and the crisis of the individual in a totally administered society, as well as artistic innovations in the novel and drama all represented new modes of address that evacuated and reconvened notions about the 'real,' about 'socialism,' and about the relationship between the two. There were many contributing factors to the transformation of cultural codes. Certainly one of them was the willingness on the part of individual writers to experiment and take risks.

A second important factor in the development of literary opposition in the GDR had to do with the *institutional* erosion of a monosemic public space. The rapprochement between the government and the Protestant Church in 1971 meant both an attempted cooptation by the regime of an institution that had heretofore remained outside of official public life and the beginning of a process whereby distinctions between private and public space in the GDR were to be blurred and finally openly and aggressively contested in the struggle for societal pluralization. The emergence of civil rights movements around issues of peace, women, ecology, and freedom of speech within and around the church provided an alternative institutional challenge to the official public sphere in the GDR. It will be one of the tasks of this book to demonstrate the mutual interplay between the breakdown of a monosemic discourse by leading cultural intellectuals within the institutions of official power, on the one hand, and the more broadly based struggle for social reform that came to the surface in the fall of 1989.

Finally, this book will concern itself with the unique role of the GDR intellectual within the socialist bloc. The differences between GDR and other Eastern European writers lie less in any innate national characteristics among the countries involved than in the preceding twelve-year histories within Europe from 1933 to 1945. The political and cultural legacies of German fascism profoundly shaped both the formation of the postwar socialist state as well as the modes of political and cultural resistance that arose to oppose it. The discursive politics of antifascism in the GDR were always doubly endowed. On the one hand, as a message of critical atonement and remembering, it offered the promise of rebirth through the building of a socioeconomic order free of the inequalities and compromises glimpsed as so central to the Federal Republic. Yet that very promise served to legitimate a Stalinist status quo whose monolithic grasp of power would precisely prohibit any such move toward greater liberation. Those intellectuals who chose to wage their struggle for a better Germany within the interstices and power structures of GDR socialism may have erred in their judgment about the possibility to do so or the support of those for whom they purportedly spoke. For this they should and will be criticized. What should not be forgotten in the post-Wall frenzy to erase the past are the historical contingencies out of which these writers spoke and what they actually accomplished regardless of any intentions.

I intend to stress the increasing importance of discourse, language, and cultural encoding as systems of interpretive communication through which power was articulated *and* contested in the GDR. The fact that writers and artists became so central both as figures of official legitimation and as a source for social change cannot be attributed simply to the traditional German reverence for the *Denker und Dichter* [thinkers and poets] as prophets and seers. It also stems more specifically from the increasing failures of official ideology in the GDR to provide a sense of value and cohesion, together with the ability of writers and artists to speak a language of 'authenticity' at a moment of crisis. Certainly this was a language that at times bound them closely to the values, institutions, and individuals with whom they were in conflict. It was also a language that permitted the development of a literature that would hold its own in the struggle for social and cultural self-expression.

PART 1: THE POLITICS OF CULTURE

1. THE WRITER AND THE
PUBLIC SPHERE

I n November 1976, the East German poet and ballad singer Wolf Biermann had his citizenship revoked and was refused readmittance to his country while on a concert tour in West Germany. Biermann, it was asserted, had provoked the GDR regime in his nationally televised concert held in Köln. The ensuing uproar in both East and West Germany led to the first political crisis in the then five-year reign of Erich Honecker. Within the GDR, the unprecedented collective and public response to Biermann's expulsion, even by writers in the Party hierarchy, clearly signaled a miscalculation by the ruling Socialist Unity Party (SED).[1] But more significantly, it also indicated a new willingness on the part of heretofore isolated individuals to assert their rights of expression publicly. The fact that a petition of protest was eventually signed by over 150 prominent artists from every walk of cultural life – many of whom risked permanent professional liability and in some cases exile – indicated the extent to which the issue of Wolf Biermann had come to represent a measuring stick for civil welfare within the population as a whole.[2]

But why Biermann and why the uproar? Viewed within the framework of *Deutschlandpolitik* [all-German politics], the case of the poet Wolf Biermann had exemplary, indeed symbolic, significance. The son of a communist in the resistance movement who had been executed by the Nazis, Biermann had emigrated to East Berlin from his native city of Hamburg, West Germany, in 1953 at the age of sixteen. His success as a poet and singer in the early 1960s led to concert appearances and growing popularity in both East and West Germany. It also got him into trouble with Party authorities. Despite his status as convinced communist, Biermann's poetic call for reform and his critique of 'real existing socialism' were seen to violate norms of accepted cultural discourse in the GDR: as of

1965 he was not permitted to publish or perform there publicly. The fact that he continued to publish all of his work in the West following this *Berufsverbot* [professional prohibition] only intensified the efforts to isolate him at home. As a poet speaking to and through the 'other' (West) Germany, Biermann had become a symbol of youthful rebellion and political change to new generations on both sides of the Wall.

However, the unprecedented response to the Biermann ousting cannot be explained merely in terms of *Deutschlandpolitik*. Looked at in relation to a larger set of events stretching from Prague 1968 to Gdansk 1980, the broadened protest was clearly part of a growing if uncoordinated effort to carve out a more flexible version of democratic pluralism from within the structures of mono-organizational socialism. To be sure, the reform movement of Alexander Dubček in Czechoslovakia and the explosion of self-determination under the aegis of Solidarnösc in Poland stand in marked contrast to the abortive efforts by a group of intellectuals to reinstate Wolf Biermann in the GDR. From its inception one of the most authoritarian and 'democratically centrist' parties within the communist bloc, the ruling elite in the GDR had continued to keep much of its repressive surveillance apparatus in place under the reign of Erich Honecker in the 1970s. Yet viewed in the light of subsequent events throughout Eastern Europe in the 1980s, the Biermann episode may indeed be seen as a fundamental turning point in the struggle for civil rights in the GDR: for many, it provided evidence for the impossibility of working within the parameters of Party reform and for the necessity to carry the fight for social change beyond the framework of individual cultural dissent into more collective forms of social organization.

In addition to political motivations, there are also social and economic realities that explain why freedom of speech and assembly were emerging as paramount concerns in all the more advanced industrial societies of Eastern Europe. Central in this regard were growing expectations stimulated both by economic growth and by the political promise that came with Khrushchev's de-Stalinization measures in the 1960s. Populations throughout the bloc became considerably less willing to postpone basic demands for self-determination, be they expressed in the choice of a product, the voicing of an idea, or even the right to travel. In the case of East Germany, increased production and higher living standards under the NÖS (Neues ökonomisches System, or New Economic System) in the 1960s had helped overcome the austerity of the *Aufbaujahre* [construction years: 1945–1961], resulting in a significant rise as well in social needs and consumer expectations.[3] It is true, of course, that the GDR's proximity to West Germany, which included continuous bombardment by Western advertising via the television and radio airwaves, presented a somewhat unique situation when compared with other socialist countries. But this, I would argue, made the GDR merely an extreme example of the rule, not its exception.

Obviously higher standards of living do not, in and of themselves, mean unrest among a population. Legitimation through consumerism rather than ideology, the so-called social contract,[4] had been one way socialist regimes sought to pacify their populations' desire for more structural change and win support for Party policy. Certainly the substantial gains under Honecker's leadership in the areas of personal income, private ownership of durable goods, social welfare spending, and housing construction had provided an effective means of social control. But the long-term impact of such a policy was at best two-sided. Increased standards of living and the satisfaction of the basics, as much as they might temporarily enhance identification with a system, just as easily spiral into increased desires for consumerism and freedom of movement, which are inevitable outgrowths of societal modernization.

A further structural reason for the growing demand for civil rights can be linked to the building of an industrial sector that became increasingly dependent upon ever more sophisticated forms of scientific training and the exchange of information. While the development of refined industries and high technology again gave the GDR a special status in this area, it is clear that within the bloc as a whole any hope to compete with the West in the age of computerism and cybernetics necessarily entailed expanding areas of higher and general education.[5] Moreover, in the process of creating such a capacity, industrial economies like the USSR, Hungary, Czechoslovakia, and the GDR had to rely increasingly on forms of communication and the development of knowledge industries that inevitably challenged the hierarchical structures of power and control inherent to 'democratic centralism.'[6] One of the important lessons of *perestroika* in the USSR under Gorbachev was the extent to which the efficient use of modern technologies increased demands for freedom in the development of horizontal as well as vertical communication systems. In this light, it is interesting to note that in defending the goals of the short-lived 'democratic movement' in the Soviet Union during the late 1960s, Andrei Sakharov prophetically argued – much in the manner of Czechoslovakian intellectuals during the spring of 1968 – on pragmatic rather than moral or even political grounds: 'Under conditions of a modern industrial society, in which the role of the intelligentsia becomes increasingly important, . . . dissension can only be described as suicidal.'[7]

However, just as important as issues of national identity or the growing significance of the intelligentsia for an understanding of the Biermann protest is the fact that the central figure himself was a poet. In the GDR, as in other socialist societies, the area of culture and in particular literature came to provide an invaluable forum for articulating the needs for pluralism and for actively organizing the groundwork for a more democratic public sphere.[8] More than any other public institution, the literary writer served as spokesperson for issues of moral, philosophical, social, and above all political significance – a role that far transcended the social function traditionally accorded the realm of belles lettres in Western capitalist societies. Thus our effort to understand the political uproar around Biermann leads us necessarily to consider more fully the unique place of literature and the writer within a rapidly changing public life. In so doing, two major topics emerge that will be central points of analysis for the remainder of this chapter.

The first concerns the evolution of public life in the GDR both within the context of the cold war and in its relation to the political and cultural legacies of Nazism and socialism. To comprehend the absolutely central role of literature and culture in the GDR as it revealed itself in the crisis around Biermann in the mid-1970s, one must grasp the institutional and discursive histories within which the literary public sphere emerged and took on the role that it did.

The second examines more specifically the unique position of literary writers in that society, with particular focus upon the changes that occurred after 1970 in their attitudes about the role of the intellectual under socialism. As officially commissioned purveyors of governmental policy, artists in the GDR were from the beginning accorded an institutional status unknown to their counterparts in the West. That some were increasingly willing to use this position to provide an alternative voice to that of the status quo says as much about the powers of poetic speech to challenge critically codified representations and officially intended meanings as it does about the structural tolerances inherent to literary discourse itself. I now examine the contradictory institutional role of the writer in the GDR as a historically constituted discursive practice.

THE EMERGENCE OF OFFICIAL PUBLIC LIFE

The officially sanctioned socialist public sphere in the GDR developed from the confluence of two separate but interlocking histories: within the German tradition, institutional legacies inherited from the Weimar Republic and the Third Reich; coming from the Soviet Union, Party-orchestrated public life as it evolved between the Bolshevik revolution and the founding of the people's republics.

Concerning German fascism, Ralf Dahrendorf in his *Gesellschaft und Demokratie in Deutschland* (Society and democracy in Germany) has argued convincingly that the twelve-year Third Reich must be understood not as a momentary seizure of political power but as a thoroughgoing transformation of the state for purposes of what he called 'modernization.' While Dahrendorf surely exaggerates the integrative impulses of the Third Reich, his emphasis upon modernization does help us understand the contradictory nature of life under fascism. If the myths of National Socialism spoke of a return to communal values and a rejection of modernity as the cornerstone of a 'new' politics, the reality of Nazi rule was profoundly the opposite in a number of important respects: Nazi *Gleichschaltung* [synchronization] as a metaphor of technology meant literally a 'gearing to the same,' a streamlining of public and state institutions to the needs of a coordinated, synchronous whole. While the burning of the Reichstag and the abolishment of parliament in 1933 declared in spectacular fashion Hitler's all-out war on civil society, that was only the beginning. What followed were the abrogation of states' rights, the integration of public bureaucracies, the virtual elimination of autonomous economic institutions and their replacement by state-controlled organizational patterns, and, finally, massive incursions into those organizations that traditionally had remained further removed from the state, such as churches, labor unions, youth groups, universities, and even the family.

The fascist accomplishments toward integration and *Gleichschaltung* provide one key institutional legacy for the building of socialist public life after the war. Liberation in 1945 in the SBZ (Sovietische Besatzungszone, or Soviet zone of occupation) did not mean, either ideologically or institutionally, a return to the status quo ante in terms of regenerating a separate civil society or other public organs of state democracy. De-Nazification and the *Aufbaujahre* saw, rather, the expropriation of large industrial corporations and private landholdings, particularly where complicity with the war machine was involved; the removal of culpable individuals from positions of public authority; and the taking over of what were perceived to be the neutral organs of the state. This latter policy was completely in keeping with Marxist-Leninist theory, which had always held the state to be merely a committee – an instrument as it were – in the hands of the ruling class and which therefore tended to discredit any separation of state and society as 'formal,' that is, 'bourgeois,' democracy. 'Real' democracy, on the other hand, was purportedly represented by the policies of the Party, which as the embodiment of the general 'proletarian will' was itself constituted as the pedagogical mediator of all social value.

The basic premises of so-called real democracy permeated every aspect of political life in the GDR and provided the official rationale for the mono-organizational authority of the SED. Although the GDR constitution guaranteed freedom of expression, freedom of assembly, and freedom of the press (but not the right to strike or the right to emigrate), these rights were only to be exercised 'in accordance with the basic principles of the constitution,' that is, in accordance with the 'leading role of the working class and its Party.' Similarly, the East German parliament, the Volkskammer, while including a number of different political parties and mass organizations, was also organized in its electoral and internal voting practices in such a way as to guarantee control by the SED.[9]

Thus, as far as state and civil society were concerned, the socialist revolution under the Socialist Unity Party of the newly founded GDR continued the process of dismantling established enclaves of tradition and civil autonomy. While these strategies contributed to genuine forms of de-Nazification by removing many of the institutional and even personal elements that had been the backbone of fascist power in Germany, they also resulted in increased integration of all public life under the auspices of Party-controlled state structures. As in the other people's democracies, the one official labor organization, the FDGB (Freier deutscher Gewerkschafts-bund, or League for Free German Unions), did not function as an autonomous collective representative of worker interests. Like many other official organizations, such as the FDJ (Freie deutsche Jugend, or Free German Youth) and DFD (Demokratischer Frauenbund Deutschlands, or Democratic Women's League of Germany), it was merely a Party formation without an independent constituency or political legitimacy in the populace as a whole.

Perhaps the most striking example of integrational modernization took place in the area of farming. In contrast to Poland and Hungary, East German agriculture was reformed with a vengeance. Begun in 1952 and accelerated with state violence in the early months of 1960 (40 percent of existing production was collectivized between January and April of that year), GDR two-step collectivization meant a radical integration of rural life into the centralized system of government and into a metropolitan lifestyle. This thorough industrialization of the land, along with regional redistricting of the five traditional states [*Länder*] into fourteen counties [*Bezirke*], further eliminated any potential resistance to central authority by ethnic, regional, or local cultures – or even a potential balance of power between city and country in the GDR.[10]

Regarding the church, the process of integration was a somewhat longer and more conflicted one. From the earliest years of the GDR, the prevailing relationship between church and state, both for the majority Protestants as well as for Catholics, was founded upon survival, internal autonomy, and gradual integration into the political life of the society. When the Protestant Church proclaimed itself 'not against, not parallel but *within* Socialism'[11] in 1971, it marked the end of 'inner emigration' and the beginning of participation and public involvement in social life. However, in both phases, in the earlier period of repression and withdrawal and then during the 1970s, the church was severely limited in its role as an articulator of social needs within the public sphere. When some church leaders began to involve themselves more actively in social issues, such as their engagement in the peace movement, against military conscription, and for civil rights, they offered a forum for other voices in the society, many of whom, at least initially, were poets and writers wishing to articulate alternative views not tolerated in the official media.

In exploring the evolution of institutional public life in the GDR, it has been important to situate it within a context of the changing post–Third Reich and cold war periods. Simply in descriptive terms, and not as a normative category in the Habermasian sense (see part 3), it is helpful to delineate three major public spheres – *Öffentlichkeiten* – as they emerged in the GDR prior to the events of 1989.[12] The first can be defined as the official public sphere under Party control, which, in Lenin's original definition, saw its task in transforming the press from an 'organ of sensation,' a mere apparatus for the latest news, into an instrument for economic and political 'reeducation of the masses.'[13] We shall discuss below (part 2) how the official literary public sphere was itself organized in the 1950s as an instrument of pedagogy for the transformation of consciousness in the struggle to build a new socialist order.

A second public sphere, unique to the GDR as an Eastern bloc nation, was defined by the role of the media coming from the Federal Republic, in particular television, which played an inestimable role in organizing, creating, orchestrating, and ultimately homogenizing the needs of the two advanced industrial societies, both in terms of consumer policies and politically in relation to each other. In very significant ways, East and West German television and radio programming were carefully structured as systems of debate and rebuttal, persuasion and its counter.[14]

A third public sphere, historically more recent in origin and the most difficult to define, consisted of the various unofficial public enclaves or counterofficial voices that sought to break into or establish dialogue with the officially dominating voices. This third category includes literary writers, the Protestant Church, the feminist, peace, ecology, and gay movements, as well as members of the underground culture scenes (jazz, rock, and punk musicians, filmmakers, artists, poets, etc.), all of whom struggled to establish semi-autonomous terrains of publicness, either partially within or wholly outside of official institutions.

These are *not* clearly distinct areas of public or official life, and it will be important to define the ways in which they interacted and overlapped in the developing struggle for control and self-assertion. As I have argued in the introduction, the line between an official and nonofficial public sphere – between dissent and approbation, critical dialogue and ultimate affirmation – was a thin, if not invisible, one, to be understood at each and every juncture as historically redetermined.

THE LITERARY PUBLIC SPHERE

What were they once, the poets and writers? Eulogists, court fools, entertainers some, spoiled and never taken seriously; prophets, Cassandras, critics, rebels and revolutionaries, the others, persecuted and feared – but all finally, homeless in their society, decoration or threat. And what are they today? 'Engineers of the soul.' Or master builders. Or inner architects. Or whatever. All metaphors fail in some way.
Rudolf Bartsch, *Die Zerreißprobe*

One of the first areas of institutional public life in the GDR where more open discussions concerning social needs and political crises did take place was that of culture and literature. To be sure, most accepted cultural production was initiated, sponsored, and controlled by the myriad state- and Party-organized bodies for the goals they deemed appropriate. Yet while literature and culture did indeed play vital roles as agencies of socialization and ideological legitimation, this very centrality helped facilitate the development historically of critical discourses and the articulation of alternative political views within the larger polity.

Certainly as an institution, the writer in the GDR bore little resemblance to his or her counterpart in a capitalist society.[15] As an integral member of what the first minister of culture, Johannes R. Becher, termed the Society of Literature (Literaturgesellschaft), the writer was part of a carefully coordinated system running from the local company library through the State Ministry of Culture to the Central Committee of the SED.[16] The society had three specific goals: to encourage participation of the working masses in the literary process; to move toward eliminating the separation between elitist and mass literature; and to further the appropriation of the literary heritage by the working class. While highly developed educational policies in the GDR led to appreciable compensatory advances and hence to the partial realization of the last two points, literary production for the most part revolved around a specialized group of the intelligentsia.

35

The one official attempt to establish a workers' writing movement, the so-called Bitterfeld movement, begun in 1959, was subsequently to be deemed a failure in terms of its claimed goal to produce a new and revolutionary literature from the ranks of the working proletariat.

A linchpin in the interlocking network of literary institutions was the German Writers Union (Deutscher Schriftstellerverband, or DSV). Founded at the Third Writers Congress in 1952, the DSV included members from every sector of the literary public sphere: most leading authors, translators of belles lettres, journalists, editors of leading literary journals, publishers, publishers' readers, critics, and literary scholars. The general function of the DSV was to act as an ideological 'transmission belt' (Lenin) between Party and writer – as a means for coordinating and developing literary creation at every level of the society. The writer Kuba's (Kurt Barthel) founding words point to its well-defined political function: 'The DSV's task is to communicate literary skills and a knowledge of society to German authors, which will enable them to create a useful literature worthy of our time, our tasks and our goals.'[17] The importance of its function as a mediating organ was made particularly clear by the fact that all the major meetings of the Writers Congresses, which served for the public presentation of new literary policy, were preceded by meetings of the Central Committee, where many of these policies were worked out in advance.

The immensely representative character of literature in general and the DSV in particular is underscored by two events of the 1950s. On 17 June 1953, striking East German workers marched directly to the offices of the DSV in East Berlin in order to express their dissatisfaction with existing work norms. The ironies of this relationship were immortalized poetically by none other than Bertolt Brecht when he wrote:

After the uprising of the 17th June
The Secretary of the Writers' Union
Had leaflets distributed in the Stalin Allee
Stating that the people
Had forfeited the confidence of the government
And could win it back only
By redoubled efforts. Would it not be easier
In that case for the government

To dissolve the people and
Elect another?[18]

A second indication of the importance attributed to literary culture in
the GDR occurred at the Fourth Writers Congress of 1956, held four weeks
prior to Khrushchev's de-Stalinization speech at the Twentieth Congress
of the Communist Party. Leading writers and critics (Georg Lukács, Anna
Seghers, Bertolt Brecht, Johannes R. Becher, etc.) voiced open dissatisfaction with the 'schematic' literary practices and policies of the preceding
period (1949–55), turning the conference into a major political event of
this tumultuous time.

But high-level policy formation was not the only mechanism linking
the writer to the society as a whole. The goals of these policies were realized through an elaborate 'contractual' system according to which artists
were commissioned to address what were deemed to be the central social
and political questions of any particular time. 'Contractors' could be the
Ministry of Culture; other cultural institutions (theater, film, television,
publishing houses); social organizations (FDGB, FDJ, DFD), or individual
factories or firms. One leading contractor for writers was the Deutscher
Fernsehfunk (the East German television network), which produced over
600 TV films per year, many of which were commissioned dramas dealing
with current events. Because of the extremely public nature of the TV
medium, collective control over the creative process in this area was particularly pronounced. A key figure in this organizational hierarchy was
the dramaturge, who as combination artistic consultant and ideological
midwife often ended up rewriting much of the material. While obviously
at one level another form of social control, the activity of the dramaturge
cannot be seen only in light of censorship. Television dramaturges (just as
readers in publishing firms) often played an absolutely vital mediating
role between the Ministry of Culture and the individual writer, helping
to negotiate the publication of ideologically controversial materials that
might otherwise never have seen the light of day. Finally, in addition to
official cultural organizations, contractual activity often included 'political' counseling by workers collectives as well as ideological guidance from
the DSV.

Officially, of course, there was no censorship in the GDR, as it was forbidden by the constitution. However, in order for a book to be published

the Ministry of Culture had to issue an 'authorization to print [*Druck-genehmigung*],' which was often granted on ideological grounds. In his discussion of the ministry's role in censorship during the latter days of the regime, Robert Darnton describes how bureaucrats in the Publishing and Book Trade section saw themselves playing an enabling role very similar to that of readers in publishing houses in their efforts to make a book ideologically palatable: 'In fact, she [the censor] thought that by authorizing books she had promoted them. Many of the manuscripts that she shepherded through the bureaucracy would never have appeared in print had she not removed phrases that were certain to provoke the wrath of the Central Committee of the Communist Party. A censor had to be familiar with the sensitivities of the men at the top of the Party and to have an ear for language that was likely to offend them.'[19] In his work (published only in the West) entitled *Der vierte Zensor* (The fourth censor), the exiled GDR writer Erich Loest described the 'genesis and death' of his novel *Es geht seinen Gang oder Mühen in unserer Ebene* (Things go their way or difficulties at our level) and in so doing spelled out four ascending levels of censorship in the GDR: self-censorship; publishing house censorship; censorship by the Ministry of Culture; and 'censorship from the highest darkness of anonymity.' To understand the function of censorship in the GDR one has to consider the hierarchy as well as interlocking nature of the four.

While considerable official emphasis has been placed upon the importance of the contractual system for the creation of culture in the GDR, it was the five major literary journals (*Sonntag, Sinn und Form, Neue Deutsche Literatur, Zeitschrift für Germanistik, Weimarer Beiträge*) and the book review section of *Neues Deutschland* that many times determined the official judgment and ultimate fate of a literary work. As the most public interpretive authority within the complicated web of the publishing process, these journals often functioned as yet another medium of constraint vis-à-vis writers who dared to deviate from cultural or political propriety. Hence it was not surprising, for example, that the famous 'lyric debates' of 1964 and 1972 resulted in particularly vitriolic attacks by leading poets against the ideological and aesthetic rigidity of the critics who wrote for these journals. On the other hand, the fact that the lyric debates took place at all illustrates how the journals themselves have periodically served as major forums for ideological conflict and dissent. For instance, under the editorship of Peter Huchel in the late 1950s and early 1960s, *Sinn und Form* published a number of heretical Marxist writings by thinkers such as Herbert Marcuse, Jean-Paul Sartre, Ernst Bloch, and Hans Mayer, all of whom implicitly or explicitly challenged official tenets of Marxist-Leninist theory.

From the perspective of their own goals, the attempts by the Party to break down the cultural stratification of bourgeois society through planned literary production can certainly be said to have been successful. If it is true that 85 percent of belles lettres in the GDR could be classified as general literature to 'provide examples for the entire nation,'[20] it is fair to say that the separation between elite and mass literature as we know it in the West had all but been eliminated by the middle of the 1960s. This is not to say that the GDR did not develop its own forms of nonserious literature. The novels of Wolfgang Schreyer, Werner Steinberg, and Karl Zuchhardt, with distribution in the hundreds of thousands, were best-sellers very much in the tradition of adventure or detective novels. But these did not contain the kind of pornography and violence of some Western mass literature, and they were exceptions, not the rule. The rule represented a new kind of literature, less technically sophisticated or modernist in its form of expression, for the most part conservative as well as politically correct in the moral and social values it communicated, but read by numbers unheard of in the West for comparable 'serious' literature. The most successful best-seller, Bruno Apitz's novel about political resistance in Auschwitz entitled *Naked among Wolves,* translated into Esperanto, went through 32 editions between 1959 and 1969 to total over 860,000 copies. Christa Wolf's *Divided Heaven,* Erik Neutsch's 900-page *Spur der Steine* (Trace of the stones), and Hermann Kant's *Die Aula* (The auditorium) all ranged above 200,000 copies within the first five years and continued to be reissued each year. With an average first edition of 15,000 to 25,000, and 25 percent of the adult population classified as book readers, it can indeed be said that the role of writers and their relationship to the public was a decidedly different one from the past.[21]

But the situation of GDR writers cannot be determined simply by reading quotas or institutional descriptions. With the growing disaffection of a small, yet highly visible group of literary intellectuals in the late 1960s, it became clear that for some the centrality of the writer within the governing hierarchy increasingly had come to mean a burden and even a nemesis. Stalin's description of the writer as 'an engineer of the soul,' referred to above in the quotation from Rudolf Bartsch's writer's novel *Die Zerreißprobe* (Stress test), is not without irony in the context in which it appears. Bartsch's character Norbert Angermann has his controversial novel *Die Beerdigung eines Gewissens* (The burial of one's conscience) vilified at a Writers Congress in front of the highest political authorities, after which it is dropped from publication. Caught between a 'contract' requiring him to depict things 'realistically' and his own private sense of reality, Angermann becomes an alcoholic dropout unable to create. It is not only censorship that keeps him from writing, it is the problem of self-censorship – the cutting edge between observable experience and a version of that experience that simply does not jibe. Rudolf Bartsch was not by any stretch of the imagination a dissident writer in the GDR. Hence, the fact that even he felt compelled to address the problems of censorship and self-censorship in a critical manner says much about the emerging 'moral' crisis among the literary intelligentsia in the late 1960s.

No one has pondered the issues of individual integrity and freedom of expression more profoundly than Christa Wolf, and her comments in a now famous interview with Hans Kaufmann articulate the connection between self-censorship and her own poetic principles. 'The mechanism of self-censorship,' Wolf says, 'which follows that of censorship, is more dangerous than the latter. It internalizes demands that can hinder the birth of literature and entangles an author in a fruitless and pointless hassle with two mutually exclusive demands: that he should write realistically, for example, and yet at the same time avoid conflicts; that he should write truthfully, and yet not believe what he sees, because it is not "typical." An author who does not remain sharply conscious of this process, who is not his own most rigorous monitor, will begin to give in, to avoid, to erase.'[22]

Wolf was not advocating some solipsistic 'subjectivity,' as critics in the East, and more recently even the West, have sometimes tried to suggest.[23] Nor was this simply a call for freedom of speech. Wolf's insistence upon the *self* as monitor sprang from a theme that has been basic to her Marxism and her art – a repudiation of that ahistorical 'unscrupulous subjectivism' (Wolf) she found to be present in an official discourse founded upon 'wishful thinking and prefabrications' rather than the critical understanding of one's own historical experience. Having just completed a novel (*Patterns of Childhood*) that implicitly questioned the official socialist version of antifascist historiography and its grasp of subjective history, Wolf argued for the validity of just such an individual view.

The year was 1974, two years prior to the Biermann expulsion, and Christa Wolf was not alone in her efforts to link the problem of censorship to writers' inability to rely on their individual perspective as mediators between historical and personal experience. At the Seventh Writers Congress of 1973, Volker Braun had introduced the section on 'Literature and Historical Consciousness' by provocatively asserting: 'Historical consciousness is consciousness of self. The reality with which we live is working history, and what we usually call history is the "object of a construction" which is loaded with "now time." '[24] Braun's references to history as a 'construction' and as loaded with 'now time' drew on the thought of the unorthodox Marxist Walter Benjamin as a means by which to challenge official Marxist-Leninist historiography. Braun's emphasis upon individual 'self-consciousness' as a starting point for any historical construction denied the absolute priority of a universalized, objective (Party) view of history upon which censorship and self-censorship had heretofore founded their rationale.

The growing conflicts in the 1970s around questions of censorship and the right of individuals to determine meaning imbued debates about culture and the role of the writer with a significance well beyond that intended by those who formulated *Kulturpolitik*. Despite its avowed function to constitute a form of mediation for official policy (i.e., to 'reform and reeducate the working people in the spirit of socialism'), it was precisely the realm of the cultural public sphere that provided a modicum of space for critical two-way discussions of social, moral, and even philosophical significance.

And why was this the case? What was it within the area of cultural discourse that such a development was facilitated? While these questions provide the working rationale for this book and hence can only be properly 'answered' in the process of elaborating individual historical case studies, let me mention a number of general hypotheses that inform my study as a whole.

The first concerns the central importance officially granted to the cultural public sphere as a mediator of political legitimation. From its very inception as a Party in the late 1940s, the struggle by the SED to appropriate and identify itself with the 'proper' cultural heritage was one means by which the ruling Party elite sought to verify its claim to be the bona fide successor to all 'progressive' and 'humanistic' traditions in the German past. Certainly the binary oppositions that informed the conceptual organization of official 'cultural policy,' particularly as it emerged in the early 1950s, provided an absolutely central value orientation for the political culture as a whole. 'Progressive,' within this scheme of things, was any tradition identified philosophically with the Enlightenment (Descartes, Kant, Hegel, Marx, etc.) or culturally with German Classicism (Goethe, Schiller, Winkelmann, Lessing, etc.). Socialism, and by extension socialist realist culture in the GDR, was the logical continuation of all that was enlightened, rational, and therefore democratic from Germany's controversial past. Opposed to this were any and all modes of ideational expression that had contributed to the 'degeneration' of the aforementioned traditions into modes of 'irrationalism' and that, so the argument went, had wittingly or unwittingly paved the way for fascism. German Romanticism; the philosophical writings of Nietzsche, Schopenhauer, and Heidegger; the Expressionist movement and various forms of modernism and avant-gardism – all served, well into the 1970s, as examples of an alternative, 'reactionary' political network, one that had purportedly found its latter-day breeding ground in the Federal Republic of Germany.

Given the profound ideological significance attributed to the 'cultural question,' it should not be surprising that literary writers within this system would occupy a particularly central and crucial position. As artists within a discourse that must perforce seek to articulate its own, 'authentic' voice, they were a vital link in the transitional chain from officially stated values to their reception into the world of private encoding. Mediating between the public and private spheres, successful and established authors in the GDR gained not only considerable political power as spokespeople for official policy but, in a number of cases, also a political independence not found in other areas of official public life. This was particularly true for those authors with international reputations, such as Bertolt Brecht, Christa Wolf, Heiner Müller, Stefan Heym, Stephan

Hermlin, Volker Braun, Irmtraud Morgner, and Christoph Hein. Precisely as individuals they were able to attain a degree of 'institutional' status in their own right: responsible directly or indirectly for representing particular social interests; vital for articulating a more variegated, pluralist public discourse; supported in a significant way by hidden constituencies within the society at large.

Admittedly, Hermann Kant, the president of the writers union, offered a somewhat caricatured perversion of this point when at the Eighth Congress of the Union of Graphic Artists (1974) he asserted: 'Anyone who devotes himself to writing in this society ends up founding, in the eyes of the public [*im Verständnis der Öffentlichkeit*], his own collective corporation (VEB [Volkseigener Betrieb]), and is viewed by the rest of society as an institution owned by the society.'[25] For the average writer, the path from the writing desk through the various Party institutions to the public was often a perilous one, entailing compromises that severely curtailed his or her public voice. This perhaps explains why the 'institutionalization' of some well-known writers has occurred in spite of, rather than with the support of, the official organs of cultural representation.

Beyond the questions of institution, there were also genre-related factors determining the status of the literary voice. In a society in which the forms of official public communication were thought to consist of 'tautologies, empty formulae and metaphors,'[26] it is small wonder that literary discourse should come to express sentiments and experiences at odds with or even peripheral to official representations. Because of their highly controversial subject matter, the Kafka and lyric debates of the 1960s, the Brecht-Lukács controversy (1968), the case of Wolf Biermann (1976), and the periodic scandals surrounding publications by Christa Wolf, Heiner Müller, Stefan Heym, and Volker Braun often evolved into major political events, involving many of the leading journals and large segments of the ideological apparatus.[27]

Yet in addition to the specific ideological content of what was being contested, the very existence of these 'debates' also said something vital about the structural function of literary discourse itself; about how the 'unreliability' and general ambivalence often associated with the meanings of cultural representation provided a rare terrain for genuine interpretive struggle. Beyond the intentions of the individual authors, it was literary discourse as discourse that opened up possibilities for a more mutually conceived dialogue between author and reader, literature and the public. While the speaker of a literary text is surely imbued with an individual authorial presence, the power of poetic speech *as a system* evolves precisely from its historically derived *potential* refusal to partake in the language of power; from its *generic* status as a seemingly genuine voice of alternative meaning. Noninstrumental in that it claims no goal beyond its own self-expression, noncodifiable in that it gravitates inexorably to that which cannot be said in expository writing, literary discourse invokes the involvement of an audience for the completion of its meaning.

Thus despite, or perhaps even because of, the fact that culture and literature came to occupy an absolutely central legitimatory place in the socialist public sphere, questions of language and style, particularly when they involved innovative technique or symbolic meaning, often generated uncomfortable modes of thought that reverberated outward into the general polity as a whole. The void created by the emptiness of officially regulated Marxist-Leninism was filled by a discourse that claimed for itself a kind of 'authenticity.'[28]

Certainly a major reason for the centrality of literature and culture was that literature provided one of the few mediations between public and private life in the GDR. Because of their relative institutional and rhetorical autonomy, writers were able to garner a considerable following, in part because they provided empirical information, critical perspectives on issues, and a look into evolving norms that were otherwise absent from public discussion anywhere else. The writer Günter Kunert spoke directly to this point when he wrote:

> Literature is a unique playground [*Tummelplatz*] for deviant views about the world and the only place where readers find things that move and really affect them. In this way, literature has become in the GDR an ersatz for information: for instance, in literary travel descriptions or even as history lesson, as we find in Christa Wolf's *Patterns of Childhood,* where for the first time in the GDR the public was informed that German fascism was not only a conspiracy between industrial capital and Herr Hitler, but that a sizable number of nice, average citizens had also been involved, even voluntarily.[29]

Thus it was often from within the literary sphere that many vital issues of everyday life were first brought into the public domain. For example, it was no accident that the first publication of Sigmund Freud was initiated by the dissident novelist and poet Franz Fühmann, whose edited anthology of Freud's writings, appearing in 1982, opened the gates for the publication of psychoanalytical literature in the GDR.[30] Similarly, the crisis of psychiatric care in East Germany found its strongest initial expression in a remarkable volume about a teenage suicide whose mother put together a semidocumentary, semibelletristic collection of letters, commentary, journal entries, and paintings narrating the institutional failures to deal with the case.[31]

The increased importance of audience involvement in the literary process was reflected theoretically as early as the late 1960s within the area of literary criticism. Leading critics alluded to the 'involvement of the reader,' to the 'subjective side of literary reception,'[32] to the relationship of literature to the 'life of the concrete subject.'[33] Admittedly, this shift to reception theory, while explicitly acknowledging the inadequacy of 'a systematic, speculative criticism based primarily on textual analysis,'[34] did not in any fundamental way analyze the discrepancies between the norms of class struggle or the 'educated nation' communicated by official cultural policy, on the one side, and the actual behavioral values of the population itself, on the other. Nevertheless, the sociological studies of Günter Lehmann[35] as well as the essays in *Gesellschaft-Literatur-Lesen*[36] did contribute to registering discrepancies and recognizing as well the extent to which the official institution of literature had lost contact with both writers and readers. It was also a further acknowledgment of the autonomous and growing significance of the artistic public sphere as a 'form of communication for working people, who find depicted therein their basic problems of life.'[37]

TOWARD A DEFINITION OF THE SOCIALIST PUBLIC SPHERE

Although I have employed the concept 'public sphere' in describing the historically evolved structures of public life in the GDR, this is not a term that appears within – or is even compatible with – official Marxist-Leninism. The reasons for such a lacuna may be traced to the fact that the notion of a public sphere as developed in theories of bourgeois liberalism carries with it a history of normative values that stand fundamentally at odds with the theory and practice of mono-organizational socialism.

Viewed normatively, the concept of the public sphere seeks to encompass all that would be entailed for constituting ideally a realm of social life in which public opinion and a public body can be formed. 'Citizens behave as a public body when they confer in an unrestricted fashion – that is, with the guarantee of freedom of assembly and association and the freedom to express and publish their opinions – about matters of general interest.'[38] In his classical work on this subject entitled *The Structural Transformation of the Public Sphere* Jürgen Habermas defines the bourgeois public sphere as the institutionalization of public space situated between the competing realms of state, the economy, and society, in which reasoned and critical discourse [*Räsonnement*] about all aspects of public life can transpire. His emphasis upon the separation of realms has served normatively as a critical means by which to evaluate the erosion of genuine public *Räsonnement* through the integrative processes of *all* contemporary modern societies, socialist or capitalist.

While Habermas grounds the notion of rational consensus and the establishing of a legally protected public space as paradigmatic for *any* future, truly democratic society, *The Structural Transformation* does not provide a prescriptive model for a postcapitalist or socialist society. Nevertheless, Habermas's discussion of Hegel and Marx on civil society touches on issues that have had implications for the evolution of socialist public life. For instance, seen from the vantage point of class struggle, the notion of a bourgeois public sphere has revealed itself, according to Marx, as a form of 'false consciousness: it hid before itself its own true character as a mask of bourgeois class interests.'[39] Only with the overthrow of the bourgeois class could socialism hope to achieve what capitalism never could: the end of the separation between public and private, the integration of the state into society, and a concomitant expansion of the public sphere into the realm of production. 'In this countermodel,' Habermas summarizes Marx, 'the criticism and control by the public were extended to that portion of the private sphere of civil society which had been granted to private persons by virtue of their power of control over the means of production – to the domain of socially necessary labor' (128).

As Habermas makes clear, what emerges in Marx's thinking on the question of civil society is a negative utopia in which politicizing the whole society (abolition of the distinction between mental and manual labor, between public and private life, and the call for a direct, mono-organizational democracy) is the end of alienation. Marx also prioritizes socially necessary labor as *the* value determinant for all questions of democracy and freedom.

> Underlying the proposal for the constitution of the Commune, the anticipation of the replacement of bourgeois parliamentarianism by a system of worker councils, was the conviction that, stripped of its political character, public authority, the administration of things and the direction of production processes, could be regulated by the laws (discovered once and for all) of political economy without extended controversies. Implicitly, socialistically emancipated public opinion was still viewed by Marx as it had once been viewed by the aristocrats: as an insight into the *ordre naturel.* (140)

It is this latter legacy that has proved dominant ideologically for the institutional history of Marxist-Leninist societies. Whether defined as superstructure or conceived as a part of the state, issues such as freedom of speech and freedom of assembly were perforce relegated to subsidiary significance when viewed in relation to the primacy of freedom from physical want. What is more, it is precisely such theoretical axioms that provided the ideological rationale for reigning Communist Parties in Eastern Europe to define the socialist public sphere only as a forum for molding 'proletarian' consciousness rather than as a locus for reasoned and critical public discourse.

A good example of how such reasoning worked itself out in theoretical practice may be found in a 1979 article entitled 'Kunst und Öffentlichkeit in der sozialistischen Gesellschaft' (Art and the public sphere in the socialist society) by the GDR literary critic Robert Weimann. To my knowledge, Weimann was the first GDR writer to employ the Habermasian concept of the public sphere for a discussion of public life under socialism.[40] Whereas most orthodox Marxist critics East and West have dismissed such a concept as 'bourgeois idealism,' Weimann sought to reappropriate it for Marxist-Leninism. Moreover, his attempt to do so revealed the limits but also the political potential of such discussions within the context of the GDR.

'The public sphere is . . . an agent of socialization,' Weimann writes programmatically, 'a moment in the organization of socialist living and thinking [*Lebens- und Denkprozesse*]. As a form of social intercourse fed by experiences of reality and by life praxis, the public sphere . . . is a high-level consciousness-forming sector of communication and value formation.'[41] Literature as the 'organization of socialist thinking,' as an area of 'value formation,' as a means for 'the molding of socialist consciousness' – Weimann's choice of language is revealing. Cast within the framework of 'historical materialism,' with the Party itself as the surrogate subject of history, the historical notion of the public sphere [*Öffentlichkeit*] as a locus for critical *Räsonnement* emerges here transformed into 'an agent of socialization.'

Viewed historically, Weimann's treatment of the public sphere was, to be sure, a sophisticated step above earlier GDR assessments of the Frankfurt School or of Western media theory. It was an attempt to appropriate and not simply to dismiss. Like Jürgen Habermas, Weimann characterizes the bourgeois public sphere approvingly (and not merely as a form of bourgeois 'false consciousness') as a once critical dimension of eighteenth-century life that had forfeited its claim to universality with the emergence of more advanced forms of market capitalism. In fact, Weimann's historical narrative conforms in many ways to similar arguments and even the language of *The Structural Transformation* as well as *Dialectic of the Enlightenment*) by Horkheimer and Adorno. In all three cases, we find the depiction of a *Verfallsgeschichte* [history of decline], in which a once pristine form of early bourgeois public life succumbs to the rise of commodity fetishism as the main destroyer of bourgeois culture.

However, where the East German parts ways with the more pessimistic outlook of the Frankfurt School is in his solution to the problem. For Weimann, it is the emergence of the Leninist party at the turn of the century, with its principles of 'partisan value formation' and 'communication for the common good,' that has provided the *only* viable alternative to the brutal inequities of bourgeois laissez-faire liberalism. What is interesting here is not the expected paean to the Leninist party as the rescuer of sacred bourgeois values. This idea we find already in Marx's notion of the proletariat as the realization of classical philosophy, a proposition that was to reemerge stillborn in Lenin and the Leninist party's perennial homage to bourgeois culture as the foundation block of socialist culture. Far more revealing is Weimann's total refusal to think historically once on the ground of socialist history itself. Why, for instance, in a modern, technically advanced social system, in which private property and forms of the market have been abolished for over sixty years, must all forms of social life still be totally 'organized' from the top down by what Weimann himself has acknowledged are *prerevolutionary* forms of party control? His silence on this subject, along with his normative juxtaposition between 'partisan value formation,' on the one hand, and 'liberal laissez-faire,' on the other, shows an obvious unwillingness to confront the historical realities that faced a society such as the Soviet Union, not to mention the far more modernized German Democratic Republic.

Yet despite the dominant role of the Party in Weimann's conceptual treatment of the public sphere, one should not underestimate the *political* importance of his contribution. Read within the context of the accelerating civil rights movement beginning in the late 1970s, Weimann's programmatic essay represented a first decisive attempt to initiate, from within the domain of official theory, a discussion of public life in the GDR. Following in the wake of the Biermann expulsion and the arrest of Rudolf Bahro in the late 1970s, this article, despite its apologetic theoretical framework, communicated a strong, unequivocal plea for the necessity of critical public discussion under socialism: 'The more we distance ourselves from seeing the socialist public sphere as the benign [*konfliktlos*] expression of a *human community* [emphasis mine] and the less we approach the public sphere voluntaristically, i.e., try to launch speedy campaigns to stamp it out of the press, the more vital the question becomes in relation to its actual given historical conditions and social bases [*Grundlagen*]' (221). The language is convoluted, the signified meaning less so. Although he mentions neither names nor dates, Weimann here distances himself critically from the policies of two earlier periods of GDR history. On the one hand, there are the 'voluntaristic' practices of the 1950s in which alternative views were 'stamped out of the press'; on the other side, we find the pseudoharmony of the 1960s, characterized by Walter Ulbricht as a 'socialist human community,' in which all antagonisms had supposedly already been overcome. By so arguing, Weimann clearly suggests the possibility of a socialist public sphere founded upon a more democratically conflictive exchange of ideas.

Even more significant for our present discussion is the fact that Weimann looked to the realm of art and literature, and in particular to the avant-garde, as a medium of public discourse that had paved the way for more active public involvement in the process of 'value formation.' Regarding contemporary prose and above all the work of the writer Christa Wolf, for instance, he suggested that fictional modes of representation had served as a model for the way people think and speak in all areas of social life, for here 'discovering for oneself is preferred to receiving things packaged, reflecting about things to simple proven facts, having an opinion to being given answers, to model illustrations' (219). Again Weimann's choice of words is revealing: 'packaging,' 'proving,' 'model illustration' pointedly refer to the disastrous edicts of official socialist realism. Moreover, his call for 'reflection [*Nachdenken*]' just as clearly valorizes Christa Wolf's highly controversial novel *Nachdenken über Christa T* (*The Quest for Christa T*) as a new, more critical mode of thinking.

Weimann's plea for a more genuine socialist public sphere within the existing structures of state and Party control reveals, albeit unwittingly, the theoretical and programmatic dilemmas of a reform strategy unable to speak about the end of one-party rule. The attempt to transform a public apparatus that was intended historically as an 'instrument for economic and political reeducation of the masses' (Lenin) into a 'crossing point in which economic, aesthetic and theoretical interests of the social ensemble confront each other politically' (215) must inevitably founder around questions of established power. Without the creation of separate and legally protected areas of public space, any attempt to broaden existing rights will always remain dependent upon the tolerance of those above. Certainly the emergence of a civil rights movement in the 1980s outside the parameters of the 'official public sphere' came as a recognition of such a reality.

CULTURAL AND PUBLIC LIFE AFTER BIERMANN

The developments immediately subsequent to the Biermann expulsion in November 1976 helped redefine the limits and potentials for public life in the GDR. Initial responses indicated a hardening of political lines by the Party regarding freedom for artists and the role of the literary public sphere. Sanctions for individual writers included expulsion from the Party and the writers union, 'permission to leave the country' (i.e., forced emigration), refusal of publication, outright censorship, and in some cases even arrest. The authors themselves reacted in varying ways: some resigned from official organizations and withdrew into private life (Christa Wolf); others protested, resulting in further punitive measures (Jürgen Fuchs, Gerulf Pannach, Christian Kunert); and not a small number chose to leave the country and emigrate to West Germany (Günter Kunert, Sarah Kirsch, Reiner Kunze, Hans Joachim Schädlich, Jurek Becker, Erich Loest, Bettina Wegner, Klaus Schlesinger, Thomas Brasch).[42]

For many intellectuals, crushing the Biermann protest meant dampening the hopes for inner-Party reform that had been generated with the arrival of Honecker in 1971 and that had become attached to the representative power and status of exceptional individuals. The fact that resistance could be so easily aborted revealed not only the underlying symbiotic relationship between author and Party (many of the most critical writers were, after all, still members of the SED) but also the willingness of the Party itself to employ any and all means in order to assert its political hegemony at a time of crisis. Isolated within the elite intelligentsia and dependent materially (but also as long-time Party members intellectually and psychologically) upon the prevailing value system for the publication of their works, even the most prestigious of these critical writers discovered how powerless they were when it came to maintaining themselves as 'institutions' of alternative views. In this regard, it is profoundly ironic that these highly politicized authors – spokespeople, as it were, for an entire realm of cultural and social experience that could not be articulated elsewhere within the social order – could be so radically and easily disenfranchised when it came to the organization of their own interests.

Yet the crushing of the individual literary voice, in some cases through forced exile, did not mean the end of the struggle for pluralist expression in the GDR. The 1980s saw the emergence of more collectively motivated and in part even institutionally recognized protoforms of autonomous public life. Central in this development was the increasingly active role of the Protestant Church, both as a forum for the public reformulation of social values at a time of a moral legitimation crisis and as a locus for other organizations concerned with issues of peace, ecology, and civil rights. By 1985 a small number of parishes had become the center of a growing political activity that was to lead to the momentous eruptions four years later. Of the 160 civil rights organizations recorded by the Stasi in June 1989, most were functioning as *Basisgruppen* [grass-roots organizations] working in close coordination with parish congregations.[43] As one pastor reported: 'The phenomenal group activities – peace and ecology groups, Third World groups, homosexual and diverse women's groups, handicapped and self-help groups of all types, human rights groups and the numerous circles made up of skilled and semiskilled laborers – situated themselves almost completely within or at the margin of the churches. Only a small percentage of the groups remained outside the churches, but even they were constantly connected within the larger religious field.'[44]

The success of the church over a ten-year period in providing an institutional as well as moral counter to the official value system came at a time when the government itself was finding it increasingly difficult to stem the tide of alienation and disaffection among vast numbers of youth within the sixteen- to thirty-year-old generation. Thus the public space established by civil rights and *Basisgruppen* activities represented a haven for those ostracized because of their political beliefs or social orientation as well as a center of resistance from within which the movement for democratic rights and the struggle for civil society were to emerge with force at the end of the 1980s.

Such developments also meant a significant change in the perception of the writer as a harbinger of social change. Whereas the 1970s had seen the emergence of a semiofficial, critical Marxist opposition under the leadership of individual cultural figures from within the institutions of cultural power (publishing houses, theaters, some official media, science academies, concerts, etc.), the failure of inner-Party reform together with the public presence of a marginally autonomous civil rights movement redefined the view of the literary public sphere. Once idealized as the vanguard in the struggle for freedom of speech, established dissident writers were now seen, particularly by the youngest group of writers to emerge in the GDR, the Prenzlauer Berg poets, as being caught in compromise with, if not ultimately co-opted by, the powers that be.

While this critique from the margins clearly pointed to the dilemmas of the inner opposition, particularly at a time of mounting crisis, it did not do justice to the continuing role of many public intellectuals in the processes of change during the final decade in the GDR. Nor did it adequately grasp the dynamic of ideological deteriorization within the system itself and the role decay was to play in the process of peaceful revolution in 1989. Particularly within the area of culture, both at the level of institutional theory and in the realm of everyday cultural practice, developments were occurring that marked a shift in the whole conception of *Kulturpolitik*.

The most important such development was the dissolving binary oppositional structure underlying the political and conceptual framework of the cultural policy system. Here good versus bad or progressive versus reactionary cultural heritages gave way to a validation of almost all (with the exception of outspokenly fascist) cultural traditions as acceptable aspects of the German past. With the introduction of such figures as Otto von Bismarck and Frederick the Great into the pantheon of the 'socialist national heritage,' along with the cautious attempts to rehabilitate the arch antirationalist Friedrich Nietzsche,[45] there appeared, by the end of the 1980s, to be precious little remaining of the once impregnable bastion of 'reactionary' German thought mapped out so confidently by Georg Lukács in his monumentally influential work *The Destruction of Reason*.

The reasons for such a breakdown may be attributed to short-term political developments as well as long-range structural changes occurring within legitimacy formation as a whole. Certainly the need by the government for political acceptance among religious groups together with the increasing militarization and 'nationalization' of the GDR in the late 1970s and 1980s would explain why 1983 saw the reclaiming of *both* Martin Luther and Otto von Bismarck as a part of 'our heritage.' Yet, as noted above, one finds at a deeper level a gradual move away from Marxist-Leninism and even political ideology itself as binding forms of value formation and national identity, together with a search for more 'pragmatic' ways of understanding one's relationship to the social order.[46] As in the past, the cultural sector not only reflected such a shift at the level of official utterance but offered a particularly vital area for the rearticulation of values guiding the system as a whole.

The dissolving of political Manichaeanism within the cultural sphere represented an important step in the move toward greater pluralism from within the official literary public sphere. Deprived of the steadfast ideological markers that had heretofore clearly signaled the limits of toleration or models for the good, writers, critics, and even the public itself were forced back upon their own initiative to rethink and in some cases reinvent the standards by which the tradition was to understand itself. To be sure, the category of socialist realism as a positive norm still existed in the GDR up until the very end, as did the epithets 'progressive' and 'reactionary.' What had changed was the absence of any enduring models [*Vorbilder*] for what these abstractions did and did not mean. What had emerged was a terrain of uncertainty and ambivalence, not only within the bounds of interpreting an individual work of art but at the highest level of value definition itself.

Thus, subsequent to the Biermann expulsion, certain writers and artists continued to articulate issues that went beyond the range of 'culture' per se and that contributed to an ever expanding and variegated official public sphere. By far the most dramatic development within the area of literature was the increasing number of outstanding women writers who clearly helped redefine the contours of a women's readership through discussions of women's issues. Institutionally, there was no 'women's movement' in the GDR, simply because the official public sphere prohibited any collective public presence that was not organized as an ideologically proper representation of the female experience. Yet the discursive space carved out by the plethora of women writers and their readerships emerging in the 1970s clearly represented a broadening of the parameters of public speech. As Angelika Bammer quite rightly argues, public political engagement of women writers 'did not take the form of political activism on behalf of women's liberation' but rather tended to be played out in the cultural sphere: 'protest was registered in the form of fictions.'[47] Not located in organizational structures or articulated in feminist theory, the voices of such writers as Brigitte Reimann, Irmtraud Morgner, Helga Schubert, Christine Wolter, Helga Königsdorf, Christa Wolf, and Gerti Tetzner defined and encouraged an inchoate resonance of solidarity and critical reflection. Thus, regardless of their role vis-à-vis the active civil rights movement, the critical women's literature of the 1970s and 1980s clearly helped forge a break with the officially prevailing Marxist value position on the women's question.[48]

The Writer and the Public Sphere

A second development from within the official cultural public sphere was a growing willingness to stand up to the censorship policies and institutional constraints imposed upon artistic speech and visual representation. Heiner Müller's outrageously provocative avant-garde production of his own *Macbeth* at the Volksbühne in 1982 brought a stinging public rebuke by Hartmut König, powerful head of the official youth organization, the FDJ, because of its 'historical pessimism' – but *not* a termination of the performances. The appearance of books by Christoph Hein (*The Distant Lover; Der Tangospieler* [The tango player]), Christa Wolf (*Accident*), Stefan Heym (*Collin*), Volker Braun (*Hinze-Kunze-Roman* [Hinze-Kunze-novel]), all of which openly defied the norms of political and aesthetic propriety on subjects ranging from Chernoble to the crisis of alienation under socialism, bore witness to the shifts in attitude and behavior occurring in all areas of cultural production, including the censorship bureau of the Ministry of Culture. Add to this the proliferation of semipublic (i.e., officially unregistered) cabaret performances, rock concerts, media showings, art exhibitions, poetry readings, and dramatic performances that were being held at 'private' homes, in church parishes, as a part of Fasching (Shrovetide carnival) celebrations, in local museums, at disco clubs, and even within Party youth gatherings and one begins to grasp the massive implosion of the borders separating public and private, official and nonofficial cultural life in the GDR.

This erosion of norms and increased cultural challenge from below surfaced, finally, in direct public attacks at the highest level of government upon the procedures of censorship within the publishing industry. At the Tenth Writers Congress held in November 1987 in East Berlin, both Günter de Bruyn and Christoph Hein vigorously condemned cultural sanctions: 'The existing official censorship of publishing houses and books, publishers and authors,' Hein said, 'is outdated, useless, paradoxical, misanthropic [*menschenfeindlich*], unpatriotic [*volksfeindlich*], illegal, and punishable.'[49] It 'infantilizes' the reader, 'undermines' the writer, 'destroys' the publisher and even the censor. In short, Hein concluded, 'Censorship must disappear immediately and totally, if we are to avoid further damage to our public life and our national honor, to our society and our state.'[50]

As a public testimony by a prominent writer, Hein's statement and the reaction to it provide an intriguing nodal point in the political evolution occurring within the GDR in the 1980s. Two years prior to the October Revolution a prominent writer excoriates the system as a whole and professionally survives to publish another day. Even more surprising, Hein's provocative remarks were followed within months by the official abolition of the censorship policy, if not a total abandonment of its existing practice. Publishers were no longer required to submit their manuscripts to the Ministry of Culture for 'permission to publish.'

Why was Hein not punished? What led to this extraordinary paralysis and even abdication at the highest levels of the apparatus? Who then was responsible for the decision to go in another direction? Like so much of what was occurring at that time, there are no monocausal answers. What we find instead is an overdetermined moment in which the myriad particles of a system suddenly undergo a subtle but significant realignment. The almost total dearth of a coherent set of cultural policy norms; the increasing failure of will on the part of bureaucrats up and down the policy ladder to enforce the long discredited criteria of a moribund ideology; a growing and inchoate determination on the part of writers, editors, publishers, critics, and even ministry censors simply to defy the enforcements of a publication system perceived now to be a paper tiger – all these elements conspired to produce an atmosphere into which Hein was to speak his portentous words.

While Hein was never an official leader in the process for social change in the 1980s, his written and spoken thoughts would continue to articulate the borders and profile of what many hoped would be the constitution of a genuine socialist public sphere. That his and similar efforts were overtaken by the events of the following years does not and should not diminish the importance of individual, in most cases isolated, writers struggling to provide an alternative way. If their efforts to establish a democratic public space within a one-party structure appear today to be naive and even misplaced, that struggle was not an insignificant part of the ongoing movement for change in the GDR.

2. VOICES FROM WITHIN:

RUDOLF BAHRO AND INTELLECTUAL

OPPOSITION IN THE GDR

The arrest of forty-one-year-old Party official Rudolf Bahro in December 1977 for the publication in the West of his monumental work *Die Alternative* (*The Alternative*) marked a unique development in the process of dissent in the German Democratic Republic.[1] For the first time a major voice of opposition came not from the artistic or scientific-academic community but directly out of the ranks of the Party apparatus. Whereas the poet Wolf Biermann or the professor Robert Havemann spoke for sectors of an intelligentsia that had traditionally found occasion to oppose the strictures of government policy, Rudolf Bahro was a product of that policy's own socialization.

A comparison with Wolf Biermann is instructive. Born within a year of each other, both men began their formal political education as totally committed communists studying philosophy at Humboldt University in East Berlin between 1953 and 1960. Here, however, the similarities end. Biermann's rapidly growing reputation in the early 1960s as a poet and enfant terrible, openly critical of government political and cultural policy, soon brought him public censure for his concerts, rejection from Party candidacy, and finally *Berufsverbot* from 1965 until his forced exile in the fall of 1976.[2] Rudolf Bahro, however, became a candidate for Party membership at age sixteen and a member at eighteen. His rapid climb to a position of responsibility paralleled and was an expression of the political learning years of the Party itself. During the period of collectivization, he defended government policy as editor of an agrarian periodical. His work as editor of a university newspaper and as a labor union official in the early 1960s culminated in the editorship of the journal *Forum*, the ideological organ of the FDJ. Here he ran into controversy for the first time, although hardly for any want of commitment to Party policy. His decision to initiate a debate about lyric poetry with a group of young experimental poets came precisely at a point in 1965 when Party officials had decided to end the period of cultural relaxation. Although his enthusiasm ultimately cost him his position and, as he himself said, his 'naïveté,'[3] it was not until the invasion of Czechoslovakia by troops of the Warsaw Pact countries three years later that he began to question the premises of the system as a whole. 'In the first hours and days after the intervention something changed in me forever. From that point on I wanted to deliver to them a reply against which they would be as helpless as we had been against their tanks' (1110). Bahro's 'reply' – nine years in the formulation – was a book that not only challenged the self-understanding of 'really existing socialism' but, beyond that, attempted a fundamental, immanent critique of Marxist-Leninism itself.

How does one explain the emergence of Rudolf Bahro within the GDR? Was he a paradigm or just another renegade, the exception or the rule? What were the historical contingencies that led to the writing of his book, and where does his development as an oppositional Party ideologue stand in relation to dissident cultural intellectuals such as Wolf Biermann, Stefan Heym, Christa Wolf, and Heiner Müller within the areas of art and literature? To answer these questions I first define areas of intellectual dissent and opposition in their relation to the officially constituted socialist public sphere within the German Democratic Republic. I then trace historically the emergence of intellectual opposition prior to the events of the 1980s. While the intent of my investigations is not a comparative study with the Soviet Union, I draw constrastive analysis where it seems useful. Finally, I discuss Rudolf Bahro's own achievement in an effort to argue that his appearance in the late 1970s can be understood as the *culmination* of a particular inner oppositional development within the ideological apparatus of the GDR. Like the writers and the poets, Bahro's notion of opposition was founded on the importance of aesthetics as a potentially subversive and profoundly liberating force within the socialist body politic.

INTELLECTUAL OPPOSITION IN THE GDR

The nature of a postrevolutionary socialist public sphere anticipated in the writings of Marx, Engels, and even Lenin bears little resemblance to

the public discourse and political institutions of real existing socialist societies. While Marx himself devoted relatively little speculation to the subject of a future society,[4] his writings in 'Critique of the Gotha Program'
and 'Civil War in France' spell out a 'dictatorship of the proletariat' in
which the oppressive power of centralized government, army, and bureaucracy would be abolished and public affairs placed in the hands of a
body elected by universal secret ballot and subject to recall at any time.
Lenin's *State and Revolution* was equally adamant if also unrealistic in its
vision of a 'withering away of the state' and the emergence of a proletarian
public sphere in which freedom of expression and self-organization were
to become constituent factors of public discourse. 'Socialism cannot be
decreed from above,' he wrote. 'Its spirit rejects the mechanical bureaucratic approach: living, creative socialism is the product of the masses
themselves.'[5]

The policies evolved during even the initial stages of the Soviet revolution stood in marked contrast to the futuristic writings of Marx and
Lenin. By replacing the Soviets with a hierarchical, centralized, and hegemonic party as the self-defining representative subject of history and by
subsequently developing a bureaucratic apparatus for the determination
and control of all social needs, the Bolsheviks soon relegated the legacy of
the Paris Commune to the realm of communist utopia.

While the Soviet model was taken over intact by most of the existing
socialist societies in Eastern Europe, its functioning and development differed in accordance with national, geopolitical, and historical realities.
East Germany's geographical location on the periphery of the Soviet bloc
as well as its constant confrontation with one of the most powerful economic forces in the capitalist world, West Germany, clearly affected the
formation of opinion and dissent. Most people had access to Western
radio and TV, and, even with the Wall, GDR borders were virtually useless
in preventing Western publications from infiltrating the country.

The formation in the USSR of Samizdat as a subpublic sphere had as one
of its impelling motivations the need to create a communications and
information network among an intelligentsia as isolated from its own
populace as it was from the outside world. Following the trial of Sinyavsky
and Daniel in 1966, Soviet dissidents came to represent a 'nation within a
nation,' an isolated group completely at odds with the system they were

opposing. Consider the following, somewhat overinflated remark by Alexander Solzhenitsyn: 'For a country to have a great writer is like having another government. That's why no regime has ever loved great writers, only minor ones.'[6] Certainly Solzhenitsyn's own development subsequent to *A Day in the Life of Ivan Denisovich* must in part be explained by his second isolation in the archipelago of political dissent, which, cut asunder from the body politic, saw its primary function as a restorative and corrective to the distortions of official history and Soviet self-image.[7]

In the GDR, the development of dissent took another course. While some authors resorted to publishing in the West, this for the most part was with official sanction and with an eye to eventual publication at home. It is also a fact that many of the most important documents of dissenting opinion appeared in official publications or were written with hopes of being published. Wolfgang Harich, who eventually did go underground prior to his arrest and incarceration in 1956, began his deliberations on an alternative Marxism with a reevaluation of Hegel published in *Deutsche Zeitschrift für Philosophie,* the major philosophical organ of the Party. The scientist Robert Havemann's early statements concerning freedom of expression appeared in *Neues Deutschland,* and even his *Dialektik ohne Dogma* (1964) was first presented in public lectures at the Humboldt University. The controversial literary writers Christa Wolf, Stefan Heym, Volker Braun, and Heiner Müller all eventually had some or all of their works published, or at least they continued to function publicly within the body politic. The point here is not that there was more tolerance in the GDR; in fact, there may well have been considerably less. Yet for reasons of its own history and because it has remained public, oppositional literature in the GDR was not comparable to the kinds of dissent that developed in other East bloc countries. Most significantly, the scope of dissent in the GDR remained much more limited within the legitimacy framework of official Marxist-Leninism. While this clearly led to the impoverishment of theoretical and artistic achievement and to restriction, it also forced open new trajectories within Marxism itself, as I show with the case of Bahro.

Again comparison with the Soviet Union is helpful. Wolfgang Leonhard has located three ideological-political frameworks within what he has delineated historically as the 'inner Soviet opposition.'[8] The first is the liberal-socialist reformers (Sakharov), who were for the most part non-

Marxist or anti-Marxist and who called for reform on the basis of existing Soviet institutions, for reinstating freedoms of speech, assembly, and organization, and for establishing a multiparty system. Ideologically, this group felt allied with the Social Democrats in the West and held to some variation of convergence theory. A second group Leonhard calls the religious-ethical reformers (Solzhenitsyn). This orientation was not only antisocialist but anticapitalist as well, looking to a return to preindustrial modes of production and to revitalizing spiritual values and a political monarchy. Third, the Marxist tradition was represented by Iwan Djuba and the historian Roy Medvedev. Staunchly anti-Stalinist, they drew their political authority from the October Revolution and the Lenin period and called for a reform of the Party and codetermination for workers.

Until shortly before its demise, only the last of the three categories delineated by Leonhard had any real relevance for the GDR. Prior to the mid-1980s, there was no sustained civil rights movement of any kind.[9] While the church provided a basis for institutional and individual resistance to the encroachments of state authority, its 'historic compromise' with the SED (officially in 1971) considerably inhibited attempts to spearhead a fundamental ideological or political alternative to the prevailing system.[10] Finally, the size of the country and the thoroughness of surveillance seriously curtailed the possibilities for any sustained development of an underground comparable to Samizdat in the Soviet Union.[11]

When talking about opposition in the GDR prior to the 1980s, we are limiting ourselves for the most part to a prescribed group within the intelligentsia;[12] more specifically, to controversies and individuals that emerged historically within the culture and legitimacy-producing sectors of social reproduction.[13] Wolfgang Harich, Robert Havemann, Rudolf Bahro, Wolfgang Heise, Heiner Müller, Christa Wolf, Wolf Biermann, and Stefan Heym were at one point all trained and sanctioned members of a political elite functioning within the broader reaches of cultural policy. Their impact says much about the historical development of the system as a whole. It is also clear that the absence of developed consumer markets in the 1950s and 1960s in a society totally vulnerable to the media manipulation of the Federal Republic necessitated highly elaborated forms of political and cultural legitimation as means of compensation. Precisely the imposition from above of an 'ideological political economy' subordinating all social and political needs to the goal-rational planning objectives of the state Party apparatus marked the people's democracies, in the phrase of Ferenc Feher, as 'systems of dictatorships over needs.'[14] These societies are 'ideological societies,' says Feher, not simply because they draw on Marxist theory as false consciousness to mystify social relationships but, at a deeper level, because the 'perverted' radical principles of their political economy (labor power as the sole defining principle of one's relation to society; all social needs expressed and defined by central planning; etc.) are constitutive structurally of the system itself.[15] In this way we can understand how, up until the mid-1960s, culture and ideology were central for the reproduction of the social system as a whole. Such an analysis also explains the potentially subversive nature of an intelligentsia that turned the radical tradition of Marxism back upon the system it would legitimate. It is this turning back upon itself of Marxism that I call the 'dialectics of legitimation.'[16]

In focusing upon intellectuals I do not wish to ignore oppositional developments in other sectors of the society or to suggest that such political and social activities were not significant for the intelligentsia. What must be emphasized, however, is that prior to the 1980s, intellectual dissidents did not succeed in linking their cause to a broader cultural identity within the body politic as a whole. In Czechoslovakia, Poland, and Hungary oppositional developments drew on national traditions to expand their political and ideological resistance to *Soviet* forms of political domination, but this did not occur in the GDR.[17]

There are important historical reasons that explain such developments. First, and most obvious, the discrediting of nationalist values in the wake of the Third Reich together with the existence of a divided Germany coded in the West as an issue of 'reunification' virtually eliminated the 'national question' as a source of leftist opposition. To call for a unique German form of socialism would have inevitably raised the question of German identity as a whole, and this the opposition was not willing to do. In refusing to do so, however, they inevitably cut themselves off from the rest of a population that did indeed see unification as a meaningful alternative to the status quo.

In this regard it must also be mentioned that since its inception in 1919, German communism has historically had difficulty separating itself from a dependency upon the Bolshevist mother party. Certainly the deployment of a 'national cultural heritage' by the SED in an effort to counter the legitimacy claims of the Federal Republic only enhanced such an impression. The SED's constant emphasis upon 'our socialist Fatherland' [*unser sozialistisches Vaterland*] as the natural heir to the progressive bourgeois culture of German Classicism as well as the revolutionary proletarian culture of the Weimar twenties was seen by most as the legitimation ploy that it was. As a statement of policy it also stood in stark contradiction to the systematic elimination in 1946 by the Soviet-sponsored Ulbricht group of any separate German road to socialism. Given the 'politics of unification,' the intellectual opposition felt unable to offer a nationalist alternative. Hence their efforts to link reform with repressed cultural traditions and an alternative Marxist discourse only served to separate them further from wider reaches of the populace.

When talking about opposition we are defining a mode of discourse prescribed within a theoretical apparatus once referred to officially as 'revisionism.' While limited as an analytical category,[18] the term 'revisionism' does separate those groups that are ideologically and politically completely at odds with a system from those who would *in some way* transform it on its own terms.[19] Moreover, what I am going to trace below might best be characterized as the attempts by dissident thinkers to recapture a Marxist cultural tradition that was at once critical and self-transforming; that functioned not as a tool of self-acclamation in the name of a corrupted positivist social science but that sought a dialectical understanding of the 'concrete totality.' While dialectical Marxism surely took some of its severest beatings in the GDR, there was a line of development from Ernst Bloch through Rudolf Bahro that suggests the tradition was not completely dead. It is this tradition that I designate the tradition of dissent.

ROBERT HAVEMANN AND THE 1950S

There was no figure in the history of the GDR with a more consistent record of resistance to state authority than the physicist Robert Havemann.[20] Himself imprisoned for anti-Nazi activities in a KPD (Kommunistische Partei Deutschlands, or Communist Party of Germany) cell during the Third Reich, Havemann drew on the moral legitimacy of his antifascist past to wage a struggle for what he called a more democratic socialism. That struggle put him on both sides of the barricades and both sides of the dialectic. During the 17 June uprisings in 1953, he was one of the first members of the SED intelligentsia literally to risk his life by facing the wrath of GDR workers when he went into the streets with a bullhorn to defend the Party cause. Conversely, following the Twentieth Congress of the Communist Party, he stood alone before his colleagues at Humboldt University and in the presence of Walter Ulbricht to call for the beginning of de-Stalinization at home and world revolution abroad. Only Ulbricht's personal intervention saved him his position.[21] Although his lectures on the dialectic in 1964 brought him ostracism, censure, expulsion from the Party and the Academy of Sciences, and finally *Berufsverbot*, he was always adamant in his defense of the GDR as a socialist country and as the only real political alternative on German soil.

But if his political behavior walked the thin line between inside and outside, his writings were equally ambivalent. More than one critic has asked whether his thought represented 'enlightened dogma or a philosophy of freedom.'[22] But the question is not whether Havemann was or was not an 'institutional revisionist' – in one sense, any of the oppositional intelligentsia who were to publish in the GDR were caught in apologetics and contradictions and to some degree would fit into that category. More important at this point is why and how Havemann was representative of a particular historical period in the GDR – the decade prior to the NÖS beginning in the early 1960s. What dimensions of his thought offered a challenge and transformation? Where did he conform?

The publication in the West of *Dialektik ohne Dogma* in 1964 was the culmination of a theoretical project that began in 1952 with Havemann's reviews of Engels's *Dialectics of Nature*[23] and his vigorous repudiation in *Deutsche Zeitschrift für Philosophie* of Party ideologue Victor Stern's critique of Einsteinian physics. An initial central concern in most of Havemann's analysis was to free the empirical sciences from the increasing constraints and encroachments visited upon them in the name of Marxist-Leninism. The canonization of Lysenko and the assaults upon 'bourgeois Einsteinism' in 1948 marked an increase of state ideological intervention into the sciences that was to have serious repercussions for key areas of production throughout the East bloc economies.[24] This campaign against 'cosmopolitanism,' as ideological coexistence came to be called, was particularly intense in the GDR, and Havemann's defense of Einstein was directed above all at keeping the sciences from inclusion in this category. Thus, rather than any fundamental resistance to state authority, Havemann's early work can be seen as a theoretical correlative to the changing demands of production within that economy from 1952 to the end of the decade. The struggle against dogma was the reverse side of the development of an economy absolutely reliant upon the most refined technologies for its very existence.

Havemann's theoretical arguments as well as their political implications are in fact largely parallel to those of the mechanists in their struggle against the philosophers during the founding years of the Soviet Union in the 1920s.[25] Both Havemann and the mechanists attacked the metaphysics and idealism of a macrodialectic divorced from the insights of positivist science. Yet in their efforts to weld the dialectic to empiricism in order to liberate theory from its codification as *Weltanschauung,* both Havemann and his forebears unwittingly prepared the internment of that theory in a new orthodoxy of productivist, scientistic Marxism.

Robert Havemann's attack on dogmatism in the early 1950s included one basic postulate that he repeated throughout his work. 'In every valid science,' he said in an article that appeared in *Neues Deutschland,* 'all knowledge is itself dialectical and materialist, whether the individual sciences are conscious of that or not.'[26] Any attempt to develop a separate philosophy or theory of dialectics outside a discipline and without a specific object of discourse will only lead to a kind of 'dogmatism' that codifies the abstractions of a Lysenko or vilifies the empiricism of an Einstein. And finally, 'because we view reality as primary, as the content that creates the forms of our consciousness, dogmatism is alien to us.'[27]

The political implications of these statements are both immediate and long term. Beyond its firm call for freedom of inquiry and the use of argument rather than coercion, Havemann develops what amounts to the first systematic critique of dogmatism at a time when it was not opportune to do so. The fact that his defense of Einstein occurs three years *before* the Twentieth Congress of the Communist Party in 1956, prior even to Stalin's death, is as significant politically as the language and conceptual gesture in which it is expressed. Havemann and his colleague Hernek ridicule the sophistry, idealism, and voluntarism of Party ideologues who lack the competence even to understand Einsteinian physics, much less discuss it: 'Victor Stern is like the philosophers of whom Donan once said, "They sit in their chairs, bring systems into their prejudices and then demand that the world behave accordingly!" '[28]

In Havemann, the Party encountered a brilliant natural scientist who was as skilled as it was at using the basic texts of Marxism as a final authority. His recourse to Engels's *Dialectics of Nature* as a means to attack dogmatism is a case in point. The grotesque distortions and sclerosis of Marxist theory in the sciences, Havemann tells us, stem from the separation of philosophy from empirical investigation: the creation of a methodological *Weltanschauung* uninformed by the reality upon which it reflects. Engels's fusion of the Hegelian dialectic with a theory of science overcomes that split by positing the dialectical processes of logical thought (universal movement of contradictions; movement of quantity to quality; the processes of quasi-automatic transformation) as *immanent* to matter itself, thus establishing a direct tie between nature, society, and the laws of nature and society as reflected in the heads of human beings. As a scientist, then, faithfully discovering the laws of the universe, Einstein is a dialectician *malgré lui* – despite the ideological implications of the relativity theory and despite the fact that Einstein was influenced in his work by that arch-'idealist,' Ernst Mach.

While Havemann's defense of scientific practice effectively countered the 'sophistry' of his Stalinist colleagues, the introduction of Engels as the basis for a nondogmatic, revitalized dialectic was a Trojan horse. While it permitted him to cut through the dogmatism of Party ideologues, Engels's *Dialectics of Nature* nevertheless helped Havemann reconstitute on a methodological level the groundwork for the very orthodoxy he believed it to refute. Havemann's reduction (with the help of Engels) of the dialectic to an inexorable objective process equally valid for nature and history reinstates the primacy of matter over mind and posits the historical process itself as an 'automatic' unfolding of subjectless history.[29] 'The dialectical logic,' Havemann writes, 'is the logic that resides in things, that we can only discover in things, in reality but not in our heads.'[30] By locating the 'dialectical logic' outside human will and by ontologizing the 'socialist dynamic' of production as a demiurge to the future, Havemann implicitly affirms the very process he would critique. Havemann's Marxist critique of state bureaucracy, Stalinist excess, the alienation of everyday life, and the calcification of critical thought necessarily and logically leaves unquestioned the technological and economic infrastructure upon which it was built and upon which it rests. Havemann's *Dialektik ohne Dogma* is in reality a dialectic without negation, wrapped and bound in syllogism. The GDR is socialist; socialist production leads to communism; Marxism is a midwife in the discovery of that process; etc.

Let us return now to the problem of dissent. What becomes clear in grasping the importance of an intellectual like Havemann is that there is a distinction to be made between confronting the inequities of life under Stalinism and developing a methodology for exploring its root causes. Havemann's recourse to Engels's *Dialectics of Nature* as a means for establishing 'objective' criteria for scientific procedure and freedom of inquiry was an absolutely vital counter to the ideological incursions occurring throughout the East bloc in the 1950s. The agreement of his 'dialectic without dogma' to certain dogmas of an 'automatic' Marxism that have been used to justify existing power relations does not in the least detract from the subjective integrity of his own persona as a focal point of intellectual and moral resistance. This distinction also helps us understand the extent to which other 'revisionists' from within the framework of theoretical Marxism often remained irrevocably bound to the apologetics of an older dialectic.

CULTURE AND THE ALIENATION DEBATES IN THE 1960S

The question of the dialectic was particularly relevant to the alienation debate that began subsequent to Khrushchev's de-Stalinization speech in 1956 and that reached its public crescendo at the Kafka Conference of May 1963 in Liblice, Czechoslovakia. In celebration of Kafka's eightieth birthday, the Czech Academy of Arts had invited leading Marxist critics and philosophers from East and West to discuss the relevance of the writer's work for socialist societies. Certainly it was obvious to all participants that the not so hidden agenda behind this literary topic included fundamental and potentially volatile political issues. Indissolubly linked to the question of Franz Kafka was the issue of alienation under socialism: to what extent did this writer's work transcend the bounds of its historical context to depict experiences contingent to all forms of modern bureaucratic reality? Ernst Fischer's electrifying opening speech in Liblice summarized quintessentially a thesis that had already become commonplace among a cadre of critical young Marxists from Poland, Czechoslovakia, Yugoslavia, and Hungary – that the appropriation of private property and the socialization of factories was only a precondition, not *the* condition, for the end of alienation.[31]

This was of course heresy, and it was no surprise that in the absence of Soviet representation at the Kafka conference it was the GDR delegation that became the defenders of the orthodox position. The four literary scholars from East Germany – Klaus Hermsdorf, Helmut Richter, Ernst Schumacher, and Werner Mittenzwei – proclaimed in various ways the ideological and artistic obsolescence of Kafka for contemporary socialist writers.[32] A premise basic to their arguments was an ideological sine qua non for 'real existing socialism.' In the words of GDR Party ideologue Manfred Buhr in the *Philosophisches Wörterbuch*, 'alienation is eliminated only with the socialist revolution and the dictatorship of the proletariat in the process of building a socialist society.'[33] Thus, where other East bloc Marxists such as Adam Schaff and Kolakowski in Poland, Karel Kosik of Czechoslovakia, and the Praxis group in Yugoslavia had returned to the early Marx and a Hegelianized dialectic as a means for breaking through positivist Marxism in order to critique the roots of bureaucracy and posit a subject as the active agent in social change, even the most unorthodox of the GDR theoreticians in the 1960s still clung steadfastly to an objectivism based on Engels's dialectics of nature.

Take, for example, the work of Wolfgang Heise, professor of aesthetics and philosophy at Humboldt University and one of the most recalcitrant and original of the philosophical deviants in the GDR.[34] If there is alienation under socialism, Heise stated in a public discussion in answer to the question 'Do we have alienation in our society?' then it is due principally to leftover remnants from the former society in the form of bureaucracy, 'attitudes of strangeness vis-à-vis the state' or 'exclusion of individuals from the conscious formation of the overall social process.'[35] Thus, while Heise is indeed willing to concede the existence of alienation under socialism, drawing upon the controversial texts concerning alienation from the early Marx and even citing the equally neglected subject-object dialectic in Hegel, like Havemann he excludes from critical consideration the socioeconomic order that is its condition. His concluding comments reinvoke the shibboleths of Marxist-Leninism in order to neutralize a controversial stand: 'The dictatorship of the proletariat is the domination of humans over humans, it is at the same time an absolutely necessary instrument through which its organizational-economic and cultural-educative function realizes and develops itself, during which time its repressive function actually withers away ... Socialism and communism are *by their very nature* an *Aufhebung* [elimination] of alienation' (emphasis added).[36]

It is this kind of tautological nightmare that helps explain why the discourses of culture and literature and not official Marxist theory increasingly became the locus for alternative views in the 1960s. For despite efforts to transport the conceptual framework of various ideological positions into the realm of cultural representation, art often remained resistant to such a function. As Bukharin, A. Tolstoy, and others repeatedly emphasized, art is not simply scientific theory; its communicative and epistemological processes cannot be reduced or simply equated with philosophical or discursive argumentation. Those cultural theorists who looked to literature as a cognitive instrument for the enlightenment of something 'other' failed to grasp the fact that formal literary representations, precisely in their being able to challenge perceptual 'horizons of expectation,' open up areas of knowing and seeing beyond and even at odds with the *content* of literary discourse.

It is, finally, the problem of cognition that really underlies the opposing positions concerning a socialist realism as they emerged from within the Marxist and socialist traditions. What distinguished Brechtian from Lukácsian aesthetics, to use one debate as an example, are not just incompatible notions of literary technique or contrasting views of the functions of art but rather fundamental differences at the level of epistemology.[37] The Lukácsian concept of aesthetic totality is unsympathetic to specifically artistic modes of perception precisely where it most faithfully adheres to the Hegelian bias that philosophy is the highest form of knowledge and art merely its mediation. Thus, for this school of thought, 'realistic' (i.e., good, progressive, etc.) literature is perforce referential – the bearer of a preformulated philosophical message. The Brechtian-formalist challenge to this locates in the practice of defamiliarization [*Verfremdung*] a notion of art as the renewal of perception, as a 'way of restoring conscious experience, of breaking through deadening and mechanical habits.'[38] For this position, literary epistemology is not the reflected 'content of knowledge' but rather a critical reorganization of one kind of experience.

With this latter view of aesthetic discourse we may more readily understand why for official Party ideologues works of literature often became 'unreliable' as vehicles of enlightenment, since even attempts to establish monosemic, binding models of communication must necessarily draw upon forms of representation that do not always translate into the ideological codifications for which they were seemingly intended. In point of fact, efforts to have them do so have historically often ended in interpretive disagreement. And it is precisely because of this continued space of interpretive uncertainty that the center of interest and conflict within the ideological sphere of state socialist societies shifted from philosophy to culture. As Herbert Marcuse convincingly argued, the establishment of Soviet Marxism as a 'descriptive' rather than 'analytical' science eliminated Marxism 'as a danger zone of philosophical transcendence.'[39] That art and literature should have moved to fill this void as potential 'zones of transcendence' in the 1960s is an important historical event necessary to understanding the dialectical function of literature in the socialist bloc. Embedded within the battles around Expressionism, Kafka or literary modernism in general were often fundamental issues concerning the maintenance or change of the political status quo.

The function of literature as a mode of immanent political opposition was particularly significant for the GDR, where theory so lamentably foundered as a radical discourse and, conversely, where creative artists continued to remain within a Marxist framework. Indeed, unlike the Soviet Union or other East bloc countries, almost every major literary dissenter posed a threat precisely because the questions raised were at once within and yet subversive of the master discourse.

LYRIC POETRY AS A 'DANGER ZONE OF TRANSCENDENCE'

In the 1960s, it was the realm of lyric poetry that provided a medium for articulating controversial attitudes and that offered the most significant challenge to official cultural policy. Prior to this time, the voice of much published poetry in the GDR had been one of collective affirmation for reigning political representations (hymns and odes to Stalin and Ulbricht, etc.), for the achievements of socialist production (the so-called tractor poems), and for a more general panegyric to the 'new society,' the 'new feeling for life [*das neue Lebensgefühl*]' in overcoming the fascist past.

To be sure, there were significant exceptions. In poems written during the last years before his death, Bertolt Brecht revealed a new-found interest in the themes of nature, sensuality, and personal experience, in contrast to the 'harsh' political poetry of his exile years, where he had once even apologized because 'we / who wished to lay the foundations of kindness / could not ourselves be kind.'[40] In addition to Brecht, a number of poems by other writers coming out of exile such as Erich Arendt and even Johannes R. Becher or postwar generation poets such as Georg Maurer, Franz Fühmann, Peter Huchel, and Stephan Hermlin set clear standards that were to provide aesthetic models for the following younger generation.

But what marks the difference between these older writers – some of whom, like Franz Fühmann, were former soldiers in the Nazi Wehrmacht quite intensively involved in searching inwardly for a reorientation in the new society – and the next generation to emerge after the building of the Wall (August 1961) was a profound shift in lyric persona and attitude.[41] The new poetic voice of the 1960s was *not* that of self-searching individuals in quest of a humanism unstained by a fascist past or a politically repressive present. Here was a collective group that experienced itself as such – a group ready to assert publicly its sense of shared 'provocation' and critical impatience with the status quo.[42]

The explosion of collective poetic energy in the 1960s by such writers as Günter Kunert, Karl Mickel, Sarah Kirsch, Rainer Kirsch, Volker Braun, Reiner Kunze, and Wolf Biermann, all of whom were born between 1933 and 1940, resulted in an unprecedented if somewhat short-lived carving out of a wider public space. In December 1962, Stephan Hermlin organized two readings by young poets at the Academy of Arts in East Berlin, bringing about a storm of public interest in such new faces as Wolf Biermann, as well as some stern reprisals on the part of the Party. Yet despite severe censure and criticism in the Party press, Biermann, for example, continued to make highly successful singing appearances in the East and West up until his public repudiation at the Eleventh Plenum in December 1965. More important, the years 1961 to 1966 saw the appearance in several anthologies, collected works, and journal publications of poems by both older and younger generation poets that registered attitudes of political deviance, aesthetic innovation, and even personal despair unheard of heretofore in the GDR. In fact, it was the publication of the most controversial of these anthologies, entitled *In diesem besseren Land* and edited by Adolf Endler and Karl Mickel in 1966, that sparked off the 'poetry debate' in the journal *Forum*.[43] Asked to respond to questions concerning the relevance of poetry to the technological revolution occurring in contemporary society, leading poets used the occasion to launch an attack on the entire value system of Marxist-Leninist productivism and its belief that technology was inevitably progressive.[44]

This brings us to the second important point about poetry in the 1960s. Beyond its function as a forum for public discussion, it was through a confrontation between, on the one hand, the values and subject matter peculiar to the lyric genre (individualism, subjectivity, nature, love) and the entrenched norms and practices of a socialist society driven by the imperatives of modernization (industrialism, progress, collectivism) that fundamental questions would be raised concerning the goals of the socialist project in general and the quality of life in the GDR. Thus it is no surprise that the problem of personal alienation, for instance, so neatly dispensed with in the seamless sophistry of Marxist-Leninist theoretical tautologies, emerges as a central thematic concern in many of the poems of the early 1960s; or even that Günter Kunert, a convinced communist, would use the poetic genre to argue that 'Marx is dead' if he does not mean more than

> snowed-in mortal remains as enshrined rain
> than
> sunshine pressed within the covers of a book
> than
> the ceremonial announcement of the weather report.[45]

But even more threatening than the content of the poems was their inherent tendency to communicate an attitude at the very level of their formal organization – the inevitable refusal of the poetic 'I' to be held cognitively responsible. Thus, what upset officialdom about the lyric poets, beyond their ideological deviation on questions of technology, alienation, historical optimism, and even Marxist-Leninism, was the seeming ambivalence of the articulated message. Critics spoke with concern about the 'dismal griping' in these works, about the 'taunting of a power that remains unnamed,' or of a worldview 'whose – often carefully honed – *undecidedness* reflects in dark images something threatening, threateningly dangerous, something horrible, mysterious, suffocating, and lethal' (emphasis added).[46]

Once again Günter Kunert serves to illustrate just how threatening and taunting to power poetic double entendre could be. In his most notorious 'parable' from this period, Kunert tells the story of an ancient monarch who forbade the making of lamps:

As unnecessary luxury
there was forbidden to be produced what people
call lamps
by King Tharsos of Xantos who
from birth
was blind[47]

The poem is about the capricious nature of rule and the naming of reality ('what *people* call lamps') as the defining of power. It is also about the use of dialectical materialism ('as unnecessary luxury') to rationalize primary and secondary needs in the interests of those in command. The poem's brilliant structure withholds and retards the giving of information, thereby inverting meaning and enhancing the ambivalent levels of association. Its tone is one of unmitigated irony.

Certainly the most openly militant and notoriously dissident of the poets during this time was Wolf Biermann. Paradoxically, his political views also placed him in many ways closest to the official positions. As was noted by his friend Rudi Dutschke, Biermann's Marxism, regardless of its potpourri of Luxemburgian spontaneity and New Left jargon, demonstrates at the categorial level a notable reverence for two basic premises of socialist orthodoxy – the Party and the state.[48] While this is indeed true, Dutschke is also aware of the extent to which Biermann's lyric persona is itself a repudiation of the strictures of orthodoxy, for its rude and re-calcitrant tone often expresses itself between the lines – in the gestures rather than the literality of language.

Unlike the GDR writers Günter Kunert, Karl Mickel, Sarah Kirsch, and Heiner Müller, Biermann's style would not be characterized as modernist or experimental. His syntactical and cognitive patterns are conventionally representational, indeed, draw their power from a proximity to everyday speech. But it is the libidinous and thoroughly sacrosanct lyric 'I' organiz-ing and permeating this discourse that cuts across the grain to cause dis-ruption. Hence Biermann's political difficulties in the GDR stemmed not only from the explicit message of his lyrics but also from the simultaneous statement and inversion of message in the posture of language.

An example of such gesture can be found in the prologue written for Fred Beyer's 1965 film version of Erik Neutsch's novel *Spur der Steine:*

Here's a DEFA-film for you to view!
So stay in your seats, such fortunes are few!
Frank Beyer is the director of the movie,
Which concerns the Party's secretary,
And the morale of the working,
The pub-boozing and shirking,
And young love in May
With tears on the way;
The disciplined Party enclosure,
With its bare-assed exposure,
In Plan-discussions engages
With heavy-duty wages.
With lies in a fugue,
With Manne Krug'
As construction brigadier,
He drinks barrels of beer.
A People's policeman
Sails right in the shit-pan;
A bureaucrat, a red-tapist,
Hurts the State, and its status.
An anarchist
Becomes communist!

A beautiful dame
Is made ill of fame;
She bears a young child
The rumors go wild.
A man cracks in two
In all this to-do.
A marriage on the rocks
We show all hard knocks.
There's no lying here! Nor distortion; that's clear
There's nothing here stylish; no glossy polish!
Here, life is coarse and open to view,
It's crazy and true, crazy and true![49]

The circus-caller narrating voice of the poem presents on one level all the arguments in favor of the film that had once elicited praise from the Party for the controversial book:[50] realistic representations of living people; the dialectic of history from the chaotic (anachronistic) personages and conditions of the *Aufbaujahre;* and finally, a candid, unschematic portrayal of the failures and problems of struggle. But Biermann goes too far – not only in what he says but in the way he says it, the way he 'sees' and does not see. The raw contradictions thrown at us by the voice of a folk singer include a level of satire and *double entendre* that are a part of this voice's history as an artistic form.

While the folk ballad originated within the fifteenth-century folk tradition, more recent poets such as Goethe, Georg Büchner, and even Bertolt Brecht all appreciated the value of rhymed couplets [*Knittelvers*] to cross-associate and invert patterns of meaning within and between lines in order to deflate the mendacity of high culture and false discourse. In Biermann's prologue there is at one level something unmediated, unsorted, unabashed in its tone. Yet at the same time it knows more than it is letting on. The short statement 'There's no lying here' suggests that somewhere else there is and refuses to explain apologetically why. Thus Biermann's objectification of self into a circus-caller is, finally, too subjective (anarchistic, etc.), for it is located outside of and remains immune to official corrective. And as he says in a later ironic footnote to the poem (published in the West): 'Following the Eleventh Plenum of the Central Committee of the SED in 1965 first the film was cleansed of this poem, and shortly thereafter the GDR was cleansed of the film.'[51]

In the works of the lyric poets in the 1960s, we find a number of different fictional traditions being tapped to interrogate and finally invert established modes of socialist communication. The fact that the most meaningful opposition emerges from the lyric and modernist traditions says as much about the continued potential from within the realm of symbolic interaction (Habermas) to subvert coercive organizations of public meaning as it does about the need to make an instrumentally rationalized Marxism the object of that subversion. The insistence in all these writers upon a poetic self that knows, sees, and represents according to the dictates of its own 'subjective' experience demonstrates a radical conceptual framework denied within the lingua franca of dialectical materialism.

RUDOLF BAHRO AND THE 1970S

Whereas the course of intellectual opposition in the GDR witnessed the impoverishment of critical potential within the premises of scientific Marxism and its subsequent emergence from the domain of aesthetic discourse, Rudolf Bahro's *Die Alternative* attempted to restore to Marxism a revolutionary cutting edge. It is in this sense that he conceived of his book as a critique, not only of the social conditions of 'really existing socialist societies' but of the theory that evolved historically to help keep them in power. This was Bahro's most important political achievement. While other Marxist critiques of Stalinism began subsequent to the October Revolution with the deformation of socialism as viewed from the narrative of historical materialism,[52] Bahro subjects that very methodological starting point to critical scrutiny. The transformation of Marxism from critique to a science of legitimation, he argues, begins with the legacy of Hegel and not with Soviet bureaucracy. Hegel in the *Phenomenology of the Spirit* bequeathed to Marxism the inextricable linking of logical and historical categories, and a thus tautologized Marxism necessarily explains its own history as a self-fulfilling prophecy. By uncoupling the logic of critical discourse from the logic and history of the process it would explain, Bahro historicizes Marx's own technological optimism as a product of nineteenth-century Enlightenment Europe and frees himself to explore what others accept as given. The result of these explorations is a systematic explosion of socialist myth. Let me adumbrate its major arguments.

First, the Soviet system is not socialism but a noncapitalist, bureaucratic structure created for the task of industrialization and based on an 'Asiatic mode of production' with its prehistory in bureaucratic despotism. Hence it cannot be understood merely as a deformation of the socialist superstructure, or as resulting from underdeveloped forces of production, or in the light of capitalist forms of distribution. Rather, it must be analyzed at the level of its labor processes.

Second, Marx and Engels underestimated the intransigence and fundamental character of the division of labor. The prevailing mode of political and social domination in real existing socialist societies is rooted in the vertical structures of work and the corresponding forms of consciousness that materially characterize and organize them. Since it is the 'absorbtion' of mental labor into the hierarchy that is crucial for maintaining and reproducing the system, it is conversely the production of 'surplus' [*überschüssiges*]' consciousness that will bring about its undoing.

Third, Marx and Engels also profoundly misunderstood the nature of the modern state. It is not epiphenomenal to society; nor will it 'wither away'; nor is it a means for social welfare and political articulation. Rather, it is an apparatus with its own hierarchy and set of institutional interests, ruling and dominating the rest of society and in 'tendentially antagonistic relationship to the immediate producers.'

Finally, the Marxist-Leninist party is obsolete as a form of political articulation and must be replaced by a Bund der Kommunisten (League of Communists) and transformed by a total cultural revolution aimed at every form of existing alienation.

Of these four major points, it is Bahro's theory of the division of labor and of consciousness that is key to the question of intellectual dissent, for it is here that he links his objective analysis to a strategy for social change. His emphasis upon intellectual labor as central to both maintaining and transforming the system in fact provides the political-economic rationale for why intellectual resistance became such a threat to the system as a whole.

Bahro's concept of consciousness recognizes aesthetics and culture as central categories for the formation of social theory. The emergence of what he calls 'subaltern' thinking within highly elaborated labor processes helps promote forms of domination and control precisely in its denial of the synthesizing and transcending qualities of *aesthetic* cognition. 'Aesthetic capacities and self-knowledge are integrally related,' says Bahro,[53] by which he means that the creative impulse to grasp and change the complexity of the social order is closely bound up with the ability to think abstractly: 'People who have taken up into their consciousness the dialectical structures of philosophy, cybernetics, mathematics and art are in principle able to grasp any kind of process, regardless of its complexity' (207–8). Given this formula, the key to social change for Bahro lies in promoting the classical education (philosophy, classical languages, mathematics) as a means of creating what he calls a philosophical-scientific 'surplus consciousness.' Reduced to its simplest formula, 'The point is to force the overproduction of consciousness [Es kommt darauf an, die Überproduktion von Bewusstsein zu forcieren]' (304).

With Bahro we have a figure of opposition who attempts to bring together the realms of culture and science in a totalizing theory of society. However, unlike other members of the literary opposition, Bahro's politicization radicalizes rather than rejects the moral and theoretical imperatives of the classical tradition. Just as his socioeconomic analysis inverts the premises of Soviet Marxism, so do his cultural politics radicalize and invert the classical heritage.

This attitude toward the classical education is particularly understandable in the light of Bahro's own development. From the very outset of his career he was intensely involved in the cultural-political life of the GDR. For instance, in 1958 he published an essay in an avant-garde journal entitled *Junge Kunst* praising Johannes R. Becher's appropriation of the German sonnet form for socialist struggle and recommending it as a national tradition upon which to build a revolutionary culture. In a poem he himself wrote at the same time, Bahro enjoins fellow bourgeois students at the university to make relevant the traditions of the classical heritage for the new society. His rhetoric draws from Baroque poetry in order to underscore the religiosity of political conversion and commitment:

Marx is with us.
                Within us arisen,
    Lenin's breath
                is uplifting
    the mass
                of repressed dreams
    right off
                their hinges:
    Young Thinkers –
                to the front line
    of class struggle.[54]

Bahro's attempt to infuse classical traditions into present situations is also evident in a cycle of poems he published five years later (1963) in *Forum*. The cycle was entitled 'Pathétique' and was dedicated to the fallen Russian cosmonaut Titov. Bahro weds Faustian striving with Beethovian pathos in an homage to scientific-political-cultural revolution:

    Brother German
How alike we both are! Side by side,
I can see myself in his walk of life.
The same yearning for the far and wide
Carries us up through galactic strife.
You are ahead? For myself, commands I make
Stronger to be and you to overtake.

Work, only work is that field unfurled,
The launch-pad, for your flight to chase
Through all the art and science of the world.
Philosophy – are questions there still open-face
Prove yourself, Queen Nuclear Physics!
And give your answer, KLEINE NACHTMUSIK!
Whence we have come and where we are going;
Whence came the earth, and whatever her fate;
Why people in throngs to the gods are still pleading
How rockets are built; when did art originate;
How 'thinking' machines are made electronic;
Which equations steer ships through space supersonic –

Universality, a boundless dream
Were we ever satisfied with a conquest?
Contemptuous are they who betray their fame
So as we began was made the behest:
Make all conquests into new foes,
Step by step becoming new heroes.[55]

Bahro's cultural classicism expresses here the hidden dream of what Marcuse has called 'affirmative culture' – the universalizing of bourgeois values; the end of alienation in a synthesis of scientific *and* artistic achievement: 'Prove yourself, Queen Nuclear Physics! / And give your answer, KLEINE NACHTMUSIK!'

When Bahro wrote these lines he had not yet lost his editorship of *Forum* for initiating the poetry debate of 1966 in which he himself attacked the modernist practices of poets like Günter Kunert for 'paralyzing intellectual and practical activity.'[56] The Warsaw Pact countries had not yet intervened in the reform developments in Czechoslovakia. Yet it is clear that the optimistic vision of an aesthetic-scientific synthesis pulsating throughout Bahro's earlier artistic efforts is still very much the dream informing the final chapters of *Die Alternative*. Herein lies the paradox within the dialectics of legitimation. Propelled by a cultural vision of unity and harmony forged within the legitimating politics of cultural heritage, Bahro's 'boundless dream of universality' drives him out and beyond the cultural-political framework cast to achieve it.

While one might affirm Bahro's understanding of the potentially revolutionary nature of the legitimatory sector, there are a number of problems emerging from *Die Alternative* that illustrate the extent to which Bahro was still deeply embedded within the premises of a discourse he wanted to subvert.

The first concerns Bahro's notion of social change. Although his theory of the 'materiality' of consciousness repudiates a base-superstructure model in which mind is merely the reflection of reality, his locating the dialectic of history in the conflict between absorbed and surplus consciousness reinstates the old labor-capital dialectic at a higher level of abstraction. Where once we had the forces of production as a demiurge that, when in contradiction with social relations, results in a leap of revolution, we now have the 'forces of consciousness' doing the very same thing. The problem lies in Bahro's notion of knowledge as a neutral mode of production. Just as Lenin's use of capitalist factory organization as a model for political and social relations under socialism failed to grasp the instrumental values of goal rationalization that underlie it, so Bahro does not interrogate his categories of consciousness to question *their* potentially repressive character at the level of cognitive organization and in the service of a Party that wants to stay in power.

What Bahro's paradigm fails to address is the extent to which the areas of instrumental rationality (science) and communicative interaction (philosophy) have to be thought through as separate and historically incompatible modes of perception and not simply synthesized at the top of the scale. To believe that the system's production of abstract mental labor is practically tantamount to creating its own gravediggers seriously underestimates the institutional and individually internalized imperatives within the framework of purposive rational action. Returning to the problem of dissent, only a theory that grasps the inherently ideological character of so-called scientific discourse can explain why opposition in the GDR has not emerged for the most part from the technocratic and theory-producing but rather from the artistic and literary communities.

However, by far the most severe criticism of Bahro to emerge in the West has to do with the *political* alternative that he indeed offers. While critical of Lenin and even of Marx, the argument goes,[57] Bahro's adherence to the 'negative utopia of the politicization of the whole society' (the end of the division between mental and manual labor; the call for the abolition of the state and for a direct mono-organizational democracy) and his stress upon intellectual creativity as a source for political change and rule (Bund der Kommunisten) link him irrevocably to the Leninist tradition precisely because such an emphasis must assume that a self-named intellectual elite will necessarily constitute itself as the sole representative for the society as a whole. The alternative to the 'Neo-Leninism' of Bahro, the argument concludes, lies in the development of a public sphere and instruments of civil society (parliament, market, juridical system, free press, etc.) that would permit the articulation of political and social needs basic to a democracy.

There are two responses to the above argument that I use to clarify my concept of 'an inner voice.' Viewed programmatically, of course, it is indeed true that Bahro's model, like much of the cultural opposition in the GDR, is 'soft' on the problems of civil society. Regardless of his repeated call for freedom of speech and democratization of public life, Bahro's whole vision of an educational mobility program clearly overlooks the questions of power and control that an emphasis upon constitutional pluralism would push to the fore. It is also the case that Bahro's plea for the 'withering away of the state' and its replacement by a mono-organizational form of direct democracy retains an ideological dimension that places it very close to strains of classical Marxist-Leninist-Stalinism.

Yet in fairness to Bahro, it should be mentioned that although he clearly does retain a belief in the necessary abolition of the state as a prerequisite for communism, he does not share Marx's idea that the state under capitalism was simply a committee in the hands of the ruling class that would disappear of its own accord with the demise of capitalism. Where Marx saw political power relations as merely another 'superstructural' phenomenon, Bahro emphasized that the abolition of private property does not mean the abolition of the political state; that the logic of political relations has an autonomy and history of its own. And clearly the political cutting edge of the *potential* reception of *Die Alternative* in the GDR had to be its critique of the Marxian notion of the state. This is the book's historical specificity against which its relevance as a political document would have to be measured. The fact that neither the dissident Bahro nor *Die Alternative* was accorded a reception in the GDR makes any further discussion of the Bahro question there politically moot.

DISSENT AND THE PUBLIC SPHERE

The question of historical context brings us to a final consideration concerning Bahro in relation to the rest of the opposition in the GDR. While it is true that Bahro, like Bloch, Harich, Biermann, Havemann, Fuchs, and others, remained very much within the framework of an 'inner Party opposition,' all were aware of the importance of civil rights or an oppositional public sphere. As early as 1956, Wolfgang Harich was negotiating a reform platform with a number of demands that became rallying points for the opposition in the GDR from that time on: transforming the Volkskammer into a democratic parliament; restoring legal guarantees; decentralizing the economy; establishing oppositional parties; and freedom of speech and cultural expression.[58]

The arrest and eight-year imprisonment of Harich meant an end to the realization of any such policies, but many of them were picked up and articulated by Robert Havemann beginning in the 1960s. Havemann's insistence upon the importance of individual liberties is best expressed in his citing of Rosa Luxemburg to the effect that 'socialism is free pluralism in all areas of social life.' In the case of Wolf Biermann, we again have a figure who, regardless of his voiced 'loyalty' to the Party (to which he was never admitted), remained in deed and poetic word an adamant symbol of resistance to authority and of freedom of speech and lifestyle.

The 'paradox' of Bahro, Biermann, and Havemann contains in nuce the paradox at the root of the inner opposition. What becomes clear in the story of the voices from within is the extent to which their success as opposition is the inverse side of their failure to establish such an opposition by revitalizing Marxism. Neither Havemann nor Bahro nor certainly Biermann will be remembered in the long run for his theoretical contributions; rather, the significance of each one's achievement rests in his symbolic 'testimony,' *as an individual,* to another way of knowing and doing. What has been clear since Bahro's leaving and Havemann's death is the extent to which books like *Die Alternative* and *Dialektik ohne Dogma* remained one-time events rather than the beginnings of something new; the extent to which the discourse of Marxism had become moribund in the GDR as the basis for alternative thought. In this same vein, it was Biermann the poet, *not* Biermann the Marxist theoretician, who truly challenged the existing discourse. It was for that reason that the cultural sector continued to provide a crucial source for a language with which both to articulate and negate the status quo.

PART 2: THE POLITICS OF MODERNISM:

A THEATER OF REVOLUTION?

3. AFFIRMATIVE AND NEGATIVE CULTURE: THE STRUGGLE FOR A TRADITION

The artistic avant-garde has always had little respect for entrenched authority, even when that authority claims for itself revolutionary intention. Its history within the traditions and institutions of socialist societies constituted a legacy of mutual distrust, sometimes open warfare, and repeated repression – but also a return of the repressed. Indeed, this continued dialectic of repression and revolt is precisely what distinguished the avant-garde in Eastern Europe from its function in postwar Western capitalist societies, where, as most critics agree, the integrative mechanisms of the culture industry had long since relegated the historical avant-garde to just that – the backwaters of cultural history.[1]

The hostility within Marxism and among socialists toward what has variously been called naturalism, modernism, decadence, formalism, or – most pejoratively – avant-gardism finds its earliest antecedents in nineteenth-century social democracy and its more programmatic beginnings in the aftermath of the October Revolution.[2] If Lenin and Trotsky differed in their individual assessments of movements such as Futurism or artists such as Vladimir Mayakovsky, they were one in their emphasis upon classical bourgeois culture as the cornerstone for any socialist culture.[3] In the words of Trotsky: 'The working class does not know the old literature, it still has to commune with it, it still has to master Pushkin, to absorb him, and so overcome him.'[4] Lenin was even more adamant in opposing Bogdanov's avant-garde Proletkult (Cult of the Proletariat) movement and calling for literacy as the first cultural priority of the revolution: 'While we have been palavering about proletarian culture and its relation to bourgeois culture, the facts indicate that not even bourgeois culture is far-ing very well with us today. . . . Proletarian culture simply has to be the systematic further development of the sum of knowledge that mankind has accrued under the yoke of capitalist, feudal, and bureaucratic social orders.'[5]

Of course, Lenin's nod to Tolstoy and the classics stemmed as much from the immediate economic and social exigencies of the postwar period as it did from any general theory of culture or even from personal taste. The process of industrialization lent priority to mass education in a society in which 70 percent of the population was illiterate. But there were important political reasons as well that explain the increased repression of the avant-garde throughout the 1920s after Lenin's death. The activities of highly vocal Left groupings around the Proletkult, Mayakovsky and the Left Futurists in LEF (Left Front of Literature), as well as the Constructivists constituted a potentially independent and hence politically threatening element within the precarious social order. Their call for self-organization and autonomy as the basis for creating any truly revolutionary culture clearly ran counter to the move toward centralization and Party control by the Bolsheviks. Seen in this light, the weaving of bourgeois tradition into the fabric of an emerging cultural policy was very much a part of Lenin's struggle in the 1920s to establish political hegemony. As such it provides an early example of traditionalist aesthetics being used as a form of political legitimation – a policy that was to reach its more elaborated codification with the entombment of the nineteenth-century novel in the prescriptive edicts on socialist realism in 1934. Thus the bourgeois realists Tolstoy, Balzac, and Thomas Mann, not Franz Kafka, James Joyce, and ultimately even Bertolt Brecht, were to provide the models for literary policy as it developed from the first Five-Year Plan (1928–33) into the postwar period, or as it was articulated in the literary theories of Andrey Zhdanov, Georg Lukács, and Johannes R. Becher.[6]

Since they viewed modernism as decadent and destructive of culture itself, Marxist theory and socialist practice have often been said to share much with conservative critics of the bourgeois mold. Both the Marxists and certain reactionary defenders of high culture, it is argued, view in the assault upon aesthetic autonomy and the diffusion of the organic work of art modernity's (capitalism's) threat to the very foundations of Enlightenment culture as the realization of reason and harmony. In opposition to such an approach, this chapter seeks to explore the dynamics of cultural struggle within the specific historical framework of a developing socialist cultural policy beginning in the Soviet Union and carrying into the GDR. While it is indeed true that avatars of philosophical idealism or biological positivism have helped shape the key schools of Marxist aesthetics (Lukács and Plekhanov), it is precisely the *function* of such ideas within a specific historical context that allow us to constitute their ultimate meaning.

In exploring historically the 'faces' of modernism within the politics of socialist culture, it is also important at the outset to distinguish my own analytical use of the terms *modernism* and *avant-garde* from their function as epithets within the discourse of official *Kulturpolitik*. For instance, in European as opposed to American discussions, the notion of the subcategory avant-garde under the rubric of modernism has served heuristically to delineate ontological differences and to help map out historical transformations within the modernist tradition generally. Matei Calinescu's designation of the avant-garde as a second, more politically and ideologically radical phase of modernism is but one way theorists have tried to deal with the seeming tension within modernism between its activist and its 'apolitical' gestures, between an aesthetic that claims to close the gap 'between art and life' and one centered on language, individual expression, and notions of autonomy.[7] Peter Bürger in fact used just such a distinction to formulate a theory of the avant-garde in which the historical rupture between 'aestheticism' (read modernism) and the 'historical avant-garde' became a watershed in the crisis of culture itself at the turn of the century. According to Bürger, aestheticism thematized and thereby brought to extreme awareness the autonomy status of art, which in turn called forth attempts to bridge the distance between art and life on the part of the avant-garde. My own discussion of modernism in the GDR retains the subcategorial distinction outlined above, that of an avant-garde and of a modernist tradition, without assigning to one or the other a privileged notion of 'the political.'[8] They are, in every case, to be historically and textually evaluated as they function within the politics of the GDR public sphere.

THE RETURN OF THE REPRESSED

The cultural policy directives regarding Formalism developed under Walter Ulbricht in the early 1950s in the GDR obviously inherited a political framework and institutional biases stemming directly from the Soviet experiences of the 1920s and 1930s. In one important way, the similarity between the goals of the Bolsheviks and those of the historical avant-garde marked their relationship as problematic. From its very inception in the October Revolution, Lenin's cultural policy, while politically at odds with the avant-garde, claimed that it was co-opting and indeed realizing, *not* repudiating, the revolutionary project of such artistic movements as Futurism, Dadaism, and Surrealism. For instance, if the advocate of production aesthetics, Boris Arvatov, called for the 'complete melding of the artistic forms of everyday life; the complete dipping of art into life'[9] to be central to a new revolutionary art, then the joining of bourgeois spirit to proletarian body in Lenin's policy also claimed to be an *Aufhebung* [sublation] of the values and ideals of affirmative culture through their absorption and further realization in everyday socialist reality. In this regard, even Walter Ulbricht's fantastic claim that the GDR was 'Faust Part 3'[10] is but a far-fetched version of that strain of the artistic avant-garde that has always sought to transcend the dichotomy of art and life. To be sure, Ulbricht's and, let us say, the Constructivist Sergey Tretyakov's notions of *Aufhebung* are themselves somewhat dichotomous. While the Russian theorist was iconoclastic in his assault upon the institution of traditional art, which he would use as 'compost'[11] for the new order, the cultural policy of the SED sought to terminate bourgeois autonomous culture and simultaneously to reinstitute it in what Johannes R. Becher has called the Literaturgesellschaft.

The first important GDR document dealing with modernism was a declaration by the Central Committee of the SED on 17 March 1951 entitled 'Der Kampf gegen den Formalismus in Kunst und Literatur, für eine fortschrittliche Kultur' (The struggle against formalism in art and literature, for a progressive German culture). The categories it employs reflect its historical origins. Formalism or 'cosmopolitanism,' we are told, is a form of 'American cultural barbarism' that, when practiced in the new society, leads to a 'rupture with art itself, a destruction of national consciousness and indirect support of the war policies of world imperialism.'[12] Important here is not the content but rather the structure of a political relationship. The rhetoric and posture in such phrases as cultural barbarism and cosmopolitanism were an obvious part of the then prevailing cold war climate and were soon to disappear with the beginning of de-Stalinization and a greater focus on political conflicts within the social order. What would not disappear was this reestablishment within GDR socialism of the classical antagonism between the institution of affirmative culture, on the one hand, and its potential subversion at the hands of some form of modernism, on the other – an antagonism transferred now into the legitimacy struggles of a 'state that is not supposed to be.'[13] The repoliticizing of culture is of course a two-edged sword. While welding 'national form to socialist content' (Ulbricht) indeed served the nationalist identity claims of the new order, it also meant that any iconoclastic alternative to that form was perforce a challenge to the larger political order. Nobody understood this dialectics of legitimation better than Bertolt Brecht, who, when summoned to the highest ministers of state to discuss the Formalist and ideological deviations of his and Paul Dessau's controversial opera *Das Verhör des Lukullus* (The trial of Lucullus), asked with characteristic double entendre: 'Where else in the world can you find a government that shows such interest in, and pays such attention to, its artists?'[14]

If one binary opposition at the heart of official cultural policy institutionalized the conflict between two 'bourgeois' traditions, high culture and high modernism, working out that conflict varied with changing historical realities in the GDR. Within the cold war culture of the early 1950s, it was Brechtian Formalism (epic theater generally, productions of *The Mother* [1932], *Lukullus,* and *Mother Courage* [1939]) and Hanns Eisler's irreverent treatment of *the* classic in his adaptation of the Faust legend that were seen indirectly to undermine the state as bearer of a humanist-democratic tradition. Similarly, negative evaluations of such avant-garde movements of the 1920s[15] as Formalism, Constructivism, Surrealism, Expressionism (which was termed protofascist), Bauhaus,[16] Dadaism, and Neue Sachlichkeit (New Objectivity), or such artists as Meyerhold, Tretyakov, John Heartfield, Franz Jung, and Walter Gropius stemmed from a perceived threat to the absolute primacy accorded German Classicism and bourgeois realism within the fledgling *Kulturpolitik*. Understandably, the 'cultural revolution' of the post-Stalin 1950s and early 1960s saw the playwrights Peter Hacks, Heiner Müller, and later Volker Braun draw precisely on the Constructivist traditions of the Soviet Union and the theatrical avant-garde of Weimar Germany (Brecht, Walter Benjamin, Berta

91

Lask, Erwin Piscator) to develop an agitprop drama critical of the socioeconomic failures of the 'construction years' and at odds with the prevailing theatrical practices of official socialist realism.[17]

Finally, emerging societal alienation within the vastly increased emphasis upon productivity throughout the East bloc during the 1960s and mediated culturally through the Kafka debate of 1963 was accompanied in the GDR by 'subjectivist' experimentation in prose (Christa Wolf's *Divided Heaven* and later *The Quest for Christa T*), a beginning reassessment of Expressionism and Franz Kafka,[18] and the poetic activities of such modernist poets as Karl Mickel, Günter Kunert, and Sarah and Rainer Kirsch.[19] Epic theater, Proletkult, Joycean stream of consciousness, Kafka, Expressionism, lyrical experimentalism – in each case the struggle was political in content and resulted in temporary restrictions. But it has also ultimately led to the acceptance of this or that model of the avant-garde or modernism as compatible with what appeared to be an ever-increasing elasticity in the notions of 'cultural heritage' and socialist realism. Thus it might have come as no surprise when, as part of the Eighth Party Congress in 1971, Secretary General Erich Honecker seemed to culminate this process with the statement, 'In the area of art and literature there are no taboos!'[20] For many, this was surely the final recognition that the avant-garde had been neutralized the way it would always be neutralized – not through repression but rather tolerance. The question we must answer now is whether this was true and, if not, what were the parameters around which the process continued into the 1970s and 1980s.

Certainly the expulsion of Wolf Biermann in November 1976 and the subsequent exiling and silencing of a number of leading poets and writers was a clear indication that taboos still existed and would be enforced. But neither Biermann nor other exiled writers like Thomas Brasch, Jürgen Fuchs, or even Jurek Becker ran into trouble primarily because of modernist tendencies in their writings. Thus let us reformulate the question: Did the avant-garde in any of its historically recognized forms and roles continue to function politically in the GDR and, if so, what did it look like and what were its premises? In this section I argue that the challenge of the avant-garde did continue to exist in the GDR and that its premises and potentialities emerged in particularly lucid form within the *theoretical and political* interface between the dramatist Bertolt Brecht and his oft-named successor, Heiner Müller.

When the fifty-year-old Bertolt Brecht arrived in East Berlin in the fall of 1948, he had completed the major body of his work as a playwright and theorist of epic drama. Moreover, his opus of over twenty-eight dramas, from *Baal* (1918), *Drums in the Night* (1919–22), *Man Is Man* (1925), and *The Threepenny Opera* (1928) through the classical works of his exile period (*The Life of Galileo*, 1938; *Mother Courage*, 1939; *The Good Woman of Sezuan*, 1938–40) had already established him as one of the major playwrights and creative innovators of the twentieth-century stage. During the ensuing eight years until his death in August 1956 Brecht was primarily active as a director of his own plays. His Berliner Ensemble, run by his wife and leading actress, Helene Weigel, soon developed into one of the major theater troupes in Europe and was to serve for decades as a medium for the realization and dissemination of his theatrical ideas.

However, despite his international reputation as a great modern playwright, at the outset Brecht and his theater were by no means universally applauded in the GDR. Up until the mid-1960s, his notions of epic theater and estrangement technique [*Verfremdungseffekt*] were generally viewed as antagonistic to the aesthetic principles of official socialist realism and to the theories laid down by the Hungarian theorist Georg Lukács. It was precisely the Berliner Ensemble's concern with experimentation and modernist techniques that led a number of younger playwrights and directors to see it as a center for alternative, avant-garde theater in the GDR.

Heiner Müller came from and was schooled in the Brecht tradition but in the course of time grew to question that tradition as a viable mode of revolutionary expression. Born in Saxony in 1929, Müller was the first of the postwar GDR playwrights to confront directly and brutally the historical realities through which he had lived.[21] Certainly the major phases of his extraordinarily prolific career have at once chronicled and helped shape pivotal developments in GDR drama itself. The early production plays (*Der Lohndrücker* [1956; The wage shark]; *The Correction*, 1959; *Der Bau* [1961; The construction]; as well as his history play about collectivization (*Die Umsiedlerin* [1961; The refugee]), appeared within the political turmoil of the construction years and represent an aesthetic and political break with the mythologies of socialist realism dominating literature at that time. When in the early 1960s controversial writers were discouraged from treating contemporary problems and Müller himself was banned

93

because of his production of *Die Umsiedlerin,* the playwright turned to classical adaptations (*Philoktet,* 1964; *Herakles 5,* 1964; *Oedipus Tyrann,* 1966; *Prometheus,* 1968; *Macbeth,* 1971) that, mutatis mutandis, turned out to be no less political or controversial than some of his earlier plays. It was also at this time that he turned more intensively to the writing of history dramas, works that attempted to deal with the legacies he felt were still present in the GDR, whether from the German (*Germania Tod in Berlin* [1971; Germania death in Berlin], *The Battle* [1974], a rewriting of *Die Umsiedlerin* as *Die Bauern* [1964; The peasants]) or Russian traditions (*Cement,* 1972). In scope of vision, political orientation, and innovative technique, Müller had clearly established himself by the early 1970s as the heir apparent to Bertolt Brecht, and the commission by Brecht's Berliner Ensemble to write the play (*Cement*) for the 1972 season seemed to have officially sealed that claim.

Yet despite or perhaps because of his debt to the maverick Brecht, Müller became increasingly skeptical over the years concerning the relevance of the Brechtian tradition for a critical theater in the socialist world. The reasons for this disenchantment may be traced both to Brecht himself and his reception in the GDR. At the level of cultural policy, it seems clear that with the canonization of Brecht in the museumlike Berliner Ensemble and with the resolution of the now famous Brecht-Lukács (modernism-traditionalism) debate at least at a standoff,[22] Brecht and the tradition he represented (montage, estrangement technique, epic theater) had become integrated into the theoretical and practicing life of socialist art.

But the problem for Müller may also be located within Brecht's own writing and thought and not simply their reception in the GDR. If the early Proletkultist Heiner Müller looked to Brecht's epic theater and objectivized notions of historical progress as the basis for his dramaturgy, Müller's later work increasingly questioned such a 'macrostructural' aesthetic for what it repressed in terms of historical and personal experience: 'Now we must concern ourselves with microstructures. For that Brecht offered forms and techniques only in his early works . . . but not in the classical plays. That is why they are so sacrosanct and boring.'[23]

Sacrosanct, boring, Müller says, *classical* – epithets that the avant-garde had always hurled at the establishment. Müller's critique of Brecht often had the attributes of such a clash. But were not both Brecht and Müller

Marxists of the avant-garde who had inverted in similar ways the precepts of orthodoxy to develop a poetics of consciousness? To answer this question we must look beyond Brecht the individual back to the artistic and political tradition he represents.

BERTOLT BRECHT AND THE AESTHETICS OF PRODUCTION

While Bertolt Brecht's writings and theatrical activity as a whole represent the most coherent 'materialist' alternative to the official aesthetics that was to emerge from the avant-garde within the socialist tradition, it is also true that much of the impetus and many of the practical models for not only Brecht but also a large number of leftist intellectuals of the Weimar period were to come from the Soviet avant-garde between 1917 and 1929. In this regard, the theoretical achievements of Walter Benjamin and Bertolt Brecht throughout the later 1920s and 1930s constitute an important link between the earlier Soviet experiences and the reemergence of that tradition in the GDR of the late 1950s and in West Germany a decade later.

Central to the whole notion of aesthetics to spring from the Russian postrevolutionary avant-garde was an integral link between cultural and social production. While the Formalist and Futurist movements and many of the leading poets (Mayakovsky, Burlyuk, Khlebnikov) were very much in evidence in the early 1900s, it was the social, political, and economic energies released by the revolution that helped reorganize their entire orientation. For instance, where the linguistic experimentalists such as Viktor Shklovsky and the Opoyaz group once sought to close the gap between life and art by subverting traditional aesthetics at the level of syntax and image in order to 'liberate' letters and words from the 'hegemony' of context, their leftist Futurist progeny aimed their attack at the very act of representation itself. Basic to the theories developed most coherently in the writings of Rodchenko, Tretyakov, and Arvatov was a notion of art, not as something autonomous and self-contained but rather as the "organization of everyday life," as an appropriation of nature as a form of material production.[24] Indeed, by recasting artistic creativity within the categories of labor power and material production, the LEF theorists strove for a materialist aesthetics that challenged the premises of bourgeois, but also implicitly Leninist, aesthetics. What linked bourgeois and Leninist notions of consciousness and art in the eyes of the avant-garde was an emphasis upon an ontology of knowledge, upon consciousness as a secondary, reflected, and passive repository for finished 'products' of thought. The Futurists questioned this by seeking to break with what Boris Arvatov pejoratively referred to as 'easel art' (art as supplementation of a disharmonized, i.e., unorganized, reality) and by establishing a threefold relationship to the forces of production at large: (1) as an activity that appropriated the physical materials and organizational principles of the industrialization of everyday life – film, radio, the other mechanical media; (2) as an activity that functioned within and dissolved the qualitative differences between the productions of everyday life – the production of useful objects, the design of objects and cities, the aesthetics of functionalism; (3) as an activity that availed itself of the formative principles of industrial and technological modes of production, above all the principle of montage.[25]

Metaphors of production and the importance of science and technology for art were, of course, not unique to the Russian avant-garde. The Italian Futurists also saw in the machine both an irreverence toward the sensibilities of traditional aesthetics and a thing of beauty in itself, and their songs of praise to technical weaponry surely anticipate the further implementation of such an 'aestheticization of politics' (Benjamin) as it developed in Italian and German fascism.[26] Even the Surrealists grasped in the concept of production an analogue to the furious and machinelike workings of the poetic unconscious.

What distinguished the Russians from either the Italian Futurists or the French Surrealists, however, was their attempt to link artistic activity directly to material societal production and thereby the activities of the artist to a whole set of 'laws,' processes, and energies perceived to be the inexorable, natural movement of history itself. This latter expansion of the concept of production was important for Bertolt Brecht as well, because he, like Arvatov and others, conceived of production aesthetics both in regard to the techniques employed and to art's relationship to the unfolding of social production as a whole. Brecht referred to socialism as 'the grand production,'[27] by which he meant a social system that would release the *entire* creative and working potentials of human beings, thus dissolving the distinctions in labor processes.[28] It is also true that Brecht's estrangement effect, while initially borrowed from and similar to Shklovsky's Formalist emphasis upon art 'making things appear strange so as to become visible,' was developed and expanded within Brecht's later range of thought into a category of mental production. As a 'technique of thinking,' artistic production 'worked' upon the seemingly natural and given world of fetishized objects and appearances in very much the way tools and machines are employed 'critically' in the appropriation of the natural.[29] Art too, then, was a force of production, a part of the 'ever proceeding emancipation of humans from nature on the ground of nature itself.'[30] Thus, while Brecht, in contrast to the LEF theorists, did not envision the dissolving of art and life into mere activity, and while he always emphasized centrally that art remained something constructed and hence second nature, his holding to and restatement of the theory of aesthetic production carried many of the political implications of the Soviet avantgarde into the landscape of the GDR.

What were the political implications of this aesthetic? Why was Proletkult, or, as it was called in the 1950s, neorappism,[31] to remain a thoroughly negative epithet within cultural policy? First, and most important, the anchoring of artistic production within the base as a coforce of production meant a repudiation of the base-superstructure model of Marxist-Leninism and with that the political infrastructure fed by socialist realism. The concept of reflection is vital for Marxist-Leninism not merely because in its seeming duplication of reality it claims to provide a more communicable ('realistic,' 'popular') representation of the world but because the representation itself is a replica of preestablished modes of being and knowing. In two interrelated ways works of art in accordance with socialist realism are the result of *prefabrication:* as works reflecting 'reality,' they present a cognitive organization after the fact, that is, one that conforms and is subordinate to a set of 'objective,' 'natural' processes. Second, the view of these processes is itself to be informed by an objective science that already 'knows' certain outcomes by virtue of the categories it employs (the inevitable arrival of socialism after the inevitable collapse of capitalism, etc.). Once given these two interfacing premises (the inevitability of 'socialist' history and the infallibility of the science that will know it), it follows that the Party can install itself as the omniscient mediator of the whole process.

Brecht's aesthetics challenges these premises in a number of important ways. Making the author into a producer (Benjamin) shifts the whole emphasis of literary epistemology from a reflected 'content of knowledge' to an active, 'critical' reorganization of experience. This in turn affects all the categories that Brecht employs. On the one hand, by grounding literary production in social production as a whole, he clearly retains the Marxian notion of the unfolding forces of production through the process of appropriating nature (*technē*), as basic to a concept of historical progress. At the same time, by making the author a producer and instituting a direct two-way relationship between an 'epic' voice of reason (producer I) and the critically reasoning audience (producer II), Brecht broadens his notion of production to include the production of meaning and consciousness as well. Brecht's more democratic emphasis upon the shared production of meaning – basic to both the concept of estrangement and the principles of the *Lehrstück* [learning play] – implicitly challenges the hierarchy of the *one* hegemonic science (Brecht speaks of his audiences as the 'children of the scientific age') and links him to the 'anarchy' of the leftist avant-garde.

This problematic link between cultural and literary production, on the one hand, and the aesthetics of modernism, on the other, was at the real heart of the so-called Expressionism debate waged in the exile journal *Das Wort* between 1937 and 1940. Ostensibly concerned with the question as to whether the conversion to fascism by such leading Expressionist poets as Gottfried Benn, Hanns Johst, and Arnolt Bronnen indicated something inherently (ontologically?) fascist about the Expressionist movement itself (Lukács's initial argument), the debate soon came to focus on the question of modernism and class struggle and, more specifically, on the issue as to whether the principles of avant-garde aesthetic production (self-reflection, antimimesis, nonrepresentation, technical experimentation, etc.) were ultimately compatible with artistic creation within the socialist tradition.[32]

Although Brecht himself never directly took part in this debate at the time (his contributions were published posthumously), the position he represented was set forth most forcefully by Hanns Eisler and Ernst Bloch. Whereas Lukács, drawing on a crude theory of mimesis, argued that any and all bourgeois art emerging in the period of imperialism (1875 to the present) was *eo ipso* 'rotten' by virtue of its rotten contextual roots, Eisler and Bloch articulated an aesthetics of production that drew the links to the evolution of industrial production in the society at large, technological developments within a specific medium, artistic technique, and structural changes occurring in the very notion of what is culture: 'Even the development of musical material is determined by the development of the forces of production. The modern piano makes possible a different kind of music from the cembalo, Wagnerian instrumentation is unthinkable without brass instruments. In our time, by virtue of sound film, the phonograph, the radio, as well as the changes of different forms of presentation, new problems of production emerge that cannot be solved simply with reference to how great Beethoven is or the rotten nature of monopoly capitalism.'[33] Eisler and Bloch's defense of Expressionism as a more 'progressive' mode of production in the ever-advancing diachrony of cultural production as a whole – despite the ideological disposition of individual Expressionists or even the thematics of their works – consciously sought to draw on the production aesthetics of the Soviet and Weimar avant-gardes as a legitimate 'heritage' for socialist culture as a whole, a strategy Brecht himself was to continue in the GDR.

Finally, while the efforts to suppress the aesthetics of modernism in the interest of traditional aesthetics were undoubtedly connected to the more general political strategy to form a united front for the struggle against fascism in the 1930s, the biases and values informing that policy had already evolved out of the processes of Stalinization at the end of the 1920s and were to remain long after Hitler's armies lay in ruins in 1945. At the basis of the conflict were fundamental questions concerning political control and freedom of expression at every level of the social order.

THE DIALECTICS OF THE AVANT-GARDE IN THE GDR:
MÜLLER VERSUS BRECHT

In our discussion of the Soviet avant-garde's aesthetics of production and its continuation in the theories and practice of Bertolt Brecht in the 1920s and 1930s, we have stressed the ways in which such an aesthetics subverts the philosophical and political precepts of a socialist realism based on the values of high culture. While such an emphasis explains well how 'self-

organization' as the thematic and operative principle of art would prove
incompatible with the structures of a Party policy devoted to mediating
all cultural meanings within the social order, it does not help us understand the potential for that very same aesthetics to be integrated into the
principles of Marxist-Leninism. This latter concern is particularly acute
for our discussion of Heiner Müller in the GDR, since his break with
Brecht represents in a larger sense a coming to terms with the political
realities embedded in the aesthetics of production. As much as the productivist avant-garde disrupted and transformed at the level of representation, its historically developed philosophical implications concerning
history and subjectivity relinked it to an apologetics for the existing socialist order. Basic to its orientation was an unquestioned acceptance of
the primacy of humans over nature – the interaction between subject
(producer, artist) and object (nature, material for representation) – as *eo
ipso* the realization of an enlightened, progressive history.

As we have seen in our discussion of Robert Havemann,[34] the binding
of a theory of production to a theory of history was also, of course, the
theoretical cornerstone of Soviet Marxism for the legitimation of existing
socialist societies. If Marxism as a *revolutionary* social theory stressed the
importance of theory (thought, consciousness, art, etc.) as the *critical*
self-consciousness of an actual revolutionary process, its transformation
into an 'objective' social theory of production grounded in the categories
of natural science meant a recasting of the subjective, history-making
element into a subcomponent of a naturalized historical process. Understanding the primacy of production for such an ontologized dialectic of
history is the key to grasping the paradoxical role of the Left opposition in
the Soviet Union of the 1920s[35] as well as the avant-garde of the same and
later periods. In all instances an emphasis upon production was seen as an
emancipatory break with scholasticized Marxism.

As much as the Proletkultists and the Futurists challenged the precepts
of a dialectic that had become sedimented in a one-way transmission of
truth, their unproblematic glorification of production must be seen as
ultimately contiguous with or even anticipatory of the later instrumen-
talizing of culture and history embodied in Stalin's famous designation of
writers and artists as 'engineers of the soul.' In the Soviet avant-garde we
find the same glorification of urbanism and technological culture that was

to provide the ideological framework for imposing a modernist, 'enlightened,' 'proletarian' revolution from above upon an agrarian society. Like the mechanists and like Stalin at a later period, the enthusiasts of Proletkult and Constructivism voiced uncritical optimism concerning the inherently uplifting and liberatory powers of Taylorism and the Americanization of culture. Thus, the fact that Tretyakov, Eisenstein, Mayakovsky, Meyerhold, and others were in opposition to and finally in various ways victims of the emerging Soviet cultural politics of the late 1920s and 1930s should not obscure the fact that their political aesthetics contained as its own internal paradox that very same 'dialectic of the Enlightenment' that was the essence of the order they tried to reform.[36]

The Brechtian aesthetics as it was introduced into the GDR contained a similar paradox. On the subversive side, its implicit emphasis upon self-organization was seen and repressed as a challenge to Party hegemony in matters cultural. In this regard, the critical treatment of Brecht and Benjamin in the GDR[37] is very much in keeping with the repression of any cultural revolutionary program that calls for self-initiative and pluralism as the constituent parts of a democratized cultural public sphere, from the Soviet avant-garde to Hans Magnus Enzensberger. Yet although Brecht himself remained to the end an 'uncomfortable' Leninist, his embrace of socialist production as the demiurge of historical progress reestablished the 'epic voice' of his later plays as the collective subject of an ultimately rational historical process.

It is this epic voice and its political implications that Müller begins to question as a viable heritage for radical expression in the GDR. The fundamental difference between the two began to emerge around 1975, when Müller made his move against what he calls the aesthetics of 'naturalism': 'the expulsion of the author from the text, of the reality of the author from the theater.'[38] Brecht is a naturalist for Müller because of his relationship to what he writes rather than because of any specific technique or style. While epic theater as an avant-garde, nonrepresentational art form repudiated the simplistic mimetic representations it saw embodied both in nineteenth-century naturalism and twentieth-century socialist realism, its sublimation of the authorial self into an epic superego, derived from the truth and telos of Marxist historiography, forfeits a radical subjectivity that Müller sees as essential for a socialist society. For Müller, the Brechtian aesthetics must be seen as the product of a historical period. Brecht's epic persona of the later plays was created within and was an expression of a minority consensus that shared an interest in the destruction of fascism (capitalism). In the course of the 1930s its collective vision was increasingly determined by theoretical premises of 'an incomplete Marxism' and propagated the values of optimism and progress. In a society like the GDR, one that prematurely claims for itself the realization of such values, such an aesthetic can become an apology in its very form. It asserts a false consensus. Its preformulated assumptions disallow a priori any expression that would challenge the collective peace. Müller's search for a new aesthetic is also a search for a new politics: instead of sovereignty he calls for doubt; in place of optimism, the expression of fear; in lieu of a collective ground in false consensus, the uncompromising voice of the subject.

Not surprisingly, Müller's differences with the Brechtian avant-garde reached their sharpest contours around the subject of fascism. Where Brecht's enlightened approach would belittle the impact of myth and irrationalism and offer as an antidote the voice of reason, Müller's 'self' (voice) is the fantasy that reason would sublimate and repress.[39] His increasing fixation in his history plays with blood, brutalizing sexuality, and even cannibalism seeks to unveil the silences of a repressed history, whether it resides in the mythologies of Greek, Renaissance, German Classical, or Marxist-Leninist representations. To this extent Müller also functions as a historian, albeit a historian of social amnesia. In his play *Germania Tod in Berlin* a character called the skull salesman, digging in a cemetery, says it directly:

> I am one of those left over. I am replanting here. UNDER FLOWERS
> AND GRASS. We work nights. Under alcohol because of infection.... I
> was a historian. A mistake in periodizing, the Thousand Year Reich
> you understand. Since history directed me to the cemeteries, to its
> theological dimensions, so to speak, I am immune to the cadaver
> smell of promises for a better world. The golden age lies behind us.[40]

Müller's negative dialectics of history bring to the surface a cultural heritage of the *deutsche Misere* [German misery] that has been repressed in the annals of official Marxist historiography. Instead of resistance fighters and positive heroes, he gives us soldiers who cannibalize each other for survival; in place of the birth of the new society on the trail of the victorious Red Army, the grotesque, painful rebirth of the old. An example from his play *Germania:* impregnated by Hitler, Joseph Goebbels as the Madonna gives birth on the stage to a horrible thalidomide wolf.[41]

The artistic tradition that Müller draws on here is clearly of Western European and not Eastern European origin, of Artaud, existentialism, Samuel Beckett; in short, 'cosmopolitanism.' Thus, it is not surprising that Eastern and Western Marxists alike accused him of a philosophical pessimism and the individualism associated with such thinking. What their critique failed to consider was the function of such an aesthetic within the 'horizon of expectation' in the GDR. Müller's cross-cut reading of German history pushed against the grain of official representations into distorted fantasies, perverted memories, sordid images – the untold stories. What this in turn entailed was breaking with an aesthetic narrator who posits reality in a sublimated, enlightened epic voice. Again Brecht was the target when Müller wrote that 'it is no longer permissible not to talk about oneself when one writes.'[42] Müller's *self* in plays such as *The Battle* or *Hamletmachine* (1977) is a repressed male history. His images indeed are not those of resistance fighters or emancipated women or even, as in Brecht, schizophrenic characters who represent historical contradictions (Shen Te and Shui Ta in *The Good Woman of Sezuan* postulating use value and exchange value; Galileo caught in the imprisonment of false and real consciousness). In Müller, dredged deep from the history of sublimated contradiction, we find the hidden psychic wreckage that enlightened, documented, 'proletarian' history has left behind.

In his book *male fantasies,* Klaus Theweleit has argued for an expanded analysis of fascism beyond the sociopolitical that would grasp it as 'rooted in the changing organization of male-female relations.'[43] The power of Müller's narration lies precisely in its production of fantasy below and beyond the level of reason. It is below the level of reason for those intellectuals who, like Brecht, have squashed that history into the narrow blocks of a rational consciousness; one that, in the words of Hegel, begins its work after the shades of night have fallen, outside of and repressing the gory underlife. But it is also beyond a level of reason in that Müller is able to catch the living fantasies of those who did fight and die and fantasize as a part of the war machine. We may call this technique antipatriarchal because it dares to constitute as the imaginary self of dramatic representation the repressed and perverted fantasy life of one group of historical males – a fantasy life that Müller believed to be still alive and well on *both* sides of the Elbe River.

And what does this say about the practicing avant-garde in the GDR of the 1970s and early 1980s? First, politicizing literature within the *Kulturpolitik* guaranteed the continuing role of the avant-garde as a political one, even when the target of revolt was one wing of the historical avant-garde itself. Second, the problem of subjectivity within socialism must be ultimately engaged with at the level of epistemology and linguistic representation, and for that reason the avant-garde had an important and viable function in exploring buried histories and hidden myths. Third, the interest in 'irrationalist' thinkers such as Lautréamont, Artaud, and even Beckett by the leftist avant-garde in the GDR was connected to the failure of rationalist and objectivist approaches within Marxism to grasp basic truths about individual human behavior and motivation. 'The trends and drives in the historical process,' wrote Müller, 'which are above all important for mass movements, have been abandoned to the right wing. I believe we must move away from this kind of overrationalizing. This is why Artaud is a productive nuisance.'[44] Finally, judgments about the political integrity of any literature can be made only in relation to its function within a particular social order. Again Heiner Müller: 'I/GDR cannot write about me without writing about GDR/politics.'[45] The realm of intimacy has been politicized. In the case of the poet, he says, this is a burden and a hope.

FROM PRAXIS TO THEORY

The struggle on the part of artists such as Heiner Müller to draw on modernist and avant-garde traditions heretofore officially repudiated, and thereby to validate them within the socialist order, did not occur in a vacuum. Rather, it was part of a process by which experimental artists have forced the question and changed the terms of discourse, not only within the practicing cultural scene but at the level of theory as well. While the time-lag between artistic breakthrough and theoretical reflection in the GDR was often a matter of years, one should not discount the importance of theoretical discourse for marking the new terrain and expanding the entire framework of debate. Take for instance the Brecht discussion. While Brecht's call in 1956 for 'small, flexible (theatrical) forms of struggle' from the agitprop movement of the Weimar Republic was recognized almost immediately, if also tentatively, on the stages of East Berlin, it was not until the late 1960s that a Brecht position could be developed theoretically within the official public sphere.[46] Werner Mittenzwei's construction of a 'Brecht-Lukács Debate' (1967),[47] together with his elaboration of an 'aesthetics of materials [*Materialästhetik*]'[48] founded upon technological innovation and the latest developments in media (film, radio, architecture), offered the first viable alternative to a classical tradition based upon the organic artwork and an aesthetics of beauty (Lukács). But beyond its narrow aesthetic implications, the theoretical validation of a Brechtian aesthetics also marked, in the words of one GDR critic, a 'turning point in the discussions concerning cultural heritage in the 1970s,' since it represented 'the first attempt from the side of Marxism to bring up the reception and the controversial interchange with the heritage of the *socialist* avant-garde after 1945 in the GDR.'[49]

It is significant that Mittenzwei does *not* use the term 'avant-garde' in his defense of a revolutionary tradition that has clearly been identified as such in discussions that were being carried on in both the Western and Eastern blocs during that time. Indeed, despite the fact that the Hungarian Laszlo Illes had introduced the notion of a 'socialist avant-garde' into the East bloc discussions as early as 1964,[50] it was not until the late 1970s that we find the term being used in the GDR at all.[51] The publication of *Künsterische Avantgarde: Annäherungen an ein unabgeschlossenes Kapitel* (The artistic avant-garde: Approaches to an unfinished chapter)[52] articulated in its title and in its preface the new perspective. Avant-garde, we are told, is a term designating a 'historical' art movement that 'arose in the force-field of the revolutionary break in the transition from capitalism to socialism.'[53]

So defined, two emphases emerge that were vital for the function of the concept in the contemporary GDR. First, there is a clear attempt to historicize the notion of the avant-garde and in so doing to prevent its application to contemporary developments. The 'historical avant-garde'[54] refers to the revolutionary period between 1900 and 1930 and includes movements such as Constructivism, Surrealism, Dadaism, Neue Sachlichkeit, and even parts of Expressionism. Regardless of the relevance of this 'heritage' for the contemporary art scene, the argument continues, the notion of a socialist avant-garde cannot be applied to developments in the GDR, since it emerged as part of a bourgeois *and* revolutionary-socialist movement in conflict with the capitalist status quo.

While such a definition does not discount the importance of formal innovation as an integral part of political innovation, narrowing the concept to a 'historical' political movement (as opposed to aesthetic and apolitical modernism) certainly suggests that the experimental activities of contemporary GDR artists are not to be designated as avant-garde: 'The thought of a *direct* re-awakening of old ideas and practices reveals itself as illusionary,' we are told in the introduction. 'The consciousness of the avant-garde's historicity is the prerequisite for its potential relevance for today.'[55] The implication here is clear: in a socialist society, there is room for only one vanguard, and that is the Party. Any attempt to resurrect the term in order to prescribe contemporary artistic developments must be seen as a challenge to the cultural authority of the status quo.

Yet historicizing the avant-garde tradition within the GDR also meant legitimizing that heritage for socialist culture, which in turn had an important impact upon artists and upon the institutions of literary criticism and culture.[56] Once a part of the official canon, heritages are there to be used in the present, and they inevitably carry political implications. For instance, the rehabilitation of such movements as Expressionism and Surrealism, with their recourse to the unconscious and to fantasy as sources for artistic creativity, inevitably expanded the framework of a rationalist and narrowly political concept of the avant-garde, which in turn changed the terms of artistic discourse in every field of endeavor. Hence, the unprecedented publication in the mid-1980s of writings by Antonin Artaud, André Breton, Max Ernst, Salvador Dali, and others in the GDR[57] was a response both to artistic practices already apparent in the cultural scene and to important signals concerning the changing tone of intellectual life in the larger society.[58] The invocation of avant-garde thinking, regardless of how it was officially interpreted and historically coded, opened up a multitude of critical issues of relevance for the contemporary society.

More important, its very presence within a pantheon of the 'past' suggested a challenge to any ingrained or established tradition that would serve merely as legitimation of the status quo.

Certainly the face-off between Bertolt Brecht and Heiner Müller came to represent one major version of the paradigm shift occurring within the politics of the socialist avant-garde. In the following three chapters, I focus specifically on three developments within GDR avant-garde theater in which the theater of Brecht and Müller as well as the constructed dialogue between the two took on cultural and political significance. In each case I show how the challenge of the avant-garde represents at once a testing of cultural norms and a critique of social relations within the body politic as a whole.

4. FROM WEIMAR TO BERLIN: REPERFORMING THE HISTORICAL AVANT-GARDE

The question is, how are we going to involve drama in the struggle for social-ism? That is the real difficulty. Our goal should be to unleash a struggle within the audience, a struggle for the new against the old. — Speech by Bertolt Brecht at the Fourth Writers Congress, January 1956, in Werner Hecht, *Brecht im Gespräch*

I n the late 1950s, a number of younger dramatists from the GDR turned to the agitprop theater movement of the 1920s as a source for poetic and political renewal. This recourse to the heretofore forbidden tradition of the Weimar avant-garde marked an important turning point in the history of contemporary play writing in East Germany. Aesthetically, the effort to reappropriate formal strategies from the heritage of modernism initiated a movement of theatrical creativity that was to produce some of the leading figures and dramatic achievements in German postwar theater over the next three decades. On a more immediate political level, the shift to what Brecht called 'smaller forms of struggle' clearly evolved out of changing institutional imperatives within the socialist public sphere: the need above all to constitute the theater as a tribune for open dialogue and as a means to engage larger segments of the populace in the political process.

The fact that the emergence of this so-called didactic theater (Ulbricht) was ultimately brought about by students of Brecht and not by the master himself cannot simply be explained by Brecht's sudden death in 1956, six months after his call for political theater at the Fourth Writers Congress. From the time of his arrival in the GDR in 1948, Brecht had found it difficult to write contemporary plays for the new society. In fact, his failure to rework the story of the legendary GDR Stakhanovite worker Hans Garbe into a *Lehrstück* [learning play] in the early 1950s grew out of the same dilemma that he had experienced as a director of Erwin Strittmatter's play *Katzgraben* with the Berliner Ensemble in 1952. Brecht's '*Katzgraben-Notes*' of that period articulate brilliantly his doubts about creating a genuinely political theater within the legitimatory framework of a socialist society: How is it possible, Brecht asked, to refashion a critical-epic method, based on a theory of negation (the estrangement effect) and developed in the struggle against capitalism and fascism, into an affirmative, agitational theater for and not against the status quo? Do the long-term social upheavals in the daily life of average people even lend themselves to dramatic representation? Can one depict the 'new infectious life feeling' under socialism without recourse to stereotypic 'positive heroes' and aesthetic clichés?[1] What is the relationship of such socialist theater, finally, to the audience and to building a critical socialist public sphere?

Similar questions had also been posed at the Writers Congress by such renowned Party intellectuals as Anna Seghers, Georg Lukács, Hans Mayer, and Johannes R. Becher in their attack on what Seghers called the growing 'schematism' in the literature of the GDR. One of the tasks of this chapter will be to indicate the reasons why and the manner in which the succeeding generation of playwrights (Heiner Müller, Peter Hacks, Helmut Baierl, Volker Braun, etc.) and *not* the writers returning from exile were ultimately to provide the first meaningful answers to such queries; but also why the efforts to engage the theater as political forum often ended in failure.

AGITATING TO AFFIRM: EARLY DIDACTIC THEATER

The public, unprecedented critique of schematism by writers such as Brecht and Seghers was not the only reason why in October 1957 the SED suddenly issued a challenge to artists to 'make use of the wealth of revolutionary tradition from the workers movement [of the 1920s] in developing an interesting socialist cultural life.'[2] This call for operative forms of struggle from the socialist heritage (agitprop groups, 'forms of the Living Newspaper,' and the 'red revues' were mentioned) and for greater political engagement from the artistic intelligentsia emerged at a time of political and economic crisis. The beginnings of de-Stalinization at the Twentieth Congress of the Communist Party (April 1956) and the ensuing uprisings in Hungary and Poland demanded of the Soviet bloc as a whole greater efforts at political legitimation. In the GDR, the Party reacted with a two-pronged strategy: in the area of foreign policy there were increased attempts to distance the GDR ideologically from the West; and the domestic front saw the introduction of a Five-Year Plan designed to encourage individual initiatives for economic growth and greater political participation from the population as a whole.

The call for a more creative, agitational *Kulturpolitik,* announced officially under the rubric 'cultural questions are questions of power,'[3] emerged from pressures to renegotiate the relationship between Party and populace within the socialist public sphere. The attack on schematism, regardless of what it said about the limitations and liabilities of socialist realism as an artistic endeavor, was, on another important political level, an open admission that in its efforts to create a truly effective, politically meaningful socialist contemporary literature in the GDR, the Party would have to speak to larger segments of the population than heretofore. Nor should we be surprised that it was the theater intelligentsia who were first called upon to broaden this appeal. As early as the founding of Otto Brahm's Volksbühne theater in the 1890s under the Sozialdemokratische Partei Deutschlands (SPD) and throughout the Weimar period within the KPD, theater had functioned in the workers movement as the most appropriate forum for creating agitpropaganda, awakening political engagement, and promoting a sense of a countertradition to bourgeois culture. Erwin Piscator's mammoth revues *Trotz alledem* (In spite of all that) (1924) and *Revue Roter Rummel* (1925) represented building blocks for a proletarian counterpublic sphere par excellence. With the help of epic materials such as documentary film, slide projections, and mass scenes and the active involvement of lay actors, thousands of young people had been drawn into the theater and mobilized for the Party. More important, the theater under Piscator established itself as a tribune for public debate, a center for the expression of alternative politics, and a podium for the voices of the disenfranchised.

In the GDR, it was Heiner Müller and Müller Hagen-Stahl who, in their documentary play of November 1957 entitled *Zehn Tage, die die Welt erschütterten* (Ten days that shook the world), first sought to utilize the Weimar tradition for postwar drama. Building on other GDR productions

111

of revolutionary drama such as Brecht's *The Days of the Commune* or the Russian Vladimir Bill-Bjelozerkowski's *Storm,* their short didactic 'scenes of the October Revolution based on the sketches by John Reed' sought to show parallels between the political transformations occurring in East Germany during that period and the achievements of the October Revolution forty years earlier.

However, just as important as the Party's immediate political goals was the related effort to take traditions that heretofore had been taboo in the GDR, namely the Weimar and Soviet avant-gardes, and make them relevant as a source of revitalization [*Neuakzentuierung*]⁴ within a moribund cultural politics. Thus, despite the fact that the Müller/Hagen-Stahl production of this 'agitprop montage'⁵ at the Berliner Volksbühne was, simply at the dramaturgical level, somewhat of a theatrical disaster, the authors were nevertheless successful in reawakening a revolutionary tradition. By deviating from the plot-, character-, and stage-centered 'theater works' of conventional socialist realism (and even Brecht's longer epic plays), they offered new possibilities for the development of a more broad-based theatrical public life.

The integral relationship between the reappropriation of the 'proletarian-revolutionary heritage' from the Weimar period and the struggle for a 'proletarian'⁶ theatrical public sphere in the GDR can perhaps best be illustrated in the genesis and reception of Heiner Müller's next play, *Der Lohndrücker.* The major theme of *Der Lohndrücker* was the story of the activist Hans Garbe, who had almost single-handedly repaired a furnace at the Siemens-Plania works in Berlin while one of the ovens was still functioning. This spectacular feat not only avoided a major production shut-down, it also created a much needed contemporary socialist myth. Thanks to Garbe's eulogization by the press, as well as the numerous literary renderings of his achievement (Eduard Claudius's *Vom schweren Anfang,* 1950, and *Menschen an unserer Seite,* 1951; Käthe Rülicke's *Hans Garbe erzählt*), the Garbe story had rapidly become a public legend that Müller now sought systematically to demystify and reexamine.

In Müller's play, the Garbe figure (his name is Balke) is anything but a positive hero. The perspective, already evident in the title, is cast negatively and focused on contradictions. In the Third Reich the worker Balke had prevented an act of sabotage against the fascist state by denouncing a resistance fighter (who appears in the present as the Party secretary Schorn). In the new society, Balke again 'betrays' his fellow workers, this time by wage sharking, that is, by achieving an extraordinary amount of work in a short amount of time and thereby driving up the work norms and deflating wages. Hence in Müller's play, Balke/Garbe is from one perspective a negative hero; a one-time denouncer whose obsessive and egotistical compulsion to work even now is disruptive to labor relations within the norm structures of socialism. Yet it is also clear from the play that Müller's goal is not to portray Balke as a villain but rather to alter the political *and* artistic perspective of traditional agitprop: Balke as 'hero of production' is viewed through the eyes and interests of *both* Party and disgruntled worker, as *both* a hero and a villain.

The ideological bifurcation of Müller's play *Der Lohndrücker* around both worker and Party interests brings us once again to the issue of critical spectatorial viewing, which was to play such a central role at every stage in the genesis of the play. Müller's double perspective is particularly obvious at the end of the first scene, for example, where we find the following stage directions: 'On the street there appears a signposter who posts a sign with the text: "SED – Party for rebuilding" on a ruined building. When he is gone a young worker comes along, stands in front of the sign, looks around, rips it down, and walks off whistling. Three workers, tired, with satchels under their arms, stomp across the sign lying on the ground.'[7] The text does not advocate an attitude for or against the Party (*or* Balke *or* the workers against Balke, etc.). On one side of the dialectical ledger, we see an official Party slogan with its fancy promises, now made hollow by the degrading postwar reality surrounding it (ruined buildings, etc.). Opposed to this is the experience of an exhausted set of workers, who at this moment constitute a negative response. But Müller does not idealize this 'antiperspective,' regardless of its political legitimacy. Indeed, in the play itself it is represented in part by one-time fascists and anticommunists. Rather, what he attempts is the confrontation of worker experience (and an often-ignored area of production), on the one hand, with the representative public offerings of the state, on the other, in order to show two sides of an ongoing conflictual process. The very interaction of such negative energies becomes the operative principle for both the dramaturgy of the play and its reception by a questioning and critical audience. Contradictions, not true (easy) answers, and a simple plot narrative are the motivating impulses for this work. Out of the disruptions at the heart of the industrial process, Müller's text seems to be saying, the new society (and the new aesthetics!) is born.

If Müller/Hagen-Stahl's *Zehn Tage, die die Welt erschütterten* is called an agitprop montage because of its outspokenly 'didactic' character, Müller's *Der Lohndrücker* offers a qualitatively different mode of reception. Instead of proselytizing, this Brechtlike *Lehrstück* implies, at the very level of its decentered perspective, that the audience is a coproducer of its interpretive meaning and not the object of a harangue. This reorientation of audience involvement assumes in turn a very different notion of publicness in a socialist society. For if Brecht's call for political theater at the Writers Congress demanded that a struggle be unleashed within the audience, 'the struggle of the new against the old,' then Müller's prologue to *Der Lohndrücker* is both a direct response to Brecht and a further development of his position. 'My play does not seek,' says Müller, 'to portray the struggle of the new against the old (which a playwright cannot decide anyway) as a victory of the new brought to completion before the closing of the final curtain; it seeks rather to displace this struggle into the audience, which will decide for itself.'[8]

Müller recasts the agitprop concept, highlighting the inner relationship between the structures of theatrical form and audience reception while inverting traditional notions of didactic theater. Formal elements such as montage or decentered characters and plot are meant to disrupt audience identification in order to establish a more equal 'partnership' with the spectators.[9] At the 1973 Brecht conference in East Berlin, Müller spoke provocatively of the necessity for a 'pluralistic audience' in socialist theater, one that is no longer structured in a bipolar fashion around 'friends on the one side and enemies on the other'[10] but rather one that seeks to create an atmosphere for critical debate and open disagreement.

The reception of Müller's *Der Lohndrücker* as well as his next play *The Correction* demonstrates both the critical potential and the political threat of such theater in the GDR of the 1950s. After its premiere in March 1958 by a studio in Leipzig, *Der Lohndrücker* was produced in Berlin at the Maxim Gorki theater by the young director Hans Dieter Mäde. Although the object of a heated and by no means uniformly negative response by the official press and even Walter Ulbricht,[11] this *Lehrstück* – conceived for just such a public reception – was nevertheless quietly dropped after just a few showings. For it was precisely the controversy itself that could not be tolerated in a public sphere immune to genuine political debate on social issues of immediate import.

A similar if somewhat more complicated reception awaited Müller's drama *The Correction*, also produced by Mäde at the Maxim Gorki. Once again the play focuses upon contradictions and historical conflicts within the area of industrial production. Bremer, a long-time Party member, is demoted from brigadier to normal laborer for attacking an engineer because of the latter's fascist past; in a subplot, a brigade attempts to retaliate for pay differentials resulting from production inefficiency. The problems and contradictions depicted in these two unresolved plot lines, together with the play's use of simple language and short, elliptical, open scenes, were intended by Müller to elicit maximum involvement from the public for the completion of meaning.

Certainly the play's genesis indicates such intention. The work was written in the winter of 1958 as a radio play following a visit by Heiner and Inge Müller to the *Kombinat* [conglomerate] Schwarze Pumpe. Workers of the Schwarze Pumpe listened to a taped reading of the first version, after which the authors discussed it with them. A transcript of what turned out to be a lively exchange appeared in the journal *Neue Deutsche Literatur*, along with the first version of the play itself. Shortly thereafter the play opened at the Maxim Gorki theater, but after one performance in front of production and Party workers from Berlin factories, the show was canceled because, as the official version would have it, 'the performance ended up making people depressed, instead of, as hoped for, more actively engaged.'[12] The Müllers wrote a second version of the play in which Bremer, the brigadier, is chastised but keeps his job and in which the contradictory, conflictual nature of the work is played down in favor of resolution and social harmony.

A comparison of the two versions of *The Correction* reveals clearly the extent to which the more pronounced 'didacticism' of the second version has actually sacrificed its potential to activate an audience. Müller's own comments also emphasize how he found 'the more sovereign (nondepressed, active) attitude' of the audience at the Schwarze Pumpe[13] that had first listened to the recording much more appropriate than the controlled and orchestrated response at the Maxim Gorki theater. When Müller himself sums up how he felt about being forced to revise the play by saying 'the self-criticism of the authors has moved into its executive phase: *The Correction* is now being corrected. The new literature can only be developed with the new audience,'[14] he is surely being ironic, but not only ironic. The central issue for Müller was not just the 'correction,' or, in this instance, the censorship of a text but rather the dialectical process through which a text is to emerge. After all, these plays did appear and were the subject of intense public debate. In this regard, such early experiments became a model of social communication and remained exceptions rather than the rule. In a later comment, Müller remarks upon the paradoxes confronting many of the theater works of this earlier period that were attempting to come to terms critically with historical processes by reactivating the deeper dialogic meaning of Brecht's *Lehrstück* tradition for living socialism: 'In a public discussion following a performance of *Der Lohndrücker* at the Maxim Gorki theater, a scene was mounted in which a worker and former member of the Sturm Abteilung (sa) asks to be admitted to membership in the Party. "It should not be left hanging in the air as to whether he is accepted or not," was one view critical of the play's inherent ambivalent character. An opposing view of another member of the audience: "What do you mean in the air? We're talking about it, aren't we?" ' Müller continues: 'Here we find two very different views concerning the function and impact of theater. For whatever reason, only one of these views prevails today: theater as a static condition. It seems to me it is high time we avail ourselves of the second one, which conceives of theater not as something static but as a process.'[15]

Müller was not the only one to use the model of the Brechtian *Lehrstück* as a means for opening up public discussion around controversial social issues. The 1950s was a time of rapid collectivization in the GDR, resulting, among other things, in a wave of farm people leaving the country for West Germany. Helmut Baierl's 'agroprop'[16] drama *Die Feststellung* (1958; The determination) is above all an attempt to present in dialogic and dialectical fashion the controversial subject of migration ('flight from the republic' [*Republikflucht*], as it was called) in all of its contradictory form and as a subject for public debate. In this play, the *Mittelbauer* [medium farmer] Finze and his wife are harassed ideologically by a Party secretary to join a local collective (LPG, Landwirtschaftliche Produktionsgenossenschaft). For economic reasons they refuse to do so and, fearing retaliation, decide to leave the country. After a number of years they return to the GDR and are asked to explain their behavior. In direct use of the Brechtian *Lehrstück,* Finze and the Party secretary, as a play within a play, switch roles and act out the original confrontation scene that had caused the Finzes to leave in the first place. By playing and thus necessarily identifying himself with the 'other' side, each side begins to 'understand' his own failings. The moral of the play is summed up in the following comment:

> A SMALL FARMER: With that the question is resolved, thank you both very much. If we had talked about these things more often, we would have saved ourselves a lot of anguish, right, Finze?
> THE FARMER: Yes, I now understand you completely . . . I am tired of just sitting on the sidelines. It's time to join up.[17]

Comparing Baierl's *Die Feststellung* with Müller's industrial *Lehrstücke,* written at approximately the same time, reveals diametrically opposed notions concerning the dramatic representation of social conflict under socialism. In the case of Müller, the contradiction exists within the context of the socioeconomic order itself: the primitive, underdeveloped, in no way 'socialist' relations of production stand in genuine, antagonistic conflict with the human needs of those living in the society. If the workers in *The Correction* juggle the norms, then this is seen in relation to failures in the area of production and not simply as the result of 'false consciousness.' In Baierl's *Die Feststellung,* on the other hand, the only problem with the Party's collectivization program is its failure to find the means of proper persuasion. Finze's resistance is not seen to emerge from any crisis of existing economic conditions (the massive economic disasters of early collectivization measures are not even mentioned) but is based rather on his inability to understand these measures as inevitable and just. By using Brecht's behaviorist-oriented *Lehrstück* as a means to provide Finze and the audience with ideological instruction, Baierl transforms what was intended by Brecht to be a vehicle for experimentation and critical questioning into an instrument of manipulation.

But does he completely? While such an analysis might seem to grasp the thematic and political message of Baierl's play at the level of its authorial intention, it does not deal with its theatrical function within the cultural framework of the late 1950s. Also important for understanding this play, as well as Herbert Keller's *Die Begegnung* (1957; The meeting), a *Lehrstück* similarly dealing with the subject of *Republikflucht*, is the fact that it evolved as a part of the amateur theater movement, 'which around 1957 experienced a remarkable growth and popularity in the GDR.'[18] The goal of this movement – like the underlying intention of the Brechtian *Lehrstück* – was to provide lay worker-actors with the opportunity to bring their daily problems onto the stage and to act them out in the manner of collective therapy. 'This play gestus,' writes the GDR critic Gudrun Klatt, 'namely learning through play-acting, being able to assume, dispense with, overcome different attitudes and thereby arrive at new attitudes [*Haltungen*] is the basis of this kind of play, which in turn strikes at a central nerve of reality.'[19] What Klatt does not mention, and the reason that a play like *Die Feststellung* can potentially take on a critical function (despite any thematically structured affirmative content: happy end = tying up all contradictions), is precisely the polyvalence factor inherent to the *Lehrstück* form itself. Basic to the Brechtian *Lehrstück* is a noncalculable, experimental character, which by encouraging actors to improvise and draw on their own life experience breaks up the traditional text-stage-audience relationship and potentially challenges conventional political meanings. Gone is the one-way street from authorial intention to audience (passive) reception, so central to political didacticism.

In Baierl's *Die Feststellung* the scene in which the Party secretary either blackmailed Finze (according to Finze) or tried to persuade him (according to the secretary) to join the LPG is played through twice, the second time, as noted above, by having each of them act the other's role. Role switching allows the text to serve as a surface for projection, offering a variety of possibilities for improvisation and for playing against the text in order to invert meaning. Thus, this historic confrontation of two diametrically opposed spheres of interest is provided a space to inject experiences and problems that cannot simply be tidied up by the narrative resolution at the play's conclusion. The textual form itself contains two competing notions of publicness and reception. On the one hand, correct consciousness as constituted in the text is given in the form of a predigested answer to the crisis: Finze 'realizes' that it ultimately lies in his interest to join the LPG. Opposed to this is the possible critical intervention on the part of a lay actor/spectator, who functions as a 'coauthor' of reality and an integral part of the decision-making process. Baierl's unresolved handling of the Brechtian *Lehrstück* illustrates paradigmatically the aporia emerging out of an attempt to employ a revolutionary/critical tradition in the service of specific Party policy.

A third important work to emerge from the didactic theater movement of the late 1950s was Peter Hacks's contemporary play *Die Sorgen und die Macht* (The cares and the power), which was written in 1958 under the title *Die Briketts* (The briquettes) and whose second and third versions saw brief productions. The most controversial aspect about this 'first attempt to present in grand form our industrial reality'[20] was its thematization of a basic contradiction between quantity and quality in the socialist mode of production: because quantity of production is the decisive factor, a briquette factory is delivering masses of inferior products to a neighboring glass factory, which in turn is unable to make glass because the briquettes will not produce the needed heat. An inversion of the basic contradiction also fails to bring about resolution. The briquette worker Max Fidorra falls in love with the poor glass worker Hede Stoll and out of love for her sees to it that the quality of his briquettes improves. Max becomes poor because of his failure to meet the norm; Hede, on the other hand, rich because of newly attained bonuses. The basic contradiction remains, and the love relationship is now in jeopardy because the male chauvinist Max cannot stand to be in a lesser position than his soon-to-be wife, Hede.

Like Heiner Müller in his industrial plays, Hacks succeeds in designing a plot in which individual characters are decentered and in which social contradictions become the basis for the play's structure. But instead of leaving the contradictions open and as material for the audience, Hacks defuses their dialectical power by resolving things with no less than two(!) dei ex machina. At the level of social relations, an invention is introduced that permits both quality *and* quantity: thus, in accordance with the mythology of a benevolent dialectical materialism, the ever progressing 'means of production' suddenly and miraculously intervene in human destiny to provide salvation. Once having resolved the 'objective' contradiction, the subjective resolution also emerges, as Wolfgang Schiwelbusch says, 'pseudodialectically as in a second grade boulevard comedy'[21] at the end of the play: Max, who heretofore has stood egotistically at odds with anything connected to the collective, suddenly has a socialist epiphany and becomes a positive collective hero.

The happy endings and pseudoresolutions in the plays of Baierl and Hacks were not enough to exempt them from attacks by the SED at the Fourth Plenum of the Central Committee in January 1959. According to Walter Ulbricht, playwrights such as Baierl, Hacks, and Müller, regardless of their good intentions, were guilty of 'sectarian tendencies,' precisely because 'in their rejection of any genuine artistic representation, they ended up trumpeting the so-called didactic *Lehrstück* as *the* socialist art form par excellence.'[22] 'Sectarian' in Ulbricht's use of the term has both aesthetic and political signification. As a formal designation, sectarian refers to avant-garde dramatic representations that eliminate strong emotions and individual characterization and in so doing indulge in a kind of esotericism and 'rationality' that can only inhibit a literary movement 'devoted to speaking to millions of human beings.'[23] In addition to Formalist elitism, sectarian in the discourse of the SED also has a pejorative political meaning derived in part from the way it functioned historically to characterize the Soviet avant-garde. Within this context, the term refers to anarchistic tendencies associated by Lenin, Plekhanov, and others with political activity based on self-initiative and modes of self-reflexivity that inevitably stand at odds with the top-down political orthodoxy of the Party.

It might seem paradoxical that four months following his denunciation of Müller and Hacks for their sectarianism Walter Ulbricht was to announce a new cultural policy modeled in many ways on the very methods and even the goals of the so-called didactic theater movement. His proclamation of the Bitterfelder Weg (Bitterfeld movement) in April 1959 called for writers to go into the factories to learn about industrial production experience firsthand in order to overcome the alienation of art and life. In point of fact, Inge and Heiner Müller and Peter Hacks had already 'gone to the base' in order to gather materials for the writing of their production plays; *Der Lohndrücker* and *Die Sorgen und die Macht* were already seasoned plays that sought to overcome the division of labor between production workers and those who produce culture. The fact that these earlier results, while initially dissatisfying to officialdom, were nevertheless usurped by the Party itself as official policy in the Bitterfeld movement says much about the function of heritage in the GDR. A theater tradition founded upon criticism and genuine contradiction cannot simply be recycled into a theater of affirmation, even when the intention is to affirm. The attempts by the Party (above all in the Bitterfeld movement) to do so, in spite of such problems, produced a number of conflicts in the 1960s.

FROM A DIDACTIC TO A DIALECTICAL CONTEMPORARY THEATER

The expression 'didactic theater,' coined by Walter Ulbricht for the agit-prop theater of the 1950s, was eventually to become accepted terminology in all the official GDR depictions of this early period. In using this term, two aspects were always emphasized. On the one hand, it was a formal designation indicating short, epic plays with montage structure, non-psychological characterization, and 'rational' treatment of its material; that is, plays that were described as having 'enlightening' or 'didactic' characteristics. Yet precisely because of their supposed 'radicalizing of structure and style,'[24] these plays were also quite often viewed simply as experimental warm-ups to what followed them. GDR critic Hermann Kähler, for example, spoke of them as a 'prelude' to the development of a genuine GDR drama, as an 'expression of a transitional phase in which artists search for new aesthetic ground.'[25] Although its general assessment is on the whole more positive than that of Kähler, the official GDR theater history *Theater in der Zeitenwende* also spoke of a 'developmental period in the expanding process of our drama' that 'revealed at the same time further tasks to be accomplished.'[26] Implicit in both characterizations was an ideological historiography that pejoratively reduced the didactic *Lehrstück* to a not quite successful warm-up exercise for the grand dialectical drama that was to follow it.

The question as to whether the flood of plays with contemporary themes written in the wake of the Bitterfeld movement in the 1960s indeed developed further or, conversely, sacrificed the revolutionary achievements of the agitprop period is something that can only be answered by a thorough analysis of individual works. While such a treatment would go

121

beyond the bounds of the present chapter, we can indicate tendencies emerging in the 1960s that sought to keep the agitprop, avant-garde theater tradition relevant for the GDR.

If one noted at the end of the 1950s a return to the 'smaller, more supple forms' of the agitprop tradition (Brecht), the succeeding decade saw a move in contemporary play writing toward a renewal of the classical epic play of much grander proportions. There were two important characteristics that prevailed in almost every work: a thematic focus upon larger-than-life individuals and a broadening of the historical perspective. These two aspects were actually quite intimately linked, as is obvious even from the titles of many of the plays emerging at that time. Strittmatter's *Die Holländerbraut* (1960; The Dutch bride), Baierl's *Frau Flinz* (1961), Peter Hacks's *Moritz Tassow* (1961), Hartmut Lange's *Marski* (1962), and Volker Braun's *Kipper Paul Bauch* (1966) are all plays whose vitalistic and legendary central characters stand as emblems for the contradictory ideological developments of an entire stage of reconstruction in the GDR. Seen from the perspective of socialist realism, the reappearance of the great individual was in part a concession to a cultural policy that emphasized emotions and characterization and that, in so doing, attempted to represent broad social developments within the framework of individual psychology. In many cases these gargantuan character portrayals also stood as historical metaphors for the necessity of superhuman achievement (Paul Bauch) or the assertion of some paradisiacal utopian future (Moritz Tassow) in a society of scarcity and inadequate production. However, the shift from didactic to historical *Zeittheater* [social theater] was by no means intended as an abandonment of the Brechtian tradition or its claim to revolutionary agitation.

For instance, Helmut Baierl's *Frau Flinz,* which premiered at the Berliner Ensemble with Helene Weigel playing the lead, attempts a socialist recasting of both the plot story and the dialectical method of Brecht's famous *Mother Courage.* If Brecht's heroine sees her three children killed because the precapitalist war economy in which she functions makes it impossible for her to reconcile family survival with profiteering, the loss of Frau Flinz's five children to the collective life of GDR socialism represents a comic, 'dialectical' reversal of the original but now 'outmoded' tragic situation. In contrast to Mother Courage, Frau Flinz's errors can finally 'be resolved in a friendly way' (with help from the Party she is made the head of an LPG) because conditions under socialism represent her true interests. As was the case with Baierl's *Die Feststellung*, we once again find a Brechtian model being affirmatively defused: historicizing means for Baierl reducing contradiction to a matter of individual consciousness and adjustment. In contrast to Brecht's theater of estrangement, Baierl's epic-historical dramaturgical structure functioned so as to *hinder* any 'critical intervention' [*eingreifendes Denken*] on the part of an audience. Insight into necessity means precisely *not* to intervene – the truth is ordained.

Trivializing and narrowing the Marxian dialectic of history with the help of the dialectical, avant-garde theater tradition of Bertolt Brecht was not unique to Baierl's plays.[27] Indeed, a whole series of agrodramas and brigade plays of the 1960s had as their philosophical starting point a view of history that presented the socialist present as *eo ipso* a resolution of all unresolved problems from the past. As might be expected, their means of proselytizing for the socialist cause consisted of treating the audience as the object of a one-way educational process.

One agrodrama that did not fit this scheme was Heiner Müller's *Die Umsiedlerin* (rewritten as *Die Bauren* [The peasants] in 1964). This historical drama consists of fifteen epic scenes and depicts in ruthless detail the brutal existence of rural life between 1945 and 1960: land reform and collectivization; the never-ending failures, conflicts, suicides, and hypocrisy; the terror, human weakness, and contradictions of historical upheaval. Müller is also ruthless in his treatment of German history: there are neither legendary heroes, like Moritz Tassow or Paul Bauch, nor do historical laws unravel inexorably to guarantee a happy end in socialism. Like Müller's brigade plays, the dynamic of his historical conception is rooted in destruction and in a *negative* force field out of which the construction process emanates. The historical description of the migration movements during the postwar period by Party Secretary Flint borders on the apocalyptic: 'Out of the east came the trekkers, refugees and settlers moving across the land like grasshoppers. They brought hunger with them, and typhus. The Red Army followed, with their bill of goods for four years of war, for human wreckage and scorched earth, but with peace and land reform too.'[28]

The poetic language and historical structure found in Heiner Müller's epic scene complexes resemble more a rambling Shakespearean history play[29] than the sparse, focused structure of agitprop drama (or even of Brecht's longer epic works). Nevertheless, at the level of reception there is a similar structure of expectancy. In both cases the text demands – by virtue of its ellipses and by the absence of an omniscient, harmonizing epic consciousness – that the audience partake in the production of meaning. Unfortunately this dialectical attitude toward audience involvement was to prove fatal for Müller's *Die Umsiedlerin*. The play premiered in the fall of 1961, shortly after the Wall was built and rural collectivization was completed, and the provocative nature of its semiotics – geared precisely to evoke controversy and audience involvement – brought about the greatest response from the Party itself. After one performance by the student theater group at the School for Economics in Karlshorst, a suburb of East Berlin, the play was withdrawn and did not 'premiere' again until fifteen years later (1976) at the Volksbühne in Berlin. As a result of the initial performance of the first version, the student theater group was dissolved, each actor had to write a self-criticism, and Müller himself was thrown out of the writers union and the Party.

The twenty-year genesis of *Die Bauern* – from the time Müller began to write the play in 1956 to its final (second) premiere at the Volksbühne – represents in many ways a paradigmatic fate for dialectical contemporary theater in its efforts to carry on the agitprop heritage in the GDR. The original student production was hailed by all who were a part of it as a model, in the spirit of the Bitterfeld movement, for experimental, collective theater, as a 'new path for amateur art.'[30] The entire production resulted from close teamwork between lay actors of the student theater and professional artists – in this case the director B. K. Tragelehn and the playwright Heiner Müller. The final text was 'written, revised and written again in conjunction with rehearsal.'[31]

But that was only the first step. For Müller the second and by far most important step was audience feedback. In an interview focusing on 'theater in a socialist society,' Müller drew upon the phrasing of GDR philosopher Wolfgang Heise in defining an ideal socialist theater as a 'laboratory of social fantasy.' To mobilize fantasy in the theater simply means to enable the public 'always to design counterimages and counterpossibilities . . . so that the spectator can imagine a different dialogue, one that might have been possible or even preferable.'[32] Müller's play *Die Bauern*, from its writing to production to final audience reception, could well have served as a model for such experimental drama. It offered the possibility for critical debate about historical events and national identity precisely at a moment when the events themselves were transpiring. The facts that such a debate never took place; that the official reviews of the student production of *Die Bauern* vilified the work as a 'completely negative image of our Republic';[33] that the play only reached its public *after* the period of collectivization had come to be viewed as a successful stage of 'early GDR history' serve to demonstrate the paradoxes and limits of dialectical theater in a nondialectical public sphere.

Heiner Müller's *Die Bauern* was not the only contemporary drama of the 1960s to be denied dialogue with the public because of political tensions and the controversial treatment of its subject matter. Peter Hacks's *Moritz Tassow* (1961), written at the same time and also an agrodrama about the beginning years of land reform, was not produced until 1965 and then was quickly removed. A similar fate befell the poet Volker Braun with his first drama *Die Kipper* (The car tippers). The initial unpublished version appeared in 1962 (*Der totale Mensch*, The total human); the second version; *Kipper Paul Bauch*, was printed in 1966 but not produced; a third version had its premier as *Die Kipper* at the Deutsches Theater in 1972. Both the Hacks and the Braun plays have as their central character strong male egos, 'total humans' as it were, whose vast energies and insatiable individual needs far exceed the time in which they live. The pig herder and first GDR hippy Moritz Tassow decides to found a land commune during the initial efforts at land reform and at a time of economic devastation. The brigadier Paul Bauch seeks to sweep aside the gray, alienating industrial realities of the 1950s in order to found communism here and now. Both fail due to their own naïveté but also because of objective conditions: the sparse, instrumental norms of 'really existing socialism.' Yet in both works we find a basic question confronting the new generation that, with the help of theater, *could have been dealt with publicly:* to what extent do individuals have the right to demand things in the present that can only be realized in the future? What about utopian needs that exceed the social framework in which they emerge?

The most controversial contemporary drama of the 1960s was Heiner

Müller's *Der Bau,* which was reworked in seven different versions. This adaptation of Erik Neutsch's extremely popular industrial novel *Spur der Steine* also deals with the conflict between subjective need and the struggles of everyday life during the construction years. It too was not premiered for over a decade after its writing until a brilliant 1980 production by Fritz Marquardt at the Volksbühne. The GDR theater scholar Frank Hörnigk said of the 'friendly' response of the audience to this 'late' premiere: 'Young people who saw the production repeatedly emphasized in discussions that the events depicted struck them as extremely foreign and antiquated – like the socialist experiences of a much earlier (and distant) generation.'[34] For these people such dramas were like history plays from a bygone past: to be celebrated (appreciated) as the repressed heritage from the classical period of the GDR avant-garde but whose semiotics no longer spoke to their reality. Thus the failure of *Der Bau* to reach its rightful audience in the 1960s, as Hörnigk emphasizes, entailed 'more than the rejection of a poetic model: rejected as well was an offer to discuss something [*ein Diskussionsangebot*] emerging from the midst of a socialist society and intended as a medium for the further development of just that society.'[35]

The institutionalized lag time in the genesis of the most important contemporary dramas of the 1960s dealing critically, that is, agitationally and dialectically, with the immediate past permits us to make a few generalizations about the function and development of the historical avant-garde heritage in the GDR. Faced with the schematism of a reified, Stalinist cultural policy in the mi-1950s, the ruling Party turned to the Weimar agitprop tradition (Brecht) and to the early Soviet avant-garde in search of new impulses to reengage a theatrical public sphere. Basic to this tradition of historical avant-gardism were three important political assumptions that were formally and thematically coupled with its system of communication: (1) a belief in the *self-initiating* proletarian worker as the subject of his or her own history and as legitimate dramatic protagonist for revolutionary theater; (2) a hope that industrial and social reality would provide transindividual (collective) energy for a new aesthetic dynamic, one that would challenge the traditional aesthetics of autonomy and (bourgeois) individualism; (3) new notions of democratic publicness that must include the coproduction of meaning and a strategy of active, critical interpretation on the part of the audience. Not surprisingly, such a theater was hardly compatible with already existing models of socialist realist drama and in time was censored accordingly. In this regard, it is important to note that later GDR literary critics, employing approaches of reception theory, began to speak out vigorously against the loss of public discussion because of such repression and even to call for a reevaluation of the earlier period.[36] Clearly, the efforts to reinaugurate the revolutionary spirit of the historical avant-garde in the GDR of the 1980s became one important means by which a once-repressed cultural heritage was to function politically within the changing political climate of that period.

Yet despite such reevaluations of the classical avant-garde, one might well speculate on the extent to which this tradition had any role at all to play in the practicing theatrical developments in the GDR of the 1980s. The complete perplexity on the part of younger viewers when confronted with the 1980 production of Müller's *Der Bau* says much about the structural transformations occurring in the aesthetic and political norms of audience reception during the final years of the GDR. Where once the production plays and historical dramas of the 1950s and 1960s could assume as their starting point general ideological acceptance of the link between individual liberation and the processes of economic and social development within the larger society as a whole, one found in the later period a literary and intellectual landscape in which historical progress had become thoroughly problematized, in which the alienated individual had become the centerpiece of dramatic interest.

This move away from a materialist notion of industrial history as the demiurge of dramatic motivation and as the basis for characterization obviously affected developments within avant-gardism as they emerged in the 1970s and 1980s. As we explore in the next two chapters, the notion of the avant-garde was no longer simply equated with a model of cultural-political forwardness (vanguardism) within which proletarian experience and an ontologized industrial progressivism could be seen as the aesthetic and political basis for an agitational or even a socially critical art. Moreover, other traditions from the heritage of European modernism became increasingly important for practicing artists, traditions that explicitly or implicitly questioned, among other things, the naive productivism and progressivism at the heart of the historical Weimar avant-garde. Surely that was the reason why authors such as Heiner Müller, Volker Braun, and Christoph Hein turned to the Surrealist movement and the Theater of the Absurd, to artists such as Antonin Artaud, Franz Kafka, Samuel Beckett, and even the young, pre-Marxist Brecht, in order to excavate – with the help of a 'constructive defeatism' (Müller) – experiences and views long kept buried by official historiography. That the semiotics of such a renewed dramatugry would continue to provoke the status quo meant that the theater was to remain a locus of public debate even in the 1980s.

5. HISTORY AGAINST ITSELF:
HEINER MÜLLER'S THEATER OF
REVOLUTION

Heiner Müller's *Mauser* (1970), *Cement* (1973), and *Der Auftrag* (1979; The mission) are plays about revolution that reach beyond their historic context to thematize conflicts peculiar to a tradition of European drama after the French Revolution. Georg Büchner's *Danton's Death*, Vsevolod Vishnevsky's *Optimistic Tragedy*, Friedrich Wolf's *The Sailors of Cattaro*, Albert Camus's *The Just*, and Bertolt Brecht's *The Measures Taken* are some of their philosophical forebears. As history plays that also draw upon the tradition of the *Lehrstück*, these three works stand with and beyond Brecht's *The Measures Taken* as a new kind of drama with which the actors-viewers are to explore the dialectics of historical change as a process of self-critical, self-educating 'carrying through of certain behaviors' (Brecht). Written in the 1970s, their premises are formed by and take issue with specific processes of political domination in the GDR during that period. More precisely, their focus upon revolution as production and as the betrayal of revolution attempts to explore the failures of socialism and the crisis of sectarian mentality within the day-to-day practices of the Leninist-Stalinist party. In so doing, they both confirm and critique, sometimes schizophrenically, the conditions upon which it rests. In refusing to resolve their contradictions, they offer the form of the *Lehrstück* as a means of carrying through and coming to terms with them.

Central themes in all three works are the relation of intellectuals to violence and the necessity for killing in the realization of revolutionary goals. In the dramatic tradition with which they are linked, these themes are often portrayed as having tragic implications. For instance, the problematic hero of Büchner's *Danton's Death* is the focal point from which the audience views an inexorable social process that 'like Saturn devours its children.' The demise of Danton is an individual tragedy – viewed albeit with ironic disdain – within an emerging historical necessity. Camus's *The Just,* written 110 years later in cold war France, poses a similar dichotomy but is even more insistent in its emphasis upon individual moral crisis. Kaliayev, the poet of love and now of revolutionary violence, stands stained and finally consumed by the 'plague' of modern political necessity. Where in Büchner's view history and objective forces belie and ultimately qualify the dilemma of individual tragedy, the existential moralist Camus is unequivocating in refusing to legitimize violence through the revolutionary ethos.

Yet, for many left-wing writers in the twentieth century, the Bolshevik Revolution meant a shift in perspective from individual to collective notions of political freedom. Vishnevsky's *Optimistic Tragedy* plays the conflict out from the other side: the tragedy is an optimistic one because the dilemma is resolved on the basis of a greater good for the greatest number. Friedrich Wolf's *The Sailors of Cattaro* and Bertolt Brecht's *The Measures Taken* are also in this tradition, but with Brecht the framework has again been altered, this time in order to abandon the notion of tragedy as a central concern. In so doing, he changed the terms of both revolutionary drama and its dramaturgical representation.

As Müller's depiction of revolution in all three plays under discussion is at the same time a dialogue with Brecht's *The Measures Taken,* it is perhaps helpful to explicate briefly the thematic and formal issues at the heart of the earlier work. In this dramatic cantata written in 1930, four Party workers have returned from an illegal mission in China and report their liquidation of a young comrade whom they had recruited to carry out a number of tasks. A control chorus invites them to act out what has happened, and the four agitators report the incidents that led to their decision, playing all the parts themselves and each taking the role of the young comrade who was killed. According to their presentation, the young comrade's inability to control his humanitarian feelings led to spontaneous acts of solidarity with the downtrodden, which in turn endangered the illegal work of the agitators and necessitated that he be eliminated without a trace so as not to threaten the larger cause. In the end, the young com-

rade himself sees the correctness of their position and asks to be liqui-
dated. He is then shot and thrown into a lime pit. After listening to their
account, the control chorus acquits the four agitators of any guilt and
signals its approval of the measures taken.

How is it that a work in which a naive young revolutionary must be
executed is not a tragedy? To begin with, *The Measures Taken* was theoretically conceived by Brecht not simply as a teaching but as the 'demonstration' of a process of contradictions; as an example lesson, not an object
lesson.[1] An object lesson would say: the young comrade was wrong in
being humane; he learned from the consequences of his error and sacrificed his life for the greater collective and the revolution. An example
lesson would say: here is the *representation* of a contradictory process and
the mental reflections of and upon that process; act out this representation. Don't learn *from* it (object lesson, theater as finished product,
uncritical acceptance of thesis), learn *through* it (example lesson, reproduction of a process, *Bei-Spiel,* critical trying out of behavior). A tragic
situation is in the play but not central to it; central to it is learning as
process. In *The Measures Taken* Brecht gives us an extreme example with
three nodal points of a situation: the tasks to be accomplished; the beliefs,
world view, and consequent behavior of the young comrade; the teaching
of the Marxist classics as the practice of the Party-collective. All of these
parts represent a force field of interaction within a given necessity; from
no single vantage point can one derive a 'correct' answer. The point of the
Lehrstück is to isolate and explore given factors of a reality as a means
of concretizing and questioning them *within the experience of the actor-
viewer,* not simply to arrive at judgments about the rectitude (for example, the final decision of the control chorus) or the falseness of any of the
constituent parts.

A look at debates within Brecht scholarship concerning *The Measures
Taken* is helpful in situating the work politically and in understanding
how Müller goes about radicalizing Brecht's learning play. Two diametrically opposed interpretations have been dominant. One of them, perhaps
best represented by Reinhold Grimm, sees the play as a tragedy dealing
with the insoluble conflict of freedom versus necessity.[2] According to this
view, a clash of absolute values inevitably leads to guilt and the tragic
death of the individual hero. The second position, as developed by Reiner

Steinweg and first publicized in the journal *alternative,* takes Brecht's theory of the learning play as its point of departure and attempts to prove that *The Measures Taken* is an *Übungstext* [exercise text], an 'example' play rather than a tragedy. Steinweg sees Brecht's work as a perfect realization of the learning play in that it provides only a model for acting out differing possibilities, and he can thus dismiss the tragedy theory as a politically motivated misunderstanding of Brecht's intent.

It is clear that both interpretations contain political implications emanating from very different historical contexts. Understanding *The Measures Taken* as a tragedy frequently served to politicize the play within cold war discourse and questions concerning Brecht's equivocating stance toward Soviet communism. In this more thematic reading, critics compared the role of the Bolshevik party to the deadly function of the cruel Olympic gods in Greek tragedy;[3] or they spoke of the nihilist Brecht's longing for total authority and of his alleged immersion in the *credo quia absurdum est* of communist doctrine;[4] or they bluntly labeled Brecht a Stalinist and saw the play as embracing the final verdict of the control chorus and hence as an apologetic anticipation of the Moscow Show Trials of the 1930s.[5]

The second interpretive strategy, reading *The Measures Taken* strictly as a 'learning' play, emanated in part from attempts to politicize Brecht's work and evolved out of its reception by the West German Left in the late 1960s. This interpretation, although obviously closer to Brecht's theoretical intentions, also reflects the political context in which it emerged. While Steinweg and the editors of *alternative* correctly criticized traditional Brecht scholarship for its anticommunist biases, their analysis failed even to consider the political problems posed thematically by *The Measures Taken.* The attempt to dismiss the aspect of tragedy altogether could thus be regarded as another form of apology vis-à-vis Brecht's politics, since it placed all the emphasis upon the work's formal structure as a drama for role playing and consciousness raising while ignoring completely the implications of the plot for Brecht's uncritical acceptance of the 'ABCs of communism' (i.e., the Marxist-Leninist party) as reflected in this play, in his work in general, or in his own life. To pose the problem in existential terms, the formalist reading of *The Measures Taken* simply occludes the central question of what it means for 'the revolution' to have to kill so there will be no more killing.

It is this legacy that Müller seeks to interrogate in all three of his revolution plays of the 1970s. His corrective to the Brechtian text offers on a structural level a purer rendering of the *Lehrstück* aesthetic, an attempt to realize intentions inherent to the form itself. However, just as important, Müller's depictions of revolution represent as well a later stage in the historical continuum of socialist experience: the meaning of revolution *after* the revolution. Thus, if Brecht's *The Measures Taken* is conceived as a prerevolutionary attempt to negate bourgeois individualism as bourgeois drama, then Müller's rewriting of that work, first in *Mauser* and then in *Cement* and *Der Auftrag,* can be regarded as the negation of the negation: a critique of an 'idealist' text from within the quotidian experience of 'revolution' itself; an exploration of the Marxist-Leninist party once it is in power.

MAUSER AND THE GDR

Shortly before his death, Brecht said that he considered *The Measures Taken* to be a model for the socialist theater of the future.[6] Heiner Müller's *Mauser* is conceived as such a *Lehrstück,* written in and for that future. The play itself presents the following events:[7] In the early 1920s in the Soviet Union an executioner named A stands before a revolutionary Party tribunal to give account of his behavior during a turbulent period. His delegated task has been to kill the 'enemies of the revolution,' one of whom was his predecessor, B, who had refused to execute a peasant because he saw in this supposed 'enemy' only a class brother and downtrodden victim. A has also been having doubts during his period in office, but the Party has insisted upon his fulfilling his duty. A increasingly senses changes occurring within himself, in particular a tendency to kill like a machine. The Party steadfastly refuses to release him from his task or even to provide him with any meaning for his work. A should be able to figure out for himself the historical justification for his mission. A continues to kill and at a certain point metamorphoses from an unfeeling killer machine into an orgiastic murderer, stomping his victims to smithereens with his boots. This 'loss of consciousness' leads to his being sentenced to death by the Party, an event to which he must now give his assent. The play ends before the execution and with no clear-cut answers, although there is compelling evidence that his final cry of 'death to the enemies of the revolution' is aimed as much at the collective (which also speaks the text) as at himself. Although a critical reworking of *The Measures Taken*, Brecht's young comrade appears in *Mauser* (as B) in only one short scene: he is reintroduced as a backdrop in order to establish a point of departure for the later play. However, unlike *The Measures Taken*, in *Mauser* there is no teleological narrative; it is even questionable whether there is any plot at all. Concrete history has been almost totally eliminated, although the events themselves are situated in the Soviet Union in the early 1920s. Knowledge and consciousness are not reached at the end but are constructed, deconstructed, and reconstructed in the course of the play. *Mauser* does not offer a solution for the audience to carry home, nor does it present the contradiction between an abstract, spontaneous humanity – proven in its consequences to be inhumane – and the revolution's claim to realize humanity in the future. Instead, throughout the play, the revolutionary mandate remains inseparably linked to the inhumanity of individual action, which is the unavoidable result of the collectively organized work of killing: 'a job like any other . . . And it was a job like no other' (127).

A must live through a contradiction that tears him apart. Desperate to escape the contradiction, he asks to be relieved of his work. But the collective does not, cannot let him go. Moreover, even if he were no longer in charge of the revolutionary tribunal, he would remain part of the collective; he would not be able to escape responsibility for killing if someone else took over his task. The chorus understands the dilemma primarily from the standpoint of the collective; A sees it only from his personal perspective. He acts as an individual, both when asking to be relieved and when fighting death, tooth and nail.

Twice A abandons the dialectic between collective and individual: first when he becomes one with his Mauser (weapon) and kills like a machine; then when he loses himself in an orgy of blood and destruction and tries to claim the bodies of the dead by trampling them with his boots in a dance of death. At the play's end, the dialectic of individual and collective is reconstituted, but the contradiction is not, cannot be resolved into harmony or reconciliation. Precisely this is the pivotal point of the play, the problem Müller refuses to soft-pedal: killing as a function of life, as a job like any other and like no other, dialectically organized by the collective and organizing the collective. Viewed from the perspective of Brecht's *Lehrstück* theory, it is mandatory that both individual and collective, actor and audience remain conscious of the insoluble contradiction between death and life, between killing and the human claim of the revolution. Thus, in *Mauser* the revolution is betrayed as soon as the individual loses this consciousness (mechanical killing) or breaks out of the collective (orgiastic killing). The fact that the text plays out the *impossibility* of such sustained consciousness is its moment of most unequivocating self-reflection. *Mauser* seeks to assert a humane perspective where the text appears its most inhumane: when the chorus demands that A, who killed for the revolution, agree to his own execution precisely because he did the work he had been asked to do.

From a dramaturgical point of view, it is significant that while in *The Measures Taken* the young comrade's death has already taken place when the work begins, *Mauser* ends prior to A's execution and with an existential refusal to acquiesce:

I do not want to die. I throw myself to the ground.
I hold fast to the earth with my hands
I lock my teeth into the earth
Which I do not want to leave. I scream. (147)

A's death is not a tragic sacrifice offered to the revolution so that it can purge itself and go on. In *Mauser,* there is no reconciliation of contradictions, no aura of tenderness and solidarity in death. If there is any unity of contradictions at all, it emerges in the consciousness of those who are destroyed by the conflict but who, because they remain within it, become the example.

Müller has radicalized *The Measures Taken* in part by dehistoricizing it. While in Brecht we have the young comrade (bourgeois intellectual turned revolutionary) in dialogue with and juxtaposed to the Party-chorus (the prerevolutionary vanguard Party replete with quotes from 'the classics' – Marx, Lenin), in Müller's play the names and many of the historical referents are gone. A is clearly any one of the collective; the problem is not a historical character in a transitional situation but the situation itself. By eliminating 'history' as a naturalist element, Müller creates the formal framework for bringing the history of the actor-viewer back into the work. Just as important, the structure of the play denies the story-plot as a separate 'narratable' entity. In *The Measures Taken* the chorus tells in lockstep the story of the young comrade in the vise-grip of retrospective narrative. In *Mauser,* Müller cuts through and breaks up the different narrated time levels to allow an intermix of narration experience with nontextual experience. Historical subjectivity and consciousness are allowed back into the play through the process of participation.

Yet there is clearly a moment of historicity emanating from the text itself. In its focus upon postrevolutionary violence, Müller's play resituates questions concerning the Leninist party to a time after the fall into power. Moreover, like his earlier industrial plays *Der Bau* and *Der Lohndrücker, Mauser* is also a work about socialist relations of production. What *Mauser* tells us is that the process of making revolution, like production itself, results in the reification of mind and body. But unlike the more 'optimistic' earlier plays, this process is now linked with death. Thus the problem of this play is not simply the loss of one's humanity by having to commit physical murder but the loss of humanity due to the inability to remain conscious and politically aware of one's actions. Within this paradigm, A would be seen losing his humanity through two opposing types of reification. Reification is loss of consciousness when A becomes a reified *object* (example: A's mechanical killing). Reification is also loss of consciousness when A becomes an unmediated *subject* (example: A's reclaiming the self in orgiastic killing):

> But when your hand became one with the revolver
> And you became one with your work
> And were no longer *conscious* of it
> That it must be done here today
> So that it must be done no longer and by no one
> Your post in our front was a gap. (145)

Müller gives a process, namely, killing as a production (a job like every other/like no other), and in this extreme form (no other) of any production (any other) he demonstrates the loss of balance, the loss of consciousness of one's production, the loss, finally, of one's subjectivity as an *inevitable* component in a system in which the means are subordinated to the goals of political process.

The depiction of reification is also the moment in which Müller's play is most clearly an expression of his experience as a playwright in the GDR. While Brecht poses as a contradiction the relationship of the Party to an outside individual and with this relationship the problem of strategy, Müller puts aside these dimensions to explore more radically the workings within the Party and within a given strategy. By closing off completely the *what* (individual-Party, correct or incorrect strategy) to focus entirely upon the existential *how* (killing as production), Müller *accepts,* in a way that Brecht cannot, the Party-collective as a given objective reality. This is his 'postrevolutionary' experience. Thus the paradox: the pureness of the form – its ahistorical play quality – presupposes the historical reality of the Marxist/Leninist party as a radical given.

But there is also another paradox. In the moment that Müller's play is most Leninist, it is also most critical of the Leninist experience. By presenting the workings of the revolutionary Party as a process of production, reification, and death, *Mauser* opens up directly the problem of fetishism under socialism. The equation of revolutionary Party work with the alienation of labor in the production process ('that it must be done here today so that it must be done no longer and by no one') points to the technicalization of mind and practice that has long been a legacy of the Leninist party. Lenin himself, prior to the Russian Revolution, referred to the Party as an 'immense factory.' His optimism that the capitalist factory as 'a means for organization'[8] could be distinguished from the capitalist factory as 'a means of exploitation' and that this form could thus be taken over unaltered as a model instrument of revolution evades the problem of instrumentalist ideology that lies at the heart of the organizational form itself.[9] It is this problematic that Müller's metaphor of revolution as production pushes to the fore. In *Mauser*, as a *Lehrstück*, we are presented with the industrialization of the Party in its extreme form as a tool with which to confront such instrumentalization.

But we are also presented with a rebellion of the body. In *The Measures Taken*, the fate of the individual human body is subordinated merely to a moment in a dialectical process; to a subtext in the telos of socialist history that, while perhaps destroyed in the momentary struggle of the class conflict, will ultimately be redeemed as part of a larger, future-oriented, better socialist order. For Müller, such a linear notion of dialectical, all-encompassing history is no longer tenable.[10] In fact, he conceives his theater as an 'attack upon such a linear notion of history,' as a 'rebellion of the body against ideas, or more precisely, the impact of ideas and the idea of history on human bodies. This is indeed the theatrical point,' Müller concludes, 'the thrusting on stage of bodies and their conflict with ideas. As long as there are ideas there are wounds; ideas inflict wounds on the body.'[11]

A's refusal – 'I am a human. A human is not a machine / Killing and killing, the same after each death / I could not do it. Give me the sleep of the machine' (143) – revolts against an ideology that would sublate questions of flesh and survival within the articulations of a better world for the generations hereafter. In *Mauser*, Müller creates a textual structure of uttered ideological discourse within which are situated the bodies – individual and collective – of ideational political life. They speak and are spoken to, act upon and are acted upon. The struggle of A to 'understand' – and his inability to do so – plays out the wounds 'inflicted' by an ideological system and the body's existential refusal to acquiesce to that system. Thus *Mauser* takes us to the center of contradiction, to the experience of mechanistic, labor-consuming, and life-destroying activity as the means to create new life; to the cutting edge between apology and historical necessity as the experienced consciousness of collective-sectarian praxis:

> Your work was bloody and like no other
> But it must be done like other work. (143)

> For killing is a science
> And must be learned so that it ceases.
> For what is natural is not natural. (131)

And precisely in this absolute seizure of contradiction, this move to the heart of fetishism, Müller opens up for socialism the exploration of a repressed history. The 'ahistorical' *Mauser* carries with it the legacy of Leninism – past and present.

HISTORY AGAINST ITSELF: MÜLLER'S *CEMENT*

Heiner Müller's *Mauser* was written to be acted out by the Party hierarchy in the GDR.[12] The fact that it was only published there a year before the fall of the Wall says much about its political potential, even if we are forced for lack of a reception to speculate about it. As a play about the postrevolutionary experience, it takes issue both with that reality and with its representations. While Brecht does not even raise the question of means and ends, Müller makes it the overriding question – at the level of the human body and with terrifying implications. A is literally torn apart. What is perhaps most devastating of all is the suggested normalcy of the situation as a depiction of everyday life under socialism.

If the austerity of the *Lehrstück* in its purity is intended to keep naturalist history at bay, Müller's next play, *Cement*, transforms the experience of the learning play into socialist history. The message is again a miserable one. Adapted from the Soviet Feodor Gladkov's famous novel *Cement* (1925) about the postrevolutionary 1920s, Müller focuses upon the hard, unequivocating, contradictory experiences of the construction years: civil war, hunger, devastation, the introduction of the NÖS, Party corruption, the destruction of family life, and the emergence of what would later be called Stalinist practices – all of which are portrayed by Gladkov as well. The fact that this novel of postwar devastation and destruction was widely read in the GDR during the immediate postwar years surely stems in part from the similarities in the experiences of these two difficult periods of history. What is interesting for us, however, are precisely the points where Müller's reading of Gladkov's *Cement* deviates from the novel, both in perspective and in plot.

Predictably, Müller's austere adaptation of Gladkov completely eliminates the latter's romantic hope for a socialist happy end to the ensuing conditions. While Gladkov tells the story of Gleb Chumalov's return from the front as a difficult but ultimately triumphant struggle of a working-class hero over material conditions and an emerging Party bureaucracy, Müller's much more brutal characterization registers the defeat of individual initiative in the face of overwhelming material odds. While Gladkov's historiographical narrative depicts Party rigidity or the corruption of individual initiative being successfully countered by the forces of industrial development and mass involvement, Müller's demonstration vignettes of postrevolutionary life refuse such Marxist 'optimism,' showing instead the reestablishment of archaic conditions. His use of classical motifs to underscore the cyclical occurrence of primal relations cuts against a linear notion of progress and reveals a more resigned perspective of political revolution from a point fifty years after the novel and the revolution itself.[13]

While the characters and plot of Müller's *Cement* are drawn almost entirely from Gladkov, the few instances where the play does deviate from the novel are significant as indicators of Müller's political concerns. They also highlight his ongoing dialogue with Brecht. For instance, the brief appearance of a young revolutionary named Makar provides a direct reference both to *Mauser* and to Brecht's *The Measures Taken*. In a scene entitled 'The Administration, or Christ the Tiger,' we find depicted a classical confrontation between the vital, spontaneous, working-class hero and the exigencies of Party discipline in the form of 'the apparatus.' Gleb Chumalov's anarchic attempts to push through changes and rebuild the cement factory are met with the real existing 'hell-machine' of Soviet bureaucracy and administration:

CHUMALOV: Comrade Chairman, I've come on important business. And I'll throw your door-keeper out of the window if he gets in my way again. It's a disgrace, Comrade Chairman. Our dead aren't even buried yet, and you already act like Generals, attacking the working class with typewriters. The Bureaucracy. You're the chairman of the executive committee, and it's harder for a working man to get into your office than to take an enemy trench. You can fight machine guns with machine guns. Maybe someone should set up a machine gun here. Comrades, you have constructed a hell-machine. It must be smashed if we are to work.

IVAGIN: You're wrong, Comrade, you can't judge us like that. This isn't 1918, a Mauser can't replace an Underwood anymore. (Laughs, alone) Soviet power needs an intact administration, even if it is bureaucratic administration. What do you want, Comrade? The Revolution can't afford anarchy, the enemy is everywhere. We need terror, merciless terror. Work among the masses is a different story. Comrade Lenin's words about the cook who has to be ready to govern the country must become popular fact.[14]

Müller's setting and dramatic juxtaposition for the scene parallel in characterization and even dialogue the chapter entitled 'The Presidium' in

Gladkov's novel, where Chumalov faces Badyin. Both the novel and the play depict in epic scope the struggle of an entrenched and beleaguered Party apparatus to cope with a deteriorating economic crisis; the use of terror and violence as the policy of survival; the monumental efforts of the righteous Gleb Chumalov to transcend the contradictions through voluntaristic, heroic deed.

However, it is not their depiction of historical crisis but the manner of its narrative resolution that defines the political chasm separating these two texts. In the Gladkov novel, the confrontation reaches its crescendo with the arrival of Shramm, the 'Chairman of the Council of People's Economy,' with 'briefcase under his arm, dressed in yellow leather from cap to boots. He had the soft face of a eunuch, with gold pince-nez perched on an effeminate nose.'[15] In her book *The Soviet Novel: History as Ritual*, Katerina Clark has indicated the ways that Gladkov's *Cement* helped to invent the 'master code' for socialist realism as it evolved and was applied in subsequent works of prose literature, particularly in the 1930s and 1940s.[16] Certainly the face-off between Gleb and Shramm offers a classic example of how fictional narrativization served to resolve into ritual the historical events occurring during that period. In his depiction of character, Gladkov employs the discourse of gender stereotype to transform an economic crisis – the absolute lack of capital accumulation – into a mythological struggle of good against bad. Inscribed upon the fictional body are the deeper ontological truths of the forces they supposedly represent. The figure of Shramm personifies the parasitic 'apparatus,' demonized as eunuchlike and effeminate, feeding off the forward-moving forces of proletarian vitality. Opposed to this impotent, degenerate form of a corrupt bureaucracy stands the powerful, 'natural' man, Gleb Chumalov, a paragon of physical strength and nonsubterfuge and in league with the 'good' bureaucrat Badyin, whose final speech and dramatic exit punctuate the forces that prevail: 'You [Schramm] are a Communist, but you have no knowledge of a worker's policy. You've neither smelt powder nor the sweat of working men. I don't care a damn for your apparatus. . . . You've got swarms of rats there who have sharpened their teeth on Soviet bread, easily earned.'[17]

In Müller's text, it is not the bureaucrat Shramm who arrives to conclude this pivotal scene but rather the soldier Makar, a nineteen-year-old member of the Cheka who has been brought in to be executed by Comrade Chibis because he has slept with a female prisoner and hence endangered the good name of revolutionary justice. In Makar, one of the few characters in Müller's play *not* found in Gladkov's novel, Brecht's 'young comrade' and A from *Mauser* are rolled into one:[18] the innocence of youth consenting to his own death in the name of a higher cause; a child of the revolution whose bourgeois lineage has been effaced by the ersatz parentage of the Party machine.

BADYIN: Have you any relatives?

MAKAR: No. Comrade Chibis is sort of like a mother and father to me in his work as Chairman of the Revolutionary Tribunal, and the Cheka is my relatives. (31)

Gleb Chumalov's ensuing confrontation with the executioner Chibis in Müller's *Cement* thematizes the legacy of Communist Party liquidation that had only begun to emerge in the early 1920s:

CHUMALOV: He's nineteen, he's still a boy. He's spent two years at the front. And now this because of a whore who handed over our comrades to the whites. What kind of a people are you? Do you have stones for hearts?

CHIBIS: . . . Our struggle has just begun, and we have a long road ahead of us. We won't reach the end on our feet, Chumalov, but the earth will have to drink all kinds of blood before we can see the goal from a distance. Some will drown in the blood of others, and there's only one certainty: We shall have more blood. Yes, I voted for the execution, too, and so did the person I'm going to shoot right now. It's my job, and I owe him and myself at least this much, that I don't turn the job over to anyone else in his case. (32)

In a later chapter of Gladkov's *Cement* there is also a conversation between Chumalov and Chibis concerning revolutionary violence, but Shramm (not an 'innocent') is the object of deliberation and Chumalov the one who suggests that there are 'swine in the Economic Council . . . asking to be shot.'[19] The logic that permeates the Gladkov text is clearly one that pervades the Brechtian text as well: the question of murder is a tactical one, rationalized narratively by the larger historical framework that will ultimately bring about justice and a world without the necessity for execution. While Brecht has the apparatus kill for the good of the whole, Gladkov advocates (even if uttered partly in jest) the killing of the 'swine' within the apparatus. A different moral emphasis in the march of socialist progress, perhaps, but the political rationale is the same: the 'rationalization' of a process that will exonerate the individual actors at the end of the realized socialist goal.

The sudden appearance of Makar in Müller's text is neither narratively motivated (he comes from nowhere and is never mentioned again) nor wrapped in the guise of historical necessity. What we have is the anachronistic portrayal of a repressed history rising up against itself. There is no compelling strategic justification offered for the execution of this hapless boy; Chibis's 'defense' in the face of Chumalov's accusation is simply to act through verbally and finally to accept stoically the responsibility for it – 'I owe him and myself at least this much' – by pulling the trigger. Nor does the text offer any certainty whatsoever about a historical telos that will bring an end to the flow of blood.

Within the historical context of Müller's *Cement,* Makar and Chibis are anachronistic because they obviously stand for a history that lies ahead: what was to come in the Moscow Show Trials (Bukharin, Zinoviev, Kamenov, Rykov) of 1937 and 1938; what was to emerge during the postwar period in the Prague trials (Slansky) of 1952; or what continued, finally, on a more mundane level every time a Party stalwart, having sacrificed any identity outside of the apparatus, was thrown up upon the block in order to agree to some form of his or her own effacement – in the name of history. Müller's rereading of Brecht and Gladkov in *Cement* historicizes precisely through its use of anachronism; pushes contemporary insight and the experiences of Stalinist terror back upon a period prior to their inception in order to deflate the myth of 'optimistic' tragedy.

Yet as much as the appearance of Makar is about political necessity, it also and at the same time highlights the other side of the *Measures/Mauser* complex: the role of left-wing intellectuals in revolutionary praxis. In conclusion, let us return for a moment to Chibis's exchange with Chumalov in Müller's play, reading it now as a testimony concerning the socialization of Chibis, the sensitive intellectual, into a hardened Party man. As a way of explaining why he must kill Makar himself, Chibis tells of an earlier experience during the civil war on the Polish front when the Reds were in retreat and a wounded friend begged to be killed so that he would not fall into enemy hands alive: 'Chibis: . . . I didn't drag him along, he was too heavy, I didn't stay with him and I didn't shoot him, I couldn't. I can hear him to this day screaming behind me. Intellectual, he screamed, dirty intellectual. Maybe that's why I joined the Cheka' (32). The shift of focus is a significant one. While Brecht's young comrade (victim as betrayer) and *Mauser*'s A (victim as victimizer) both struggle to reconcile the conflicting dictates of individual and collective need, the Makar scene in Müller's *Cement* bifurcates the 'problem' into two separate characters: Chibis the executioner and Makar the victim. Moreover, it is Chibis the executioner *and* intellectual who now occupies center stage, both dramatically and philosophically. He is a killer who has avowedly joined the postrevolutionary Cheka in order to harness the self and further the cause.

Again, a comparison with the novel reveals Müller's emphasis. In the Gladkov text, Chibis remains a strangely enigmatic figure as viewed through the uncomprehending, narrating eyes of the pristine Gleb Chumalov: 'Gleb raised his eyebrows, waiting for Chibis to speak. Childlike tears and behind them a leaping demon. Such eyes do not sleep at night; they can see through walls. Chibis had a language of his own which would never be uttered; with strange incomprehensible words which dissolved into a childlike smile.'[20] Müller penetrates Chibis's 'gray mask' as portrayed by Gladkov to give us the terms of that 'indistinct black dot' (Gladkov) of inner self. We do not learn the inner secrets of his 'language,' to be sure, but rather the historical rationale for the mask, for Chibis's character armor. Chibis's ability to function in the 'hell-machine' (Müller's term, not Gladkov's) of the Party apparatus is bought at the price of his own identity. His stoic acceptance of 'my job,' his 'upright gait,' as it has more recently been redescribed,[21] has taken its very deep toll. Yes, Chibis avowedly pulls the trigger now, but the target is himself.

THE THEATER OF THE REVOLUTION IS OVER

In the light of Müller's evolving concern with intellectuals and power, it is important to explore his treatment of that theme in his one other drama of the 1970s that dealt extensively with socialist revolution: *Der Auftrag*. In the period prior to writing it, Müller had reached a crisis in his work. His 'history' plays subsequent to *Cement* (*Germania Tod in Berlin, The Life of Gundling,* and *Lessing Sleep's Dream Scream*) had increasingly questioned the possibility of history as drama and finally even of authorship itself. The short antidrama *Hamletmachine,* written in 1977, is a text, barely a text, in which the writing subject self-destructs into a series of monologic identities: Shakespeare, Ophelia, Hamlet, father, mother, whore, and son. It has been described as the 'self-reflection of the Marxist intellectual mirrored in the Hamlet tragedy.'[22] One would only add, at the end of his creative rope. The rest, Müller seems wont to say, is authorial silence.

Similar to the works of a number of other German writers of the 1970s, Heiner Müller's *Der Auftrag* could be seen as the author's attempt to locate in Third World revolution a way out of political solipsism; a means to renegotiate the link between history and drama. But the differences between Müller and, for example, a West bloc revolutionary writer like Peter Weiss are more revealing than their similarities. *Der Auftrag,* subtitled 'memory of a revolution,' deals with the failure of revolution, not its incipient realization. And it is Müller's confrontation, indeed, poetic, assertion of that failure that propelled him to write again. In stark contrast to Weiss's unequivocating submersion of authorial persona into the epic perspective of collective black Africa in *The Lusitanian Bogey* and his reabsorption of that voice back through the framework of Marxist epistemology, Müller's *Der Auftrag,* based on a short story by Anna Seghers,[23] is explicitly about the crisis of white, First and Second World left-wing intellectuals.

Briefly, the context (I purposely avoid the use of the term *plot*): three emissaries of the French revolutionary government of 1789 are sent to the British colony of Jamaica in an unsuccessful attempt to organize an uprising of the slaves for the French Republic. The play begins with the reading of a letter from the peasant Galloudec – one of the three – to Antoine, the man who contracted them in the name of the Convent to do the mission and who is now in hiding because Napoleon has come to power. In the letter, Galloudec cancels the mission and reports that his black comrade Sasportas has been hanged and that the third revolutionary, a white man named Debuisson, has betrayed the cause. Heiner Müller's ensuing fragmentary and elusive treatment of this material is less a representation of events than a montage of pantomime, abbreviated dialogue, Surrealist dream sequence, poetic chant, and finally long, unbroken prose monologue – all of which address in various ways the portentous utterance of Sasportas that 'the theater of white revolution is over.' The line, of course, can and should be read in two ways: one stressing the end of white revolution, the other of its theatrical representation. In the interactions of the three revolutionaries with each other and with the mother country, Müller plays out black-white relations on both a geopolitical and personal scale. The not-so-veiled analogies between Napoleon and Stalin, postrevolutionary France and post-Leninist Russia mark the different stages of 'white' revolution as the return of a paradigm vis-à-vis the colonies. In this sense, Müller's play could be seen as a somewhat negative answer to Weiss's more optimistic vision of socialist–Third World solidarity. Written from within the East bloc and from a considerably more sober time of world politics at the end of the 1970s, Müller's allegorical broken contract/task (the German title *Der Auftrag* contains both those meanings) resonates with implications concerning national self-interest and betrayal of the Third World; implications that seem to challenge not only ideological shibboleths of Soviet foreign policy but the very infrastructure of Marxist historiography as well.

But surely such an allegorical reading is much too simple, for Müller's play does not present a thesis and in that sense is not primarily 'about' the failure of socialist solidarity with the Third World. Much more in the spirit of the *Lehrstück*,[24] it, like *Mauser,* the Makar scene from *Cement,* and even *Hamletmachine,* seeks rather to explore a crisis of consciousness among leftist intellectuals. Thus, if there is a relation to be found to a writer such as Peter Weiss, then it is only to the extent that Müller dramatizes his own severe inner doubts, much in the way that Weiss did in his pre-Marxist play *Marat/Sade.* It is also in this regard that *Der Auftrag* has been compared to two other plays about white revolution, Brecht's *The Measures Taken*[25] and Büchner's *Danton's Death.* For example, when the emissaries arrive in Jamaica, they are masked, much the way the comrades in Brecht's play are when they arrive in China and for similar reasons. However, while for Brecht masks are mainly a tactical maneuver, Müller uses them to explore dimensions of identity. The white intellectual Debuisson, for instance, returns to Jamaica masked as himself. 'I am who

I was,' he says upon arrival, 'Debuisson, son of a slaveholder in Jamaica, heir to a plantation with four hundred slaves. I have returned home into the lap of my family . . . after the horrors of the revolution have opened my eyes to the eternal truth that everything old is better than anything new.'[26] Are mask and self identical? Debuisson will struggle with that question and answer it finally in the affirmative. The black Sasportas, 'masked' as a slave, does not have that privilege. Although he also is two selves, revolutionary and slave, both must lead inexorably to a kind of death. Revolution is not a choice, it is a condition of his blackness. As Galloudec says: 'I know Sasportas, that you play the most difficult role, it is written onto your body.'[27] The race question, not the class question, is central here. But the race question is not just skin-deep, and this is where Büchner comes in.

Hans-Thies Lehmann has shown well the parallels between Büchner's Danton and Müller's Debuisson,[28] both caught between a commitment to revolutionary action, on the one hand, and a melancholic compulsion toward sexual fulfillment, loss of self, and, in Debuisson's case, literally a crawl back into the womb, on the other. Upon arrival at his 'home' court, Debuisson is greeted by his former lover, FirstLove (ErsteLiebe), who tells a story about freed slaves crawling back to their former plantation-owner begging to be reinstated as slaves: 'Behold the human being: his first home is the mother, a prison house.' At this point servant slaves raise Debuisson's mother's skirts high above her head for all to see. 'Here it lies, gaping wide, the homeland,' FirstLove continues. 'Here it yawns, that lap of the family. Just say one word if you want to return and she'll stuff you back in, the idiot, the eternal mother.'[29]

Müller's images and fantasies as well as his juxtaposition of bodily and historical truth remind us not only of Büchner's *Danton* but also again of Peter Weiss's *Marat/Sade*. Yet where the dualism between sexual and political freedom for Büchner and the pre-Marxist Weiss remains constituted as the dilemma of the European Enlightenment – the aporia of white revolution – Müller posits in black Sasportas an alternative: not Sasportas as a figure (this would be a dialectical-dramatic and representational resolution) but Sasportas as the externalized and internalized 'other,' as an absolute negation. He is there in all the speeches, as much a projected, 'actor' in the *Traumarbeit/Traumspiel* of Debuisson (as men-

147

tioned, the play is subtitled a 'memory') as an objectively constituted, ontologically centered dramatic character.

For example, following Debuisson's arrival at the court, he is placed upon the throne (with FirstLove as his footstool) and told that 'the theater of revolution has opened.' What ensues is a nonsense pantomime play, part Beckett, part Büchner, featuring 'SasportasRobespierre' and 'GalloudecDanton' and acted *out* by the 'masked' black and peasant themselves (the plays within the play and displaced/inverted identities are legion here). The grand theater of revolution reveals itself as nothing but an absurdist farce in which the two revolutionaries play football with decapitated masked heads and ridicule each other as the hapless, vice-riddled clowns of a failed revolution: 'GalloudecDanton: The theater of revolution has opened. Attraction: the man with the missing genitals. Maximilian the Great. Moralmax. The Chairfarter. The masturbator from Arras. The bloody Robespierre.'[30] At the conclusion of the 'play,' Sasportas replaces Debuisson on the throne to utter the epic summation of the now accumulating levels of reference: 'The theater of white revolution is over. We condemn you to death Victor Debuisson. Because your skin is white. Because your thoughts are white. Because your eyes have seen the beauty of our sisters . . . The trouble with all of you is, you can't die. And for that reason you kill everything around you. For your dead ordered world in which intoxication has no place. For your revolution without sex.'[31] Sasportas's double 'role' is an important one. As a player in *Der Auftrag* and as Sasportas/Robespierre in the farce, he is but one of the equally flawed components of a flawed revolution. But replacing Debuisson as 'spectator' of his own play, he then voices Debuisson/Müller's self-reflections concerning the larger questions. It is the theater of *white* revolution that is over, thematically and formally: impaled upon the immutable dualities of the white revolutionary intellectual; reduced from the epic grandeur of historical tragedy (*Danton's Death*) to an absurdist nonrepresentational farce (*Waiting for Godot?*). Yet the black revolutionary Sasportas can and does die, regardless of any moral strength or failing as a character. Unlike Debuisson, *his* body and history are one. And it is from the configuration of meanings that he generates in this play that any future revolutionary theater must emerge.

Müller's reutilization of Brecht's *The Measures Taken* takes a number of turns in *Der Auftrag*, and it is helpful now as a way of summation to review some of these in the light of the central problems of this chapter. Simply at the level of story, for instance, it is clear that Müller's play is indeed, as Arlene Teraoka has cogently argued, a deconstructive reading of the earlier text: the donning of masks in order to conceal their task; the series of 'tests' that are to probe the revolutionary commitment of the young comrade; even the direct thematization of repressing their feelings as Galloudec and Sasportas (here the young comrade) are led by Debuisson (here the Party/control chorus) through the process of emotional denial and acceptance of revolutionary instrumentalism to reenact and reinvent the Brechtian model within yet another dimension of socialist history.[32]

But once again it is the reversals that are important. For instance, Victor Debuisson, the representative of the Party (control chorus) and a voice of historical reason, is revealed here as a paragon of intellectual privilege and out and out betrayal. While in Brecht's *The Measures Taken* the 'traitor' is the comrade who in acting spontaneously breaks with Party omniscience and endangers the larger cause, in Müller's *Der Auftrag* Debuisson's betrayal lies in his absolute adherence to the survival dictates of the 'Party,' whose function in this play will be condemned as a breach of contract. Thus, while the intellectual Chibis in Müller's *Cement* joins the Cheka in order to harden himself and stoically carry on the dictates of (a potentially unreasonable) historical reason, Debuisson's cynical withdrawal reveals the entire model itself as bankrupt and wanting.

What is the model that is increasingly put into question by Müller's re-readings of Brecht's *The Measures Taken?* First, and most obviously rooted in the experience of real existing socialism in the GDR, there is a profound questioning concerning the 'leading role of the Party' and in particular the role of socialist societies as harbingers of meaningful revolutionary change, both domestically and in the face of Third World insurgence. Müller's depiction of the Party (collective) in all three plays reads against the grain of Brecht's ultimate reverence for the 'classics' and their institutionalization, to question, each time at a deeper level, the forms of ossification and corruption that have undermined the socialist project as a whole. *Mauser* and *Cement* raise insistently the repressed historical issue of Stalinism, which Müller asserts was to remain a major 'silence' in

Brecht's own politics and work, beginning with his exile in Hollywood and carrying over into his role in the GDR.[33] In *Der Auftrag*, Müller looks at the effects of such a process within the sphere of 'proletarian internationalism.' Official communist policy would have it that the fate of the Third World is linked historically to the liberation struggles of the metropolitan proletariat, which in turn finds its primary leadership in the dictates of the homeland of international revolution, the Soviet Union. Debuisson/Antoine's betrayal is the privilege of the white revolutionary who can abandon the cause at any time, whether it is Paris of the nineteenth century or Moscow of the twentieth, whether it is under Napoleon or Stalin.

At the philosophical and aesthetic level, Müller's critique of the Brechtian *Lehrstück The Measures Taken* constitutes a repudiation of basic tenets of Marxist theory. While the Brechtian aesthetic remains tied to an Enlightenment notion of history that would link the material advance of society to a betterment of the human condition, Müller's theater of revolution posits the revolt of the body against such an abstraction of ideas and offers in the figure of Sasportas a repudiation of this political model. Perhaps it is ironic that Müller's employment of the *Lehrstück* form is finally what permits such a questioning of the model, as GDR Germanist Frank Hörnigk emphasized when he wrote: 'Precisely the impression of closed and finished solutions in a work of art are what must be avoided (for Müller) both at the level of form and content. *Such an impression cannot exist for Müller aesthetically because he is unable to locate it in reality*' (emphasis in the original).[34] Having abandoned the 'closed and finished solutions' of Marxist history, Müller opens up for critical questioning a legacy of brutalization that in many ways found its staunchest ideological justification precisely in the categories of that historiography.

6. PATRICIDE OR REGENERATION?:

BRECHT VS. BRECHT

IN THE 1980s

What began in the mid-1970s as a somewhat heretical assertion that Brecht's plays were nothing more than a 'constant,
liturgical repetition of what one already knows'[1] was soon to
become common dramaturgical parlance within the avant-
garde theater establishments of both East and West Germany. 'Brecht is
dead,' was the Nietzschean pronouncement of Hellmut Karasek in *Der
Spiegel*,[2] to which the celebrated 'Brecht-Killer'[3] and East German heir
apparent Heiner Müller could only add that it was, in all due respect,
a *Vatermord* [patricide].[4] Statistics would bear all this out. Whereas 1967
saw twenty separate new Brecht productions in the GDR,[5] this number had
dropped to eight by 1985, three of which were of *The Threepenny Opera*
and two of *The Guns of Carrar*[6] – not exactly the center of the classical
Brechtian canon. If that is not enough, one need only cite the burial of old
Bertolt Brecht as a classicist by the Brecht progeny in the Berliner Ensemble. 'Brecht's theater works of the mature period,' the GDR critic Christoph
Funke offered by way of historical explanation, 'make a tired-out, worn-
down impression. The clearer, the more intelligent, the more logical and
coherent the Brechtian text, the less it seems to offer today in the way of
critical intellectual challenge.'[7] Speaking from the towers of academic literary criticism, Werner Mittenzwei even went so far as to call the move
away from Brecht a moment in the 'emancipation process of socialist
literature,' the initiation of which he ascribed to 'the aesthetic dethrone-
ment of Brecht by his students.'[8]

While such hyperbolic metaphors of patricide and internment serve
well as signals of crisis, a closer look at the actual function of Brecht within

the GDR beginning in the 1970s reveals a somewhat more complicated picture. To be sure, a growing number of artists and critics alike spoke openly and even cantankerously of 'Brecht fatigue'; of the aesthetically paralyzing impact of the Brecht *Modelle* from the 1950s and 1960s on the entire contemporary theatrical landscape; even of the irrelevance of the mature, enlightened, finished works for the post-1968 generation in the GDR.[9] But the venom in most cases was directed as much at the historical canonization of the *Stückeschreiber* [play writer, as he liked to call himself] as an expression of a prevailing cultural political hegemony as it was at the author and the works themselves. Once a thorn in the side of the Aristotelian-Stanislavski-dominated theatrical status quo, the official Brecht had come to stand for a particular kind of 'knowing-it-all' [*Besserwisserei*] and establishment control. However, what also becomes increasingly clear is that there were more Brechts than just this official one. Moreover, they were at war with one another.

As illustration of the inherently internecine nature of the signifier Brecht in the GDR, I should like to discuss two highly controversial GDR Brecht productions of the 1980s. I use these events to delineate a number of ramifications of the Brecht discussion in the GDR, which I organize around the following questions: What do these productions and the response to them tell us about the relevance of Brecht's works for theatrical practice in the GDR in the 1980s? What was the importance of the changing reception of Brecht in the GDR historically for questions concerning the ongoing reassessment of modernism and the avant-garde in that society? Finally, within what ideological framework did experimental theater continue to provide a space for political articulation within the public sphere?

In February 1982, the director Friedo Solter of the Deutsches Theater in East Berlin left the capital to direct the first GDR production of Brecht's very early play *Baal* (1919) at the Städtische Bühnen in Erfurth. The choice of *Baal* is significant not only because of its recourse to the early Brecht, which with the exception of *Man Is Man* (a transitional play from Brecht's early phase to his Marxist work) had for the most part remained unexplored territory in the GDR,[10] but because Solter had turned away from Brecht's own officially sanitized version of the text to draw from the 1918/19 versions in which the language was considerably more vital, the gesture infinitely more anarchistic. In the 1954 edition of his collected works published two years before his death, Brecht had warned readers that the 'asocial' *Baal* would cause those who had not learned to think dialectically all sorts of problems: 'they will find therein little more than the glorification of egomania.'[11] Clearly the older Marxist was seeking to prevent in later readings of this play any pubescent identification with this Nietzschean *Kraftmensch* [person of power]. Hence it is all the more interesting that Solter's excavation of the earlier versions, together with his whole conception for this first GDR production, was guided by a positive, not a negative, appropriation of 'the Baalic world feeling [*das Baalesche Weltgefühl*]' for socialism.

What emerges in the 1982 Erfurth production is a Baal whose destructive energies and sexual vitality, while still seen as nihilistically shocking and hence asocial, nevertheless offer preferable behavioral alternatives to a stagnated status quo. The actor Klaus Schieff's characterization gives us an older, balding, mustached, and basically lovable figure (the resemblance to Wolf Biermann was unmistakable) whose antics clearly evolve out of rebellion against rather than merely narcissistic isolation from. 'Aren't you afraid of the power of society, which you have as your enemy?' Baal is asked. 'I thrive on animosity' is the reply.[12]

The targets of this animosity range from hypocritical bourgeois morality to misuse of the environment. In a dispute with Eckhart over the ruination of the landscape, Baal almost sounds like a member of the environmental movement: 'In forty-nine years you can eliminate the term forest from your vocabulary. And human beings will be gone too.'[13] Baal's women are no longer merely victims but take part actively and aggressively in the general uproar and prevailing sensuality. His lover Eckhart is an avuncular, grey-bearded vagabond philosopher (the homoerotic dimension is eviscerated) who like Baal forms a part of a somewhat aging, late 1960s counterculture. Thus, in Solter's production, Baal's asocial behavior is socially motivated, takes on the contours of a coherent, acceptable attack upon the establishment. In the final scene the recalcitrant hero is swept from the stage by his fellow actors dressed like street cleaners. A 'disturbance factor' has been eliminated, the society stands accused.

Asked in an interview about his interest in doing *Baal* in the GDR, Solter stressed the importance of the early Brecht as a source of revitalization at a time of cultural stagnation. 'We in this society have outdone ourselves in terms of enlightenment, in terms of dogma, in terms of reducing everything to one simple message,' Solter says with remarkable candor. 'Brecht's later plays were written at a time . . . when one needed a few solid slogans and dogmas . . . but when you've done that sort of thing year after year the way we have, then you need a new lever.'[14] Solter's detailed praise of the potentials of *Baal* and the pre-Marxist Brecht implicitly constructs a 'Brecht model' in direct and obvious critical contrast to the establishment one. There is something 'wild,' 'uncomplicated,' 'unpremeditated,' and refreshingly 'unorthodox' in this Brecht, Solter says: 'no firm structures . . . no logical, inexorable unfolding of plot . . . no grand thought scheme [*Schemata des Denkens*] . . . What we find is real life [*es ist Lebenshaltung drin*]!'[15]

The ironies here are striking. In word if not exactly in letter, Solter's formulations reenact Brecht's own revolt against the theatrical status quo of the Weimar Republic fifty years before. In Solter's scheme, the closed, narrative-centered, overly didactic qualities of the older Brecht had become in the GDR what once were the attributes of Aristotelian theater to the playwright himself.

What emerges with clarity in both the production and the discussions around it is the extent to which the recourse to the early Brecht in the GDR entailed at once an attack on the GDR Brecht industry as well as a repudiation of those later works that had become encased in classicism. The problem, in other words, lay with the mature texts qua texts, as well as the way they had lent themselves to appropriation as forms of official legitimation. Solter's production of *Baal* brought out both these dimensions, which were important for the Brecht tug of war and its impact on theater life in the 1980s.

At the political level, the message seemed to be that Brecht's theater was appropriate for a postwar period in which there was a need for enlightenment with aesthetic means. Where the classical Brechtian model once was a challenge to the entrenched political and ideological leftovers from the previous historical period, where the 'grand scheme' was once necessary for a broader picture, such answers had come to have an inhibiting effect. Refreshing about the early plays was precisely a 'life attitude' where questions rather than answers, where creative destruction were the call of the day. Again Solter: 'There are academic grades now for Marxist-Leninism, for the study of the state. This thinking in grades [*Zensuren*] has something very narrow and inhibiting about it.'[16] In the GDR, Brecht wittingly or unwittingly had become associated with an entrenched worldview in which the predictable outcome of the socialist revolution provided a catechism of prestructured knowledge in a world suddenly demanding a new set of answers – and questions.

Solter's stress upon the early Brecht being rich in textual fragmentation, unexpected leaps, logical contradictions, and openness was intended to provide avenues for creative exploration that the more rounded, rational, 'classical' texts simply denied. In place of a historical emplotment, which despite its claim to epic contradiction and audience involvement would still resolve its questions harmoniously, Solter emphasized the *political* effectiveness of an aesthetics grounded in improvisation, play, and fantasy. The very fragmented, unresolved nature of the text itself was seen to undermine the hegemony of central concepts and engage the audience and the actors in the process of experimentation and resolution.

The emphasis upon improvisation and play is certainly what linked Solter's interpretation to the work of his renowned younger colleague at the Deutsches Theater, Alexander Lang, whose 1983 production of *Roundheads and Peakedheads* (only the third postwar production in German) caused an even greater sensation than did Solter's *Baal*. A former actor at the Berliner Ensemble before going to the Deutsches Theater, Lang rapidly built a name for himself through a number of highly innovative productions of such works as Büchner's *Danton's Death*, Shakespeare's *Midsummer Night's Dream*, Ernst Toller's *Der entfesselte Wotan* (The Unchained Wotan), and the GDR playwright Christoph Hein's *The True Story of Ah Q*. What marked Lang's style in all of these works and earned him the epithet *Regieindividualist* [directorial individualist][17] was a notable disdain for textual integrity, an emphasis upon the comic, the playful, upon fantasy as the seat of realism, together with a strong belief in the active, autonomous role of the actor in the collective construction of a dramatic production. None of these qualities had been particularly a mainstay of the realist or even the Brechtian theater tradition in the GDR, and so it was a source of some surprise that the keeper of the grail in the personage of Brecht's daughter Barbara Berg-Schall even granted him the rights to produce the play in the first place.[18] Needless to say, Lang realized her worst fears.

There could not have been a more incongruous combination than the architect of what came to be called 'comedic theater' [*komödiantisches Theater*][19] in the GDR and Brecht's rather weighty allegory about fascism, racism, and class struggle, written just as Hitler was coming to power (1932–34). Lang's first step was radical textual incision, which, while solving a lot of dramaturgical problems, earned him the enmity of those who stand for the 'integrity of the text': he repressed and even eliminated the racist and class conflict elements of the play. The de Guzmann plot line about the rich Jew who is momentarily persecuted on the basis of race but at a moment of crisis is able to rejoin his capitalist class brothers and continue his life as exploiter is pushed into the background; the historical alternative to the present social order in the form of the revolutionary 'sickle' movement (i.e., the finally triumphant Communist Party) is eliminated completely. The play had originally been a study of how Hitler used race to blind momentarily the proletariat to their true revolutionary interests so that the bourgeois class could maintain its power. Lang's revisions suppressed what history had revealed as Marxist myth in order to explore the problem of manipulation in mass society. In so doing he stripped the play of its limited historical context as a crude socioeconomic allegory of the rise of Hitler in the spirit of the Dimitroff theory[20] and placed it squarely into the process of political power relations in the contemporary world – East and West.

Lang's underlying dramatic conception for this play was as radical as his textual emendations. The entire production takes place in a gray, walled-in arena that resembles at once a bull ring, a circus, a theater, a marketplace – in any case, an open locus of mass gathering, where individuals lose their identity and where the seductive formation of public taste and behavior historically prevails. The dictator Iberin is dressed in a striped shirt and jogging pants and perched on a bike. His speeches to the *Volk*, delivered in lilting Saxon accent (the allusion to Walter Ulbricht was not missed by anyone), resemble more the exhortations of an exercise leader in a sports camp than the demagoguery of Adolf Hitler. The Chaplinesque tenant farmer Callas, with white clown face and red nose, gallops around the 'ring' like a circus horse in chase of his whip: a petit bourgeois run amok, brought now under control, not through any ideology of *Volk* or race relations but simply by the binding formations inherent to the collective activities and institutional life in an advanced industrial society. What marks the performance of all these characters and the production as a whole is a sense of physical activity, slapstick, constant movement – but above all play.

A number of things emerged from Alexander Lang's staging of *Roundheads* that illustrate new approaches to Brecht occurring in the GDR during the 1980s. First was the importance of confronting the power of the then existing Brecht image by making changes in the text. Lang, like Brecht himself in both his adaptations [*Bearbeitungen*] and in productions, was audacious enough to revise or even remove dimensions of a thematic plot line in order to bring into the foreground dimensions of a play that for historical reasons had become relevant topics of the day.[21] His focus upon the seductiveness of the little person through mechanisms of mass manipulation highlighted an element in this and other plays from Brecht's mature period that still spoke directly to audiences in socialist and capitalist societies alike. More important, by eliminating the somewhat heavy-handed reference to the Communist Party as the alternative lying in the historical wings, Lang cut away a ballast from the work that identified Brecht in the minds of GDR viewers with what Friedo Solter called an 'I-can-go-home-and-rest-assured' attitude. In 1934, mention of the sickle movement meant a utopian glimmer of the future at a moment when all progressive forces were being swept aside by the brown hordes. In 1983, in a state in which questions of class struggle under capitalism and their 'eventual' resolution inevitably served as ideological justification for the status quo, the allegorical sickle movement suggested, rightly or wrongly, the easy answer. Lang's position was that unless they are cracked open and shaken up and revamped and attacked anew, Brecht's epic plays from the mature period inevitably become, again in the words of Christoph Funke, a 'confirmation of certified knowledge [*Bestätigung eines gesichterten Wissens*].'[22] Thus it is no accident that Lang looked to a little-known play (no model exists) and to differing versions of that play to construct a text that would bring a breath of fresh air and even sacrilege into the Brecht aura. And it is equally unsurprising that such behavior should have him called to task for a lack of 'fidelity to the work' and for what a number of GDR critics referred to pejoratively as *Regietheater* [director's theater].[23]

Lang also sought to reconceptualize the 'heavy' political Brecht as commedia dell'arte. The director's innovative scene design, along with his use of masks and employment of circus motifs, brought an aspect of the visual and a sense of lightness and play to a Brechtian text that, in the mixed metaphor of one critic, 'could well send the signal that breaks the camel's back, particularly in that it takes place only 100 meters from the stuffy museum of the Berliner Ensemble.'[24] Circus elements and slapstick theater or an emphasis upon sport or even the geste of Charlie Chaplin's little tramp were, of course, not foreign to Brecht himself. In plays such as *Man Is Man, Rise and Fall of the Town Mahagonny, Threepenny Opera,* and *In the Jungle of the Cities,* Bertolt Brecht had employed a semiotics drawn from the domain of mass culture that was at once a parody and an incorporation of that medium for his own epic work. But this again was more the early Brecht. The prevailing image of the later Brecht in the GDR was imprinted differently, emerging from the struggles of exile and with the visage and rigor of that experience. The gray austerity of Mother Courage pulling her *Planwagen* across the stage of Europe bespoke a message of dark times with relevance for the construction years, not the 1980s. Lang's production of *Roundheads* made the play's subtitle, 'a fairy tale of horror [*ein Greuelmärchen*],' the dominant conceptual metaphor of a reinterpretation in which the central conflict was no longer labor versus capital or even rationalism versus irrationalism but rather the free play of fantasy as a liberating force and its subversion at the hands of collective culture industries. What it also communicated, above all by giving the actor free rein in physically countering and subverting the Brechtian text, was a fearless audacity vis-à-vis the official Brecht image. Lang: 'The basic motivation for me and the actors is curiosity. Curiosity about the playwright, his text and its translation into a comic mode. If I know everything in advance, it all gets boring.'[25]

The productions by Solter and Lang did not stand in a vacuum but emerged out of more general developments within the area of theater and cultural politics. In drawing conclusions about the meaning of the political controversy around Brecht it is important to situate them within such a larger framework.

The rebellion against Brecht in the GDR was at the same time a rebellion against what the theater critic Joachim Fiebach called a 'closed socialist model for art' that prevailed in the 1950s and 1960s.[26] Central to this model was a belief that one could use theater as a means for the formation of political consciousness; but even more important, that there was a clear and direct translatable relationship between scientific and aesthetic cognition. As progenitor of a Theater of the Scientific Age, Brecht's epic drama as a total system became synonymous with a notion of art in which grand philosophical and sociological questions could be posed *and* answered within the medium of aesthetic representation. Regardless of the extent to which Brecht himself had once challenged conventional models of socialist realism or as an artist was rooted in the tradition of modernism, his dialectical theater was nevertheless seen as an aesthetic analogue to the 'totality' thinking at the heart of Marxist-Leninism, where answers are pregiven by the very questions asked.

It should come as no surprise that in repudiating such 'all-encompassing models [*übergreifende Modelle*],'[27] practicing artists would rediscover the early Brecht. Rather than a 'progressive' notion of history grounded in the teachings of the Marxist classics and propelled forward by the actions of a social class, we find the naked, anarchistic individual whose destructive energies disrupt historical continuity and explode into the open new possibilities; in place of dramatic structures, which both mirror and call forth intervention into the social conditions of a world that can be rationally grasped and politically resolved, we are offered fragmented images whose inner relationship is symbolic and lyrical rather than cognitive; and instead of an epic *epistēmē*, which despite the existence of dark times will still promise us 'a perfect world [*eine heile Welt*],' we find only 'searching, not yet knowing' (Solter) and negation as life-giving principle. While constructing a binary of an early versus a late Brecht served to sublimate the very real contradictions and inconsistencies within even the later Brecht, it is nevertheless this sublimated image against which battle was being fought.

The assertion of internecine struggles being waged within the signifier of Bertolt Brecht and the recourse now to the early Brecht as a source of aesthetic renewal brings us finally to the role of Bertolt Brecht in the larger discussions of modernism and the development of the avant-garde in the GDR. Certainly it is a well-known fact that Brecht had been central to the development of experimental and avant-garde theater in the GDR since the very outset of cultural life in the postwar period. His early productions of *Mother Courage* in 1949 and *The Mother* in 1951 were points of controversy because of their challenge to established notions of socialist realism; just as his and Paul Dessau's pacifist, twelve-tone opera *The Trial of Lukullus* in 1951 had set the framework for a whole new direction in modernist music and musical theater in that society. As discussed in chapter 4, when in the late 1950s a group of younger playwrights (Heiner Müller, Peter Hacks, and subsequently Volker Braun) turned to the agitprop theater tradition of the Soviet and Weimar avant-gardes as a source of political and aesthetic renewal, it was Brecht's own earlier public pleas for 'small, flexible forms of struggle . . . as we once had in the agitprop movement' that had helped legitimate and pave the way for that kind of experimental theater.[28]

Thus our look back at the history of Brecht in the GDR reveals a figure poised on both sides of the struggle for avant-garde theater. While the epic models of the 1950s offered the first alternatives to the hegemony of socialist realist theater, it was precisely this model that in turn bore the brunt of attack as some writers sought a slightly earlier or less orthodox version to fuel their efforts for theatrical change. Which of these configurations constitutes, finally, the 'real' Brecht? The answer, of course, as more recent theoretical debates have taught us, is none. Or, rather, that any 'real' Brecht must emanate precisely in the process of slippage so central to the evolution of his work; in that inevitably contradictory authorial persona who would seem to invite canonization at the very moment he would offer the means for its decanonization. Certainly such a process has been Brecht's most important legacy historically within the development of avant-garde theater and theory in the GDR.

Viewed from such a perspective, it is possible to locate two significant reevaluations and reappropriations of Brecht that have had an impact on new theatrical directions in the GDR. Returning to our discussions in chapters 3 and 4, the first important shift in the signifier entailed a move away from the classical Bertolt Brecht (*The Life of Galileo*, *The Good Woman of Sezuan*, *Mother Courage*, etc.) to the discovery of the *Lehrstück* [learning play] from Brecht's agitprop theater days of the late Weimar period. While the first efforts in this regard were indeed initiated by dramatists in the late 1950s and early 1960s as a part of the so-called didactic theater movement, it was not until Werner Mittenzwei's articles entitled 'Die Brecht-Lukács Debatte' (1968; The Brecht-Lukács debate) and 'Brecht und die Schicksale der Materialästhetik' (1975) that the fruits of Brecht's agitprop legacy would be formulated into a more general theory of avant-gardism capable of confronting the antimodernist predilections of the prevailing Lukácsian aesthetic.

Two emphases emerge in Mittenzwei's explication that became central tenets for the embryonic avant-garde debate of that time. At the most general level, Brechtian *Lehrstück* theory, in conjunction with Walter Benjamin's essay 'The Author as Producer' and Hanns Eisler's and Ernst Bloch's writings on avant-garde from the exile period, provides the theoretical underpinnings for an 'aesthetics of materials' founded upon an analogue between material and aesthetic production in which the 'new' media such as film, radio, and television represent 'progressive,' more 'collective' and industrially produced forms of experimental art. More relevant for theater, Brecht's agitprop legacy was seen as encouraging a theatrical practice in which short, formally experimental works would evoke active, critical audience participation; works whose 'operative' nature was designed to challenge both the more traditionally structured forms of classical socialist drama as well as the character- and plot-centered structures of Brecht's own epic plays.

What is paradigmatic about Mittenzwei's use of Brecht to elaborate a theory of the avant-garde heretofore unacceptable within the realm of socialist theory is precisely the inverted time lag it reveals between practice and theory. For in fact, by the time of its tentative articulation (1968–75), a number of the leading playwrights in the GDR had already pointedly distanced themselves from even the agitprop Brecht in their search for theatrical models less overtly 'didactic' and 'rational' in their orientation. For example, Peter Hacks's call for a 'postrevolutionary dramaturgy' in 1965 spoke for a number of playwrights who would turn to aesthetically centered, 'poetic' models of expression no longer grounded in sociological explication and scientific premise.[29] 'Science does not know everything,' wrote Hacks ten years later in an even more direct attack upon Brecht's notion of 'scientific' theater, 'and where it does know something, it is not worth much for art.'[30]

But it is the playwright Heiner Müller who has most pointedly articulated the evolving second shift within the Brecht signifier in his attempted recovery of Brecht's early, pre-Marxist writings and in particular through his discussion of Bertolt Brecht's little-known dramatic fragment *Fatzer*.[31] Between 1927 and 1932 Brecht had worked on this *Lehrstück*, which deals with four soldiers in World War I who desert battle, hole up in a little room, and wait for the revolution. *Fatzer* ends when three of the soldiers execute the central character – 'yes, you ought / at least to change yourself / by no longer being / here at all'[32] – and finally themselves are discovered and shot. The profound pessimism concerning any resolution to the historical situation, combined with the assertion of ego as the material wellspring for a viable social struggle, are the reasons for Müller that Brecht was never able to finish the work: '*Fatzer* had to remain a fragment,' Müller writes programmatically, 'because, if he had not broken it off, he would never have written again. For the final insight of the play – that for a long time to come there will be no victors in this world, only vanquished – well, one simply cannot keep writing with this kind of an insight . . . *Fatzer* is the best thing that has ever been written for the twentieth-century stage in this century, and the best by Brecht.'[33]

For Heiner Müller of the 1980s (as opposed to his earlier fascination with the *Lehrstück*), Brecht's turn to Marxism in the late 1920s and to an agitprop dramaturgy founded upon the securities of the 'teachings of the classics' about the outcome of class struggle repressed the insights of his pre-Marxist, more intuitive, more experimental and fragmented aesthetic stance. While historically understandable, given the growing onset of fascism, three things get lost in the process that Müller hopes to see reclaimed for contemporary GDR theater. Not surprisingly, they are qualities that also form the foundation for both the Solter and Lang productions discussed above.

The first concerns the way that certain things seem to drop out of sight for Brecht in terms of what he perceives of social reality. For instance, the concept of the individual in a mass society – clearly not a constituent dimension of 'orthodox Marxism' – is nevertheless very much a central theme throughout the early Brecht (*Man Is Man, Fatzer,* etc.). In Müller's view the playwright's later invocation of class categories led to abandoning such a perspective and hence to an impoverishment of detail, a removal of self and subjectivity, a standing above the material that he was treating. As soon as Marxism is bound to the existence of the state, Müller argues, it goes through a process of reduction. Brecht's binding of his Marxist theater to official socialist history (Marxist theories of fascism, etc.) resulted in a similar kind of reduction, one that obscured his view of any social phenomena lying outside those paradigms. Certainly Alexander Lang's production of *Roundheads* implicitly takes part in such a critique of Brecht, precisely by abandoning the models of class and socialist history in the original version of the play to focus on the hopeless fate of the 'little person' in mass society.

A second blind spot to emerge from the more enlightened Marxist Brecht, in Müller's view, can be traced in his increasing focus upon the positive at the expense of the negative. Central to Brecht's early plays (*Baal, Drums in the Night, In the Jungle of the Cities*) as well as *Fatzer* was a sense of 'destruction,' of evil and the asocial as the potential for something new. Again Müller: 'Society can get a great deal of good from the presentation of asocial behavioral patterns. Representing the asocial releases more impulses than any kind of good example.'[34] Friedo Solter's production of *Baal* was clearly conceived to tap the nihilism of the early Brecht, which Heiner Müller has theorized into a new, more vital avant-garde tradition for contemporary socialist theater.

Finally, most important for Müller about *Fatzer* is precisely its tentative, fragmented, experimental character. Closed theater with closed answers, even if Marxist answers, he argued, prohibits the audience from critical involvement, prevents it from seeing reality as an ongoing process. The unfinished, unrhymed nature of Brecht's early work stands for Müller as a critique of the more facile solutions offered by the agitprop as well as the classical, epic plays that were to succeed it.

The very existence of such lively interchange within the dramatic and theoretical heritage of Bertolt Brecht speaks to his continued life and not his complete demise in the GDR of the 1980s. Whether one looks to the younger Brecht to counter the old, as did Solter and Müller, or urges more playful, less text-centered approaches to the classical epic works, following Alexander Lang, it is clear that Bertolt Brecht remained a part of avant-garde theatrical developments – even as an object of assault. For what transcended the validity of the textual canon or established production models was the critical spirit of the Brechtian method, a method that was aimed not only at the social conditions of an unjust world but at those very forms of representation that would claim to confront them. That GDR playwrights and theater directors directed this method against the figure of Brecht himself seems a fitting tribute to their acknowledged teacher. After all, isn't that what *Vatermord* is really all about?

PART 3: THE POLITICS OF THE IRRATIONAL

7. LITTLE RED RIDING HOOD IN THE GDR:

FOLKLORE, MASS CULTURE, AND THE AVANT-GARDE

I n September 1960, the West German periodical *Der Monat* published an article by Sabine Brandt entitled 'Rotkäppchen und der Klassenkampf' (Little Red Riding Hood and the class struggle). The author, a former journalist from the GDR living in the West, recounted in fairy-tale-like wonder her efforts to publish the first GDR edition of the Grimms' *Kinder- und Hausmärchen* (Children and household tales) in the immediate postwar period. Brandt's initial inquiry at the Central Institute for Pedagogy as to why there were Russian, Uzbekian, Albanian, Korean, Indonesian, even Eskimo and African but no German fairy tales published in East Germany brought forth a response that told much about the 'trials and tribulations'[1] of the folklore tradition in the early days of the German Democratic Republic:

> The comrade preschool instructor looked at me as though I had said something obscene. 'The Socialist Unity Party,' she explained, 'wants to bring its children up to be builders of a peace-loving, democratic Germany. Young pioneers need models. Are Hansel and Gretel, who end up burning a witch in an oven, really able to serve as models? And what about the seven dwarves, who force the evil queen to dance in burning slippers? These are folktales, to be sure, but unfortunately they bear the stamp of their reactionary bourgeois recorders: flight from reality and an obsession with the uncanny, the sick, the perverse. I would advise you to keep your hands off. This is a hot potato!'[2]

As was often the case in those early days, the ideological winds were quickly to shift. The initiation of the first Five-Year Plan in 1950, together with cold war tensions and the growing separation of the two German states, was accompanied by increasingly vitriolic attacks against 'cosmopolitanism' and 'Anglo-American imperialist' incursions within the realm of culture. The fight, in other words, was for nothing less than the rightful claim to the national heritage, and it was clear with the increasing emphasis upon national identity in the GDR that the Grimms would have to be included in the accepted canon.

In July 1952, participants at a conference held in the Hotel Johannishof in East Berlin sketched the outlines for rehabilitation and finalized concrete plans for a new edition of Grimms' fairy tales. Contrary to previous assessments, the fairy tales were now seen as important documents of class struggle, 'a fantastic revolution of the suffering people against the suppression of their feudal masters and bourgeois property relations.'[3] To be sure, there were ideological difficulties with individual tales, but these were to be attributed to the falsifications of 'bourgeois ideologues' and would soon be eliminated by the planned publication of *Kinder- und Hausmärchen* by the Kinderbuch Publishing House. In fact, the two-volume edition[4] that appeared shortly thereafter contained a number of revisions and deletions to make the stories conform to prevailing socialist sensibilities: 'Hansel and Gretel' was dropped completely; the witch in 'Two Brothers' did not perish in a fire but self-detonated because of her own poisonous personality; prayers and baptisms were eliminated; daughters of kings were transformed into peasants. In short, the editors Walther Pollatschek and Hans Siebert sanitized the stories along the lines of domesticated proletarian good behavior, much the same way the Grimms themselves had rewritten and reworked the original versions to conform to the norms of bourgeois morality some 140 years before.[5] In both cases, the effect was to deradicalize the tales by bowdlerizing the elements of the fantastic, the uncanny, the grotesque, and the obscene.[6]

Yet fairy tales remain subversive and utopian, not because they ritually reinvent the social order as an ideal type of the status quo but because the logic of their narrative reality as a projected fantasy of the 'other' explodes the paradigms of propriety to explore a forbidden world. Take, for example, the tale entitled 'Tischlein deck dich' ('The Table, the Ass, and the Stick'). In the original version, three sons of a poor and hard-working tailor are thrown out into the world to make their way the best they can, and they eventually do so with surprising success. After many ups and downs they return with a magic table that will provide an unlimited source of food, a donkey that will regurgitate upon command an equally unlimited supply of money, and a stick in a sack with which to protect their bounty. The underlying 'intention' of this tale, as Ernst Bloch has argued, is a utopian world without cares [*Schlaraffenland*] suggesting in its outline a future socialist order: 'it is as though we can already hear a social fairy tale of the state, simpler in its provision of goods, yet more nourishing than all others.'[7]

The real existing socialist version of 'The Table, the Ass, and the Stick' published in the GDR in the construction years of the early 1950s could not afford the implications of such early retirement. Bored with their bourgeois life of luxury, the three sons happily go back to a life of productivity in the form of manual labor, and in the end 'each carried out his work better than ever before.'[8] The message of immediate gratification in the older tale was simply too threatening, given the proximity of the rapidly growing West German economic miracle and the needs of domestic production in the GDR.

A focus upon the historical contingencies governing the reception of folk tales and the folk tradition in the GDR leads us to two central issues that are key for an understanding of the function of folklore in that society and that are the topic of this chapter. The first concerns the potential threat to the self-proclaimed 'rationalist' *Kulturpolitik* by a genre of discourse that is centered around the world of dreams, fantasy, the fantastic, the mystical, and the uncanny. The fact that folklore emerged out of the ambience of nineteenth-century Romanticism had a profound effect upon the 'meaning' accorded it within the evolving historical interchange between cultural policy and literary production. The guidelines developed to legislate the fantastic and, conversely, the role that the fairy tale genre went on to play as a mode of political articulation (for example, among avant-garde writers) can only be properly understood in light of long-range historical codings accorded to the folk tradition within German intellectual and socialist history.

A second concern connected with the function of folklore in the GDR was its deemed importance for the development of a popular culture, or *Volkstümlichkeit*. If one of the premises of socialist realism was that culture be made accessible to many, then it is certainly understandable that the introduction of folk traditions in the GDR became closely linked to the hope for a rejuvenated mass culture: 'broad circles of our cultural public sphere, indeed, all culturally interested working people,' wrote a leading folklorist, Wolfgang Steinitz, in 1953, 'expect a lot from the science of German folklore, namely, the reacquaintance with their own traditions, which had become buried under capitalism.'[9] As we see in our discussion of the German folk song movement in the 1950s, strategies of folklore reception were closely bound up with the struggle to stem the inflowing tide of Western mass culture.

NINETEENTH-CENTURY FOLKLORISM AND ITS MARXIST RECEPTION

The cultural politicians of the SED were not the first Marxists to be concerned about the pedagogic use or nonuse value of the folk traditions for more contemporary sensibilities. In 1839, the young Friedrich Engels wrote of the *Volksbuch* that its task was 'to make more clear for the working people their moral feelings, to bring to consciousness their sense of strength, justice and freedom, to awaken in them courage and love for the Fatherland.'[10] Nor was Engels averse to a little censorship if folk traditions threatened or challenged his own somewhat philistine notions of proper decorum. For instance, although he loved Gottfried von Strassburg's *Tristan* for its 'poetic value,' he nevertheless felt that its basic message came down to a blanket exoneration of adultery, 'and to put that sort of thing in the hands of the people is very questionable indeed.'[11]

But the problems surrounding the folk and fairy tale tradition in the GDR in 1950 did not just stem from long-standing socialist conservatism, be it the prudishness of the Pietist's son Engels or the anti-Romantic predilections of the classicist Franz Mehring. In the over 100 years between the writing of *The Communist Manifesto* and the founding of the 'first peasant and Workers State on German soil' lay the continued historical politicizing of the folklore tradition as it emerged out of the struggles for national unification. It was during this period that we note a split in the political coding of folklore ideology that was to affect the reception of this tradition in the twentieth century, on the Left and on the Right.

On the one hand, the folk tradition continued to be viewed, as it had been in the eighteenth-century Enlightenment and Sturm und Drang movements (Herder, the young Goethe), as a rational and progressive form of bourgeois emancipation and nationalism emerging from a preindustrial, artisanal culture with its stress on democratic, populist orientations. *Volk* in this sense was a sociological category, one that stressed agrarian modes of work and community in social opposition to either the feudal aristocracy or the emergent bourgeois urban and industrial culture of early capitalism.

Opposed to this more sociological reading of the folk tradition was the transformation of folklore discourse, beginning within Romanticism, into a mystical and irrational ersatz religion with chauvinistic overtones. In fact, more than was the case for any other cultural tradition, it was the advocates of *Volkstümlichkeit* who were among the most active (and successful) 'co-producers of that seductive ideology of the organic community, of the natural-primitive notion of folklore [*Volkstum*]'[12] that emerged in the intellectual ambience of German Romanticism and reached its political apotheosis in the Third Reich. In its transformation from a philosophy of tradition to a political ideology, the growing obsession with folklore in the nineteenth century came increasingly to help constitute a cultural and political climate within which mythologies of folk, nation, and finally race were to compensate for a failed and crisis-ridden history: the threat of the French Revolution and the wars with Napoleon; the failure of bourgeois (1848) and socialist (1918–19) revolutions; the retardation of national unification; the disruptive and accelerated rush from an agrarian to a modern industrialized society.

The fate of the brothers Grimm is illustrative in this regard, for a look at the process of their reception in the nineteenth and early twentieth centuries offers important insight into what folklore actually came to 'mean' in the crucial years of its political formation. Certainly on the basis of their self-conception and in the light of their political views and even actions, Jakob and Wilhelm Grimm were typical of a number of moderately liberal intellectuals immersed in a time of political and ideological transition.[13] As members of the Göttinger Seven, they were dismissed from their positions at the university at Göttingen in 1837 because they spoke out against the abrogation of the constitution by the new regent.[14] It is also true that their emphasis upon a scientific and rationally grounded study of language and literature, together with their stress upon language (rather than simply *Geist*) as the foundation of a national folk culture, linked them philosophically with the traditions of the Enlightenment and humanism as opposed to such chauvinist thinkers as Adam von Müller, Achim von Arnim, and Turnvater Jahn. Indeed, they felt themselves a part of the progressive traditions of folklore research and theory formation at the beginning of the nineteenth century, one that stressed the foundation of a nationalist consciousness that could overcome the feudal and reactionary political structures of the time in order to establish a more democratic and egalitarian social order. Yet despite a decided liberal orientation, many of their views were at the same time compatible with and ultimately even helped shape the shifts that were occurring toward a more conservative folklore ideology during the period.

Let us consider, for instance, their view of history. Whereas the more empirically and socially oriented theories of Vico, Herder, and Karl Philip Moritz conceived of *Volkspoesie* as the national expression of language and culture at a particular stage of its historical development, the Grimms posited the origination of what they called *Volksgeist* [spirit of the people] outside of any historical or social context in a vaguely defined prefeudal, organic 'community of estates [*Ständegemeinschaft*]' of early Germanic times. Thus their turn to history entailed in fact a transformation of history into myth, a dissolution of temporal and political contingencies into a 'timeless time' (Schlegel) in which history is elided with nature.

For our consideration of folklore reception in the GDR, this shift is a vital one. In the face of a 'disenchanted world' (Weber), one that increasingly came to understand itself in terms of progress, science, the rational organization of everyday life, and so on, the discovery of folklore came to mean a restoration of something lost and a leap outside the coordinates of politics and modernity. For Marxists in particular, the emphasis upon *Volksgeist* would thus be seen as a rebellion against the very forces of material production and modernization that were for them the sine qua non of human existence.

The Grimms' naturalization of history into Teutonic myth, their positing of a 'lost poetic paradise' prior to the fall into contemporary reality, introduced paradigms of a newly mythologized history that saw the redemption of the German *Volk* through a return to a 'Nordic' past. Thus, the concept of the *Volk*, heretofore primarily a category of linguistic/

literary tradition or bourgeois emancipation, was transformed into a requisite of *national* rebirth and the means for reversing the failed telos of a 'Europeanized' history. For the Grimms, the 'Nordic' becomes 'the Mythos, the energizing principle, promising national integrity and historical rejuvenation in one.'[15] It also provided one more revision of German history around a binary opposition that pitted some form of primitivism against modernity. Christianity, the Enlightenment, industrialization, *Zivilisation* (as opposed to *Kultur*), *Gesellschaft* [society] (as opposed to *Gemeinschaft* [community][16]), liberal parliamentarianism – all were forms of modernization that were seen to have alienated the Germans from their Teutonic-Nordic collective selves.

Thus, although the Grimms themselves did not share many of the more militantly chauvinist and racist views of their contemporaries, and although the eventual fascist notion of a 'fighting *Volk* community' united behind the Führer had little to do with the idyllic rural *Volk* community represented by the world of the fairy tales,[17] the general philosophical orientation of their research fit very much into the political climate George Mosse has so aptly characterized as the 'crisis of German ideology.'[18]

The linking of folklore research and folklore tradition to *volkisch* ideology and the philosophical tenets of German Romanticism had a profound effect upon the initial reception and coding of the folklore tradition in the GDR. Central to the premises of the *Kulturpolitik* as it was developed by the KPD in exile and constituted by the SED in the early postwar years was the valorization of German Classicism and the philosophical principles of the Enlightenment as the appropriate heritage for any new German socialist culture.[19] It is no secret that the key thinker to develop the link between German Classicism and theories of bourgeois and socialist realism was the Hungarian Marxist Georg Lukács. And not surprisingly, it was his disparaging views of both Romanticism and philosophical 'irrationalism' that were to prevail in the GDR well into the 1960s; that is, well beyond the period of his fall from favor and subsequent official repudiation as a revisionist because of his role in the Hungarian uprising in 1956.

Whereas Lukács's writings, starting in the early 1930s, established the tradition of Goethe and Schiller as the cultural and philosophical centerpiece for an antifascist aesthetics, it was his critiques of the irrationalist tradition (Romanticism, Schelling, Schopenhauer, Nietzsche, Expressionism, etc.), culminating in his magnum opus *The Destruction of Reason*, that lent massive philosophical underpinning to what became the prevailing binary opposition of GDR official (and unofficial) thinking about the history of German philosophy for the preceding 150 years. Indeed, the compelling lucidity of his argumentation was only enhanced by his equally simplistic reduction of the history of German thought into two qualitatively distinct diachronic traditions.

On the one side of Lukács's scheme was the tradition of irrationalism, which through its abandonment of the subject-object dialectic, privileging of subjective experience, and apologetic defense of the most reactionary political and social movements at the beginning of the nineteenth century set in motion the process of a 'destruction of reason.' For Lukács, this tradition begins with Schelling and Schopenhauer and leads via such thinkers and traditions as Nietzsche, Kierkegaard, Wilhelm Dilthey, Max Weber, *Lebensphilosophie* (philosophy of life: Simmel, Spengler), and social Darwinism inexorably to the apotheosis of irrationalism in the Third Reich. Needless to say, it includes all forms of *volkisch* and racist thought as only the more overtly manifest variations of a deeper trend.

Opposed to this were the beleaguered forces of rationalism, [*Vernunft*], starting with Kant and Hegel within German idealism and continuing under the aegis of the working-class movement developed in the dialectical materialism of Marx, Engels, Lenin, and Franz Mehring. Without elaborating on the sometimes brilliant internal exegesis of the various positions, three critical points should be made about the historical impact of these concepts upon the evolution of *Kulturpolitik* as well as the reception of folklore traditions in the GDR.

First, Lukács's ideas became an absolutely invaluable palliative for a whole generation of German leftist intellectuals (East and West) who were in search of an explanation of fascism that would go beyond the economistic theories of Dimitroff (fascism as the highest stage of capitalism) and deal with the specificity of the German experience as a total socioeconomic and cultural phenomenon. His political bifurcation of cultural thought into Enlightenment and anti-Enlightenment traditions offered not only a convenient coding of German history but, more significantly, an even more appropriate means by which to legitimate the political status quo as a necessary alternative to the failed past.

Given the above development, it should not be surprising that the division of culture into rational and irrational traditions also had a direct impact upon the coding of fairy tales and folklore in the GDR. As we shall see below, the effort to purge folklore of its irrationalist past and imbue it with the great classical-progressive heritage was a clear recognition of the importance of folk traditions for both educational and cultural-political purposes.

But there is a third point to be made concerning the binary opposition of GDR cultural policy as it emerged in the 1950s. The hypostatization of the Enlightenment (and with it Marxism) as the absolute arbiter of reason and rationality in history precluded, of course, from the outset any consideration of the extent to which the Marxian notions of progress based on the development of the forces of production and modernization had themselves attained the status of myth: in the service of a repressive political power; justifying in the name of reason and progress the destruction of the environment, the political legislation of everyday life, or the curtailing of fantasy. To anticipate a later argument in this chapter, certainly one of the reasons that some members of the avant-garde in East Germany looked to folklore traditions and paradigms of myth as a means to critique the status quo has much to do with the ideologically repressive function concepts such as industrial progress and Marxist enlightenment came to play in the interests of a ruling elite.

Given the historical and ideological coding of folklore, it is easy to understand why the rehabilitation of the Grimms in the 1950s entailed, in the words of the GDR biographer Leo Stern, recapturing an image that had been 'aesthetically sublimated for generations' in order to show a 'clear political engagement for the cause of the people, for the cause of freedom, progress, democracy and humanism.'[20] If, on the one hand, Stern's insistently 'objective' depiction of the brothers included a reverse sublimation, obfuscating their more ambivalent positions vis-à-vis the *Volksseele* [soul of the people], it did, on the other hand, conform to the reformulation of policy toward folklore that was occurring in the GDR at that time. Whereas earlier treatments had relegated folklore to the area of irrationalism, the task was now to be a rescue operation for the democratic, humanist, nationalist tradition. As was the case in the Soviet Union and other socialist societies, the study of folklore [*Volkskunde*] in the GDR was now expanded to include ethnography.[21] Whereas folklore traditionally had been confined in Germany to the institution of *Germanistik*, that is, to a focus upon written and spoken language as the basis of cultural tradition, the 1950s saw East German folklorists directing more and more of their research toward the material products of culture (tools, utensils, housing, currency, etc.). This anthropological broadening of the discipline brought with it a redefinition of terms and methodological reorientation that had political implications for the recasting of *Volk* and folklore within the society at large.

First, the emphasis upon material products instead of language shifted the focus of studying folklore away from a fixation upon questions of national and spiritual identity and at the same time brought the concept of labor as a heuristic category into the foreground of folklore research. The work of Wolfgang Jacobeit and Reinhardt Pietsch at the Humboldt University in Berlin on European agrarian ethnography (Jacobeit) and the fishing communities of Rügen (Pietsch) opened up areas of concentration that had an impact upon the study of folklore in West Germany as well.[22] It also resulted in significant rewriting of folklore research history around what Jacobeit called a 'two-track development.'[23] The one 'reactionary' path, according to Jacobeit, concerned itself with *Volksseele* and *Volksgeistigkeit* [spirituality of the people] and was 'in no small way' responsible for the misuse of folklore studies in the Third Reich. Opposed to this was a distinctly identifiable Enlightenment tradition that was grounded in an 'all-encompassing view, one that included work and economy and that aimed at an underlying image of a historical 'Vox populi' based on language, regional history, and folklore as an interdisciplinary totality.'[24]

While the new emphasis in folklore research resulted in a healthy introduction of anthropological and sociological categories into a study historically contaminated with racist and nationalist mysticism, the emphasis upon a sociological approach and folklore as a part of the Enlightenment tradition opened the way for subsuming folklore into the more general category of working-class history. This conjoining of folk history and working-class history tended to occlude distinctions between industrial and preindustrial modes of cultural life and in so doing to play down the extent to which the 'fantastic' folklore discourse stood very much at odds with processes of modernization and the rational precepts of the Enlightenment. Whereas the interest in folklore has traditionally been motivated by a 'homesickness for a lost paradise of the world primeval, for the simple life,'[25] and in that regard has often entailed a critique if not repudiation of contemporary civilization, the dialectical materialist approach now simply elided folklore tradition with the long history of 'working-class struggles' that had begun against feudalism and that led to the founding of the GDR itself. Wolfgang Steinitz's extensive research in the 1950s on working-class folk songs and the inclusion of 'proletarian everyday life' in folklore research in the 1960s are two examples of this broader shift in orientation. Hand in hand with Steinitz's reorientation was the creation, at a more general cultural-political level, of the German folk song movement.

FROM SOCIALIST *VOLKSLIED* TO SOCIALIST ROCK

The political implications of bifurcating folklore into good and bad traditions and subsuming its Enlightenment side into Marxist-Leninist historiography can only be fully understood when viewed within the larger framework of East-West relations in the 1950s. The changes in cultural policy were directly connected to the cold war crisis evolving between the two German states. The cultural, political, economic, and finally military integration of the eastern and western zones into the two alliance systems, together with the insistent and not unconvincing claim by West Germany to be the only legitimate representative of all German interests, increasingly came to threaten a GDR policy that held to the pretense of an antifascist, democratic united front as the basis for eventual unification, or at least neutralization, in Central Europe.

Of particular difficulty for the SED at this time was the enormously seductive impact of Western mass media and avant-garde art movements upon the cultural life of East Germany. In the now famous document of the Central Committee of March 1951 entitled 'The Struggle against Formalism in Art and Literature,'[26] outlines of cultural contestation were spelled out that were to dominate and structure the terms of political discourse until the end of the decade. Emanating from the West, it was argued, were the destructive influences of 'decadence' and 'kitsch,' which

177

'brutalized the tastes of the broad masses of people' and 'fulfilled a concrete function in the interest of antihumanist imperialism and its politics of war-mongering.'[27]

The rhetorical vehemence of the Formalism document is not simply the expression of cold war stalemate or the anti-imperialist posturing of a country on the frontier of the Soviet bloc. It is that surely, but it is also more. It bespeaks graphically the extreme frustration, indeed helplessness, of a fledgling regime forced to derive its political and cultural legitimation in proximity to the most burgeoning capitalist economy in postwar Europe, one that claimed to be the only representative of Germany as a whole. Let it be remembered that the main terrain of struggle between East and West Germany as the selected showcases for the two world systems took place for the most part within the then open city of Berlin; and that, official de-Nazification programs on both sides notwithstanding, economic recovery and modernization were viewed by much of the German populace in the East and the West as the *only* real path to an overcoming of the fascist past. Given that political reality, it should come as a paradox but as no surprise that the main strategy of a Marxist government founded upon an ideology of progress would be a critique of cultural modernity in both its avant-garde and mass cultural forms; and that the alternative offered by the GDR to Western culture would be some version of a rejuvenated 'national culture.' In fact, it had no other choice.

The regime felt particularly vulnerable in the area of popular music. While serious music from the West with formalist or modernist tendencies was said to give voice to a 'life-detesting nihilism,' it was above all through mass cultural forms such as 'boogie-woogie' and 'hit-tune kitsch' that the Americans were said to 'poison the minds of the working people and prepare indirectly for war.'[28] An initial effort to counter these incursions in the GDR came through the founding of the 'new German folksong movement,' led by the poet and cultural minister Johannes R. Becher and the composer Hanns Eisler, both of whom had collaborated to write the national anthem. 'These folksongs,' intoned Walter Ulbricht in a speech inaugurating the first Five-Year Plan (1950) in the GDR, 'are an expression of what is beautiful and new in our society. They inspire our youth and working people to new and greater heights of achievement.'[29]

Hanns Eisler himself, who in the 1930s had collaborated with Bertolt

Brecht to produce some of the now classical revolutionary songs during the political struggles of the Weimar Republic, was less sanguine than Ulbricht but still hopeful about creating a latter-day socialist folk tradition that could resist or even survive within the incursions of Western culture. In his 'Brief an West Deutschland' (Letter to West Germany), published in the GDR journal *Sinn und Form* in December 1951, Eisler addresses what appear to be queries of Western musicians who seem perplexed that the former student of the modernist composer Schönberg would allow himself to be compromised: 'You write,' begins Eisler, ' "we scarcely know here what to make of your discussion on music. Explain to us (composers, musicologists and music lovers) just this once exactly what the starting point for your thinking is." I will try, but forgive me if I begin by going back somewhat in history.'[30] Eisler's answer, as Hans Mayer has argued, is itself a 'historical text that cannot be read verbatim,'[31] for its 'cunning' attempt to negotiate a compromise between the realms of avant-garde and popular culture offers, finally, a glaring illustration of the impossibility of creating synthetic forms of contemporary folk culture out of the rubble of tradition and in the face of the Western culture industry.

The first half of Eisler's essay, drawing on his and Adorno's *Composing for the Films* as well as Adorno and Horkheimer's *Dialectic of the Enlightenment*, analyzes well the crisis of music in advanced industrial societies. Too well. The commodification of all art forms by monopolized industries, Eisler argues, has led to a split within the area of musical production between 'serious' and 'light.' Where the former speaks only to elitist audiences with the privilege of a musical education, the latter is consumed unthinkingly by an audience of musical illiterates, systematically socialized into appreciating nothing better. Eisler's closed system will scarcely tolerate the abrupt, somewhat optimistic solution he offers at the end of his essay, even if it is to result from a socialist planned economy:

> You misunderstand our striving for popular culture [*Volkstümlichkeit*] as naiveté, emotional outpouring or as certain customs and mores which no longer correspond to our times. However, once we become aware that the most advanced segment of the people – its heart – is the working populace, popular culture means something qualitatively different. For workers are not naive; they learn quickly, have their own customs and mores, which though differing in their

international peculiarities, are international in content. They crave innovation, for they know how important it is to change things, restructure them, and to use many kinds of methods . . . These people need a new popular culture.[32]

Eisler's feeble resolution to the crisis of contemporary culture is not simply the hollow posturing of an official representative of GDR culture writing in an official journal of cultural policy. It also genuinely represents the long-held, sublimated dream of the historical, leftist avant-garde that the realization of socialism must lead to the *Aufhebung* of the divisions within bourgeois culture (the separation of art and life, high and low art, avant-garde and traditional culture, avant-garde and mass culture, etc.), out of which would emerge, phoenixlike, a new and genuine *Volkstümlichkeit*. For Eisler as well as Bertolt Brecht in 1951, the ingredients were there in the GDR: despite the rubble, despite the remnants of fascism, despite the hardening of political positions and the growing Stalinization of the cultural policy – and despite the impact of Western culture.

What were these ingredients? First and foremost, in conformity with the notion of a distinctly separate and politically enlightened strand of folk tradition, both believed that the proletariat offered the basis for a 'qualitatively different' creation of culture, that the working class was almost ontologically receptive to new artistic forms. In an essay entitled 'Volkstümlichkeit und Realismus' (Popularity and realism), written in 1938 as a response to Georg Lukács's more orthodox views concerning avant-garde art and published posthumously in *Sinn und Form* in 1958, Brecht argued that the masses are willing and able to understand the boldest, most original, and most complex means of expression as long as the work gives voice to their interests. His essay criticizes forcefully those who would create a folk art by lowering aesthetic standards and concludes: 'If we wish to have a living and combative literature, which is fully engaged with reality and fully grasps reality, a truly popular literature, we must keep step with the rapid development of reality. The great working masses are already on the move. The industry and brutality of their enemies is proof of it.'[33]

Although Brecht and Eisler reveal a decidedly idealized notion of the working class, such ideas were not in conformity with the historically evolved official position on working-class culture (Lenin felt that the proletariat could create no culture of its own prior to the overthrow of capitalism). On the contrary, in many ways they paralleled and were influenced by the controversial views developed within the earlier Soviet avant-garde and Proletkult movements. Like certain artists and theorists of the 1920s such as Arvatov, Tretyakov, and Mayakovsky, Brecht and Eisler put primary emphasis upon technological innovation and the development of the means of production as the creative source for any new socialist folk culture.[34] For artists these offered new media and materials for both artistic experimentation and mass distribution, which, at one and the same time, would revolutionize and democratize, renew and simplify the production of art in advanced societies. The ideal audience for such a new art would have to be the proletariat, socialized through its proximity to production into an appreciation, in Eisler's words, a 'craving,' for innovation. 'New popular culture,' Eisler wrote in conclusion to his letter, 'is the conversion of the new into the simple. Without becoming vulgar, it will establish community with a language that the inexperienced will understand.'[35]

History has shown that Brecht and Eisler were wrong on all counts. Their own efforts to write *Volkslieder* were a momentous failure, both aesthetically and as works that sought to achieve 'popular' appeal. Brecht himself had been adamant in his criticism of the anachronistic romantic longings for modern folk songs encouraged by the official cultural policy. In 1952 he remarked: 'While the folk song says something complicated in a simple way, the modern imitators say something simplistic in a simple way. Besides, the populace does not wish to be popular [Außerdem wünscht das Volk nicht tümlich zu sein].'[36] Yet in his own efforts to write children's folk songs [*Kinderlieder*], it is clear that Brecht himself never came close to the poetic power and richness of his and Eisler's songs written at the beginning of the 1930s and that he even looked at the whole undertaking as a kind of occasional writing. In a note from Brecht's *Arbeitsjournal*, we find the following cryptic remark: 'am finishing off by the bushel children's songs for Eisler. Handicraft work.'[37]

The cycle of Brecht's *Kinderlieder* opens with a poem entitled 'The Story of Mother Courage,' a three-stanza rendering of the play *Mother Courage and Her Children*, which Brecht had written in 1939 and which had been staged as the inaugural production of his newly founded Berliner Ensemble in 1949. The play tells with Brechtian estrangement and double entendre of the heroic/nonheroic struggle of the mother who sells herself to the system of barter to save her children – and, learning nothing, loses all three. What in the dramatic version stands as both tragedy and an ironic *Aufhebung* of tragedy with the help of an audience that must learn what the play cannot 'teach' – a brilliant regrounding of the seventeenth-century folktale as Marxist antiparable – becomes in the children's folk song version a somewhat weighty lesson about the wrongs of war. The 'once upon a time' beginning of stanza 1 about the trader woman who goes to war moves quickly to the unconcealed, unilinear truth of the lesson:

> Sie hatte keine Furcht vorm Kriege
> Wollt machen ihren Schnitt
> Und nahm, daß sie auch was kriegten
> Ihre drei Kinder mit.[38]

The sloppiness of the *Kriege/kriegten* rhyme is indicative of a larger kind of intellectual indolence and heavy-handedness pervading all these verses. Brecht has lost the sense of ambivalence, of play and naïveté so central to his dialectics of history, that links him, as few other modern writers, to the seventeenth century and the folk tradition.

In the long run, then, Brecht's and Eisler's folk songs of this period suffered the same fate as the entire folk song movement: as historical relics they remain interesting documents of an unsuccessful and ultimately apologetic attempt to generate from above a meaningful alternative to the Western culture industry. The route taken from this point on was to be in the opposite direction. Any viable forms of *Volkskultur* would be patterned after Western mass culture. From now on, jazz, pop, rock, and disco music would be the 'folk' material out of which would be forged socialist variants of the Western scene.

THE WISDOM OF THE FAIRY TALE

The failure of both the traditionalists and the avant-garde to create a folk art in the 1950s as a 'popular' socialist alternative to the growing influence of Western mass culture did not mean a disappearance of folklore and the folk tradition from the cultural scene of the GDR. Certainly one of the most vital aspects of the GDR publishing world continued to be the area of children's literature, and not a small number of major authors wrote novels, tales, and poetry for children drawing in part or whole from folk traditions. In some cases, the resultant works transcended the somewhat 'safe' ghetto of children's literature to speak to people of all age groups. There were also instances where such works came to serve as a vehicle for challenging and criticizing the status quo.

This *Umfunktionierung* [reutilization] of folklore for purposes of political critique or the expression of forbidden fantasy in modern society was not new to the socialist tradition. In the 1920s, for instance, a large number of Expressionist and Dadaist writers, several of them on the Left or affiliated with the Communist Party, turned to the fairy tale genre as a means of artistic experimentation or social protest. Hugo Ball, Béla Balázs, Edwin Hoernle, Carl Maria Graf, and Ernst Bloch are just a few of the Left avant-garde of the Weimar period who saw in the writing and reception of fairy tales an oppositional form of culture.[39]

It is significant that virtually none of this leftist fairy tale heritage was republished in the GDR but that nevertheless certain GDR writers felt compelled to draw on the tradition of fairy tales and folklore to offer alternative fantasies or voice critical ideas. There is, of course, a connection between these two things. Marxists such as Bloch, Balázs, Benjamin, Hoernle, and even Brecht have represented a tradition within Marxism and Marxist aesthetics that has at various historical times been forced into an uncomfortable, occasionally even subversive relationship to official Marxist-Leninism. Their adherence to fantasy and consciousness as material, generative forces within the historical process; their questioning of historical materialism with its stress upon material progress as the sole motor of history; their emphasis upon artistic experimentation for the creation of socialist culture; finally, their repudiation of both the Enlightenment and the German Classical heritages as the only philosophical and aesthetic source for a progressive cultural policy have made them controversial figures within the pantheon of socialist thinkers. That such 'uncomfortable' theorists and artists have turned to the fairy tale as an important source for their ideas is not accidental. Beyond their general interest or creative need, it has to do with a rebellion against the strictures of the aforementioned binary opposition that has prevailed in Marxist thinking since the end of the nineteenth century. It should thus not be surprising that critical and potentially critical thinkers in the GDR have looked in this direction as well.

One of the first GDR writers to appropriate fairy tales in his artistic work was the poet Franz Fühmann. Born in 1921, Fühmann found his way to the GDR via service as a soldier in the Nazi Wehrmacht and subsequent rehabilitation as a prisoner of war in the Soviet Union after his capture at Stalingrad in 1944. Fühmann's earliest writings, the most important of which was a long epic poem entitled 'Die Fahrt nach Stalingrad' (The journey to Stalingrad), tell enthusiastically of his transformation from Nazi to communist. Stalingrad, that city Fühmann came to view as a barometer for his entire life, not only taught him the horror of war and the joy of redemption but also gave him a sense of what John Flores has described as the 'ultimate rationality of imaginative fantasy.'[40]

> City Stalingrad, may I see you again
> you city, which saved for me my fatherland
> and which let me love, and whispered verses to me
> and which taught me to understand fairy tales
> and all dreams which pass down through the woods
> into the blue future and Germany's happiness.[41]

Although deeply influenced initially by the writings of Georg Lukács, it was the fairy tale in particular and the tradition of Romanticism that provided Fühmann the greatest resources for his creative energy. To be sure, his first fairy tale poems mark some of the worst examples of empty socialist-realist platitude to be published in those days, telling, for instance, of giants who, having slain all the dragons, remain nevertheless vigilant, never at peace: 'They wander ever forth into azure days / into the dawn without dusk.'[42]

But in the poems entitled 'Die Weisheit der Märchen' (The wisdom of the fairy tale) and 'Die Richtung der Märchen' (The direction of the fairy tale), both of which appeared in the late 1950s, Fühmann indicates a shift in his use of the fairy tale that signals an importantly different attitude about the potential of aesthetics as a medium of social expression. His fairy tale poems no longer serve as allegories for great socialist truths (heroes slaying dragons symbolic of the defeat of fascism). What he has discovered, rather, is the semiotics of the genre itself as a philosophical metaphor for a mode of dialectical thinking and living:

I bow deeply before the wisdom of the people
to which we give thanks
that in the fairy tale
things go dialectically.[43]

While Fühmann was to continue to change and develop, becoming one of
the most important and critically respected writers in the GDR, no single
stanza or statement better sums up what was to become the guiding principle of his thought. The dialectics of folklore, for Fühmann, was as much
the uneven, cunning, and unpredictable rendering of objective reality as it
was a way of grasping metaphorically the importance of fantasy. As the
basis of his aesthetics, the adherence to Romantic and folk traditions set
him increasingly at odds with the official cultural policy. It is also not
surprising that his views about fairy tales and aesthetics have linked him
often, in the eyes of critics, to the Marxist renegade Ernst Bloch.

As has often been noted, the fairy tale is an absolutely vital part of
Bloch's Marxism, appearing, for example, as one of the key philosophical
components of utopian thinking in the final section of Bloch's magnum
opus *Das Prinzip Hoffnung* (The principle of hope).[44] Like Fühmann's
later fairy tale poems, Bloch sees in the 'wisdom' of fairy tales a prophetic
and dialectical thinking that transcends the more analytical dimensions
of economistic Marxism: 'Marxism in all its analyses the coldest detective
nonetheless takes the fairy tale seriously, the dream of a Golden Age practically.'[45] The wisdom of the fairy tale is revolutionary because it is directed beyond the obstacles that it sets up. 'Fantastic as the fairy tale is,'
Bloch says, 'in the overcoming of difficulties it is forever wise; courage and
cunning meet with success in an entirely different way than in life.'[46]

It is clear that Fühmann's look to the fairy tale and his own reliance
upon Romanticism and Romantic writers emerge from shifting political
predilections similar to those of Ernst Bloch. Both find in the counterlogic
of the fairy tale the unlocking of creative energies and utopian strivings
that are sensed to be sorely lacking in the Enlightenment versions of traditional Marxism or in the established aesthetics of a cultural policy
grounded exclusively in classicism. Both are driven thereby – Bloch quite
consciously as a theoretical strategy, Fühmann less intentionally through
his exploration of the dialectical power of fantasy – into challenging the
paradigms of the discourse in which they operate.

This becomes even clearer in Fühmann's prose writings of the ensuing years. In the novella *Strelch* (1960), for instance, the narrator is on a one-day excursion to a small island when he observes the almost diabolical fairy-tale-like fantasies of a group of schoolchildren. Some of the children act out the fairy tales, others tell them to each other. Of particular concern to the narrator are the constant attempts of the teachers to terminate such behavior and bring the children into line:

> Why are there people in our society who have such a hostile attitude toward any kind of poetry? I wondered. Was it a kind of envy for a gift that they themselves did not possess? The feeling of being excluded? The uncertainty or even fear about a world which they could not measure? Or was it a poverty and narrowness of the soul, which heaps hate upon anything which does not reflect one's own image? Or the sad heritage of the past or a terribly misunderstood philosophy or all this taken together?[47]

The narrator's simple query in *Strelch* names with clarity and prosaic understatement a number of causes that have led to the negative valorization of myth, folklore, and fantasy in the GDR: fears concerning the legacies of fascism as well as adherence to the strictures of an overly rationalist Marxist-Leninism and the demands of the scientific-technical revolution. All have helped to create an atmosphere of fear and oppression that must crush as threatening to the 'rational' order all that is unpredictable and not conventionally creative. It is for that reason that Fühmann looked to fairy tales as a source of rejuvenation, not only for artists but for all those who strive to experience 'what people can be if the sacred labor of everyday life were to be united with the sacred fantasy of leisure time.'[48] This is Fühmann's utopia.

Franz Fühmann, of course, was not the only member of the literary avant-garde to reappropriate folk tradition and in particular the fairy tale for purposes of dialectical inversion. Beginning in the 1960s, an increasing number of leading authors in the GDR turned to the fairy tale to express themes that went beyond the historical thematics and even formal codes of the genre.[49] As noted earlier, the initial rehabilitation of the fairy tale had been geared primarily toward children as a means of the 'education and formation of socialist personalities.' While such pedagogical focus was to continue into the present, the fairy tale was now seen also as an 'adult' genre for purposes of satire, parable, and the grotesque.[50]

The reasons for renewed interest in the fairy tale were both genre-related and historical. As a short prose form, its variegated narrative and coding systems provided freedoms for literary experiments that easily transcended the more narrow confines of the officially constituted realistic genres, such as the novel. In the fairy tale, the comic and the tragic, the grotesque, the absurd, and the realistic could be easily combined as a legitimate realization of the form itself. In their reutilization of the folk tale, one notes, moreover, an interesting parallel between GDR authors and those Romantic poets of the nineteenth century who also refashioned the traditional *Volksmärchen* into what have come to be called *Kunstmärchen*. As was the case with such writers as Ludwig Tieck, Clemens Brentano, and E. T. A. Hoffmann, we note in the GDR fairy tale a stylized reappropriation of traditional motifs, topoi, and stereotypical characters, one in which more personal, less collective modes of narration were employed to express individual fantasies and criticize social conditions.

Yet beyond the question of genre, there are more immediate historical reasons for the emergence of the fantastic fairy tale during the waning years of the Ulbricht era (late 1960s). The sudden spate of books, essays, articles, and treatises arguing for the importance of the fantastic and fantasy as significant dimensions of literary production[51] were clearly part of a more general thematic shift toward subjectivity, the idiosyncratic, the problems of private life, and the individual that was occurring in greater frequency throughout the literary landscape of the time.[52] Certainly an important dimension of this shift for the entire structure of cultural policy was the reevaluation of the Romantic heritage by GDR authors and literary theorists alike in the 1970s.[53] Once linked to the most reactionary historical tendencies, nineteenth-century writers such as Kleist and Hölderlin, E. T. A. Hoffmann and Jean Paul, Gunderode and Bettina von Arnim suddenly were looked to not merely as literary models to be emulated but as articulating experiences that spoke directly to the contemporary society. As Peter Hohendahl has emphasized, for Christa Wolf the Romantic consciousness 'anticipates' the situation in the GDR: 'its suffering under instrumental rationality, its suffering in an economic system in which success is bought at the cost of eliminating the particular.'[54] Hohendahl's use of such terms as 'instrumental rationality' and the 'particular' link (in a way Christa Wolf would not consciously have done) the re-evaluation of fantasy and Romanticism occurring within the realm of literature to a critical position close to the one developed by Horkheimer and Adorno in their *Dialectic of the Enlightenment.* The problems being addressed by the 'Romantic consciousness' (alienation, subjectivity, so the argument goes) derive in response to processes of modernization that lie at the very heart of *all* advanced industrial societies, whether socialist or capitalist. Once the unquestioned cornerstone of all that is progressive and humane, the Enlightenment itself and with it the scientific-techno-logical revolution, the demiurge of Marxist historiography, are now seen to be complicit as forms of social oppression.

While the writers of fiction were among the first to address the issues of instrumental rationality and subjectivity under socialism, such discus-sions were not unique to the realm of literature. The fact that sociologists and cultural historians in the GDR were raising fundamental questions about the adequacy of dialectical materialism – in particular its class para-digms – for grasping the more differentiated needs and groupings of con-temporary society clearly signaled that the role of the individual under socialism was being rethought in all realms of the social order.[55] The limits of the scientific-technical revolution, the more insistent emergence of what was once defined and made structurally harmless as the women's question, indeed, the problem of self-initiative and self-creativity vis-à-vis continued bureaucratic stagnation, production inefficiency, and curtail-ment of individual freedoms moved now into the foreground even of of-ficial deliberation. Thus the rediscovery of the fairy tale, viewed in the larger context, emerged in tandem with a reconceptualization of the whole nature of subjectivity in a society that could no longer derive its identity within the framework of prevailing epistemologies.

As an expression of 'subjectivity,' the contemporary fairy tales them-selves ranged from direct social criticism of life in the GDR to the simple expression of the absurdly fantastic, which, precisely because it had no reliably decipherable metaphorical 'meaning,' deviates radically from the norms of 'realistic' discourse. An anthology of fairy tales by leading GDR writers[56] includes a story by Irmtraud Morgner entitled 'Die Sendung' (The shipment) in which an East Berlin zoo receives a box from an unknown 'Asian' land with a king in it instead of the expected exotic animal. The ensuing bureaucratic disarray lays bare administrative, ideological, and even moral absurdities of life under 'democratic centralism.' The zoo director suspects 'provocation,' the animal keeper counters with the argument that the failure to execute or incarcerate a king should not cast doubt on 'the revolutionary intentions of the senders,' since it could mean 'a complicated domestic political situation.' The refusal of the king to eat when served standing forces the keeper to provide him (kneeling) with food from the Exquisit stores on East Berlin's Park Avenue, Unter den Linden (for the socialist aristocracy). The momentous decision to remove the king from initial 'quarantine' and display him with the 'other' animals comes from the realization 'of a certain pedagogical value' to be gained, and so on.

The function of this Surrealistic parable is not crudely allegorical but estranging. No particular persons or institutions are being mirrored or satirized per se, yet in the tradition of Brecht and even Kafka, the absurdly complicated behavioral and thought processes unleashed by the improbable event make strange – and thereby comically 'familiar' – the social contradictions, political inequities, and, above all, labyrinthine linguistic rationalizations that are the reality of everyday life under socialism. Is the older monarchical order that far removed from the new one? The end of the story underscores some doubt: on Sundays the king is allowed to dress up in a trench coat and leather shoes and take walks in the park. 'The clothing makes him unnoticeable in the crowd; without his collar and chain no one would even recognize him as a king.'[57]

The above tale by Morgner was extracted from her novel *Leben und Abenteuer der Troubadora Beatrix nach Zeugnissen ihrer Spielfrau Laura* (Life and adventures of Troubadora Beatriz as chronicled by her minstrel Laura), which tells the fantastic legend of Beatriz de Dia, a medieval troubadour who enters the GDR in the late 1960s after having awakened in France from an 810-year sleep. The 'fantastic' in this case is constituted most pronouncedly by Beatriz's provocative forms of female bonding, which threaten the patriarchal socialist order simply as an assertion of a world without male dependency. As Biddy Martin has argued, 'Beatriz brings the fantastic, the extravagant, the impossible and the erotic to bear on the apparently "natural" order, its discursive underpinnings and its literary representations.'[58]

While Morgner is one of the few writers, male or female, to locate sexual oppression and patriarchy at the level of psychosexual relations, she is not the only one to employ the 'extravagant and impossible' world of the fairy tale to thematize the dilemma of women in a society that has officially (economically) solved the problem. The question as to why the women's issue would be rethematized in a genre historically geared to 'glorify passivity, dependency, and self-sacrifice as a heroine's cardinal virtues'[59] points us back precisely to the confrontation between potentially incompatible discourses, in this case the discourse of fairy tales and that of official Marxism-Leninism, that defined our initial deliberations. Let us then pursue an answer to this question as a means of summarizing some of the main concerns we have voiced in this chapter.

In her fairy tale 'Lauf weg – kehr um' (Run away – come back), Monika Helmecke tells of a hard-working housewife named Elizabeth who, when offered by a magic fairy the fulfillment of any wish, requests two separate lives to be lived simultaneously: in the one, continued existence as wife and mother; in the other, the freedom to pursue at will, alone and unencumbered, her secret desire to compose an opera for children. After a schizophrenic year of 'running away and coming back,' the two worlds have become so separated that she is unable to recall the laughter of children needed for her composition and decides joyfully to return to her original life. A happy ending? One wonders. The resolution of Helmecke's dystopic fantasy, while tearfully affirming the family idyll as the seat of nonalienation, is at the same time an unwitting indictment of the liberated model upon which GDR socialism rests. The personal and the professional can coexist, Helmecke suggests, but for the beleaguered GDR woman who must perform both at the same time only at a loss of self-fulfillment and creativity.

The increasing employment of the fantastic, and in particular the fairy tale, to explore myths of gender difference, sexual preference, and role playing under socialism indicates the extent to which women writers in the GDR, like their socialist predecessors in the Weimar Republic, were able to reappropriate the genre for purposes of self-articulation.[60] In so doing, emphases emerged that tell us much about the dialectic of dominant and counterdiscourses in this society.

On one level, the fairy tale functioned allegorically to comment upon social inequities of role definition. Whereas women in the GDR were officially granted unprecedented social and economic equality, fairy tales explored ways that traditional expectations furthered patriarchal behavioral patterns within the areas of private and family life. Fantasies of female bonding or of liberation from the strains of motherhood and monogamy clearly reflect back upon ways that the microstructural bases of power and oppression were held intact through traditional sexual and gender arrangements.

But beyond their critique of social institutions, the feminist fairy tale as a discourse served to challenge deeper-lying values inherent to the very epistemological value system of Marxist-Leninist philosophy. The freedom of fantasy and the interpretive free play at the heart of the genre, once coded pejoratively as irrationalist, opened up a realm for subjectivity and self-definition foreign to, if not at odds with, the more pragmatic and instrumental framework of enlightenment Marxism. If the needs of the collective and models of totality and material progress led to the suppression of particularist interest and subjectivity within socialist discourse, then what Bloch has called the 'wisdom' of the fairy tale functioned to disrupt such one-sidedness. Certainly the vitality of the genre in the literary landscape of the 1970s was but one more example of how a radical reappropriation of a once demonized discourse both initiated and reflected changes in political and social values in the GDR.

8. THE DESTRUCTION OR THE PROMOTION OF REASON?: NIETZSCHE IN THE GDR

Although light years apart in ideological orientation, Wolfgang Harich, East Germany's most ardent advocate for a revival of cultural Stalinism, and Allan Bloom, the conservative American *Kulturprophet*, agreed on one thing: it is the Nietzscheanization of the Left (Bloom's term) that poses one of the gravest threats to the basic values of coherent culture and even democracy in the contemporary world. In a 1987 article excoriating the 'revision of the Marxist Nietzsche image,' Harich cataloged the devastating impact that the philosopher has had upon intellectual life in the twentieth century. 'There is absolutely no evidence for the fact that national or world culture is indebted to Nietzsche in any way for contributions of lasting value,' Harich intoned. 'In every respect his influence has been a detrimental [*schädlich*] one.'[1] One of the saddest examples of this for Harich was the writer Thomas Mann, who, like many of the *Bildungsbürger* [educated citizens] of his time with 'amateur interests' in philosophy, 'allowed the Schopenhauer fad, the Nietzsche cult and the sensationalism around Sigmund Freud to keep him from even being aware of Germany's Classical . . . philosophical heritage running from Leibniz to Feuerbach' (1050).

While this chapter is about Nietzsche in the GDR and not in the United States, I bring Bloom into the picture simply to stress a similarity in the way the reception of Nietzsche in two very different cultural and social environments has served to articulate processes of polarization and stigmatization, which in turn have taken on considerable political significance within the two body politics as a whole. Beyond the very different ideological meanings intended (Bloom only indirectly associates Nietzsche with the rise of fascism), in both cases the philosopher is seen to represent a threat to cultural identity. For Bloom, Nietzsche poses a challenge to the sanctity of what he calls 'our country's extreme Enlightenment universalism.'[2] For Harich, who follows Lukács, he represents a threat to the tradition of dialectical reason running from Socrates via Descartes to Leibniz, Feuerbach, Hegel, Marx, and finally Lenin. The qualities of Nietzsche's thought that led him to be viewed as a catalyst for what Harich and Bloom would both agree is a 'destruction of reason' will only be of secondary concern in this discussion. Of primary focus is what Nietzsche had come to signify in the cultural wars of the GDR – and why the topic emerged at the time that it did.

First to the most recent debate. In May 1986 the cultural journal *Sinn und Form* published an article by Heinz Pepperle in which the author spelled out what he very cautiously called a more differentiated version of the Marxist Nietzsche image. Pepperle sought to question some of the basic Marxist 'truths' established over the years by such venerable Party thinkers as Franz Mehring, Hans Günther, Georg Lukács, and, more recently, the GDR Nietzsche ideologue, Heinz Malorny.[3] In abbreviated form, Pepperle's major points were the following: Nietzsche was not, as many Marxists have argued, a protofascist thinker but someone whose political significance has been inflated and abused by the Left and the Right over the years. He hated anti-Semitism, was anti-German to the core, and would, in Thomas Mann's words, have gotten nothing but a 'migraine headache' at the very sight of the brown hordes of the fascist movement. Moreover, as much as Nietzsche and Marx would have parted ways on such questions as socialism, the workers movement, progress in history, reason in history, dialectical thinking, and the primacy of the Enlightenment, there were also astounding parallels between the two concerning their critiques of ideology and, in particular, their respective critiques of religion and bourgeois liberalism.

Clearly Pepperle's article was launched as a trial balloon by pro-Nietzsche supporters in order to test the readiness for the three or so planned Nietzsche editions waiting to be published in the GDR in the early 1980s.[4] Wolfgang Harich's attempt to abort the publication project one year later was just as clearly intended to initiate, finally, a public debate on the Nietzsche question and all that he had come to represent. A number of crucial issues emerged from Harich's extraordinary performance and the just as extraordinary responses to it that are important markers concerning the status of both the 'renegade' philosopher Nietzsche as well as the changing contours of cultural life in the GDR.

NIETZSCHE AND THE PUBLIC SPHERE

The first and most important aspect of the Nietzsche exchange in the late 1980s had to do quite simply with freedom of speech in the GDR. It was not just Harich's excessively authoritarian tone that conjured up memories of the not-so-distant horrors of a totally repressive *Kulturpolitik*. He even had the audacity to call for an *increase* in censorship, for instance, by suggesting that the official GDR edition of Thomas Mann's works was unconstitutional [*verfassungswidrig*] because it included publication of the author's highly polemical, Nietzschean essay of 1916 entitled 'Betrachtungen eines Unpolitischen' (Views of a nonpolitical man). The reason Mann's 'youthful work' (Mann was forty-one when he wrote this) as well as similar 'signs of decay' such as Expressionism, Futurism, Russian 'pseudo-avant-gardism,' and other forms of 'cultural decomposition [*Kulturzersetzung*]' must be banned from public consumption in the GDR is summarized in Harich's strongly-worded recommendation to expunge Nietzscheanism and return to the eighteenth century as a model for cultural health. 'A society cannot sink any lower culturally than by making knowledge of Nietzsche a criterion for general education,' Harich wrote. 'The entire works of Christian Wolff (1679–1754), the Latin ones included, are more relevant than any Nietzschean aphorism. It should be viewed as a basic rule of mental health [*geistige Hygiene*] to consider this man not worthy of even being quoted. There is nothing more destructive to one's orientation in the world of today or tomorrow than to want to learn anything from him' (1036).

It was a credit to the individual respondents, but also a sign of the changing times, that many of the replies to Harich did not even deign to deal with his hyperbolic arguments, focusing instead on the political implications of Harich's statements. Thomas Böhme questioned the elitist principles of a position that divided groups into, on the one hand, the initiated few who 'controlled the cabinets of poison [*Giftschränke*] within archives and libraries and decided what others should and should not read' and, on the other, 'a general population who was expected to consume what was predigested and already defused.'[5] Stefan Richter raised a politically more provocative question concerning the importance of critical dialogue for public life under socialism: 'Can a society that is in need of an interested public sphere, one based on the ability to make sovereign judgments and form one's own critical opinions, in all seriousness even consider such a model of discourse?'[6]

The writer Stephan Hermlin proved most outspoken in this regard, choosing the meeting of the writers union in November 1987 to vilify a notion of *Kulturpolitik* based on 'prohibitions' and 'destruction' and concluding with an unprecedented public assessment of the devastating impact of Stalinist cultural practices: 'What is going on here [in Harich's attack] and affecting us all is a reactionary turn back in the direction of obsolete political positions, positions that for untold hundreds of progressive artists in many lands have brought about total destruction of their work and even led to their death, and that have also resulted in the disgraceful situation that socialist societies are being compared to fascism.'[7] Hermlin's very powerful acknowledgments represented for that time a new level of 'coming to terms with the past' in the GDR as it affected human rights under socialism.

Of course, it might be argued that what was really being performed in the Nietzsche exchange was the enactment of a debate that should have taken place twenty or thirty years before: Harich, as the Stalinist mastodon in the closet, was trotted out to propagate and defend political views that were clearly out of touch with the contemporary situation and, because of the absurdity and extremity of their position, served to legitimate the newly enlightened status quo. But that, I would argue, is itself a reductionist, monolinear view of political processes that presupposes an absolute top-down Party control, one that in fact no longer existed in the GDR of the 1980s, if it ever had in the first place. In fact, as was patently clear from subsequent publications in the official ideological journal *Deutsche Zeitschrift für Philosophie*[8] and by the Central Institute for Philosophy at the Academy of Sciences, Harich's position was not so out of date as one would like to have believed. Unfortunately, the powers he represented were still very much a part of a political dialogue that was absolutely vital to the transformation of political life within the era of Soviet *glasnost* – again, a coming to terms with the not so distant socialist past as well.

This brings us to our second point: the challenge of the Nietzsche discussion, beyond the question of civil rights and freedom of speech, to the institutional structures of the *Kulturpolitik* itself. Toward the end of his essay, Harich asserted that the present Nietzsche craze throughout the Western world finds its way into the GDR at a particularly vulnerable moment due 'to a certain willingness to approach problematic figures of German history, like Luther, Frederick II, and Bismarck, in a more liberal way than heretofore' (1052). This Nietzsche fad, Harich continues, thus 'joins up with a creeping tendency toward undermining cultural political "basic principles," . . . "basic principles" that should not be seen as being simply Stalinist' (1052).

Harich's linking of the Nietzsche question to a more general erosion of cultural political principles points, if only obliquely, to a long tradition of socialist value formation in which the reception of Friedrich Nietzsche has played a highly significant role. Beginning even prior to the philosopher's death in 1900, the critique of Nietzsche by the establishment socialist Left had sought to create an ideological repository for all that socialism was not meant to represent. This evolving Nietzsche image projected a configuration of pejorative otherness that helped construct characteristics of socialist identity and proper ideological decorum. Let us now look at this prehistory in light of its impact on the GDR debate.

FROM MEHRING TO MALORNY: A HISTORY OF
NIETZSCHE RECEPTION

The most important initial voice in the official reception of Nietzsche within German socialism was that of Social Democratic Party ideologue Franz Mehring. In the early 1890s, he sketched a reading of Nietzsche as 'philosopher of monopoly capitalism'[9] that was to provide a model for the numerous subsequent interpretations by Social Democratic and Communist Party cultural authorities. Mehring's critique traced out Nietzsche's philosophy as both an expression of and a formative contributor to the development of capitalist ideologies of exploitation and aggression. Whereas following the 1848 revolution Schopenhauerian pessimism became the philosophy 'of a moneyed and philistine bourgeoisie that wanted nothing more than peace and quiet,' Nietzsche, in contrast, was to 'place his laurel wreath on exploitation and high finance.'[10] His praise of the *Übermensch*, Mehring argues, his belief in a will to power, and his scorn for the 'herd people' were nothing more than the clarion call of an emerging pannationalist, imperialist class whose espoused philosophy was devoted to ruthlessly advancing exploitation at all costs. Inspired by a 'morality of aristocracy' [*Herrenmoral*] 'beyond good and evil,' such a view of the world had nothing but disdain for the simple values of 'civic responsibility, good will, respect, diligence, moderation, patience, and modesty.'[11]

A number of arguments and emphases emerge in Mehring's original presentation that were to reappear, thinly disguised, in numerous later interpretations of Nietzsche within the socialist camp. The most important, perhaps, is the linking of Nietzsche with history itself, as both harbinger and reflection of an internal spiritual biography of 'the' bourgeoisie. For instance, although in the 1930s Georg Lukács was to repudiate Franz Mehring for his romantic anticapitalism,[12] the Hungarian's characterization of Nietzsche as a major 'forerunner of fascist aesthetics'[13] and of fascist philosophy reproduced salient features of Mehring's original model for a dialectical materialist analysis of German nineteenth-century intellectual history. While Mehring had isolated Schopenhauer, Eduard von Hartmann, and Nietzsche as representatives of an anti-Hegelian evolution of bourgeois thought from 'pessimistic' petty capital to a 'philosophy of monopoly capital,'[14] Lukács extended the mapping backward and forward in time, with Nietzsche again as linchpin. Beginning with the Romantics and Schelling, Lukács argued, German philosophy becomes bifurcated into rationalist and irrationalist strands: on the one hand, the dialectical thinkers, such as Hegel, Lassalle, and Marx, whose wholesome adherence to a subject-object totality articulates notions of progress, science, enlightenment, and rationalism that have been central to the forward-looking ideologies of the upward-striving elements within an enlightened bourgeoisie; opposed to this, a tearing asunder of such a dialectic and the privileging of irrationalist, subjective, antihumanist modes of thinking that have come to characterize late capitalism in its period of cultural decline.[15] Friedrich Nietzsche's glorification of brutality and egotism, Lukács concluded, goes hand in hand with the move of the bourgeois social class to imperialist and finally fascist policies of domination. Thus both Mehring and Lukács link the figure of Nietzsche to narratives of spiritual decay in order to construct an identity of socialist morality as everything that Nietzsche is not.

Although more differentiated official readings of Nietzsche in the GDR sought to rehabilitate Mehring's socioeconomic approach by opposing it to Lukács's rather crude identification of this philosopher with fascism, their ultimate linking of Nietzsche with imperialism retained the allegation of his one-sided allegiance to a discourse of bourgeois power.[16] For instance, GDR scholar Franz Malorny concedes that Nietzsche's views about race, German nationalism, and specifically the Jews were diametrically opposed to those of Hitler and the race ideologue Alfred Rosenberg,[17] yet Malorny's emphasis upon the 'inner' relationship between Nietzsche's thought and ideologies of irrationalism and fascism recapitulates much of the official Lukácsian line and the historiographical message implicit within it. Similarly, the Soviet scholar S. F. Odujev's *Auf den Spuren Zarathustras* (1971; In search of Zarathustra), appearing in the GDR in 1977, does not even mention Lukács by name (except for one entry in the bibliography). Yet his argument that 'Nietzsche's mysticism provides a theoretical model for the indirect apology of the capitalist world order and imperialist enslavement'[18] clearly owes a methodological debt to Lukács's *The Destruction of Reason*.

It can be argued, of course, that the depiction of Nietzsche by Mehring, Lukács, Odujev, and Malorny entailed highly selective readings of the philosopher's thought. For example, the notion of Nietzsche as the quintessential voice of nineteenth-century, antidemocratic (antisocialist), imperialist ideology – a kind of 'right-wing super Bismarck [*Über-Bismarck*],' as one critic has characterized him – profoundly ignores the extent to which Nietzsche became increasingly *and aggressively* opposed to a politics of nationalism after 1870.[19] His brief, early approval of Prussian policies gave way to deep misgivings during the Franco-Prussian War, resulting in antinationalist outbursts against the Second Reich for its, in Nietzsche's words, 'extirpation of the German spirit in favor of the German Reich.'[20] By no stretch of the imagination did Nietzsche understand his attack in terms of Left-Right politics or as anything but a repudiation, on cultural grounds, of the Bismarckian state and its cultural vulgarity and encroachments.

A similar argument can be made for Nietzsche's supposed anticommunism: his obvious disdain for social democracy should not be taken out of the historical context of his assault upon nineteenth-century modes of cultural modernity. For Nietzsche, capitalism and socialism shared in the mediocrity and leveling processes of contemporary industrial society and were equally moral products of a secularized Christianity, which Nietzsche hoped to see overcome through cultural renewal. Subsequent efforts to theatricalize Nietzsche into a strident anticommunist before the fact fail to grasp the extent to which Nietzsche's arguments also *anticipated* similar critiques of social democracy by left-wing intellectuals such as Lenin, Trotsky, Lukács, and Walter Benjamin.

But the concern is not whether any reading of Nietzsche remains faithful to some originary intent or hermeneutic truth, which taken to an extreme is itself a phantasm of classical philology. Of interest is the nature and function of these official readings of Nietzsche within the political life of the major parties on the Left.[21] As will be discussed at length below, it is important to emphasize that there has been and continues to be a powerful counterreading of Nietzsche from within the ranks of the unofficial Left, one that has sought to rescue him for socialism. In fact, the one-sidedness of Mehring's harsh critique of Nietzsche in 1891 emerges in part as a result of his efforts to *counter* the pro-Nietzsche views of people close to or within the Social Democratic Party of his time.[22] For instance, Otto Brahm, a founder of the Freie Bühne and later director of the Deutsches Theater in Berlin, was known for his outspoken views concerning the aesthetically conservative positions of the social democratic cultural bureaucracy, in particular August Bebel and Mehring himself. Mehring in turn devoted a significant part of his diatribe against Nietzsche in *Kapital und Presse* to attacking both Brahm and Paul Lindau, a naturalist playwright who had once described Nietzsche as a 'social philosopher of socialism.' What is important is not the specifics of sectarian politics within the Social Democratic Party but the fact that Nietzsche, even during his lifetime, had already become a terrain of interpretive contestation in the process of ideological identity formation and the struggle for political power: for the meaning of power and the power of meaning.

The Destruction or the Promotion of Reason?

If all of this reminds us that divergent readings of any thinker are generated by real political conflict, in the case of Nietzsche in the GDR we are confronted with a philosopher whose challenge to state socialism was seen to be centrally connected to questions of historical and cultural identity. The link between Nietzsche and history was particularly important as a means to clarify opposing cultural traditions for purposes of political legitimation. The association of Nietzsche with irrationalism, individualism, antisocialism/communism, nationalism, Romanticism, aesthetic subjectivism, barbarism, and so on, was clearly part of a larger political strategy devoted to creating a monolithic 'imperialist' Nietzsche. As a cultural cult figure, identified with an entire strand of historical-intellectual development deemed antagonistic to socialism at the level of cultural tradition, Nietzsche could be made representative of a *Sonderweg* [special path] of German history.[23]

The notion of a German *Sonderweg*, of course, was not unique to the historiography of the GDR. Western historians as diverse as Gordon Craig, Karl Dietrich Bracher, Ralf Dahrendorf, Heinrich August Winkler, and Hans Ulrich-Wehler have stressed the uniqueness of the German path to modernity as a way of explaining the emergence of Hitler. The lateness of industrialization, the failed bourgeois revolution of 1848, the rapid economic expansion after 1871 – all are seen as part of an 'unnatural' cataclysmic leap from agrarianism into modernity. Just as prominent for some are the cultural and ideational forms of specialty and uniqueness that were to accompany such a late development: the rejection of a superficial *Zivilisation* (Kant), typical of France and England, in the name of German *Kultur* with its emphasis upon the 'unpolitical' (Thomas Mann), upon *Gemeinschaft* [community] instead of *Gesellschaft* [society] (Tönnies), upon the dark, creative, 'irrational,' spiritual side of a deeper legacy; or the ridicule of liberalism and democracy for their preponderance of mediocrity in the name of protonationalist sympathies of autocracy and genius. While scholars recently have begun to question the legitimacy of such a special path, stressing either the normalcy of German nineteenth-century history or the uniqueness of any national development, it is clear that the *Sonderweg* thesis has served to legitimize the 'Westernization' (i.e., normalization) of the Federal Republic as the only path away from fascism.[24]

A similar process, with a significantly different set of categories and conclusions, can be traced in the GDR. Like those Western scholars who located in the early nineteenth century the emergence of what Helmut Plessner once called 'die verspätete Nation [the belated nation],'[25] the Lukács-inspired *Sonderweg* thesis developed in the GDR found in German Romanticism the onset of a destruction of reason. Taken at such a general level, there would indeed seem to be important parallels between Plessner, Wehler, Winkler, and even Kracauer, on the one hand, and Georg Lukács and Heinz Malorny, on the other, all of whom were committed to some form of a 'from Schelling (Nietzsche, Caligari, etc.) to Hitler' thesis of German cultural history as the inexorable march of a particular strand of pathological *Geist* from Romanticism into Nazism.

What is noteworthy about the GDR is the extent to which its version of the *Sonderweg* thesis helped create a foundational narrative that was to dominate political and cultural policy formation until its very collapse in November 1989. Moreover, in the socialist rendition of *Sonderweg* there are *two* coexistent paths of German history, not just one. The aberrant version of an irrationalist, demonic development leading to the triumph of imperialist and fascist forms of domination is countered by a second, democratic one. This alternate historical strain, with its origins in the German Enlightenment and its further development in nineteenth-century social democracy, the struggles of the Communist Party throughout the 1920s and into exile in the 1930s, and the coming of socialism in the GDR, helped develop the ideological rationale for the postwar division of Germany. Indeed, this story of a schizophrenic separation of national self, the Romulus and Remus of German identity, is more than simply an allegory about Germany's special route to national forms of modernity; more than an explanation for the rise of Nazism. It becomes the very raison d'être for the existence of the GDR itself. If the dominance of the irrational path led from 'the destruction of the humanist spirit within the flowering period of classical bourgeois philosophy and literature in Germany'[26] to the repression of democratic, bourgeois liberal and socialist traditions and impulses through 1945, then the establishment of the 'first German state for peasants and workers' represented the historical alternative to such a despicable special path.

The Destruction or the Promotion of Reason?

This bifurcation of German history brings us back to the importance of Friedrich Nietzsche. More than any other figure to emerge from the 'swamp' of irrationalist, antidialectical intellectual history, Nietzsche provides the central organizing cultural topos for German degeneracy and barbarism. Even during his lifetime, his reputed rejection of the Enlightenment and humanism helped label him as the antipode to that 'good' path of German intellectual history emanating from German Classicism. Indeed, within the philosophical discourse of late-nineteenth-century imperialism, his writings are said by socialists to have transformed the inchoate Romanticism of the early part of the century into a philosophy of aggression, which in its pseudocritique of capitalism in the name of capitalism was all the more insidious for its appeal to the masses. Writing about the Marxist reception of Nietzsche, Denis Sweet quite rightly emphasizes how, within the ambience of nineteenth-century philosophy, Nietzsche is distinguished from all the other Romantic critics of capitalist, industrialized society. They emphasized the *good side* of modern society (industrialization, scientific progress, rationalization) while condemning it in totality as bad and yearning for a return to a precapitalist state. 'Nietzsche does just the opposite. He praises the *bad side* of capitalism (domination, constant struggle for a living, elitist ideology of a master race, social Darwinism) while positing an extrapolated version of this society in the future where all the contradictions have been resolved through intensification of precisely this bad side.'[27]

Certainly the centrality of Nietzsche for the socialist version of Germany's special historical path is furthered immensely by his featured role within European fascism. Mussolini, Hitler, and the intellectual leadership in Italy and Germany gave active allegiance to the philosopher as foundational for their political movements. 'Friedrich Nietzsche,' wrote Alfred Rosenberg, 'represented the desperate cry of repressed millions . . . The fact that finally there was someone who suddenly in fanatic outrage destroyed all values . . . sent a breath of relief throughout the souls of all searching Europeans.'[28] The renowned Nietzsche specialist at Humboldt University, Alfred Bäumler, found in Nietzsche the unifying figure for the 'liberation of the German spirit' and the politics of a 'new type.' Bäumler's historiographical mapping sharpened the line of succession in a way that was to prove particularly providential for the Marxist historians. 'The

German state of the future,' Bäumler writes, 'will not be a continuation of Bismarck's creation [which Bäumler considers a Christian *Kleindeutschland* (Germany writ small)], but will be born again from the spirit of Nietzsche and the spirit of the great war.'[29]

Given the centrality of Nietzsche's reception in the Third Reich, it is little wonder that the socialist constructions of a deviant *Sonderweg* would highlight the importance of Nietzsche's role as forerunner and paradigm for a right-wing heritage. More than Houston Stewart Chamberlain, Oswald Spengler, Ludwig Klages, Ernst Jünger, Gottfried Benn, and even Martin Heidegger, Nietzsche became a historical watershed for historical continuity and the special path.

This was also to have relevance for the period after 1945. Nietzsche's role as prime marker for a German ideological *Sonderweg* does not end with the demise of the Third Reich. His 'renaissance' in the Federal Republic is characterized by East German scholars as evidence that the historical spirit that he had come to represent during the first half of the century had found its nesting ground on the other side of the Elbe.[30] This 'rehabilitation,' in fact, is repeatedly cited as a chief weapon of Western ideological cold war strategy and provided one of the significant means by which the cultural politics of the GDR was able to distinguish itself from the capitalist West; by which the GDR affirmed its difference and identity vis-à-vis the Federal Republic.

THE OTHER NIETZSCHE – FOR ANOTHER SOCIALISM?

But the function of Nietzsche in the GDR was not just a matter of officially constructing a proper foreign policy image, directed for purposes of legitimation toward the outside. Equally important, particularly during the 1980s, was the role that Nietzsche came to play in the struggle for cultural change within the evolving policy and interpretive practices of the GDR itself. For some, the absence of Nietzsche within the corpus of accepted bourgeois tradition had come to suggest a lack of maturity on the part of the GDR state apparatus.[31] Regardless of his own questionable politics, the argument went, Nietzsche's influence upon artists and thinkers of every persuasion was simply too vast for him to be excluded from the pantheon of the past. For others, many of them poets and literary critics, there were more positive reasons for the publication of Nietzsche in the GDR. Aware of contemporary discussions occurring in the West, particularly in the writings of and around Foucault and Derrida, these intellectuals shared a sense that a dialogue between Nietzsche and Marx, or, at the very least, a rethinking of the Nietzsche question, would provide a critical revitalization of the cultural identity. Indeed, viewed from the perspective of a reassessment of Marxism, Nietzsche's critique of the Enlightenment touched on major epistemological, historical, and cultural issues within the Marxist paradigm that some saw in need of revision and rethinking.

As emphasized earlier, the revisionist reading of Nietzsche within the socialist camp did not originate in the GDR. Rather, it was present from the inception of official socialism itself and has included major intellectuals affiliated with the Social Democratic and Communist Parties for the last 100 years. In the Soviet Union, for example, the first Bolshevist cultural commissar, Anatoly Lunacharsky, and his brother-in-law, the Proletcultist Alexander Bogdanov, were deeply influenced by Nietzsche's notions of cultural revolution, an ideological deviation for which they were attacked repeatedly by Lenin, Plekhanov, and others. Whereas the official party position stressed Nietzsche's unrepentant 'individualism,' with Zarathustra representing the epitome of bourgeois selfishness and egotism, both Lunacharsky and Bogdanov glimpsed in the figure of the *Übermensch* a potential for collectivist vision and cultural renewal. Of particular importance for Lunacharsky was Nietzsche's influence as prophet and seer:

> Nietzsche taught that man is free to create illusions and fantasies providing they lead forward along the path of creative achievements, to the growth of powers, to the sovereign of power over Nature. Even if the vision should prove unrealizable, even if the ideal should prove to be beyond the powers, all that matters is that man should be bold and struggle to advance. Take away from a man such an illusion and, if he is strong, he will create another, even more beautiful, for himself. And who knows but that what awaits him may not be more beautiful than any vision.[32]

Nietzsche's influence on Lunacharsky is evident both in the latter's poetic endeavors and in his formation of cultural policy. For example, one of his best-known plays, *Faust and the City*, depicts the development of an 'ultraindividualist' from an attitude of aristocratic amoralism to one of social commitment. The proletariat is represented as an amalgam of Nietzsche and Marx: the collectivist realization of a dynamism and a cultural creativity that Lunacharsky glimpsed in the vitalist energies of the *Übermensch* Zarathustra.

Similar themes are found in the writings of the Proletcultist Alexander Bogdanov. Although Bogdanov, unlike Nietzsche, viewed the proletariat as a force capable of creating genuine culture, it is Nietzsche's writings on the herd that helped the Russian distinguish between the malleable, submissive, yet threatening 'masses' (as depicted, for example, in Gustav Le Bon's classic definition of the 'crowd' in modern society) and a truly class-conscious, politically active working-class collectivism. As the first of his 'laws of a new conscience,' a kind of proletarian ten commandments, Bogdanov writes,

There shall be no herd instinct.

A passive, submissive attitude has more to do with the petty bourgeois fear of being different than with true collectivism. A faceless being brings nothing to a collective but mechanical force, thereby increasing its inertia. In rejecting the herd instinct, a collectivist coincides with the individualist; he differs, however, insofar as the individualist thinks only of 'me and thine' whereas the collectivist attempts to elevate and perfect the collective, and, in so doing, maintain and develop his individuality together with the collective.[33]

Lunacharsky's and Bogdanov's recourse to Nietzsche in order to supplement the Marxist paradigm contained a number of ingredients that have come to characterize a 'Nietzschean Left' within twentieth-century European socialism.[34] Central to this mode of thought was a concern for the 'subjective' dimension of human experience within the historical process; a radical critique of scientism and positivism; an understanding of culture and fantasy as integral to any revolutionary process; and, finally, a visionary, utopian view of a nonalienated social order. In each instance, the thought of Nietzsche was seen as a possible corrective and addition, as a critique in a positive sense, *not* as a cancellation or negation of the Marxian project.

The positive reception of Nietzsche within the ranks of German socialism, while virtually nonexistent among official party ideologues, articulated themes similar to those developed by Lunacharsky and Bogdanov. We could mention the writings of the feminist Lily Braun as well as the anarchists Willy Hellpach and Bruno Wille or the activities of a group of radicals called the Jungen.[35] Certainly one of the best examples of a positive reception of Nietzsche within German communism is found in the writings of Ernst Bloch, a Marxist philosopher whose life work was dedicated to enriching dialectical materialism through an appropriation – rather than a critical repudiation – of religious and mythical 'heritages.'

Significant for our present discussion is Bloch's unique treatment of both Nietzsche and fascism. In a now classical text entitled *Heritage of Our Times (Erbschaft dieser Zeit)*, written as a collection of essays over a period of eleven years and published in 1935, Bloch sought to recast the regnant leftist view of fascist ideology.[36] Whereas orthodox Marxist critiques of ideology tended to measure cultural and ideational phenomena against what they saw as enlightened notions of reason and scientific progress, Bloch looked beyond a merely cognitive, historically teleological understanding of *textual* representations to the unconscious sedimentation of social experience out of which and to which they spoke. Methodologically, his highly idiosyncratic readings of artistic and political icons pushed against the grain of monolithic interpretive practice to grasp the multiplicity of contradictory 'meanings' inherent in *any* discursive tradition. In so doing, he developed a mode of writing and reading that struck implicitly at the very underpinnings of what people like Lukács were saying about the relationship between irrationalism and politics. Instead of dismissing myth, Romanticism, and religion as per se 'reactionary,' that is, as expressive of a desire simply to retreat to a golden past, Bloch attempted to mine those 'nonsynchronous' traditions for what they revealed about the contemporary social unconscious, about 'a yearning for the true self to which humanity strives to return,'[37] about collective dreams and the hope for a nonalienated, utopian better world. In accordance with such views, fascist ideology for Bloch was not simply an instrument of deception but also and at the very same moment contained 'an element of an older, romantic contradiction to capitalism, which misses things in present-day life and longs for something vaguely different' (2).

Viewed within the context of the rise of fascism in the 1920s and 1930s, Bloch's essay entitled 'Nietzsche's Impulse' can be read at one level as a vigorous rebuttal of all those 'Socratic' Marxists who have refused to acknowledge the subversive, eminently contradictory dimension of the Nietzschean message. In the figure of Dionysus, for example, Bloch sees 'not merely the unrestrained reflex of monopoly capital,' so central to the writings of Mehring and Lukács, but, in addition, a fulminating revolt against the 'zero point of mechanical existence': 'Dionysus as a symbol of abstractly fantastic escape into anarchy: only here do we grasp Nietzsche's serious impact on the age. Only here did Nietzsche express his age in watchwords, in watchwords of an indistinct countermovement of the "subject" against the objectivity which it finds to exist' (325). Bloch does not deny the image of an 'imperialist' Nietzsche as one possible reading of the 'power content' of his later works: 'Neither monopoly capitalism nor imperialistic war lack an understanding of this will to power, of course' (328). Of concern, however, is the failure of such a reading to countenance the *ambivalence* of meaning inherent, particularly, in mythic or literary representation: 'Yet even in his final phase – after *Übermensch* and Dionysus – Nietzsche ideologizes not merely imperialism, but a formal upward tendency, an indeterminate content, as well' (328). Nietzsche's 'impulse' is mythopoetic, not logically discursive. His evocation of the Dionysian creed reverberates archaic past *and* utopian future, regressive atavism *and* the dream of a better, even socialist world. Thus for Bloch Dionysus is not only a 'mere earlier level of consciousness, smeared with blood, an Ananke in labor and a murderous nature' but at the same time 'a symbol of the one unarrived, unbecome in man, . . . a god of fermentation, but of the wine-seeking, light-calling kind' (327).

Bloch's plea for a 'dialectical' poetic literary, written during the growing fascist hagiography and Marxist demonization of Nietzsche, bears the markings of that aporiatic historical time. His own vision of the two Nietzsches – the imperialist and the revolutionary – remains throughout the essay *absolutely unmediated conceptually.* Bloch does not seek to defend the philosopher or exonerate him of anything. Nor does he draw from Nietzsche, as later Critical Theory will do, a critique of the Enlightenment that would throw open to question the very possibility of a non-instrumental, liberatory reason. What he does do is shift the focus of textual interpretation from an attempt to explicate a purported *unified* and *essential* authorial message to the process by which the 'meanings' of texts are forever renegotiated as part of their historical contextualization. For instance, if there is a 'creative' utopia in Nietzsche, Bloch argues, then it is a 'private one, one tinged with aristocratic reaction and disguised, a romantic utopia, without contact with history, let alone with the decisive class today; *but history makes its contact for itself, the cunning of reason is great*' (emphasis added) (328). Regardless of Nietzsche's origins or even intentions, the highly ambivalent text itself, released into a contradictory social world, remains a 'mixture of blasting powder and incense, of tomorrow and the primeval day before yesterday' (327) to be used, we are told (with the help of Hegel's cunning of reason), historically – with the help also of the critical intellectual, thinking about heritages dialectically.

Bloch's plea for a differentiated view of Nietzschean philosophy provides a primer for how to read against the grain of simplistic critiques of ideology, how critically to reinvent a legacy within the sediments of a historical present. Certainly Nietzsche's own mode of writing provided a rich terrain for such a deconstructive reading. As a creator of contemporary myth who breaks the mold of prevailing ideological and epistemological dualisms (left vs. right, modern vs. premodern, aesthetic vs. expository writing, mythological vs. Enlightenment, rational vs. irrational, etc.), Nietzsche's importance for Bloch, and in Bloch's view for Marxism, lay precisely in the way he forces a rethinking of the reading strategies of all cultural heritages for purposes of political rearticulation. Beyond and even at odds with its political content, Nietzsche's style conveys a shift in epistemological emphasis that is a political emphasis as well. Bloch's phrase 'Nietzsche's impulse' suggests a blurring of boundaries and a use of language no longer founded simply upon transcendent propositions: the poetic ambivalence communicated by Dionysian and Zarathustrian thought militates against the Procrustean bed of systematic philosophy, remains highly multifaceted, polyvocal. Moreover, it is precisely this quality of indeterminacy that blunts the hammer and tongs of a one-sided interpretation in the spirit of Marxian Socraticism, one that could evoke the kind of dialectical reading that Bloch would call for.

NIETZSCHE AND THE POLITICS OF IDENTITY

Bloch's situating of the Nietzsche essay at the conclusion of a book devoted to reassessing the political potential of religious and romantic anticapitalist heritages was clearly of strategic importance within the cultural politics of the exile and postexile period. While his defense of Nietzsche was to have little effect upon Nietzsche's almost total denigration within the Marxist camp, it did suggest contours of reception – in particular through its emphasis upon historicization and the importance of poetic ambivalence and contradiction, and its schizophrenic view of Nietzsche himself – that were to be taken up, albeit belatedly, in the GDR. Although Bloch had chosen to return from American exile to the GDR after the war, his 'ideological deviations' led to conflicts with the Party in the early 1950s and culminated, finally, in his decision to emigrate to West Germany in 1961.

One cultural critic to draw on Bloch's and Walter Benjamin's methodological legacies was Renate Reschke, whose unpublished dissertation of 1983 called for a 'historically exact reassessment' of the 'one-sided' image of Nietzsche still dominant even at the beginning of the 1980s.[38] Reschke's position, presented publicly at a 1980 Nietzsche conference in West Germany[39] and elaborated further in a 1983 article published in the *Weimarer Beiträge*,[40] articulates the radical turn in the treatment of Nietzsche beginning in the late 1970s that assumedly also contributed to Harich's almost hysterical concern about Nietzsche inroads in the GDR. At the broadest and politically most provocative level, she argues explicitly for a revision of the Nietzsche image, implicitly for his inclusion in the canon of the 'bourgeois heritage.' 'It simply isn't enough,' she writes, 'to characterize Nietzsche's work merely as a philosophy of the negative contrast. A critique based only on a disdainful wave of the hand underestimates its immanently critical potential and abandons him to our ideological enemies.'[41]

Several points of emphasis converge in Reschke's contributions that are key to understanding how and why the reassessment of Nietzsche was emerging in the GDR. The first points to the disparate and even conflicting structures of discourse within the rapidly shifting cultural policy formation during the 1980s. As a member of the Cultural Sciences and Aesthetics Department at Humboldt University, Reschke's emphasis upon Nietzsche's decisive role as a critic of bourgeois culture was part of a move by the humanist establishments to wrest exclusive control for interpreting Nietzsche from Party 'philosophers' such as Heinz Malorny and Manfred

Buhr at the Academy of Sciences. Against their overtly *political*, philosophically systematic readings emphasizing the affirmative and apologetic nature of Nietzsche the philosopher of power, Reschke stresses the rebellious and contradictory thrust of his thinking as a critic of bourgeois culture. However, this is not advanced simply as an institutional imperative, intended to separate Nietzsche the political philosopher from the aesthetician of poetic discourse. Rather, her argument seeks to open up the importance of understanding Nietzsche's *style* as an integral part of his thought structures in their entirety: 'Of importance is the mostly metaphorical conceptualization of his statements, the philosophical substance of his metaphors as well as the poetic variables in his choice of concepts . . . To take Nietzsche literally is one sure way of misunderstanding him. Not to do so also' (24–25).

Reschke's call for an 'immanent' ideological criticism sensitive to the historical nuances of Nietzsche's language speaks against those who would reduce his 'meaning' to 'isolated statements taken out of context,' laid across a grid of ideological proposition. Like Bloch, Reschke would emphasize the complexity and contradictory nature of the philosopher-poet's prose and by so doing critique from her side the 'undialectical' shortcomings of Marxism's unilinear methods of ideology critique.

A similar line of argument can be traced in the writing of Eike Middell, a literary historian at the Academy of Sciences who in 1985 offered the first differentiated historicizing of Lukács's (and by proxy Malorny's) position by arguing that the Hungarian's limited depiction of Nietzsche's as a forerunner of fascism was really an attack upon the Nazi's reception of the philosopher, not a treatment of Nietzsche himself.[42] Had Lukács looked at Nietzsche in relation to the former's own aesthetic predilections, Middell concludes, he would have found numerous points of agreement, whether in Nietzsche's attack upon decadence and the loss of totality in modern art or in their shared disdain toward aspects of mass culture as represented in the work of Richard Wagner. Instead, Lukács's reductive view of Nietzsche, in which 'the unifying element, the systematic moment lies in the social content of his thought: in the fight against socialism' has resulted in 'an essentially critical-literary interpretation of Nietzsche giving way to a philosophical-programmatic one.'[43] Middell's juxtaposition of 'critical-literary' and 'philosophical-programmatic' conveys important methodological implications. Like Reschke and Bloch, he also finds fault with an abstract Marxism that 'functionalizes' Nietzsche into a monolithic representative of a metaphysical power politics, one that ignores the richness of his metaphorical language and refuses to acknowledge the parallels between Nietzsche's *Kulturkritik* and similar views emerging on the Left.

But the implications of a 'critical-literary' appreciation of Nietzsche's contradictory message open up political considerations that potentially challenge the very framework within which 'official critics' such as Middell and Reschke would even be able to operate. It is one thing to suggest that the prevailing interpretation of Nietzsche has ignored a 'progressive' aspect of his critique of bourgeois culture. It is quite another to question the very epistemological foundations upon which such systematic-philosophical critiques of ideology have tended to operate and to intimate thereby that Marxism has something to learn or that it might even be nourished by attendance to Nietzsche's thought.

The writings of Reschke and Middell tread perilously close to the thin line separating an assertion about the unhistoric nature of some forms of Marxist interpretation from a more fundamental critique of Marxism in its entirety. Yet they also, finally, do enunciate where they will not cross that line. For instance, while Reschke is careful to call for a differentiating concretization of Nietzsche's metaphors in the 'context of their intellectual complexity,' she is well aware of the political implications involved in Nietzsche's influence upon classical Critical Theory or more recent modes of Neo-Marxist, poststructuralist, and postmodernist thought prevailing in the West. What was important about Nietzsche for the Frankfurt School, for instance, quite apart from Critical Theory's distance from Nietzsche's overtly political views concerning power and subjectivity, was their affinity to crucial methodological issues concerning a critique of modernity and a theory of epistemological self-reflection. Fifty years before the publication of *Dialectic of Enlightenment*, Nietzsche saw that the Enlightenment had turned into its opposite, that the grand belief in a 'cure for the world through knowledge, in a life guided by science' results finally in the triumph of a 'higher egotism' based on an increase of property and power.

In terms of epistemology, Nietzsche was equally prescient in his attack on the metaphysical separation of a rational, truth-seeking *epistēmē*, on the one hand, and interests of utility and power emanating from the need to dominate nature, on the other. He also recognized that the relation between subject and object, between reflection and the world 'is forever historically determined anew, namely on the basis of determinate existing conditions, interests and valuations.'[44] It is clear that Adorno especially was deeply influenced by Nietzsche, not only concerning philosophical and epistemological questions but also regarding the importance of aphoristic, essayistic style for the *content* of philosophical discourse.

Thus, given the growing positive reception of Nietzsche by poststructuralists and Neo-Marxists in the West, it is of little surprise that Reschke's 'necessary debate' with the 'modern, bourgeois Nietzsche-reception' would focus on the challenge of such a development for Marxism. While one part of her critique faults in particular the tendency to absolutize Nietzsche's position into either a prophecy for Dionysian revolution (certain Lacanian readings) or to find in his views of language a linguistic turn in the spirit of deconstruction, she reserves her severest attack for those on the Left whose 'disappointment' with Marxist theory had led them away from Marx to Nietzsche. For Reschke, examples for such thinking are to be found throughout European and Anglo-American thought: 'The history of emancipation in the twentieth century has more to learn from the horrors of Nietzsche than the hopes of Karl Marx,' writes Günther Rohrmoser, enunciating a view prevalent within West German discussions according to which the philosopher of individualism, not the dialectical materialist, had truly grasped the problems of alienation, the loss of agency, and the limits of science in the contemporary world.[45] The French poststructuralists (Foucault and Derrida) are even more radical in their assertion that, rather than Hegel or Marx, it is Nietzsche's thought and tradition, with its critique of all metaphysical totalities and 'master narratives' (Lyotard), that hold the only real hope for a genuine democratic order or postmodernist art.

If Reschke, in her defense of Marx, quite rightly emphasizes the one-sidedness and lack of historical contextualization in some Western attempts to make out of Nietzsche a 'Kryptosocialist,' she is also just as obstinate in her refusal to acknowledge that Nietzsche has anything constructive to say about the failings of Marxism itself. Here we see the *limits* of even the most enlightened revision of Nietzsche in the GDR. Reschke is quite open to speaking about Marx and Nietzsche as 'alien brothers' in their critique of the capitalist order at the end of the nineteenth century. She is not, however, willing or institutionally able to acknowledge that post-Stalinist Marxism has anything to learn from Nietzsche, whether it be about the limits of Enlightenment or the centrality of the cultural question. In fact, her 'contextualizing' of those post-1968 Western leftists who have turned from Marx to Nietzsche illustrates a classical leftist denial mechanism that often emerges when the question of another thinker borders on the inadequacies of Marxism itself: the 'spectacular' discovery of Nietzsche by leftist bourgeois ideologists is for Reschke simply a reaction formation emanating from their own failure to make use of Marxist theory in the struggle against capitalism. Citing Hans Heinz Holz's remark that 'Nietzsche serves as an alibi in order to repress Marx,'[46] Reschke is even more aggressive in imputing false motives: 'behind the assertion concerning the purported inability of Marxist theory to solve acute human problems lies an attempt to defame all those who, moved by Marxist ideas, have committed themselves to social change.'[47] No mention here of the horrendous failure of Marxism around questions of gender, ecology, the Holocaust, and individual freedoms. No acknowledgment either concerning the implications from within Reschke's own literary-critical method for a critique of Marx emanating from Nietzsche's own thought.

Having defined the borders of Nietzsche reception within the literary-critical establishment, it seems necessary to reiterate that the primary task for the Nietzsche revisionists was to open up discussions of Nietzsche in the GDR within the area of *Kulturpolitik*. Again Reschke is helpful for an understanding of these broader political dimensions. More important than simply rehistoricizing or normalizing Nietzsche was understanding his significance as a figure of influence and appropriation for leading avant-garde thinkers and artists on the Left political scene – Johannes R. Becher, Anna Seghers, Bertolt Brecht, Walter Benjamin, Ernst Bloch, Lu Märten – whose 'differentiated relation to the bourgeois, or more precisely late bourgeois heritage . . . furthered the development of Marxist positions.'[48] Clearly, the absolute centrality of Nietzsche for so many of the bourgeois and even socialist writers at the center of the official canon provided a continued dilemma for those who would want to repudiate him.

The issue of Nietzsche and the canon brings us back to the *Kulturpolitik* and its relation to social change and identity. The constant questioning and reinscribing of the socialist canon beginning in the 1960s had resulted in major rehabilitations in every area of cultural life. As already mentioned, by the late 1980s Martin Luther, the Prussian tradition, Frederick the Great, Otto von Bismarck, German Romanticism, Heinrich von Kleist, Franz Kafka, Hermann Hesse, Expressionist painting and literature, Weimar modernism (Dadaism, Neue Sachlichkeit, Bauhaus), French Surrealism, the early Soviet avant-garde, Sigmund Freud, and James Joyce had all been brought into the ever-expanding orbit of legitimate socialist heritage. This is where Nietzsche comes in – with a vengeance. For in point of fact, this 'philosopher of irrationalism' was virtually the last of the once-demonized representatives of the negative – read reactionary, bourgeois, prefascist, 'other' – canon. With his inclusion in the socialist fold, not only was the canon itself threatened but all that such a binary opposition had come to represent when constituted as the basis of political life.

What disturbed not only Harich but also such official voices of Marxist-Leninism as Manfred Buhr about the Nietzsche debate of the late 1980s was its relation to issues of political legitimation. Indeed, Buhr's reply to Harich, while critical of the latter's one-sidedness, focused precisely on that issue when he wrote:

> There is no reason that I can see for a 'reevaluation' of Nietzsche and his impact. And there is even less of a reason for a recantation of the fundamental premises of a Marxist antifascist Nietzsche image. The consequence of such a move would mean an undermining of the antifascist tradition, which is an essential and indispensable [*unverzichtbar*] characteristic of our state and which we cannot afford to neglect simply because we do *not* want to surrender our very selves [das wir nicht vernachlässigen können, weil wir *nicht* uns selber aufgeben wollen].[49]

'Weil wir *nicht* uns selber aufgeben wollen.' No single sentence in this entire debate articulates more explicitly what was at stake in the ongoing Nietzsche discussion in the GDR. For Manfred Buhr in 1988, the Nietzsche question was no longer a matter of rational argument concerning the merits of an individual case or the hermeneutical interpretation of specific philosophical texts. What was of concern was the question of national identity and political power. Without the demonization of Nietzsche and all that such a stigmatization represents, one entire strategy of socialist historiography was thrown into disarray. At the center of that historiography, as we noted in our discussion of the German *Sonderweg*, was a belief that there are absolute, lasting objective values that result inexorably from the telos of socialist history; that as part of such an unbroken linear continuity, the working-class movement and its various political state formations are *eo ipso* antifascist; and, finally, that given such a linkage, the problem of the fascist past and *Vergangenheitsbewältigung* belong essentially on the other side of the border in West Germany. When Manfred Buhr emphatically states that Nietzsche 'does *not* belong to our heritage, to the heritage of the working class, to the heritage of the antifascist state GDR [gehört *nicht* zu unserem Erbe, zum Erbe der Arbeiterklasse, zum Erbe des antifaschistischen Staates DDR]'[50] he is simply asserting the primacy of cultural identity for political viability and Nietzsche's connection to that.

In the summer of 1989, the head of the GDR's Academy of Sciences Otto Reinhold issued a statement that subsequently became known as the Reinhold thesis. The core of his argument held that socialism was the sole reason for the existence of the GDR; that if socialism disappeared then the GDR would have to disappear also. Speaking in extraordinarily bold and prescient terms about the 'national question,' only months prior to the collapse of the state, Reinhold drew a direct connection between political identity and national raison d'être. Manfred Buhr's linking of Nietzsche to the GDR's antifascist identity provides the cultural correlative to the Reinhold thesis: without the demonization of Nietzsche, there can be no coherent *Kulturpolitik*. As such, it helps us understand the *public* significance of the Nietzsche debate – despite its forensic and rhetorical shabbiness – as a last-ditch effort to plug the dam. The fight for and against Nietzsche stands as a final war by proxy in the struggle for fundamental social change.

But what, one might still ask, has this got to do with Nietzsche's own writings per se? Why the insistence upon Marx or Nietzsche? What is it beyond Nietzsche's particular elitist views (the anti-Semite Richard Wagner remained very much a part of the socialist canon) or his reception by the Nazis (who had sought to appropriate Hegel for their cause as well) that has made *this* thinker such a thorn in the side of the socialist status quo? The answer to this question moves us closer again to the writings of Allan Bloom. For it is not so much Nietzsche's individual views on this or that subject that are the ultimate threat but rather his 'unreliability [*Unverbindlichkeit*],' his 'relativism,' his utter and absolute disdain for all absolutes, including the absolute of reason itself, that is ultimately the destabilizing and provocative dimension. It is in this light that we must understand the extent to which the difference between Marx *or* Nietzsche and Marx *and* Nietzsche looms as a profoundly political one. Seen no longer as mutually exclusive opposites, the notion of reading Marx through the eyes of Nietzsche, a practice with a venerable Marxist tradition from Bloch to the Frankfurt School, is most problematic for GDR officialdom because of its potential critique (and even revision!) of Marxism around questions of history and epistemology. As a critique of history, as we have seen already with Benjamin, it would entail a reading against the grain not only of monolinear historiography but of history in the *singular* with an integral subject as its agent and cognizance. More important, it would also mean the taking apart of a binary opposition that has enabled Marxism to become the sine qua non for reason, truth, totality, but most important, political and cultural identity. 'Weil wir *nicht* uns selber aufgeben wollen.'

The parallels between the Marxist Wolfgang Harich and the conservative Allan Bloom emerge most strikingly then in the way Nietzsche is structured in relation to the evolution of Enlightenment thought and notions of a universal Classical heritage. Although their end points are diametrically opposed, both Harich and Bloom find in the 'Nietzscheanization of the Left' a subjectivizing of value orientation (which Bloom calls 'nihilism American style') and a dissolution of national character. On the other hand, what unites the critics of both – and the critics are by no means uniformly Nietzschean – is a shared sense of the threat that such a universalizing of the canon has for questions of democracy, genuine pluralism, and cultural-political otherness. The battle for the enlargement of the canon in the GDR was indeed an assault upon a particular kind of reason. Whether this in turn would have led to the development of meaningful alternatives was not to be known in the GDR. With the exception of one poem, Nietzsche's writings remained unpublished through the demise of the regime itself.[51]

EPILOGUE:

THE STASI AND

THE POETS

The removal of an unjust regime, the liberation from the supervision of a secret police that penetrates everything and that, with petty-cold perfection, outdoes anything that Foucault's image of a panoptic society had ever sought to grasp about our reality – that is what is normatively decisive about this 'revolution.' — Jürgen Habermas, *Vergangenheit als Zukunft*

The three major post-Wall debates about the political and moral legacy of East German literary culture were all framed by controversies involving the writer and the 'secret police.' The first occurred in June 1990, when the belated publication of Christa Wolf's fictional 'story' *Was bleibt,* written in 1979 and depicting a female writer's harassment by the Stasi, resulted in strong public rebuke of the author for her depiction of self as victim and her failure to speak out against state repression during the decade prior to the fall of the regime. The following year the issue of the Stasi and the poets was brought to the fore again when it was revealed that two leaders of the younger poetic underground, Sascha Anderson and Rainer Schedlinski, had been working as 'unofficial informants [IM].'[1] Not surprisingly, to have the leading spokesperson and chief literary entrepreneur of the dissident Prenzlauer Berg artists, Sascha Anderson, outed as a Stasi agent was taken by some as further proof of an all-pervasive, ever-corrupting control of GDR intellectuals from above.[2]

But the Anderson scandal would not be the end of it. The revelations in January 1993 that Christa Wolf and Heiner Müller had also spoken with the Stasi, the former over a three-year period, seemed to confirm once and for all the moral and political bankruptcy of the literary avant-garde in the GDR. It was one thing for Müller and Wolf to have naively worked within a dictatorial system in hopes of reforming it; quite another to have crossed the line into a realm of unadulterated evil. For in the social imaginary of post–cold war and post-Wall German politics, the Stasi had become precisely that: a metaphorical monster whose tentacles enveloped and indeed poisoned every aspect of East German public and private life. Again Habermas:

> Today this sovereign authority, organized to perfection by German professionalism, is symbolized in the image of the *Krake* [octopus]. This image also expresses the feeling on the part of those who are caught up in it that freeing oneself is not simply a matter of a single act of liberation but rather a process of gradual decontamination [*Entgiftung*] in which no one knows how long it will last. One slays a dragon, an octopus simply perishes [*verendet*] – and not everything caught in its clutches is let go of. Therefore some things survive that are not particularly worth keeping. The new beginning is burdened with false continuities.[3]

The image of the Stasi as *Krake* did not originate with Jürgen Habermas. In March 1990, three months prior to the interview in which both of the above quotes appear, *Der Spiegel* ran a cover story entitled 'The Long Arm of the Stasi' with a giant picture of a sinister-looking octopus looming out of the dark with a tiny East German flag clutched in one massive tentacle.[4] In the phantasm of the culture industry and the frenzy of post-Wall allegations, the GDR had already become metamorphosed into the Stasi as a monster sea serpent.

However, what is significant because uncharacteristic of Habermas is the somewhat frivolous slippage of metaphor as he struggles to articulate the uniquely horrifying, yet equally pedestrian, nature of power configuration in the GDR. On the one hand, we find the familiar tropes from an Orwellian world of mind control and a one-dimensionally deformed bureaucracy: the Foucaultian panoptic eye, detached from the violent body, which with 'petty-cold perfection' and 'German professionalism' penetrates to the very core of its would-be knowing victim. Here is the logic of modernization run amok; the Weberian iron cage, coded now Teutonic-

ally and in the service of dictatorship, as a monument of absolute philistine efficiency. If there is evil here it is characterized, in Hannah Arendt's
sense of the term, by its banality.

Yet coexistent with its aura of technological perfection is an image of
the Stasi as gargantuan and mythological, as evil incarnate. Indeed, the
figure that will *reembody* this apparatus emerges out of a very different
tropic system. The sinister *Krake* is a metaphysical beast from the oceanic
depths whose formidable powers to invade and infect an organism would
seem to defy any hope for the kind of purgative quick fix suggested in the
notions of 'revolution' or 'liberation.' There is something not so much
premodern as antediluvian in the depiction of a body politic released by
a dying serpent and subject to the slow and painful process of decon-
tamination. Such an image shifts the emphasis from a clinical focus upon
spatial control (the panopticon) to the problem of a temporal rehabilitation that must allow for the organism to restore and purify itself, morally
and psychologically, over time.

The point, of course, is not to delimit the 'meaning' of the Stasi inter-
pretively to one signifying system or form of discursive analysis. Nor is it
important whether either of these metaphorical families has anything to
do with the 'reality' of a surveillance system that had become mired in
inefficiency and overproduction; whose capacity to gather trivia had rendered it increasingly incapable of 'knowing what it knew.' Rather, the
tension in Habermas's mixing of metaphor reminds us of the often contradictory meanings and projections circulating around the process of
Stasi revelation. The story of the Stasi and the poets does not just tell of
individual literary figures or the empirical workings of an intelligence
service. It is also about reconstructing and reclaiming one's history; the
nature of complicity, control, and dissent in the processes of everyday GDR
life; the search for new and different norms of morality and value; and
confronting the twin legacies of fascism and Stalinism. Understanding the
story of the Stasi and the poets takes us to the very heart of questions
concerning the relationship of intellectuals to the Stalinist state.

WHAT HAPPENED?

In comparing the Stasi connections and activities of Christa Wolf, Heiner
Müller, Sascha Anderson, and Rainer Schedlinski, notable differences

emerge that are important for evaluating them individually and as representative of different generational experiences. In the cases of Anderson and Schedlinski, it is clear that they both took an active and damaging role in reporting on the activities and views of friends and colleagues, some of whom were on the front lines of political resistance in the GDR. Anderson worked as an IM for approximately twenty years, beginning as a seventeen year old in 1970 and continuing even after his exile to the Federal Republic in 1986.[5] A prolific poet and social extrovert, he was the center of an enormously active scene of writers and artists, facilitating the development of the entire Prenzlauer Berg movement through contacts and publication arrangements both inside the GDR and with Western publishing houses. Simply by talking casually about his own day to day experiences, which is all that Anderson claimed (or wanted to believe) he was doing, he was in a position to provide a virtual panorama of information and interpretive impression about a whole generation of young intellectuals in the GDR. But Anderson, who operated under the code names David Menzel, Fritz Müller, and Peters, did more than just talk. In contrast to his highly allusive and esoteric fictional writing, Anderson's numerous written IM reports were a model of thoroughness, clarity, and precision, offering a wealth of potentially incriminating detail. Since his discovery in November 1991, Anderson has either denied having worked 'officially' for the Stasi (despite overwhelming evidence to the contrary) or sought to belittle the allegations being made against him.

Rainer Schedlinski was considerably less well known than Anderson, if in some quarters more respected as a sophisticated theorist of postmodern culture. Under the code name Gerhard he worked for the Stasi from 1974 until 1989. His reports differ markedly from Anderson's in their general dearth of empirical information, as well as in their emphasis upon subjective interpretive impression. Schedlinski has used this difference to claim that he purposely avoided providing any 'information' that might incriminate anyone. One look at a Stasi report based on Gerhard's recounting of a New Year's Eve party at the house of dissident Lutz Rathenow reveals how thin the line can be between fact and interpretive fancy:

> Rathenow then set off some giant fireworks with his son and after that everybody played 'monopoly.' A few days later Rathenow sent to the IM [i.e., Schedlinski] by way of Detlev Opitz the following items:

1 Copy of 'Dialog' with articles massively antagonistic toward the GDR (Schädlich, Duwe, Fuchs)

2 Copies of 'Ost-West-Diskussionsforum' Nos. 3 and 4 as well as other written materials of Western origin that he had gotten hold of illegally.[6]

The possession of any one of these materials would have been grounds for arrest, if the security system were so disposed. But had the Stasi intervened at this point, it would probably have destroyed its own elaborate system of surveillance and control. Convincing Schedlinski and Anderson that as informers they themselves were actually using the Stasi for their own purposes was one of the means this organization employed to keep the upper hand. Since the revelations, neither Anderson nor Schedlinski has seemed able or willing to acknowledge the enormity of their actions. Anderson often 'lied' about his activities or said it didn't matter anyway.[7] Schedlinski has 'confessed' publicly on several occasions, excusing himself at every turn.[8]

Regarding the Stasi's contacts with Heiner Müller and Christa Wolf, there is no evidence to date that either of them ever informed on friends or colleagues or divulged information that was not already available from other published sources or the public media.[9] The archival material in the case of Müller consists of a few index cards and some handwritten notes that indicate that during the 1980s he was registered first as IM Cement, in what was called a *Vorlauf* [preparatory status], and later as IM Heiner. To date no IM files for Müller have been found, nor has he appeared in anyone else's file as an IM. In an interview with *Spiegel TV*, Müller admitted to speaking with the Stasi and gave as his reasons a desire to lobby for the publication of his work in the GDR as well as an attempt to criticize and influence what he considered to be the disastrous domestic politics of the Honecker regime during the Gorbachev era. He also confessed to seeking 'material' about the working methods of an organization that had remained a mystery to the population at large.

The motivations and circumstances in the case of Christa Wolf are markedly different.[10] Unlike Müller, there is an IM file record of her contacts with the Stasi containing for the most part reports of conversations. These meetings occurred over thirty years prior to the time of the revelations, from 1959 to 1962, when as a committed member of the Party she was rapidly becoming a leading figure within the literary socialist public sphere. While the 'voice' to emerge from the file clearly adheres to the sectarian rhetoric of SED cultural policy of the 1950s, the information given to the Stasi (for example, about the politically misguided and 'labile' attitudes of other writers) did not differ, in tone or content, from the views she was expressing publicly as a literary critic writing in the mainstream press. Furthermore, although Wolf knowingly took the code name of Margarete, she appears to have written only one report and to have eventually insisted that her meetings with the Stasi take place at her home in the presence of her husband, rather than in a 'conspiratorial apartment,' as was the usual practice. While the latter does not excuse Wolf of anything, the 'normalizing' of the situation (an admitted Stasi strategy) does help explain why Wolf was able to repress any memory of having worked officially as an IM or of the fact that she had a code name. It is also clear from written comments by her interrogators about her excessive 'caution' and 'discretion' that she was not giving them much of what they needed, which may explain why they decided to close her file.

Three years following this episode Wolf was to emerge as an outspoken critic of the regime's domestic policies, and by 1968 the Stasi had opened a 'victim' file on her and her husband, Gerhard, under the code name *Doppelzüngler* [forked tongue] that by 1980 had expanded to forty-two volumes. Wolf discovered the existence of Margarete while reading her victim file in the spring of 1992. The reason she gave for waiting nine months before announcing it publicly had to do with her fear of the witch hunt atmosphere that 'would block rather than promote a debate about the complex reality of the GDR as well as self-critical working through of our experiences in this country.'[11]

GENERATIONAL DIFFERENCES AND THE LANGUAGE OF POWER

While neither Wolf nor Müller were found guilty of the sorts of behavior attributed to Anderson and Schedlinski, there were aspects of all the cases and their aftermath that reopened important issues about the highly complicated and ambivalent status of literary dissidence in the GDR. Indeed, the seemingly oxymoronic notion of a *Stasidichter* [Stasi poet] threw into question the very identity of GDR dissidents as the bearers of a genuine, antifascist alternative to the Stalinist version propagated by the regime. Was it possible to work 'inside' an authoritarian system in any critically viable way? Was there even a credible distinction to be made between 'inside' and 'outside'? What had been the role of language and rhetoric and, metonymically, the poet in defining difference and power?

It is significant that the framing of the discussion around inside and outside, language and power had already emerged in the GDR with the radical disavowal of any working within the system by Prenzlauer Berg poets in the late 1970s. The political role of this group is important, less for its programmatic positions than for the questions these poets asked. As a rhetorical strategy, I stage a debate between the 'older' and 'younger' oppositional generations, loosely defined, as a way of exploring the historical presence of alternative voices within what since 1989 has increasingly come to be characterized as a monolithic, closed society, one devoid of any alterity or disruptive fervor and more totalitarian in some ways than the Third Reich. As the exposition to such a discursive drama and as a summary of major arguments in this book, I briefly outline a history of literary opposition in the GDR as it emerged prior to the 1980s.

In its initial period, GDR literature was centered within the official Party institutions and the discourse of Marxist-Leninism. From 1949 to roughly the middle 1960s, most major and minor writers viewed themselves as integral members and even as spokespeople for the official socialist public sphere. They published in major journals and publishing houses, participated in the state writers organizations, produced their stage and television plays as part of an orchestrated public life. The writer, it was held, spoke as a mediator of social values and served to enlighten and communicate, in an aesthetic medium, policies forged within the higher reaches of the Party hierarchy.

To be sure, even in the 1950s there were 'uncomfortable' writers, such as Peter Huchel, Erich Arendt, Peter Hacks, Heiner Müller, and Günter Kunert, whose aesthetic proclivities or ideological nonconformity challenged or wished to broaden the norms of official aesthetic doctrine. But if these few experimentalists were in any way oppositional, then it was only by virtue of stylistic transgression. They did not consciously question the epistemological premise that linked one's knowledge of reality to the collective reproduction of the system in its entirety. Nor did their view of history contest the notion that the development of industrial production, technology, and science inevitably led to the emancipation of the society as a whole. What they did suggest – and this was the *limit* of their non-conformity – was the necessity for a greater plurality of 'progressive' cultural voices within the body politic: not the end of one-party hegemony, or even the legal guarantee of freedom of speech, but a kinder, gentler articulation of monolithic rule.

The period from the mid-1960s through the Biermann expulsion in 1976 marked a significant turning point in the nature of dissent and opposition among the literati in East Germany. Whereas most writers in the earlier period had sought merely to broaden the framework of debate within a structure of shared ideological values concerning the primacy of production, the inevitability of socialist history, and the validity of proletarian truth, a number of leading writers now began to question those discursive paradigms. At the center of their critique was a repudiation of the instrumental reason guiding official socialist policy. What these writers had begun to understand is the extent to which the *language* of a supposedly progressive, scientifically rationalized, dialectical materialism was irrevocably linked to repressive structures of power in the GDR, and that any genuine struggle for social change would also mean a recasting of the entire value system around which it would cohere.

Perhaps it should not be surprising that intellectuals such as Kunert, Braun, Müller, Wolf, and Morgner, while critical of official ideology, would nevertheless choose to ground their critiques in the language of a deviant Marxism. The first GDR publication of the early writings of Marx in 1968,[12] coupled with growing reference to such unorthodox thinkers as Jean-Paul Sartre, Walter Benjamin, Ernst Bloch, Antonio Gramsci, the Frankfurt School, and even the young Georg Lukács, provided a medium with which to launch an assault from within the framework of Marxism in order to transform the entire tradition itself. Thus the GDR dissidents of the 1970s were caught in the classic aporia of the 'renegade.'[13] Committed to speaking within the ever-shifting boundaries of a permissible public voice, they drew upon a discourse that they hoped would at once be acceptable to and yet subversive of the language of power itself.

It is precisely this symbiotic discursive status that proved so repugnant and unacceptable to the youngest and, as it turns out, last generation of opposition to emerge in the GDR. Born for the most part in the 1950s, which is to say subsequent to the founding of the GDR, the Prenzlauer Berg writers and artists defined themselves in opposition to the older, now established literary generation precisely in terms of what they saw as the latter's naive attempt to fight from within to reform the system.

A strong articulation of this position may be found in an essay by the poet Uwe Kolbe entitled 'Die Heimat der Dissidenten: Nachbemerkungen zum Phantom der DDR-Opposition' (The homeland of dissidents: After-thoughts concerning the phantom of GDR opposition), written after 1989, in which the author bluntly states that there never was an opposition in the GDR. Kolbe compares East German intellectuals to their colleagues in the rest of the Eastern bloc and finds the former wanting in the extreme. While Soviet and Eastern European oppositional writers risked their lives in unequivocating struggle against the system as a whole, often ending up in jails and insane asylums, the East German 'dissident' elite articulated the dream of reform socialism – a utopian third way between Stalinism and capitalism, beyond the existing two-bloc system. In contrast to the genuine 'antisocialist' opposition of a Václav Havel, who precisely because he had refused compromise with the foreign Soviet dictatorship was morally and politically able to unify a postcommunist Czechoslovakia, leading GDR writers unmasked themselves as hopelessly out of touch with the needs of the general populace. Exemplary for Kolbe of such naïveté was Christa Wolf's plea to a downtrodden GDR populace on the very eve of total collapse: 'Help us build a truly democratic society,' she intoned, 'one that will retain the vision of a democratic socialism' (34).

For Kolbe and the other poet dissidents, even the most radical forms of intellectual resistance throughout the postwar GDR cannot be called genuine opposition. This is true of Wolf Biermann, who was prohibited from making public appearances for twelve years and then exiled; or the physicist Robert Havemann, who lived his latter days under house arrest and permanent harassment; or even Jürgen Fuchs and Rudolf Bahro, both of whom were jailed and then exiled into West Germany, Bahro for his book *Die Alternative*, which critiques real existing socialism, and Fuchs for his protest of the Biermann affair. To Kolbe and others, none of these people represent an opposition. The reason for this is very simple: Havemann,

227

Biermann, Fuchs, and Bahro, the writers Brecht, Müller, Wolf, Heym, and
Franz Fühmann, regardless of their physical or mental suffering and despite their desire for fundamental political change, were *dissidents* acting out of a desire to build an alternative form of socialism. Dissidents
then were those who had been excommunicated but remained true to the
Marxist faith. More important for our present analysis, dissidents for
Kolbe were those renegades whose very effort to speak in the language of
the 'faith' at the moment of its greatest corruption lent a powerful legitimacy to the status quo.

In response to Uwe Kolbe, let me reiterate arguments that have been at
the core of this book. The tendency of East German intellectuals to speak
within an alternative Marxist discourse was clearly connected to their
situation vis-à-vis German fascism and the history of the Third Reich.
Whereas other East bloc intellectuals drew upon nationalist and religious
discourses to articulate an anticommunist and/or anti-Soviet form of
resistance, the coupling of nationalism with the ideology and criminality
of Nazism during the Third Reich had effectively foreclosed any move to
such a tradition within German postwar political culture. Seen from this
perspective, the appeal of Marxism for dissident intellectuals in East *and*
West Germany may be viewed historically as a logical means by which
they strove to open up an oppositional discursive space within the frozen
contours of central European cold war culture: in the West, between a
conservative, potentially nationalist anticommunism on the Right, and a
helpless, ultimately apologetic anti-anticommunism on the Left; in the
GDR, between existing forms of Stalinism and a restoration of what were
perceived to be the capitalist conditions that had led to Nazism in the first
place.

In the GDR the turn toward a critical Marxism permitted an incipient
intellectual opposition the means by which to challenge the prevailing
Marxist-Leninist dogmas concerning gender, ecology, freedom of speech,
the role of science, and technological/industrial progress and to do so as
potentially constituent of civil society and within the framework of an
existing socialist public sphere. To that extent, Kolbe is absolutely right
when he borrows the language of ecclesiastical history to label the East
German dissidents *Abtrünnige* [defectors from the faith]. Like Luther,
their original intent was very much a move toward reformation and revi-

sion and not a total abandonment of doctrinal adherence or even a break with the institutional church. And like Luther again, the political consequences of such heresy led them far afield of their imagined political goals. Certainly it was the existence of such a heretical discourse that provided the language and means for public dialogue and that in turn was initially to help galvanize a broadly based civil rights movement around issues of peace, freedom of speech, freedom to worship, juridical due process, ecology, feminism, gay rights, and freedom to assemble. Simply to dismiss the East German literary opposition on the basis of their philosophical roots within a political culture of Marxism or their efforts to work from within is to ignore their *function* within the evolution of a much broader, democratizing process.

Yet having made that point, I would nevertheless maintain that there is more to be learned from pursuing our staged confrontation between the two generations. For what is important about the younger generational poets is precisely the radicality with which this group of intellectuals has stressed the issues of discourse and power for an understanding of the complicated process of political articulation within a system devoid of officially constituted structures of civil society. Their reading of Foucault and Deleuze/Guattari onto the discursive network of real existing, that is to say, real discursive socialism opens up a dimension of the opposition question that forces us to explore more thoroughly issues of complicity and resistance beginning at the level of the speech act itself.

CONTOURS OF ACCOUNTABILITY: MÜLLER AND WOLF TAKE STOCK

Focusing on the question of complicity and speech within the framework of our debate and in the light of Stasi allegations, let us return for a moment to those two authors who because of their fame as writers and as public political personae have most come to represent the paradigm of GDR literary dissidence in its now classical phase: Heiner Müller and Christa Wolf. While the poetic and political voices of Müller and Wolf are different in many significant respects, their shared generational experiences and institutional relations to the state are not. Born in 1929 immediately prior to the Third Reich, Müller and Wolf were socialized under two dictatorships in ways that shaped much of their intellectual and political lives: regardless of any perceived shortcomings, the highly authoritarian forms of GDR antifascism remained for both authors the necessary antidote to what was feared to be a probable return to fascism under conditions of capitalism. Moreover, both saw their work develop into increasingly critical and even dangerously confrontational exchanges with the status quo.

Following 1989, Müller and Wolf both published 'autobiographical' works that sought to explore that inchoate subliminal region of social life where an individual self and the power of the state become proximate; where the political as a language of being is imbibed and reinvented in the struggle to constitute a separate identity or even to justify one's location within a set of conflicting and not easily observable political coordinates. In both these texts, one 'fictional' (Wolf) and the other in the form of staged self-interviews (Müller), the issue of the poet and the Stasi re-emerges at a deeper register as the question concerning the extent to which one is able to trace in memory and through language the contours of accountability in relation to a state and a Party with which one is at once profoundly at odds and deeply entangled – and whose absent presence after unification continued to provide the defining framework for political self-understanding.

In Müller's *Krieg ohne Schlacht: Leben in zwei Diktaturen* (War without battle: Life under two dictatorships), the 'voice' of the author appears at times almost compulsively driven to explain its relationship to the ruling elite and the reasons for having preferred to stay in the GDR. 'Partisan commitment to the GDR was connected to Brecht,' he says emphatically. 'Brecht was the legitimation for why one could be for the GDR . . . a proof for the superiority of the system was its better literature. I never thought about leaving.'[14] As articulated here, Müller's choice to stay in the GDR does not emanate from a set of political beliefs or social values. Whereas writers such as Franz Fühmann, Christa Wolf, Stefan Hermlin, and Günter Kunert often stressed how the moral authority of an antifascist leadership that had actually engaged in the struggle against Nazism had provided the basis for their initial commitment to the GDR, for Müller the dramatist the GDR supplied *Erfahrungsdruck* [pressure of experience] for his production of literature:

Living in the GDR was above all living in a material. It's like architecture, architecture also has more to do with the state than painting does, and drama also has more to do with the state than other literary genres. Here there's a particular relationship to power, a fascination with power, a rubbing up against power and taking part in power, even perhaps submitting oneself to power in order to take part. . . . For a dramatist a dictatorship is more colorful than life in a democracy. (113)

Several points emerge in the above citation that are significant for understanding Müller's own highly dramatized, intensely performative relationship to the GDR. First, the playwright's elaborate representation of the premodern, semifeudal, even Elizabethan conditions of real existing socialist dictatorship, familiar enough from the highly allegorical staging of his own version of *Macbeth* in 1982, unfolds an almost physically erotic relationship to 'power,' revealing much about its seductive pull on intellectuals, particularly male intellectuals, in the GDR. Müller also contrasts the fate of the socialist writer to the less 'colorful' life of a writer under capitalist liberal democracy, whose market-mediated relationship to the status quo operates within a highly insulated buffer zone in relation to the state. In the GDR, writers were more vulnerable precisely because of their proximity to power. This is not, of course, due to any disposition over the means of state security or their participation in political decision making; rather, it stemmed from the importance of the role writers played in generating a language of legitimation. Given the accelerating devaluation of official ideology as a means for constituting political consensus in the 1970s, the writer in the GDR became increasingly vital as a medium for the creation of 'authentic' speech in a world of nonspeech. Indeed, it was precisely within this area of a growing discursive power vacuum that literary discourse was able to provide what for Müller becomes an erogenous zone within the interstices of power; a place, in his own highly metaphorical formulation, where poet and power 'rub up' against one another, where one 'submits oneself in order to take part.'

If the sensual gratification of cavorting with state power provided titillation at times, the direct and altogether personal violence of state oppression also delivered the terror, and thereby the 'material,' for Müller's work as a professional dramatist. His emphasis upon the priority of mate-

rial over political attitude or moral stance as the starting point for his production as a thinker and writer appears repeatedly throughout his other
autobiographical writings and is a familiar theme in much of his work.
For instance, asked about his fascination with the archconservative Carl
Schmitt, Müller replies: 'Carl Schmitt is theater. His texts are performances. I am not interested in whether he is right or not' (272). Similarly,
in response to a question concerning Ernst Jünger receiving the Goethe
prize in 1982 we are told that 'for me Jünger was never a hero . . . I am
interested in his literature. I can't read things morally, just as I can't write
morally' (281).

Müller's theory of an aesthetics of material is basic to his self-understanding as a political artist. Like Brecht, who preferred the 'bourgeois'
works of Franz Kafka and the Expressionist Georg Kaiser to the political
correctness of nineteenth-century naturalism or even socialist realism,
Müller too claims to be drawn by properties inherent to the solution
of formal aesthetic problems; by their performative dimension, rather
than any overriding interest in the political or philosophical views of the
authors.

Particularly revealing in this regard are the comments he makes about
his major clash with the Party around the production of his play *Die
Umsiedlerin* in 1961. Müller's dramatic depiction of the brutal and anarchic collectivization campaign in the province of Mecklenburg (which
premiered in most untimely fashion four weeks subsequent to the building of the Wall) so infuriated the Party that the production was canceled
after one performance and Müller himself expelled from the official writers union and denied publication rights in the GDR. What becomes significant in Müller's autobiographical recounting of the events is not the severity of the punishment or even the cowardice of his literary colleagues,
many of whom denounced him publicly and almost all of whom, with the
exception of Peter Hacks and Hans Bunge, voted for his expulsion. Far
more striking is Müller's description of how he subsequently stood before
his colleagues to practice self-criticism:

> I looked at the whole thing as dramatic material, I myself was also
> material, my self-criticism is material for me. It was a mistake to
> believe that I was a political writer. (183)

It definitely had an aspect of the theater about it, how people simply walked right by me without saying hello. I was not hurt by that, I observed the whole thing with detached interest. (181).

At one level, the voice of the text can be rightfully accused of massive denial, topped off with a touch of apologetics. Faced initially with the full terror of the state, Müller's subsequent narration of the events resorts to self-aggrandizing, ironic distance, at once stylizing himself performatively as above the fear and shame of the moment, but also playing down the fact that other writers had ended up in jail for far lesser 'crimes.'

Yet what we also see in the above is the extent to which Müller's 'erotic' relationship to the state indeed derived from his being permitted to perform and take part; from being provided the truly dramatic material of what was a moment of extreme humiliation for himself and the entire literary community. Moreover, as is obvious from the text of his self-criticism, which he still refuses to disavow, this was born precisely out of his strong bond to the system: 'I wanted to write a play that would be useful for socialism . . . My wish was a hard discussion. A discussion that would help me to keep working on a higher plane, more than before, better than before, productively.'[15] In his subsequent twenty-eight years in the GDR, Heiner Müller's position was never really to change. He remained to the very end, as he acknowledged when confronted with the Stasi allegations, dedicated to dialogue. Paradoxically, however, it was always his unsuccessful efforts to achieve a genuine dialogue with power – and the 'material' such failures and humiliation provided him as a performer of his own abjection – that kept him 'working on a higher plane.' What better source for his hapless representation of intellectuals in such figures as the young Frederick the Great or Hamlet in *Hamletmachine*? And what better testimony to his own *discursive* seduction to power than Müller's anecdotal insight into the fate of socialist renegade intellectuals from Bukharin down to the author himself?

If a criminal is blamed for something unfairly he will not refute it, he simply says nothing. An intellectual, on the other hand, can't hold back if he is blamed for something unfairly. He can't stop himself from disagreeing. And at that moment he joins the game/play [*Spiel*], the dialogue begins, and you've got him. An intellectual al-

233

ways wants to play a part, all you have to do is offer him a part. That is the point about Bukharin, the point about the Moscow Trials. That's how you get an intellectual. A criminal knows better. (184)

That, unfortunately, is not the only point about the Moscow Show Trials, where the raw savagery of Soviet state power and Stalinist paranoia simply ground up any form of 'participation,' regardless of individual attitudes concerning dialogue or criminality. But it is, interestingly, a most revealing confessional point about Müller himself, as well as others of his generation. For in fact, the double bind of many GDR intellectuals lay very much in their inability to accept themselves as having been criminalized. The most profound forms of public mistreatment and humiliation were viewed by many right to the very end as part of a dialogic process in which the powers that be might be brought to see the error of *their* ways.

Christa Wolf's first post-Wall publication reveals a similar narrative compulsion. In *Was bleibt*, written about a time of crisis between the exile of Wolf Biermann in 1976 and the expulsion of other authors from the writers union in 1979, Wolf portrays a day in the life of a female author being observed by the Stasi: three uniformed men sit in a car in front of her house, ostentatiously watching and waiting. In the highly volatile post-Wall atmosphere in which it appeared, this work was either criticized for its self-serving glorification of Wolf herself as victim, or it was praised as posing 'a radical critique of real existing socialism.'[16] As Herbert Lehnert has rightly argued, certainly any blanket identification of Christa Wolf with the central figure ignores the obvious 'fictionality' of the text and leads to a distorted reading of the story itself.[17]

Of interest to me is less the question of the text's 'critical' attitude toward the state, although clearly that is a theme of the book, than what it reveals about the narrator/writer's tortured struggle to situate herself – cognitively, emotionally, psychically – in relation to a system within which she is both willing participant and an object of ostracism. In my view this text is not concerned at all with establishing complicity or resistance; with whether the writer is a fellow traveler or a victim of persecution. What it seeks instead is to confront the *already* internalized discursive 'system' as a functioning and invasive presence in the mental processes of *this* intellectual's everyday life.

Wolf presents the phenomenology of surveillance as a process of shared communication. If Foucault's panoptic eye registers the power of the look as one-sided, epistemological upper-hand, in *Was bleibt* the viewer/Stasi is also the viewed: 'And so I stood, as I did every morning, behind the curtain that had been put there so that I could hide behind it, stood and looked, I hoped unseen, across to the parking place on the other side of the Friedrichstraße. . . . By the way, they weren't there.'[18] This is a game of cat and mouse, played out within a regime of domesticated terror, told by a narrator/author who must perforce deny the full implications of the violence unfolding before and within her. One night the 'victim' flashes a light in the window in an attempt to signal her pursuers, 'whereupon they blinked their car lights three times in return. They had a sense of humor. We went to bed that night a little more relaxed, a little less intimidated' (20). On other occasions, the narrator/author catches herself wanting to bring them hot tea (19); or not wishing to demonize the 'three gentlemen' by thinking of them in 'leather coats' (18); or simply boastful of the fact that from her window above she is able to notice a balding spot on one of the officers, 'even before his own wife might have, who has never gotten a chance to view him from this angle' (16).

This narrative compulsion to domesticate and dedemonize is significant, because it shifts the focus from a simple depiction of victim and victimizer to the more complicated question concerning the victim's own *investment* as speaker and actor in the social text. This work explores the fragile fault lines binding and separating the self in relation to an apparatus with which the central figure had once considered herself at one. The story's internal dialogue entails a struggle to press against the truth of an author's persecution and what an acceptance of that truth would mean for her own political and moral identity/ies. Her desire to understand and even nurture her oppressors, converse with them about the weather and their family life, her 'shameful need to get along with any kind of people' (20) give startling voice to the gendered mechanisms of internalization and rationalization that have *self-admittedly* hindered the acquisition of a new 'language that is there in my ear, but not yet on my tongue' (7).

Rather than a record of repression, this is the search for 'another' voice as a means for finding another self. If her story begins with anxieties concerning the Stasi sitting in front of the house, the centerpiece of this work is the struggle to come to terms with the Stasi within. In a 1974 interview, Wolf spoke of the 'mechanism of self-censorship' as more dangerous than the official censor, 'for it internalizes constraints which can hinder the birth of literature' and 'entangles an author in mutually exclusive demands.'[19] *Was bleibt* radicalizes and works through this insight performatively in a fictional internal dialogue among competing voices of the self, one of which is her 'self-censor' (52) (now serving as her *better* self rather than as a 'mechanism' of outer control), whom she intermittently calls 'Judge,' 'Partner,' and 'Companion.' 'Incensed I demanded to know who had placed him [the Companion] there and he answered calmly: you yourself sister' (56–57). The succeeding passage brings us to the nexus of inner and outer forms of censorship and control: 'I myself. It took me a long time to get beyond those two words. I myself. Which of the multiple beings, of which "I myself" constructed me? The one that wanted to know itself? The one that protected itself? Or that third one, that was always tempted to dance to the same tune as the young gentleman out there in front of my door?' (57). By splitting the 'I,' the narrator deconstructs a single self and with it the authority of 'that third one always tempted to dance to the same tune,' and does so as a prerequisite for moving forward. The acknowledgment of a fragmented, multiple identity, once the marker of an alienated being, now provides the regenerative terrain for discursive renewal.

In their 'autobiographical' works, Heiner Müller and Christa Wolf have sought to confront the rhetorical and dialogic grounds of the writer's relationship to the state. Müller's self-stylization as cynical performer in the drama of his own abjection would seem a distant cry from Wolf's depiction of a highly personal, tentatively groping struggle to extract oneself from / extract from oneself 'that third one [*jenen Dritten*]' (57). What links the two, however, is an effort to explore the extent to which separation / opposition of self had to begin in dialogue with and even subjection to the (internalized) powers that be. It also confirms even as it challenges the radical critique by the Prenzlauer Berg poets of the older dissidents.

PRENZLAUER BERG AND BEYOND

What then would be a 'genuine' opposition in the eyes of the newest generation? In her preface to the poetry anthology of young writers from the Prenzlauer Berg subculture entitled *Berührung ist nur eine Rander-*

scheinung (Touching is only a marginal thing), Elke Erb articulates what amounts to a manifesto concerning the younger generation vis-à-vis their elders, one that proves helpful for understanding the self-declared differences between the two:

> The new literature reflects a social consciousness that no longer wants or is even able to be the object of an inherited civilization. . . . They [the authors] refuse to be infantilized by its utopian contents and they resist its compromises. Nor are they seduced into feckless criticism and confrontation. Their social maturity is the result of a total withdrawal [*Austritt*] from the authoritarian system, an absolute release from the tutelage of subordinated meanings.[20]

The 'maturity' of the Prenzlauer Berg poets, in Erb's definition, reverses the Freudian-inspired paradigm whereby emotional and political sovereignty would occur through internalization, in all of its dialectical complexity, of the ideological superego. Whereas the elders like Wolf, Müller, Heym, and Biermann remain 'infantilized' by their compromisings with the socialist *Vater-Staat* as well as through their adherence to the telos of a utopian *Geschichtsphilosophie* [philosophy of history], the young ones dare to stage their *Vatermord* not as an act of aggression, but rather as an evacuation from any kind of historical continuity or paternal heritage: no confrontation, no shared linguistic space, no Hegelian *Aufhebung*. 'I attempted not to live in this system,' says Sascha Anderson in his notorious interview in *Die Zeit.* 'Perhaps it was wrong, but it was a kind of defence [*Abwehr*].'[21] Schedlinski describes this relationship narcissistically in terms suggesting a kind of Habermasian uncoupling of system and *Lebenswelt*: 'What the others do does not interest me, what my friends think is important.'

Central to this construction of an autonomous second culture, one that is oblivious to and disdainful of all state institutions, was the priority attributed to a critique of language as a *prerequisite* for a critique of social and ideological structures. In contradistinction to the older dissident writers who were said to labor in 'the web of public lies [das Gespinst der öffentlichen Lüge],'[22] the Prenzlauer Berg poets saw themselves driven to the margins of society, *outside* the 'dictatorship of linguistic simulations' and immune to the conventions of a language that bind the speaker 'to a hermetic discourse, robbing him/her of the freedom of his/her senses.'[23] Only a language free from the clichés of ideological polarities, a language, finally, in close proximity to the material 'thingness' of things, can break the vicious circularity of discursive oppression. Gert Neumann's notion of 'clandestine' speech, a poetics of silence speaking between the signs, at once signals the absolute bankruptcy of the language of power while claiming to restore and reconnect a relationship between language and truth, public and private speech.[24]

Having established the premises of the linguistic critique emerging from the younger generation, let us return now to our staged debate and to the question concerning literary opposition as it emerged in the GDR of the 1970s and 1980s. First, it is clear, at one level, that what the Prenzlauer Berg poets were able to see and thematize in both their theory and their poetry – in a way that Müller, Wolf, Hein, and others were not – was the extent to which the decay of ideology [*Ideologieverfall*] had severely discredited *any* form of Marxism as a positioned discourse of opposition. This is not to underestimate the important role of the socialist literary opposition historically, nor does it ignore the significance of their own 'poetic speech' as a locus of authentic alterity. Rather, it recognizes the extent to which the ultimately *symbiotic* relationship of this inner opposition to the central powers substantially inhibited writers like Wolf, Heym, Braun, and even Christoph Hein from *actively* calling for modes of reform that lay outside of or at ideological variance with the normative discourse of socialist institutional life: for the abolition of censorship, for a multiparty system, for a genuinely representative parliament, for total freedom of speech, for the institution of civil society.

As a second point, it is also the case that the linguistic turn within the 'Prenzlauer Berg connection' (Endler) made them far more sensitive to the bipolar deep structures of a classically articulated, dialectical discourse and its potential for communicating beyond or even in contradiction to what it thinks it is communicating. Schedlinski's essay about the 'dilemma of the Enlightenment' presents us with an elaborate critique of what he calls 'the enlightened discourse of protest [der aufklärerisch-protestie-rende Diskurs],' which in his view is always limited to articulating what the ruling discourse has always already been silent about – and for that reason is always contained as a mirror reflection of a higher discursive power.[25] The young poet offers an incisive, indeed brilliant linguistic variation on Marcuse's somewhat shopworn theory of repressive tolerance, turning it now against socialist as well as capitalist forms of discursive control. Significantly, he also reveals in his rhetorical turns a fundamental dislocation lying at the heart of the younger poetic credo.

What intrigues me about the Prenzlauer Berg poets is not that they claimed to be the only real opposition in the GDR while simultaneously some of their leadership was consorting with the Stasi. It is clear that most members of this group were *not* involved in IM activities, and the evidence does not show, as some journalists were wont to argue, that the Stasi completely controlled or corrupted the poets' activities.[26] Of far greater importance is the contradiction at the very basis of their notion of what it means to launch an opposition in the first place. On the one hand, they ridicule the older generation for believing in confrontational dialogue and, employing a discourse theory rooted in French poststructuralism, present a 'radical' critique of the 'encrastic' (Barthes) language and metanarratives (Lyotard) of the socialist status quo and its power to subvert any potential resistance. In accordance with this position and in agreement with Foucault, there is no such thing as a linguistic Archimedean point outside of or marginal to a dominant discourse from which to speak the 'truth.' Any discourse, regardless of its intention or political gesture, is situated necessarily within the interstices of power. It is through language and language alone that one is interpolated into the system. The poet Stefan Döring makes this abundantly clear when he says: 'Durch die Sprache wird Person erzogen, hat man die Sprache gefressen, dann auch die Ordnung [People are formed by language – if one has devoured the language, then one has eaten the order as well]'.[27]

Yet as much as these poets go beyond the linguistic innocence of the older generation (which in their eyes still clung to the possibility of an 'enlightened discourse of protest'), their own self-stylizations reveal them asserting nolens volens the viability of a self-conscious, autonomous, subject-centered, indeed Archimedean locus outside of the dominant discourse and within which to develop an 'authentic' language. When Gerhard Wolf and Elke Erb, both GDR poet-critics from the older generation, wax euphoric about this 'second culture,' which 'as an independent artistic movement'[28] had seemingly transcended the confines of a feckless clinch with the SED power structure, they are not just projecting themselves as an older generation that has been worn down by their own failures of resistance. They represent as well the illusions of the upstarts, who in stylizing their poetic struggles into the status of the 'Outcast,'[29] have repressed the basic insight of their own highly theorized experience: that there is no such thing as the absolute outside, spatially or linguistically.

If we examine the actual function of the Prenzlauer Berg poets, we see that the forms of revolt are positioned in an obvious contextual relationship to the prevailing discourse, as well as to the institutionalized formations of power in the GDR. For example, as a result of their proliferating modes of distribution and performance, these poets were able to create a counterpublic sphere that, while tolerated and even infiltrated by the Stasi, nevertheless marked out a powerful cultural articulation precisely as a response to what they viewed as 'the one-dimensionality of the prevailing discourse' in the GDR.[30] Underground journals such as *Mikado, UND, SCHADEN,* and *ariadnefabrik* were integrated into an emerging network of semipublic (unofficial) readings, exhibitions, film showings, concerts, cabarets, performances, etc., that saw itself as an expression of a new kind of 'autarkic urban feeling':[31] an assertion of 'autonomy,' 'authenticity,' and 'critical life practice' that became 'a resistance against and at the same time a contradictory product of a centralized, administered, and increasingly alienated public sphere.'[32] This contradictory dimension is important. Clearly these poets' *sense* of autonomy provided an important impetus to an organizational formation that, while thoroughly under the surveillance of the security apparatus, nevertheless was able to self-define a cultural position within the breakdown of cultural legitimacy as a whole. The official decision to tolerate (i.e., not repress) such activities was simply the other side of a growing helplessness on the part of the regime to itself negotiate satisfactory modes of productive culture within a deteriorating state apparatus.

But even at the level of poetic utterance, the Prenzlauer Berg poets were in dialogue, regardless of their disavowal of any participatory role within what they disparagingly called a *Gesprächskultur* [culture of conversation]. Despite Gert Neumann's articulated refusal to speak, his call for a 'language of nonpower' and a 'voice of silence' *spoke* nevertheless from within and against a culture in which 'conversations take place, in order to numb thought.'[33] Michael Thulin's insightful analysis of a 'critique of language' as 'counter-culture' catalogs a manifesto of the various 'intentions' driving what he would even call the 'language critical school of Prenzlauer Berg Berlin/DDR": these poets are against 'the false appearance of linguistic continuity,' 'the everyday language of power,' 'the authoritarian institution of meaning,' and so on.[34]

Even a language of silence, it would seem, must define itself against the distorted discursive system that has necessitated it. In this regard the position of the younger generation poets remained a paradox. Their failure to accept the essentially contextual and ultimately political relationship between poet and state led to dangerous naïveté on the part of those who wanted to resist the state by claiming to ignore it. Conversely, their aggressive *Sprachkritik* profoundly understood the extent to which 'all social norms are at the same time norms of language'[35] and in so doing had much to say to a generation of older writers struggling to reach, in Christa Wolf's terms, 'a language that is there in my ear, but not yet on my tongue.'

Our image of the Stasi as *Krake* at the outset of this epilogue served metaphorically to conjure up a post-Wall GDR body politic released from the grasp of a dying organism and subject to the slow, painful process of social and political renewal. Important about such a reading for the present analysis was less a notion of the Stasi as evil incarnate, as was often enunciated in the Western press, than what such an image communicated about the all-embracing, thoroughly internalized nature of social control under the conditions of a modern society. The Foucaultian panoptic society has been vastly outdone, it would seem, by a social organization in which there can be no pristine, 'outside' subject whose body and mind might elude the grasp (or the gaze?) of political involvement. The fact that oft-proclaimed dissident writers, many of whom saw themselves at varying 'odds' with the status quo, were nevertheless found implicated *discursively* in the workings of the system contains an important lesson about the immanent nature of any relationship in that society. Certainly such an insight has been central to the argument of this book. The activities of individual oppositional writers of any generation in the GDR must be judged in light of the historical context from which they spoke. The powers of their speech were always part of a double-edged evolutionary process: on the one hand, they were the enabled voice of a self-legitimating status quo; at the same time, they sought to articulate, from within the interstices of official language and power relationships, the challenge to a repressive system. Like language itself, this system will release its hold not through a single act of revolutionary rupture or conscious renewal but by means of a gradual working through of its forty-year experience over time. Certainly GDR writers of all generations will continue to play a role in any such process.

NOTES

INTRODUCTION: THE POWERS OF SPEECH

1. In addition to the writers Christoph Hein, Stefan Heym, Christa Wolf, and Heiner Müller, other speakers included the well-known lawyer Gregor Gysi, later first party secretary of the SED; Markus Wolf, former general in the Ministry for State Security; Günter Schabowski, head of the SED in Berlin; and Pastor Friedrich Schorlemmer, a leading figure in the oppositional movement.

2. See *die tageszeitung*, 11 November 1989, for speeches by Christoph Hein, Stefan Heym, and Christa Wolf.

3. *die tageszeitung*, 26 November 1989.

4. See Schirrmacher, ' "Dem Druck des härteren, strengeren Lebens standhalten" '; Greiner, 'Was bleibt? Bleibt was?'

5. For anthologies of articles dealing with the debate, see Deiritz and Krauss, eds., *Der deutsch-deutsche Literaturstreit*; Anz, ed., *Es geht nicht*; and *New German Critique* 52 (1991).

6. For the views of exiled GDR writers living in the West who were extremely critical of the writers who remained, refuting the notion that they in any way helped prepare the way for the October Revolution, see Schneider, 'Das Ende der Kunst?'; Maron, 'Die Schriftsteller und das Volk'; and Schädlich, 'Tanz im Ketten.' Schädlich characterizes GDR writers as performing 'literary acrobatics . . . in order to help the rulers rule.'

7. Schneider, *The German Comedy*, 78.

8. See note 4.

9. See, in particular, Schirrmacher, 'Abschied von der Literatur'; Greiner, 'Die deutsche Gesinnungsästhetik'; and Bohrer, 'Kulturschutzgebiet der DDR.'

10. The term 'repressive tolerance' was coined by Herbert Marcuse in order to describe how capitalist democracies make use of freedom of speech as a way of obfuscating their practices of economic and imperialist repression. See Marcuse, 'Repressive Tolerance.'

11. Tökes, *Dissent in the USSR*, 24–25

12. Stone, 'The Sakharov Campaign,' 3.

13. De Bruyn, 'On the German Cultural Nation,' 60.

14. Günter Grass has argued forcibly, before and after the fall of the Wall, for the acknowledgment of two German states but one German *Kulturnation*. Moreover, in light of the increased interest in GDR literature in the West during the 1970s, both Fritz Raddatz and Hans Mayer came to disavow their earlier asser-

243

tions that there were two culturally and politically distinct German litera-
tures: Mayer, 'Stationen der deutschen Literatur,' and Raddatz, 'Gedanken zur
Nationalliteratur.'

15. In 'Whose German Literature?' Herminghouse argues that the move toward
cultural unity must be seen as the Federal Republic recognizing the statehood
of the GDR and thereby renouncing its claim to sole representation of German
nationhood: 'In diminishing its insistence on unification as a political nation,
the Federal Republic shifted its emphasis to the maintenance of a more subjective sense of cultural unity by moving toward intensification of intra-
German cultural relations' (7). While clearly there was a shift in policy within
the 'Federal Republic,' one should not lose sight of what such a liberalizing
rapprochement meant in terms of a challenge to more conservative notions of
Kultur and aesthetic autonomy still very much a part of West German cultural
politics. It was this latter position that was to emerge with such force in the
Christa Wolf debate.

16. See my 'Crossing Borders.'

17. Reich-Ranicki, *Zur Literatur der DDR*. This book consists of a collection of
essays written between 1963 and 1973, most of them for *Die Zeit*, in which the
author explores GDR authors in light of 'commonality' and 'separation.' It
should also be mentioned that in 1987 Reich-Ranicki was extremely critical
of Christa Wolf for her remarks about the Federal Republic made during a
speech presenting Thomas Brasch with the Kleist prize. At that time he spoke
disparagingly of her as a 'provincial' writer who had only produced one major
work (*The Quest for Christa T*). Reich-Ranicki, 'Macht Verfolgung kreativ?'

18. Dubiel, 'Linke Trauerarbeit,' 484.

19. Dubiel's formulation of a mourning as critique is helpful here: 'The fact that
an ersatz candidate for a comprehensive alternative socialist politics [*Ord-
nungspolitik*] is not available, that the transformation to a noncapitalist condition can no longer be conceived within the framework of a revolutionary
rupture, that every structural reorganization of society must be accepted by
people who are motivated in complex ways and oriented toward pluralism,
that there is no metapolitical guarantee of civilizing regression and that questions of ecology and gender have a dimension of their own are all part of the
thinking that the Left must first have internalized if their phantasy wishes to
be free again for a new project' (ibid., 489–90).

20. For a critique of Dubiel's application of Alexander and Margarethe Mitscherlich's 'inability to mourn model' to the GDR, see Jay, 'Once More an Inability to
Mourn,' where he writes: 'Whereas it was easy for the Mitscherlichs to identify
the unmourned lost object of the post-Nazi era with the figure of Hitler, in the

case of left-liberal attachment to the GDR, no such clear-cut equivalent is apparent' (74).

21. *Hineingeboren* [simply born into] is a phrase used to characterize the attitude of a generation of GDR writers born after 1950 and derives from a collection of poetry by Uwe Kolbe entitled *Hineingeboren*.

22. Müller, interview 'Jetzt ist da eine Einheitssoße,' 141.

23. Kunert, interview, 208–9.

24. Wolf, *Im Dialog*, 136.

25. Fühmann, 'Zweiundzwanzig Tage,' 478.

26. Quoted in Emmerich, *Kleine Literaturgeschichte der DDR* (1981), 207–8.

27. Kohlhaase, *die tageszeitung*.

28. Ludz, *Mechanismen der Herrschaftssicherung*, 9.

29. Clark, *The Soviet Novel*, xiii.

30. See Emmerich, 'Affirmation – Utopie – Melancholie,' 332–35.

31. See Emmerich, *Kleine Literaturgeschichte der DDR* (1989); Fischbach, ed., *Literaturpolitik*; Mayer-Burger, *Entwicklung*.

32. Cf. Raddatz, *Traditionen und Tendenzen*.

33. See Jäger, *Sozialliteraten*.

34. See Köhler-Hausmann, *Literaturbetrieb*; Rüther, ed., *Kulturbetrieb*.

35. Cf. Grunenberg, *Aufbruch der inneren Mauer*; Hanke, *Alltag und Politik*; Helwig, *Die DDR- Gesellschaft*.

36. LaCapra, *Rethinking Intellectual History*, 19.

37. See chap. 8.

38. Zima, 'Der Mythos der Monosemie,' 78.

39. Foucault speaks of 'those forms of discourse that lie at the origins of a certain number of new verbal acts, which are reiterated, transformed or discussed' (*The Archaeology of Knowledge*, 220).

40. White, *Metahistory*.

41. See Bhabha, ed., *Nation and Narration* for a helpful study that sees nation as 'an agency of *ambivalent* narration that holds culture as its most productive position' (3). Also important is Anderson, *Imagined Communities*.

42. Key in this regard was Erich Honecker's incarceration by the Nazis in the Brandenburg-Görden jail from 1937 to 1945. It has been often mentioned that the dissident physicist Robert Havemann was also in Brandenburg-Görden at the same time. See Lippmann, *Honecker*, 31–40.

43. The phrase 'master plot' is used by Katerina Clark to define the emergence of a narrative formula basic to the Soviet novel of the 1930s. The 'shaping pattern' she describes is not 'invented' or simply imposed from above as an edict of socialist realist policy but rather emerges from a number of different political

and cultural sources: 'One cannot analyze either the dynamic of the master plot's evolution or the meanings of its formulaic components without looking at its relations both to politics and ideology, on the one hand, and to literary traditions on the other' (*The Soviet Novel*, 6).

44. Emmerich, 'Affirmation – Utopie – Melancholie,' 334. While I fail to find a clearly delineated concept of 'counterdiscourse' or 'countertext' in the writings of Foucault, there is certainly a recognition of the importance of such modernist sensibilities as Nietzsche, Bataille, and Artaud as writers who destabilize.

45. See Nägele, 'Trauer, Tropen and Phantasmen,' for an interesting treatment of this 'genre' and its importance as a means of political disruption.

46. Berendse, *Die 'Sächsische Dichterschule*,' 4.

47. See chap. 2.

48. See Antonia Grunenberg's excellent article 'In den Räumen der Sprache,' where she writes about Neumann and other poets 'suffering because of language and because of the unbridgeable difference between signifikant and signifikat' (208).

49. Thulin, 'Sprache und Sprachkritik,' 234.

50. Grunenberg, 'In den Räumen der Sprache,' 207.

51. Schedlinski, *die arroganz der ohnmacht*, 7.

52. Kolbe, 'Die Heimat der Dissidenten,' 33–39.

53. Not accidentally, the anthology of essays on and by the young poets edited by Heinz Ludwig Arnold was entitled 'The Other Language: New GDR Literature of the 1980s.'

54. Wolf, 'gegen sprache mit sprache / mit-sprache gegen-sprache,' 15–25.

55. See chap. 9.

56. Schirrmacher, 'Verdacht und Verrat.'

57. Greiner, 'Die Falle des Entweder-Oder.'

58. Antonia Grunenberg has argued that a large part of the literature to emerge in the 1970s and 1980s 'was as far from socialist realism as the author of *Cassandra* was from Eugene Marlitt' (*Aufbruch der inneren Mauer*, 220).

59. See Emmerich, 'Gleichzeitigkeit.'

CHAPTER 1: THE WRITER AND THE PUBLIC SPHERE

1. An open letter to the Central Committee of the SED was submitted to *Neues Deutschland*, Reuters, and France Presse protesting the expatriation of Biermann. The letter was never published in the GDR but received wide distribution in the West. This document was initially signed by Sarah Kirsch, Christa Wolf, Volker Braun, Franz Fühmann, Stephan Hermlin, Stefan Heym, Günter

Kunert, Heiner Müller, Rolf Schneider, Gerhard Wolf, Jurek Becker, Rainer Kirsch, Günter de Bruyn, Erich Arendt, Fritz Cremer, and Eckehard Schall. The latter two, together with Volker Braun, withdrew their signatures later but did not disassociate themselves from the contents of the letter. For 'documentations' of the events, see *Deutschland Archiv* 12, no. 9; Mytze, 'Über Wolf Biermann'; Roos, *Exil;* and *New German Critique* 10 (Winter 1977).

2. For an English language version of the petition, see Woods, *Opposition in the GDR*, 139.

3. Although living standards lagged behind those of the Federal Republic, between 1960 and 1970 the proportion of GDR households with a television set rose from 17 percent to 69 percent, those who possessed a refrigerator from 6 percent to 56 percent, and those owning a washing machine from 6 percent to 54 percent. Staritz, *Geschichte der DDR*, 166.

4. See Sodaro, 'Limits to Dissent in the GDR,' where he argues that 'the SED's relative success in maintaining the social contract with GDR citizens has probably been the most decisive element preventing the development of acute social discontent' (199). What this argument fails to grasp is the extent to which the 'social contract' entailed pricing policies and structural changes that inevitably *increased* pressures over the long run for continued modernization.

5. For a discussion of the 'increased functional importance in the unfolding of the advanced socialist society [of the] East German *Intelligenz*,' see 'Intellectuals and System Change.'

6. See Ludz, *The Changing Party Elite*, who argues for the importance of an 'institutionalized counterelite,' which he saw emerging in the GDR as a result of the development of highly technical and scientific areas of the economy. Others, such as Baylis, *The Technical Intelligentsia* (73–82), have argued that the managerial revolution is at best a gradual and conformist one. My argument is a much more general emphasis upon the impact of developing 'knowledge industries' on increasing demands for freedom of speech.

7. Gerstenmeier, *The Voices of the Silent*, 493–504.

8. It is significant that in the oppositional movements, the Czech playwright Vačlev Havel and the GDR conductor Kurt Masur played key organizational roles as trusted spokespeople at particularly delicate transitional moments.

9. Elections to the Volkskammer were designed so as to limit the voters' choice to accepting or rejecting a single list of candidates drawn up by the National Front, a body that acknowledged the leading role of the SED. Although the SED only had 127 of the 550 seats, the fact that many of the members of the Volkskammer, such as trade unions and the FDJ, were also SED members guaranteed the SED an indirect majority. For a discussion of the 'official East German

view' of such issues as 'opposition,' 'democratic centralism,' and 'public criticism,' see Woods, *Opposition in the* GDR, particularly the initial section of the introduction (3–7) as well as the documents on the 'official East German view' (75–88).

10. For a thorough discussion of GDR agricultural policies prior to the building of the Wall, see Tümler, Mertel, and Blum, *Die Agrarpolitik;* Immler, *Agrarpolitik in der DDR.*

11. Quoted in *DDR Handbuch*, 593.

12. See Süss, 'Revolution und Öffentlichkeit,' 907–25.

13. Süss, 'Revolution und Öffentlichkeit,' 911.

14. In his *die arroganz der ohnmacht* Schedlinski discusses the extent to which oppositional discourse in the GDR was controlled and in part created by the West German media, thus robbing the East Germans of any potentially indigenous 'second language' (28–29).

15. For a detailed treatment of the institutional structure of literary production, distribution, and reception in the GDR, see Köhler-Hausmann, *Literaturbetrieb,* 81–144.

16. Becher, *Von der Größe unserer Literatur,* 276.

17. Quoted in Schubbe, ed., *Dokumente zur Kunst-, Literatur- und Kulturpolitik der SED,* 236.

18. Brecht, 'The Solution,' 440.

19. Darnton, *Berlin Journal,* 204. See also Wichner and Wiesner, eds., *Ausstellungsbuch,* for examples and discussions of individual cases of censorship in the GDR based on an exhibition entitled 'Censorship in the German Democratic Republic: History, Practice and "Aesthetic" of the Hindrance of Literature' held at the Literaturhaus in Berlin from 17 March to 1 May 1991.

20. Joho, 'Das hohe Ziel,' 18.

21. For more detailed and recent statistical information on the publication of 'best-sellers' in the GDR, see Köhler-Hausmann, *Literaturbetrieb,* 81–94.

22. Wolf, interview (1974), 102.

23. The attack upon Christa Wolf by Ulrich Greiner in the aftermath of the opening up of GDR borders stressed above all the overly 'subjective' and therefore ultimately apologetic nature of her writerly 'tone.' Greiner, 'Mangel an Feingefühl.'

24. Braun, discussion, 79.

25. Kant, 'Unsere Worte wirken in der Klassenauseinandersetzung,' 29.

26. In his *Mechanismen der Herrschaftssicherung,* Ludz offers a systematic analysis of official metaphors and analogies based on empirical data from textbooks and lexika from the GDR.

27. One of the most interesting examples of such a scandal was the uproar that emerged around Christa Wolf's novel *Divided Heaven* (*Der geteilte Himmel*) in 1964. Because the literary establishment was actually undecided as to whether the book was ideologically acceptable or not, there emerged a genuine (not merely an orchestrated) debate as to its merits and faults. See Reso, "*Der geteilte Himmel*" for a 'documentation' of the controversy.

28. The GDR writer Christa Wolf alluded to this function in an interview when she spoke of the reception of her novel *Kein Ort. Nirgends* (*No Place on Earth*) in both East and West Germany: 'Now it is really the case that official institutions [i.e., official institutional discourse] are unable to grasp conceptually the essential things in life, they slip through the perfect structures; and there are now generations, mostly younger than I, who are aware of this. The "authentic" in life is not satisfied by what both German states have to offer in terms of "welfare" – there is a need for poetry in life. A need for things that are not directly measurable in statistics. And here literature serves as a means of self-assertion . . . self-affirmation and a vehicle for yearning.' Wolf, interview (1982), 126.

29. Kunert, *Diesseits des Erinnerns*, 185.

30. A number of other GDR editions of Freud appeared subsequent to Fühmann's publication. See Nitsche, 'Freuds vorsichtiges Erscheinen' and Kapferer, 'Zur Psychoanalyse-Diskussion.'

31. Muthesius, *Flucht in die Wolken.*

32. See Hohendahl, 'Ästhetik und Sozialismus.'

33. Schlenstedt, 'Funktion der Literatur,' 37. Schlenstedt was one of the first literary critics to open up this discussion in the GDR.

34. Hohendahl, 'The Use Value of Contemporary and Future Literary Criticism,' 14.

35. Lehmann, 'Grundfragen,' 99.

36. Manfred Neumann, Dieter Schlenstedt, Karlheinz Barck, Dieter Kliche, and Rosemarie Lenzer authored this extremely important attempt on the part of East German scholars to appropriate Western reception theory in order to develop a Marxist reception theory for the GDR. See also Mandelkow, 'Rezeptionsästhetik,' and Bathrick, 'The Politics of Reception Theory.'

37. Weimann, 'Kunst und Öffentlichkeit,' 217.

38. Habermas, 'The Public Sphere,' 49.

39. Habermas, *The Structural Transformation of the Public Sphere*, 124. Hereafter cited in text.

40. In 1982, the fictional writer and essayist Christoph Hein delivered an address entitled 'Öffentlich arbeiten' (Working publicly) at a meeting of the Berlin

section of the Schriftstellerverband, where he argued that 'publicness is not a particular form of culture but its precondition. The public sphere does not mean a "limited public sphere," which conceptually doesn't make any sense. Nor does it mean a "public sphere for the chosen." ' This essay was published in 1987 in Hein, *Öffentlich arbeiten*, 34–38.

41. Weimann, 'Kunst und Öffentlichkeit,' 221. Hereafter cited in text.

42. See Rosellini, *Wolf Biermann*, for an extensive discussion of the various responses to Biermann's expulsion.

43. Mitter and Wolle, *Ich liebe Euch doch alle!*, 46–71.

44. Neubert, 'Protestantische Aufklärung,' 5.

45. See Sweet, 'Friedrich Nietzsche in the GDR,' where he writes that 'even if no clear contours have yet emerged, it is nonetheless already apparent that the official relegation of Nietzsche to "unbrauchbares Erbe" (useless cultural heritage) has become less adamant' (237).

46. See Grunenberg, 'Aspekte.'

47. Bammer, 'The American Feminist Reception,' 18–19. See also Lennox, ' "Nun ja!" '

48. Süss has defined the role of the literary public sphere (*Teilöffentlichkeit*) as an important 'intellectual preparation for an inner break with the system' ('Revolution und Öffentlichkeit,' 911).

49. Hein, discussion, 228.

50. Hein, discussion, 231. Following his excoriation of censorship, Hein turned with brilliant tongue in cheek to what censorship had unwittingly created in the area of belles lettres. I quote from his remarks, printed under the rubric 'Ein Dank an die Presse' (Words of gratitude for the press): 'I want to thank our press and the media for their untiring work, which in no small way has been responsible for the great impact of literature in the GDR . . . Their caution when reporting news and the absolute reliability of the consensus with which they express their opinions has created a situation in which there is scarcely a citizen of our country who has to spend any of his time dealing with it. The average reader is diverted only for a few minutes by current events and then can turn once again to our books, where he finds not only entertainment and stories, but also much that he has come to expect in terms of the new and the true' (233).

CHAPTER 2: VOICES FROM WITHIN

1. Bahro, *Die Alternative*. All subsequent quotations will be cited in the text.

2. See chap. 1.

3. Bahro, 'Die Herrschaft des Apparats,' 1105.

4. See Ollman, 'Marx's Vision of Communism.'

5. Lenin, 'Reply to a Question,' 283.

6. Quoted in Rothberg, *The Heirs of Stalin*, 349.

7. My emphasis upon the separation between official and oppositional discourses in the Soviet Union does not mean to disagree with Jeffrey Goldfarb in his *On Cultural Freedom* when he argues that 'the line between officially supported propagandist expression and officially repressed dissident expression cannot be drawn as neatly as these and many other similar studies imply.' What is important about the GDR is that virtually all oppositional discourse came directly out of official Party institutions and never even claimed to institutionalize itself in a second (underground, Samizdat) social sphere.

8. Leonhard, *Am Vorabend einer neuen Revolution*, 126–36.

9. The efforts in the 1970s, for example, of the physician Karl-Heinz Nitschke of Ries to organize an appeal to the United Nations for the right to emigrate must be seen as an isolated act rather than a large-scale coordinated movement.

10. The emergence of the Protestant Church as an alternative public sphere for the peace movement is discussed in chap. 1. Certainly the extremely positive reception – 'with beat band and long-haired youth' – given Wolf Biermann in the Nicolai Church in Prenzlau shortly before his expulsion hinted even in 1976 at the potential of the church to be a locus of youthful resistance and also probably contributed to the decision to deny Biermann his return to the country. See Biermann's letter to his mother in *Der Spiegel*, 'Es gibt ein Leben vor dem Tod,' for an account of his experience.

11. The publication in the West of the 'underground writings' of various literary writers, such as the Jena group in 1978, does not belie the fact that these groups remained isolated phenomena and were often forced to leave as soon as they went public in any way.

12. In his *Opposition in the GDR*, Woods locates three forms of opposition: dissident intellectuals, GDR citizens who wish to leave the GDR, and the unofficial peace movement.

13. Sodaro is correct in arguing that unlike other Eastern European societies, the scientific intelligentsia in the GDR has been essentially co-opted by the regime 'and shows no indications of wishing to jeopardize its stake in the existing system by joining with dissidents from other elements of the intelligentsia or by encouraging dissent among the masses' (Sodaro, 'Limits to Dissent in the GDR,' 89).

14. Feher, 'The Dictatorship over Needs,' 31.

15. Feher, 'The Dictatorship over Needs,' 32.

16. See Bathrick, 'The Dialectics of Legitimation.'

17. See Arato, 'Understanding Bureaucratic Centralism,' for a discussion of national tradition within the Stalinist system as the 'terrain of . . . confrontation of statist pressure and cultural submission or resistance' (77).

18. The complete lack of any unanimity on the meaning of this category among Western scholars is particularly in evidence in the collection of essays entitled *Revisionism – Essays on the History of Marxist Ideas*, ed. Labedz.

19. In his 'Dissent and Political Change,' Shtromas has argued for the importance of 'objective' rather than simply 'subjective' criteria for assessing dissidence. Regardless of one's desire for 'within-system change,' he says, reformers who struggle for socialist legality or freedom of assembly and speech are striving objectively for 'system rejective' change. I find that distinction to be much too absolute and have chosen therefore to focus only on the *intentions* of the figures I treat. For example, Gorbachev's call for socialist legality and freedom of election certainly could not be defined as system rejective change.

20. The following discussion focuses on a few exemplary figures from the different periods up through the 1970s and is not intended as an all-inclusive treatment of opposition in the GDR. For texts dealing with a more historical overview of GDR opposition, see the works by Jänicke, Fricke, Allen, Sodaro, and Woods.

21. Havemann discusses this experience in detail in *Fragen Antworten Fragen*.

22. Ludz, 'Freiheitsphilosophie,' 424ff.

23. Havemann, '*Dialektik der Natur.*'

24. The Aesopian debates within the scientific community of the Soviet Union are treated extensively if somewhat naively and uncritically in Graham, *Science and Philosophy*. For an attempted Marxist critique of Lysenko and Lysenkoism, see LeCourt, *Proletarian Science?*

25. See Joravsky, *Soviet Marxism and Natural Science*.

26. Havemann, 'Meinungsstreit,' 22.

27. Havemann, 'Meinungsstreit,' 24.

28. Havemann, 'Über philosophische Probleme,' 681.

29. For an excellent discussion of 'scientific Marxism,' see Jacoby, 'Towards a Critique of Automatic Marxism.'

30. Havemann, 'Über philosophische Probleme,' 682.

31. Fischer, 'Kafka Konferenz,' 159.

32. For a thorough discussion of the different positions represented by the GDR delegation and the debate's importance for the 'modernism' discussion in the GDR, see Erbe, *Die verfemte Moderne*, 88–105.

33. Buhr, 'Entfremdung.'

34. Like Robert Havemann and Erich Honecker, Heise had been incarcerated under the Nazis. I should also emphasize that in the 1970s Heise was to become a major intellectual figure of alternative thinking in the GDR who was to have a powerful impact upon such oppositional figures as Heiner Müller and Rudolf Bahro.

35. Heise, forum.

36. Heise, 'Über die Entfremdung,' 702.

37. For a thorough discussion of this debate, see Lunn, *Marxism and Modernism*.

38. Jameson, *The Prison-House*, 51.

39. Marcuse, *Soviet Marxism*, 112.

40. Brecht, *Gesammelte Werke*, 9: 725.

41. Franz Fühmann links the end of a certain kind of lyric poetry at the end of the 1950s with the failure of de-Stalinization in the GDR. Fühmann, *Essays*, 443ff.

42. For excellent discussions of this movement, see Emmerich, *Kleine Literaturgeschichte der DDR* (1989); Flores, *Poetry in East Germany*.

43. Endler and Mickel, eds., *In diesem besseren Land*.

44. See Raddatz, *Traditionen und Tendenzen;* Rosellini, 'Poetry and Criticism'; and Bathrick, 'Die Zerstörung oder der Anfang' for discussions of the debate.

45. Kunert, *Verkündigung des Wetters*, 86.

46. Kurt Hager, *Forum* 15–16 (1966). Cited in Jäger, *Kultur und Politik*, 128.

47. Kunert, *Der ungebetene Gast*, 75.

48. Dutschke, 'Offener Brief an Wolf,' 71ff.

49. Biermann, *Für meine Genossen*, 25.

50. An example of such a review is Schulz, '*Spur der Steine* – Eine Betrachtung.'

51. Biermann, *Für meine Genossen*, 25.

52. For a critique of such theories, see Carlo, 'The Socio-Economic Nature of the USSR.'

53. Bahro, *Die Alternative*, 170. Hereafter cited in text.

54. Bahro, 'An die Studenten,' 45–46.

55. Bahro, 'Wozu wir diesen Dichter brauchen,' 14–15. The word play in the title is made possible by the fact that Titov's first name is 'German.'

56. Bahro, 'Wozu wir diesen Dichter brauchen,' 10.

57. See Arato and Vajda, 'The Limits of Leninist Opposition.' This was a reply to an earlier version of the present chapter: Bathrick, 'The Politics of Culture: Rudolf Bahro and Opposition in the GDR.' For similar critiques of Bahro, see Sodaro, 'Limits to Dissent in the GDR," 100–102; and *Deutschland Archiv* 11 (November 1978): 1160–81.

58. As reported in *Frankfurter Allgemeine Zeitung*, 21 March 1957.

CHAPTER 3: AFFIRMATIVE AND NEGATIVE CULTURE

1. Critics in both Europe (Hans Magnus Enzensberger) and the United States (Leslie Fiedler, Irving Howe, and more recently the postmodernist position) have proclaimed the 'death of the avant-garde'; their view has been elaborated into a 'theory of the avant-garde' by the West German scholar Peter Bürger in his *Theory of the Avant-Garde* (*Theorie der Avant-Garde*).

2. Franz Mehring, the socialist historian and leading SPD ideologue, was particularly outspoken and influential in his attack upon such modernist movements as naturalism and equally adamant in his defense of Schillerian drama as the model for revolutionary proletarian art. See Fülberth, *Proletarische Partei*, 40–83.

3. Trotsky was sympathetic to Futurism and Mayakovsky, Lenin was not.

4. Trotsky, *Literature and Revolution*, 130.

5. Lenin, 'Pages from a Diary' and 'The Tasks of the Youth Leagues.'

6. See Gallas, *Marxistische Literaturtheorie*, 11–30, 135–78.

7. See Calinescu, *Faces of Modernity*.

8. In his discussion of modernism in the GDR ('The "Good New" and "Bad New"'), Hermand uses the distinction between the traditions of bourgeois modernism and socialist avant-garde (Heine, Brecht, the early Müller, Braun) in order to warn against forms of modernism that are 'formalistic in the bad sense of the word.'

9. Arvatov, *Kunst und Produktion*, 27.

10. In a speech before the National Council of the National Front on 25 March 1962.

11. Tretyakov, *Die Arbeit*, 22.

12. 'Der Kampf gegen den Formalismus in Kunst und Literatur, für eine fortschrittliche deutsche Kultur.'

13. Subtitle of an early widely read book on the GDR by the West German scholar Ernst Riechert, *Das zweite Deutschland – Ein Staat, der nicht sein darf*.

14. Quoted in Rühle, *Das gefesselte Theater*, 243.

15. See Klatt, 'Proletarisch-revolutionäres Erbe als Angebot' and 'Schwierigkeiten mit der Avantgarde' for informative and moderately critical discussions of the reception of the Weimar avant-garde in the GDR.

16. There was a 'Bauhaus debate' in the GDR in 1950. See *Für einen fortschrittlichen Städtebau*. For a more recent GDR reevaluation of the Bauhaus tradition and of Neue Sachlichkeit, see Hirdina, *Pathos der Sachlichkeit*.

17. See chap. 4.

18. 1968 saw the GDR publication of Kurt Pinthus's 1919 Expressionist anthology of lyric poetry *Menschheitsdämmerung*. In his introduction, Werner Mitten-

zwei suggests that a more open attitude toward this movement might have something to do with the 'perspective of a new social order, that of the socialist human society.' 'Socialist human community' was the epithet Ulbricht used to describe GDR socialism of the 1960s, in which the emphasis was on community instead of conflict and which clearly has an Expressionist ring to it.

The two major Kafka studies to appear in the GDR were Hermsdorf, *Kafka: Weltbild und Roman* (1961) and Richter, *Franz Kafka: Werk und Entwurf* (1962).

19. See Erbe, *Die verfemte Moderne*, 55–110.

20. Repr. in *Neues Deutschland*, 18 December 1971.

21. See Schulz, *Heiner Müller*, for an excellent introduction to the major themes in Müller's work.

22. For a discussion in English of the Brecht-Lukács controversy, see Lunn, *Marxism and Modernism*, 75–148.

23. Müller, *Die Zeit*, 17 March 1978.

24. See Gaßner and Gillen, *Zwischen Revolutionskunst und Sozialistischem Realismus*, for an excellent collection of documents and writings from this period.

25. Arvatov, *Kunst und Produktion*, 52–64.

26. See Hewitt, *Fascist Modernism*.

27. Brecht, *Arbeitsjournal*, 1: 247.

28. For a thorough if somewhat uncritical discussion of production aesthetics and its relationship to Brecht, see Brüggemann, 'Aspekte.'

29. Brecht, *Gesammelte Werke*, 20: 76.

30. Brüggemann, 'Aspekte,' 121.

31. RAPP was the Russian Association of Proletarian Writers at the end of the 1920s and beginning of the 1930s. The reference to RAPP at this later stage clearly uses it as generic for all the avant-garde groupings from the Proletkultists through LEF, regardless of their political differences on any number of issues.

32. See Schmitt, ed., *Die Expressionismusdebatte*; Bathrick, 'Moderne Kunst und Klassenkampf'; Schonauer, 'Expressionismus und Faschismus.'

33. Eisler and Bloch, 'Die Kunst zu erben.'

34. See chap. 2.

35. See Jacoby, 'Towards a Critique of Automatic Marxism,' 119ff.

36. In his book *Gesamtwerk Stalin: Die gespaltene Kultur in der Sowjet Union*, Groys has also suggested an affiliation between Stalinist programs of socialist realism and the Soviet avant-garde of the 1920s: 'The Stalin period realized the dream of the avant-garde to organize the entirety of social life according to an

artistic plan, although not of course the way the avant-garde itself had envisioned it' (14). While both the avant-garde and socialist realism share notions of the universalizing of art, this was also to be found in other modernist movements (Bauhaus, etc.). My point about productivism puts less emphasis than Groys upon the totalitarian dimension inherent in the notion of 'turning life into art.' Rather, I focus on the potentially manipulative optimism to be found in the belief that production as well as production aesthetics were *eo ipso* a positive thing.

37. See Bathrick, 'Reading Walter Benjamin.'
38. Müller, *Theater-Arbeit*, 125.
39. For an excellent comparison of Müller and Brecht, see Fehervary, 'Enlightenment and Entanglement.'
40. Müller, *Germania Tod in Berlin*, 57.
41. Müller, *Theater-Arbeit*, 63.
42. Müller, *Die Zeit*, 17 March 1978.
43. Theweleit, *male fantasies*, 1: 79.
44. Müller, interview (1976), 61.
45. Müller, *Die Zeit*, 17 March 1978.
46. Hecht, *Brecht im Gespräch*, 169.
47. Mittenzwei, 'Die Brecht-Lukács Debatte," 13ff.
48. Mittenzwei, 'Brecht und die Schicksale der Materialästhetik.'
49. Klatt, 'Proletarisch-revolutionäres Erbe als Angebot,' 245. Klatt is one of the first GDR scholars to refer openly and critically to the repression of the 'socialist avant-garde heritage' (Weimar avant-garde), stressing in particular the ignoring of such figures as John Heartfield well into the late 1950s.
50. Illes, 'Vieilles querelles.'
51. To my knowledge, the first publication in which the term was used as a neutral substantive, and not simply pejoratively (*avantgardistisch, Avantgardismus*), was Schlenstedt, 'Problem Avantgarde.'
52. *Künstlerische Avantgarde: Annäherungen an ein unabgeschlossenes Kapitel* was a collection of essays, many of which had been delivered at an international conference commemorating the sixtieth anniversary of the October Revolution held in Berlin in October 1977.
53. *Künstlerische Avantgarde*, 9.
54. The GDR critics borrow this term as well as the theoretical underpinnings for much of their analysis from the West German Marxist Peter Bürger's *Theory of the Avant-garde*.
55. *Künstlerische Avantgarde*, 18, emphasis added.
56. In his essay 'Theorie und Praxis des Erbens,' Hohendahl shows how the 're-

habilitation of the avant-garde' (36) in the GDR has helped lead to what he calls a 'structural change of heritage theory' (38).

57. Barck, ed., *Surrealismus in Paris.* In addition to his afterword to this edition, Barck also contributed an essay on Surrealism to the *Künstlerische Avantgarde* volume, in which he calls for a 'differentiation in the relation between the artistic and political avant-garde' (the title of his piece).

58. The influence of Surrealism, Expressionism, and Dadaism on contemporary GDR artists was particularly apparent at the national exhibition of GDR art in 1982. See the catalog entitled *IX. Kunstausstellung der DDR.*

CHAPTER 4: FROM WEIMAR TO BERLIN

1. Brecht, *Gesammelte Werke*, 16: 780.

2. Schubbe, ed., *Dokumente*, 504.

3. Schubbe, ed., *Dokumente*, 508–11.

4. Klatt, 'Proletarisch-revolutionäres Erbe als Angebot,' speaks of the 'new accentuations in the attitude toward heritage around 1956/57' (250).

5. Mittenzwei, ed., *Theater in der Zeitenwende.* In this official East German theater history, one finds the following definition of 'didactic' theater in the GDR: 'The didactic theater of the 1950s emerges in three different versions: as agitprop montage, *Lehrstück*, and in the form of the short epic theater play' (2: 42).

6. See Greiner, 'Arbeitswelt,' where Greiner speaks quite rightfully of the literary development of the 1950s in the GDR as 'anticipating the realization of a proletarian public sphere' but remains much too optimistic concerning the potential development of the structural conditions for a proletarian public sphere in that society.

7. Müller, *Geschichten aus der Produktion 1*, 16.

8. Müller, *Geschichten aus der Produktion 1*, 15.

9. See Klatt, 'Erfahrungen,' who emphasizes that in 'didactic' theater 'the spectator is *not* treated as an object of education, that he is *not* educated or manipulated by an educator. The intention rather was a genuine partnerlike relationship, whose objective material basis was founded upon political and social changes in the revolutionary process itself" (54).

10. Hecht, *Brecht 73*, 202.

11. See Ulbricht's laudatory speech at the fifth party conference of 1958, repr. in Schubbe, ed., *Dokumente*, 534.

12. Cited by Müller in *Geschichten aus der Produktion 1*, 62.

13. Müller, *Geschichten aus der Produktion 1*, 62.

14. Müller, *Geschichten aus der Produktion 1*, 62.

15. Müller, *Theater-Arbeit*, 121.
16. See my essay 'Argroprop.'
17. Baierl, *Die Feststellung*, 238.
18. Klatt, 'Erfahrungen,' 47.
19. Klatt, 'Erfahrungen,' 58.
20. Hacks, 'Eine Neufassung,' 329.
21. Schiwelbusch, *Sozialistisches Drama*, 69.
22. Schubbe, ed., *Dokumente*, 543.
23. Schubbe, ed., *Dokumente*, 543.
24. Mittenzwei, *Theater in der Zeitenwende*, 2: 56.
25. Kähler, *Gegenwart*, 18.
26. Mittenzwei, *Theater in der Zeitenwende*, 2: 18.
27. Emmerich, *Kleine Literaturgeschichte der* DDR (1981), 108.
28. Müller, *Die Umsiedlerin*, 50.
29. See Schulz, *Heiner Müller*, 46ff.
30. Quoted from Streisand, 'Frühe Stücke Heiner Müllers,' 144. Streisand discusses the reception of this play on the basis of protocols from the archive at the Hochschule für Ökonomie in Karlshorst, Berlin.
31. Streisand, 'Frühe Stücke Heiner Müller,' 144.
32. Müller, *Rotwelsch*, 111.
33. Quoted in Streisand, 'Frühe Stücke Heiner Müllers,' 146.
34. Hörnigk, '*Bau* – Stellen,' 52.
35. Hörnigk, '*Bau* – Stellen,' 52.
36. The important publications in this regard are the already mentioned works by Klatt, Hörnigk, and Streisand as well as Schlenstedt, *Wirkungsästhetische Analysen*; Mittenzwei, 'Brecht und die Schicksale der Materialästhetik.'

CHAPTER 5: HISTORY AGAINST ITSELF

1. For a more thorough discussion of *The Measures Taken* as a *Lehrstück*, see Steinweg, *Das Lehrstück*, and Steinweg's articles in *alternative* 78–79 (June–August 1971).
2. See Grimm, 'Ideologische Tragödie.'
3. See Wiese, *Zwischen Utopie und Wirklichkeit*.
4. See Esslin, *Brecht*.
5. See Fischer, *Stalin and German Communism*. Of Brecht's conversion to communism in the 1920s, Fischer, herself a victim of the sectarian struggles within the KPD, wrote, 'From this overall negation, from this cynical withdrawal from all values, from this bitter empty nihilism, Brecht collapsed into the polar opposite – the adoration of the discipline and hierarchical order of the

German Communist Party. Hypnotized by its totalitarian and terrorist features, he became the most original poet the Party ever possessed' (616).

6. In a conversation with Manfred Wekwerth, cited by Steinweg, *Das Lehrstück*, 123.

7. An English version of the play appeared in *New German Critique* 8 (spring 1976): 122–56, trans. Helen Fehervary and Marc D. Silberman. Quotes from *Mauser* will be cited in the text by page number and refer to the English version.

8. Lenin, 'One Step Forward,' 391.

9. See George, 'Forgetting Lenin.'

10. See Vassen, 'Der Tod des Körpers,' for a discussion of the shift in Müller's writing from a focus upon the laboring body (*animal laborans*) to the politics of the body as a locus of sexuality and death.

11. Müller, *Rotwelsch*, 38.

12. According to Schulz, *Heiner Müller*, 115.

13. In an author's note, Müller wrote that '*Cement* is not a period play, it is about revolution. It does not aim at ethnological accuracy but at (Socialist) integration. The Russian Revolution has changed not only Novorossiysk but the world. The decor and costumes should not depict an era; they should project the blueprint of the world in which we live' (*Geschichten aus der Produktion 2*, 133).

14. Müller, *Cement*, 27. Subsequent references to the play will be cited in the text and will be based on this edition.

15. Gladkov, *Cement*, 101.

16. Clark, *The Soviet Novel*, 69–82.

17. Clark, *The Soviet Novel*, 101.

18. In his review of *Cement*, the East German theater critic Ernst Schumacher suggested that Müller was trying to use this scene to sneak *Mauser* in [*hineinmausern*], which, as Genia Schulz has pointed out, was not without the irony that since *Mauser* had not been published in the GDR, this was the first that some people had ever heard of it.

19. Gladkov, *Cement*, 103.

20. Gladkov, *Cement*, 103.

21. See Bloch, 'How Can We Understand?'

22. Schulz, *Heiner Müller*, 149.

23. Seghers, 'Das Licht.'

24. See Hörnigk, 'Erinnerungen,' 155. Hörnigk emphasizes the importance of this work as a learning play also for a GDR audience, 'whose willingness to join in the production of meaning is assumed.'

25. See Teraoka, *The Silence of Entropy*, for an excellent comparison of the two plays.
26. Müller, *Der Auftrag*, 16. This play has appeared in English under the title *The Task* in *Hamletmachine*, by Heiner Müller, ed. and trans. Carl Weber (New York: Performing Arts Journal Publications, 1984), 81–102.
27. Müller, *Der Auftrag*, 17.
28. See Lehmann, 'Dramatische Form.' I am indebted to Lehmann for a number of central points in my discussion of this play.
29. Müller, *Der Auftrag*, 19.
30. Müller, *Der Auftrag*, 22.
31. Müller, *Der Auftrag*, 23.
32. See the discussion by Teraoka, *The Silence of Entropy*.
33. Müller, *Rotwelsch*, 140–41. Müller wrote of Brecht: 'Being driven out of Germany meant for Brecht a distancing from the class struggle there and at the same time the impossibility of carrying on his work in the Soviet Union: emigration into classicism . . . Hollywood became the Weimar of the German antifascist emigration. The necessity to be silent about Stalin (since as long as Hitler was in power, Stalin's name stood for the Soviet Union) forced Brecht into the generalities of the parable form in his plays. . . . The situation of the GDR within both a national and international context did not permit a way out of this dilemma.'
34. Hörnigk, 'Erinnerungen,' 159.

CHAPTER 6: PATRICIDE OR REGENERATION

1. Benjamin Henrichs writing in *Die Zeit*, 7 May 1976.
2. Karasek in *Der Spiegel*, 216ff.
3. *Theater heute* 1 (January 1984): 61. Caption introducing interview with Heiner Müller.
4. Müller, interview (1984), 61–62.
5. Mihan, 'Brecht,' 319.
6. Kraft, 'Brecht,' 5–6.
7. Funke, 'Der allwissende Brecht?' 16.
8. Mittenzwei, *Der Realismus-Streit um Brecht*, 150–52.
9. In a discussion in *Theater der Zeit* (November 1985) entitled 'Wo liegen unsere Maßstäbe?' the director Peter Waschninsky asserted: 'There is no actor today in the theater who would presumably put up with an authority like Brecht. My generation has been marked by the 1968 period' (21).
10. There was one production of *In the Jungle of the Cities* at the Berliner Ensemble in 1971 and one production of *Edward the Second* at the Deutsches Na-

tional Theater in Dresden in 1968 before the Solter production of *Baal* and two later productions of *Drums in the Night* by Christoph Schroth, one in Schwerin (1982) and one at the Berliner Ensemble in Berlin (1983).

11. Brecht, *Gesammelte Werke,* 17: 947.
12. Cited by Riewalt, 'Ein grüner Baal,' 22.
13. Riewalt, 'Ein grüner Baal,' 22.
14. Solter, interview, 14.
15. Solter, interview, 14.
16. Solter, interview, 15.
17. Hecht, 'Die Innenseite,' 40.
18. In his interview in *Theater der Zeit* 2 (1983), Lang pointedly expresses his gratitude for permission to do the play (15).
19. See a second interview about this play entitled 'Für ein komödiantisches Theater: Gespräch mit Alexander Lang,' *Theater der Zeit* 5 (1983): 21–25.
20. According to the theory of A. Dimitroff as defined at the Thirteenth Plenum of the Executive Committee of the Communist International, fascism was merely the 'open, terroristic dictatorship of the most reactionary, the most chauvinist, the most imperialist elements of finance capitalism.' See Mendel, *Essential Works,* 412.
21. Brecht's most famous and controversial adaptations at the Berliner Ensemble in the early 1950s included Goethe's *Urfaust,* Lenz's *Der Hofmeister,* Shakespeare's *Coriolanus,* and George Farquhar's *The Recruiting Officer.* In each case Brecht was attacked for his sacrilegious treatment of the classical heritage and disdain for 'textual integrity' because of his efforts to bring out elements of these works that would reflect a more contemporary view. It is ironic that virtually the same criticisms were hurled at Alexander Lang at the Brecht Symposium of 1985, in which a session was devoted to the *Roundheads* production. See *Brecht 85,* 77–104.
22. Funke, 'Der allwissende Brecht?' 17.
23. Hecht, 'Die Innenseite,' 40. See also the article by Jürgen Schebera, which offers a slightly more differentiated critique of Lang's production as an 'example' of the new Regietheater.
24. *Deutschland Archiv* 15, no. 12 (1982): 1261.
25. Interview with Lang, *Theater der Zeit* 2 (1983): 16.
26. Fiebach, 'Wo liegen?' 24.
27. Fiebach, 'Wo liegen?' 24.
28. Speech given by Brecht at the Fourth Writers Congress in 1956. Hecht, *Brecht im Gespräch,* 169. See chap. 4 for a discussion of this movement.
29. See Hacks, *Das Poetische.*

30. Hacks, 'Über *Adam und Eva*,' 157.
31. Brecht's *Fatzer* was published for the first time in *Theater Heute* 4 (1976): 48–57.
32. Brecht, *Fatzer*, 56.
33. Müller, interview (1984), 61–62.
34. Müller, 'Es gilt,' 51.

CHAPTER 7: LITTLE RED RIDING HOOD IN THE GDR

1. See Zipes, *The Trials and Tribulations*, for an excellent treatment of the historical reception of Little Red Riding Hood over a 300-year period.
2. Brandt, 'Rotkäppchen,' 65.
3. Brandt, 'Rotkäppchen,' 66.
4. Edited by Walther Pollatschek and Hans Siebert (Berlin: Kinderbuch Verlag, 1952).
5. See Zipes, *Fairy Tales*, 43–70 for a discussion of the Grimms' own revisions of different texts.
6. Particularly interesting in this regard was the publication of a manual entitled *Was sind Märchen?* accompanying the Kinderbuch edition as a 'short introduction for educators, teachers, scout leaders and parents' by Hans Siebert. As one of the editors of the edition, Siebert offers a guide for reading in order that the fairy tales will 'serve the democratic education of our children for the peaceful process of rebuilding' (5).
7. Bloch, *Das Prinzip Hoffnung*, 1: 415.
8. Grimm, 'Tischlein deck dich,' in Grimm, *Kinder- und Hausmärchen*, 1: 185.
9. Steinitz, *Die volkskundliche Arbeit*, 34.
10. Marx and Engels, *Über Kunst und Literatur*, 401.
11. Marx and Engels, *Über Kunst und Literatur*, 408.
12. Emmerich, *Zur Kritik*, 13.
13. Emmerich, *Zur Kritik*, 13. Emmerich gives a comprehensive discussion of the ambivalent ideological position of the Grimms in the nineteenth century.
14. GDR scholars cited this as one of the significant proofs that the Grimms were basically progressive. See Stern, *Der geistige und politische Standort*, and Jacobeit, *Bäuerliche Arbeit*.
15. Emmerich, *Zur Kritik*, 43.
16. See Tönnies, *Gemeinschaft und Gesellschaft*.
17. Kamenetsky, 'Folklore and Ideology,' 169.
18. Mosse, *The Crisis of German Ideology*.
19. See Gallas, *Marxistische Literaturtheorie*, for a discussion of Lukács's role in the German debates at the end of the 1920s and beginning of the 1930s.

20. Stern, *Der geistige und politische Standort*, 26. See also Woeller's Habilitationsschrift 'Der soziale Gehalt' for an early attempt (1955) to counter what she saw as those 'circles who up to now have either shown no interest whatsoever in the fairy tale or who with superficial arguments have categorically rejected it' (1).

21. For two GDR discussions of the history of folklore research in the GDR, see Weissel, 'Zum Gegenstand,' and Strohbach, Weinhold, and Weissel, 'Volkskundliche Forschungen.'

22. See Weber-Kellermann, *Deutsche Volkskunde*, for a discussion of developments in GDR research from a West German perspective.

23. Jacobeit, *Bäuerliche Arbeit*, 149.

24. Jacobeit, *Bäuerliche Arbeit*, 149.

25. Weiß, *Volkskunde der Schweiz*. Quoted in Emmerich, *Zur Kritik*, 22.

26. In Schubbe, ed., *Dokumente*, 178–86.

27. Schubbe, ed., *Dokumente*, 181–82.

28. Schubbe, ed., *Dokumente*, 185.

29. Repr. in ibid., 150.

30. Repr. as Eisler, 'Letter to a Musician.'

31. Mayer, 'An Aesthetic Debate,' 58.

32. Eisler, 'Letter to a Musician,' 69.

33. Brecht, *Gesammelte Werke*, 19: 331.

34. See chap. 3 of this book.

35. Eisler, 'Letter to a Musician,' 70.

36. Brecht, *Gesammelte Werke*, 19: 505.

37. Brecht, *Arbeitsjournal*, 2: 928.

38. Brecht, *Gesammelte Werke*, 10: 970:
    She had no fear of the war
    Simply wanted her cut
    And took, so they would get something too
    Her three children along.

39. See Doller, Richter, and Zipes, eds., *Es wird einmal*, for a reprint edition of many of these fairy tales. For an English version, see Zipes, *Utopian Tales*.

40. Flores, *Poetry in East Germany*, 94.

41. Fühmann, *Die Richtung*, 98:
    Stadt Stalingrad, ich darf dich wiedersehen
    du Stadt, die mir mein Vaterland errettet
    und die mich lieben lässt, und die mir Verse zuraunt
    und die die Märchen mich verstehen lehrte
    und alle Träume, die hinab die Wälder gehn
    zur blauen Zukunft und zu Deutschlands Glück.

42. Fühmann, *Die Nelke Nikos,* 39.
43. Fühmann, *Die Richtung,* 149:
    Ich verneige mich tief vor der Weisheit des Volkes,
    der wir es danken,
    daß es im Märchen
    dialektisch zugeht.
44. Bausinger, 'Möglichkeiten,' 21.
45. Bloch, *Das Prinzip Hoffnung,* 3: 1621.
46. Bloch, *Das Prinzip Hoffnung,* 1: 411.
47. Fühmann, "Strelch," 358.
48. Fühmann, "Strelch," 370.
49. Two important anthologies of contemporary fairy tales to appear in the GDR are Walther and Wolter, eds., *Die Rettung,* and Schnitzler and Wolter, eds., *Die Tarnkappe.* Leading GDR authors who have written or looked to the fairy tale to write about contemporary concerns include Anna Seghers, Günher Kunert, Christa Wolf, Peter Hacks, Stefan Heym, Rainer Kirsch, Sarah Kirsch, Helga Schütz, and Jurij Brezan.
50. See the afterword by Horst Heidtmann to the anthology of GDR fairy tales put out in West Germany by the Luchterhand publishing house: *Die Verbesserung des Menschen,* 185–90.
51. Some examples from the GDR: Lehmann, *Phantasie und künstlerische Arbeit;* Weimann, *Phantasie und Nachahmung;* Batt, 'Realität und Phantasie.'
52. See Nägele, 'Trauer, Tropen und Phantasmen,' for an excellent discussion of the 'fantasy' literature to appear in the GDR starting in the late 1960s. See also Heidtmann, *Utopisch-phantastische Literatur,* for a treatment of the 'utopian-fantasy' literature as represented by the GDR science fiction novel. Heidtmann notes that for the period 1970 to 1980 'just as many works appeared as in the entire twenty-five years previous' (78).
53. See Herminghouse, 'Die Wiederentdeckung der Romantik' and 'The Rediscovery of Romanticism.'
54. Hohendahl, 'Theorie und Praxis des Erbens,' 31.
55. See in particular the writings of Irene Dölling, whose attempts to elaborate a 'Cultural Theory of the Personality' in *Individuum und Kultur* reflect theoretical developments that have been occurring in GDR cultural theory since the mid-1960s.
56. Heidtmann, *Utopisch-phantastische Literatur,* 7–9.
57. Heidtmann, *Utopisch-phantastische Literatur,* 9.
58. Martin, 'Socialist Patriarchy,' 61.
59. Rowe, 'Feminism,' 239.

60. One of the most interesting works of fantasy to appear in the GDR was a book entitled *Blitz aus heiterem Himmel* (Like a bolt of lightning), edited by Edith Anderson, in which leading male and female writers wrote stories in which main characters experienced a sudden change of gender. The controversial nature of such fantasies was revealed in both the prepublication and postpublication uproar that emerged around this book. See Edith Anderson's extremely evocative description of her struggle with the Hinstorff publishing house to get the book published: 'Genesis and Adventures.'

CHAPTER 8: THE DESTRUCTION OR THE PROMOTION OF REASON?

1. Harich, 'Revision,' 1048. Hereafter cited in text.

2. Bloom, *The Closing*, 154.

3. Pepperle, 'Revision,' 934–69.

4. See Sweet, 'Friedrich Nietzsche in the GDR,' for a more detailed discussion of the publishing history of Nietzsche in the GDR.

5. Böhme, 'Das Erbe,' 187.

6. Richter, 'Spektakular und belastet,' 199.

7. Hermlin, 'Von älteren Tönen,' 181.

8. The following articles appeared in *Deutsche Zeitschrift für Philosophie* 36, no. 9 (1988): Gerlach, 'Friedrich Nietzsche – ein Philosoph für alle und keinen?'; Gedo, 'Marx oder Nietzsche? Die Gegenwärtigkeit einer beharrenden Alternative'; Malorny, 'Zur gegenwärtigen Auseinandersetzungen um die Philosophie Friedrich Nietzsches.' See Harich, 'Mehr Respekt vor Lukács!' *Kultur und Gesellschaft* 11–12 (1988) for an even more vicious attack upon Eike Middell, Günther Lehmann, Werner Mittenzwei, and others who had been critical of Lukács in recent discussions.

9. Mehring, 'Die Lessing-Legende,' 363.

10. Mehring, *Kapital und Presse*, 120.

11. Mehring, 'Die Lessing-Legende,' 364.

12. Lukács, 'Franz Mehring,' 387.

13. Lukács, 'Nietzsche als Vorläufer.'

14. Mehring, 'Die Lessing-Legende,' 363.

15. See chap. 7 for an elaboration of the Lukácsian position as related to the *Kulturpolitik*.

16. Ernst Behler argues that the GDR treatment of Nietzsche offered a fundamental revision of the Lukácsian position (Behler, 'Nietzsche,' 80–81). I find the changes to be more superficial, as I indicate below.

17. See Malorny, 'Friedrich Nietzsche.'

18. Odujev, *Auf den Spuren Zarathustras*, 429.

19. Ottmann, 'Anti-Lukács,' 576.
20. Nietzsche, *Unzeitgemässe Betrachtungen*, 160–61.
21. For an excellent treatment of the reception of Nietzsche by the German socialist Left and Right, see Ascheim, *The Nietzsche Legacy*, 165–200.
22. For a thorough treatment of Nietzsche in relation to Mehring and other intellectuals in and around the Social Democratic Party, see Thomas, *Nietzsche*, 7–47.
23. I am indebted to Ottmann's essay 'Anti-Lukács' for the link between Nietzsche reception and the *Sonderweg* debate.
24. See Blackbourn and Eley, *Mythen*.
25. Plessner, *Die verspätete Nation*.
26. Malorny, 'Friedrich Nietzsche,' 281.
27. Sweet, 'Friedrich Nietzsche in the DDR,' 230.
28. Rosenberg, *Der Mythos*, 530.
29. Bäumler, *Nietzsche*, 181.
30. See Kaufhold, 'Zur Nietzsche-Rezeption.'
31. For a representative view of this position, see the essays cited above by Richter, Böhme, Hermlin, and Pepperle.
32. This quotation was taken from Tait, 'Lunacharsky,' 282. All subsequent quotations of Lunacharsky will be from this article and will be cited in the text.
33. This quotation was taken from Sochor, 'A. A. Bogdonov,' 305. All subsequent quotations from Bogdanov will refer to this article and will be cited in the text.
34. See Bathrick, 'Marx und/oder Nietzsche.' Two general points are important for the present discussion. First, one must emphasize the distinction between Marx or Nietzsche and Marx and Nietzsche, the former referring to those who would find only binary opposition between the two, the latter suggesting some sort of synthesis. The second important point, also in the title, is the relationship between the emergence of a Nietzschean critique and a crisis of Marxism.
35. Ascheim, *The Nietzsche Legacy*, 166–76.
36. Bloch, *Heritage*. All subsequent quotations from *Heritage* will refer to this publication and will be cited in the text.
37. Rabinbach, 'Unclaimed Heritage,' 8. Rabinbach, who gives an excellent account of the philosophical dimension of Bloch's analysis of fascism, is less concerned with Bloch's reading of Nietzsche et al. as itself a theory of reading and reception.
38. Reschke, 'Die anspornende Verachtung.'
39. Reschke, discussion, 98–100.
40. Reschke, 'Kritische Aneignung,' 1190–215.

41. Reschke, 'Die anspornende Verachtung,' 13. Hereafter cited in text.
42. Middell, 'Totalität und Dekadenz,' 558–72.
43. Middell, 'Totalität und Dekadenz,' 561.
44. Pütz, 'Nietzsche,' 108. See also Schmidt, 'Zur Frage der Dialektik'; Maurer, 'Nietzsche und die kritische Theorie'; Habermas, 'The Entwinement of Myth and Enlightenment.'
45. Rohrmoser, *Nietzsche*, 16.
46. Holz, 'Die Flucht.'
47. Reschke, 'Kritische Aneignung,' 1207.
48. Reschke, discussion, 99.
49. Buhr, 'Es geht um das Phänomen Nietzsche!' 202.
50. Buhr, 'Es geht um das Phänomen Nietzsche!' 203.
51. Nietzsche, 'Ein Tanzlied,' 504–6. In addition, edition Leipzig published a special edition of *Ecce Homo*, which was available mainly for export and a few bibliophiles inside the GDR.

EPILOGUE: THE STASI AND THE POETS

1. The German term for this is *Inoffizieller Mitarbeiter* (unofficial coworker) and is often signified by the initials IM, which I shall be using in my subsequent discussion.
2. Schirrmacher, 'Verdacht und Verrat.'
3. Habermas, *Vergangenheit als Zukunft*, 45–46. See the published English translation of this work entitled *The Past as Future*. I have chosen to give my own translation.
4. *Der Spiegel*, 26 March 1990.
5. For an excellent discussion in English of the Anderson and Schedlinski affairs, see Kramer, 'Letter from Europe.'
6. Rathenow, ' "Operativer Vorgang Assistent": Stasi.'
7. See Fuchs and Hensel, 'Heraus aus der Lüge.'
8. Schedlinski, ' "Dem Druck, immer mehr sagen zu müssen." '
9. See Jäger, 'Auskünfte.'
10. For full documentation of Wolf's Stasi files between 1959 and 1962 as well as the discussions subsequent to their revelation in January 1993, see Vinke, ed., *Akteneinsicht Christa Wolf*.
11. Wolf, 'Eine Auskunft.'
12. Marx and Engels, *Werke*.
13. See Rohrwasser, *Der Stalinismus*, for a historical discussion of the 'renegade' within official communism.
14. Müller, *Krieg ohne Schlacht*, 112. Hereafter cited in text.

15. Reprinted in ibid. under the title 'Selbstkritik Heiner Müllers (an die Abteilung Kultur beim Zentralkomitee der SED)' (Heiner Müller's self-criticism [to the Department of Culture of the Central Committee of the SED]), 407–10.

16. Huyssen, 'After the Wall,' 124.

17. Lehnert, 'Fiktionalität,' 423–44.

18. Wolf, *Was bleibt,* 10. Hereafter cited in text.

19. Wolf, interview (1974), 102.

20. Erb, preface, 14–15.

21. Anderson, 'Interview.'

22. Grunenberg, 'In den Räumen der Sprache,' 207.

23. Thulin, 'Sprache und Sprachkritik,' 236–37.

24. Neumann, *Die Klandestinität der Kesselreiniger.*

25. Schedlinski, *die arroganz der ohnmacht,* 18–28.

26. Corino, 'Vom Leichengift der Grube.'

27. Döring, 'Introview,' 100.

28. Wolf, 'gegen sprache mit sprache,' 15.

29. Berendse, 'Outcast in Berlin.'

30. Thulin, 'Sprache und Sprachkritik,' 237.

31. Schedlinski, 'zwischen nostalgie und utopie,' 29.

32. Böthig, '*Differenz und Revolte,*' 80.

33. Neumann, 'Geheimsprache "Klandestinität," ' 135.

34. Thulin, 'Sprache und Sprachkritik,' 237.

35. Thulin, 'Sprache und Sprachkritik,' 240.

SELECTED BIBLIOGRAPHY

Adorno, Theodor, and Max Horkheimer. *Dialectic of the Enlightenment.* New York: Basic Books, 1947.

Anderson, Benedict. *Imagined Communities.* London: Verso–New Left, 1983.

Anderson, Edith, ed. *Blitz aus heiterem Himmel.* Rostock: Hinstorff, 1975.

——. 'Genesis and Adventures of the Anthology *Blitz aus heiterem Himmel.*' In *Studies in GDR Culture and Society 4,* ed. Gerber et al., 1–14.

Anderson, Sascha. *Interview. Die Zeit,* 1 November 1991.

Anz, Thomas, ed. *Es geht nicht um Christa Wolf.* München: Edition Spangenberg, 1991.

Arato, Andrew. 'Understanding Bureaucratic Centralism.' *Telos* 35 (spring 1978): 73–87.

Arato, Andrew, and Milhaly Vajda. 'The Limits of Leninist Opposition.' *New German Critique* 19 (winter 1980): 167–76.

Arnold, Heinz Ludwig, ed. *Die andere Sprache. Neue DDR-Literatur der 80er Jahre.* Special issue. München: Text und Kritik, 1990.

Arvatov, Boris. *Kunst und Produktion – Entwurf einer proletarisch-avantgardistischen Ästhetik. (1921–1930),* ed. Hans Günther and Karla Hielscher. München: Hanser, 1972.

Ascheim, Stephan. *The Nietzsche Legacy in Germany 1890–1990.* Berkeley: U of California P, 1992.

Bahro, Rudolf. *The Alternative: Critique of Real Existing Socialism.* London: New Left Books, 1980.

——. *Die Alternative: Zur Kritik des real existierenden Sozialismus.* Frankfurt am Main: Europäische Verlagsanstalt, 1977.

——. 'An die Studenten meiner Universität.' *Junge Kunst* 1 (1958): 45–48.

——. 'Die Herrschaft des Apparats muß gründlich ideologisch unterminiert werden: Rudolf Bahro interviewt sich selbst.' *Deutschland Archiv* 10, no.10 (1977): 1105–14.

——. 'Wozu wir diesen Dichter brauchen.' *Forum* 20 (1963): 10–18.

Baierl, Helmut. *Die Feststellung. Sozialistische Dramatik,* ed. Karl-Heinz Schmidt. Berlin: Henschel, 1968, 207–37.

Bammer, Angelika. 'The American Feminist Reception of GDR Literature (with a Glance at West Germany).' *GDR Bulletin* 16, no.2 (fall 1990): 18–24.

Barck, Karlheinz, ed. *Surrealismus in Paris: 1919–1939.* Leipzig: Reclam, 1986.

Barck, Karlheinz, Dieter Schlenstedt, and Wolfgang Thierse, eds. *Künstlerische*

Bibliography

Avantgarde: Annäherungen an ein unabgeschlossenes Kapitel. Berlin: Akademie, 1979.

Bartsch, Rudolf. *Die Zerreißprobe.* Berlin and Weimar: Aufbau, 1969.

Bathrick, David. 'Agroprop: Kollektivismus und Drama in der DDR.' In *Geschichte im Gegenwartsdrama,* ed. Reinhold Grimm and Jost Hermand. Stuttgart: W. Kohlhammer, 1976, 96–110.

——. 'Crossing Borders: The End of the Cold War Intellectual?' *German Politics and Society* 27 (1992): 77–87.

——. 'The Dialectics of Legitimation: Brecht in the GDR.' *New German Critique* 2 (spring 1974): 90–103.

——. 'Marx und/oder Nietzsche: Anmerkungen zur Krise des Marxismus.' In *Karl Marx und Friedrich Nietzsche,* ed. Reinhold Grimm and Jost Hermand. Königstein/Ts.: Athenäum, 1978, 119–35. (Coauthored with Paul Breines.)

——. 'Moderne Kunst und Klassenkampf.' In *Exil und innere Emigration,* ed. Reinhold Grimm and Jost Hermand. Frankfurt am Main: Athenäum, 1972, 89–109.

——. 'The Politics of Reception Theory in the GDR.' *Minnesota Review* 5 (fall 1975): 3–24.

——. 'Reading Walter Benjamin from East to West.' *Colloquia Germanica* 3 (1979): 246–55.

——. ' "The Theatre of the White Revolution Is Over": The Third World in the Works of Peter Weiss and Heiner Müller.' In *Blacks and German Culture,* ed. Reinhold Grimm and Jost Hermand. Madison: U of Wisconsin P, 1986, 135–49.

——. 'Die Zerstörung oder der Anfang von Vernunft. Lyrik und Naturbeherrschung in der DDR.' In *Natur und Natürlichkeit: Stationen des Grünen in der deutschen Literatur,* ed. Reinhold Grimm and Jost Hermand. Königstein/Ts.: Athenäum, 1981, 150–67.

Batt, Kurt. 'Realität und Phantasie: Tendenzen in der Erzählliteratur der DDR.' *Neue Deutsche Literatur* 2 (1976): 10–28.

Bäumler, Alfred. *Nietzsche der Philosoph und Politiker.* Leipzig: Reclam, 1931.

Bausinger, Hermann. 'Möglichkeiten des Märchens in der Gegenwart.' In *Märchen, Mythos, Dichtung: Festschrift Friedrich von der Leyen,* ed. Hugo Kuhn and Kurt Schier. München, 1963, 15–30.

Baylis, Thomas. *The Technical Intelligentsia and the East German Elite.* Berkeley: U of California P, 1974.

Becher, Johannes R. *Von der Größe unserer Literatur.* Leipzig: Reclam, 1971.

Behler, Ernst. 'Nietzsche in der marxistischen Kritik Osteuropas.' *Nietzsche-Studien* 10–11 (1981–82): 80–96.

Berendse, Gerrit-Jan. *Die 'Sächsische Dichterschule': Lyrik in der DDR der sechziger und siebziger Jahre.* Frankfurt am Main: Peter Lang, 1990.

——. 'Outcast in Berlin. Opposition durch Erziehung bei der jüngeren Generation.' *Zeitschrift für Germanistik. Neue Folge* 1 (1991): 21–27.

Bhabha, Homi K., ed. *Nation and Narration*. New York: Routledge, 1990.

Biermann, Wolf. *Für meine Genossen*. Berlin: Wagenbach, 1972.

——. 'Es gibt ein Leben vor dem Tod.' *Der Spiegel* 39 (1976): 207–9.

Blackbourn, David, and Geoff Eley. *Mythen deutscher Geschichtsschreibung: Die gescheiterte bürgerliche Revolution von 1848*. Frankfurt am Main: Ullstein, 1980.

Bloch, Ernst. *Heritage of Our Times*, trans. Neville Plaice and Stephen Plaice. Berkeley: U of California P, 1990.

——. *Das Prinzip Hoffnung*, vols.1–3. Frankfurt am Main: Suhrkamp, 1959.

Bloch, Jan Robert. 'How Can We Understand the Bends in the Upward Gait?' *New German Critique* 42 (fall 1988): 9–40.

Bloom, Allan. *The Closing of the American Mind*. New York: Simon, 1987.

Böhme, Thomas. 'Das Erbe verfügbar besitzen.' *Sinn und Form* 40, no.1 (1988): 186–89.

Bohrer, Karl Heinz. 'Kulturschutzgebiet der DDR.' *Merkur* 500 (October–November 1990): 1015–18.

Böthig, Peter. '*Differenz und Revolte*. Literatur aus der DDR in den 80er Jahren. Untersuchungen an den Rändern eines Diskurses.' Ph.D. diss., Humboldt University, Berlin, 1994.

Brandt, Sabine. 'Rotkäppchen und der Klassenkampf.' *Der Monat* 144 (September 1960): 65–74.

Braun, Volker. Discussion. In *VII. Schriftsteller Kongress der Deutschen Demokratischen Republik: Protokoll (Arbeitsgruppen)*. Berlin: Aufbau, 1974, 76–84.

Brecht 85: Zur Ästhetik Brechts, Dokumentation, Protokoll der Brecht-Tage 1985 10.– 13. Februar Schriftenreihe des Brecht-Zentrums der DDR, vol.5. Berlin: Henschel, 1986.

Brecht, Bertolt. *Arbeitsjournal 1938–1955*, vols.1–2. Frankfurt am Main: Suhrkamp, 1973.

——. *Baal*, trans. Eric Bentley and Martin Esslin. *Baal. A Man's a Man. The Elephant Calf. Three Plays*, ed. Eric Bentley. New York: Grove, 1964, 17–95.

——. *Fatzer*. *Theater Heute* 4 (1976): 48–57.

——. *Galileo*, trans. Charles Laughton, ed. Eric Bentley. New York: Grove, 1966.

——. *Gesammelte Werke*, vols.1–20. Frankfurt am Main: Suhrkamp, 1967.

——. *The Measures Taken*, trans. Eric Bentley. In *The Jewish Wife and Other Short Plays*. New York: Grove, 1965, 75–108.

——. *Roundheads and Peakedheads*, trans. N. Goold-Verschoyle. In *Jungle of Cities and Other Plays*. New York: Grove, 1968, 167–269.

——. 'The Solution,' trans. Derek Bowman. In *Poems*, ed. John Willett and Ralph Manheim with the cooperation of Erich Fried. London: Methuen, 1976, 440.

Bibliography

Brüggemann, Heinz. 'Aspekte einer marxistischen Produktions-Ästhetik.' In *Literaturwissenschaft und Sozialwissenschaften*, vol.4, ed. Heinz Schlaffer. Stuttgart: Metzler, 1974, 109–44.

Buhr, Manfred. 'Entfremdung.' In *Philosophisches Wörterbuch*, ed. Georg Klaus and Manfred Buhr. Leipzig: Dietz, 1964.

——. 'Es geht um das Phänomen Nietzsche! Unsystematische Bemerkungen anläßlich unproduktiver Polemik und halbierter Empörung.' *Sinn und Form* 40, no.1 (1988): 200–211.

Bürger, Peter. *Theory of the Avant-Garde*, trans. Michael Shaw. Minneapolis: U of Minnesota P, 1984.

Calinescu, Matei. *Faces of Modernity: Avant-Garde, Decadence, Kitsch*. Bloomington: Indiana UP, 1977.

Carlo, Antonio. 'The Socio-Economic Nature of the USSR.' *Telos* 21 (fall 1974): 2–86.

Clark, Katerina. *The Soviet Novel: History as Ritual*. Chicago: U of Chicago P, 1985.

Corino, Karl. 'Vom Leichengruft der Grube. Die DDR-Literatur hat an Glaubwürdigkeit verloren. Eine Entgegnung.' *Süddeutsche Zeitung*, 12 June 1991.

Dahrendorf, Ralf. *Gesellschaft und Demokratie in Deutschland*. München: DTV, 1971.

Darnton, Robert. *Berlin Journal 1989–1990*. New York: Norton, 1991.

Deutschland Archiv 12, no.9 (1979). Special issue on Wolf Biermann.

DDR Handbuch. Published by Bundesministerium für innerdeutsche Beziehungen. Köln: Wissenschaft und Politik, 1979.

de Bruyn, Günter. 'On the German Cultural Nation.' *New German Critique* 52 (winter 1991): 60–66.

Deiritz, Karl, and Hannes Krauss, eds. *Der deutsch-deutsche Literaturstreit oder 'Freunde: es spricht sich schlecht mit gebundener Zunge.'* Frankfurt am Main: Luchterhand, 1991.

'Der Kampf gegen den Formalismus in Kunst und Literatur für eine fortschrittliche deutsche Kultur.' *Dokumente der SED*, vol.3. Berlin: Dietz, 1952.

Doller, Bernd, Dieter Richter, and Jack Zipes, eds. *Es wird einmal: Soziale Märchen der 20er Jahre*. München: Weismann, 1983.

Dölling, Irene. *Individuum und Kultur*. Berlin: Dietz, 1986.

Döring, Stefan. Interview. 'Introview: Egmont Hesse – Stefan Döring.' In Hesse, ed., *Sprache & Antwort*, 96–102.

Dubiel, Helmut. 'Linke Trauerarbeit.' *Merkur* 496 (June 1990): 482–91.

Dutschke, Rudi. 'Offener Brief an Wolf.' In *Wolf Biermann: Liedermacher und Sozialist*, ed. Thomas Rothschild. Reinbek: Rowohlt, 1976, 67–84.

Eisler, Hanns. 'Letter to a Musician,' trans. Jack Zipes. *New German Critique* 2 (spring 1974): 63–67.

Eisler, Hanns, and Ernst Bloch. 'Die Kunst zu erben.' *alternative* 12 (1967–68): 216–18.

Emmerich, Wolfgang. 'Affirmation – Utopie – Melancholie: Versuch einer Bilanz von vierzig Jahren DDR-Literatur.' *German Studies Review* 14, no.2 (May 1991): 325–44.

——. 'Gleichzeitigkeit. Vormoderne, Moderne und Postmoderne in der Literatur der DDR.' In *Bestandaufnahme Gegenwartsliteratur: Bundesrepublik Deutschland Deutsche Demokratische Republik Österreich Schweiz*, ed. Heinz Ludwig Arnold. München: Edition Text u. Kritik, 193–211.

——. *Kleine Literaturgeschichte der DDR*. Darmstadt: Luchterhand, 1981.

——. *Kleine Literaturgeschichte der DDR*. Expanded ed. Frankfurt am Main: Luchterhand, 1989.

——. *Zur Kritik der Volkstumideologie*. Frankfurt am Main: Suhrkamp, 1971.

Endler, Adolf, and Karl Mickel, eds. *In diesem besseren Land*. Halle: Mitteldeutscher Verlag, 1966.

Erb, Elke. Preface. In *Berührung ist nur eine Randerscheinung. Neue Literatur aus der DDR*, ed. Elke Erb and Sascha Anderson. Köln: Kiepenheuer & Witsch, 1985, 11–17.

Erbe, Günter. *Die verfemte Moderne: Die Auseinandersetzung mit dem 'Modernismus' in Kulturpolitik, Literaturwissenschaft und Literatur der DDR*. Opladen: Westdeutscher Verlag, 1992.

Esslin, Martin. *Brecht: The Man and His Work*. Garden City: Anchor, 1971.

Feher, Ferenc. 'The Dictatorship over Needs.' *Telos* 35 (spring 1978): 31–42.

Fehervary, Helen. 'Enlightenment and Entanglement: History and Aesthetics in Bertolt Brecht and Heiner Müller.' *New German Critique* 8 (spring 1976): 80–109.

Fiebach, Joachim. Discussion. 'Wo liegen die Maßstäbe?' *Theater der Zeit* 11 (1985): 20–21.

——. *Inseln der Unordnung. Fünf Versuche zu Heiner Müllers Theatertexten*. Berlin: Henschel, 1990.

Fischbach, Helmut, ed. *Literaturpolitik und Literaturkritik in der DDR*. Frankfurt am Main: Diesterweg, 1976.

Fischer, Ernst. 'Kafka Konferenz.' In *Franz Kafka: Aus Prager Sicht*, ed. Eduard Goldstücker et al. Berlin: Voltaire, 1966, 157–68.

Fischer, Ruth. *Stalin and German Communism*. Cambridge: Harvard UP, 1948.

Flores, John. *Poetry in East Germany: Adjustments, Visions, and Provocations*. New Haven: Yale UP, 1971.

Foucault, Michel. *The Archeology of Knowledge*, trans. A. M. Sheridan Smith. New York: Pantheon, 1972.

Bibliography

Fricke, Karl Wilhelm. *Opposition und Widerstand in der* DDR. Köln: Wissenschaft und Politik, 1984.

Fuchs, Jürgen, and Klaus Hensel. 'Heraus aus der Lüge und Ehrlichkeit herstellen: Der Schriftsteller und die Stasi-Spitzel.' *Frankfurter Rundschau,* 21 December 1991.

Fühmann, Franz. 'Strelch.' In *Erzählungen 1955–1975.* Rostock: Hinstorff, 1977.

——. *Essays, Gespräche, Aufsätze 1964–1981.* Rostock: Hinstorff, 1983.

——. *Die Nelke Nikos.* Berlin: Aufbau, 1953.

——. *Die Richtung der Märchen.* Berlin: Aufbau, 1962.

——. 'Zweiundzwanzig Tage oder die Hälfte des Lebens.' In *Das Judenauto.* Rostock: Hinstorff, 1979.

Fülberth, Georg. *Proletarische Partei und bürgerliche Literatur.* Neuwied: Luchterhand, 1972.

Für einen fortschrittlichen Städtebau, für eine neue deutsche Architektur. Grundsätze und Beiträge zu einer Diskussion. Leipzig: Deutsche Bauarchitektur, 1951.

Funke, Christoph. 'Der allwissende Brecht? – Fragen an die Lebendigkeit eines Klassikers.' In *Brecht 85,* 16–23.

Gallas, Helga. *Marxistische Literaturtheorie.* Neuwied: Luchterhand, 1971.

Gaßner, Hubertus, and Eckhart Gillen. *Zwischen Revolutionskunst und sozialistischem Realismus: Dokumente und Kommentare, Kunstdebatten in der Sowjetunion von 1917 bis 1934.* Köln: DuMont, 1979.

Gedo, Andras. 'Marx oder Nietzsche? Die Gegenwärtigkeit einer beharrenden Alternative.' *Deutsche Zeitschrift für Philosophie* 36, no.9 (1988): 787–90.

George, Francois. 'Forgetting Lenin.' *Telos* 18 (winter 1973–74): 53–88.

Gerber, Margy, et al., eds. *Studies in* GDR *Culture and Society 4: Selected Papers from the Ninth New Hampshire Symposium on the German Democratic Republic.* Lanham: UP of America, 1984.

Gerlach, Hans-Martin. 'Friedrich Nietzsche – Ein Philosoph für alle und keinen?' *Deutsche Zeitschrift für Philosophie* 36, no.9, (1988): 777–86.

Gerstenmeier, Cornelia. *The Voices of the Silent.* New York: Hart, 1972.

Gladkov, Feodor Vasilievich. *Cement,* trans. A. S. Arthur and C. Ashleigh. New York: International, 1929.

Goldfarb, Jeffrey. *On Cultural Freedom: An Exploration of Public Life in Poland and America.* Chicago: U of Chicago P, 1982.

Graham, Loren R. *Science and Philosophy in the Soviet Union.* New York: Knopf, 1972.

Greiner, Bernhard. 'Arbeitswelt als Perspektive literarischer Öffentlichkeit in der DDR.' *Handbuch zur deutschen Arbeiterliteratur,* vol.11, ed. Heinz Ludwig Arnold. München and Wien, 1983, 337–84.

Bibliography

Greiner, Ulrich. 'Die deutsche Gesinnungsästhetik.' *Die Zeit*, 2 November 1990.

———. 'Die Falle des Entweder-Oder: In der Stasi Debatte wird altes Unrecht durch neues Unrecht ersetzt.' *Die Zeit*, 31 October 1992.

———. 'Mangel an Feingefühl.' *Die Zeit*, 1 June 1990.

———. 'Was bleibt? Bleibt was?' *Die Zeit*, 1 June 1990.

Grimm, Jakob, and Wilhelm Grimm. *Kinder- und Hausmärchen*, ed. Walter Polatschek and Hans Siebert. Berlin: Kinderbuch, 1952.

Grimm, Reinhold. 'Ideologische Tragödie und Tragödie der Ideologie: Versuch über ein Lehrstück von Brecht.' *Zeitschrift für Deutsche Philologie* 78 (1959): 394–424.

Groys, Boris. *Gesamtwerk Stalin: Die gespaltene Kultur in der Sowjet Union*, trans. Gabriele Leopold. München: Hanser, 1988.

Grunenberg, Antonia. 'Aspekte sozialer, kultureller und politischer Identität in der DDR.' In *Die beiden deutschen Staaten im Ost-West Verhältnis: Fünfzehnte Tagung der DDR-Forschung in der Bundesrepublik Deutschland 1. bis 4. Juni 1982*, ed. Ilse Spittmann-Rühle and Gisela Helwig. Köln: Edition Deutschland Archiv, 1982, 149–63.

———. *Aufbruch der inneren Mauer: Politik und Kultur in der DDR 1971–1990*. Bremen: Edition Temmen, 1990.

———. 'In den Räumen der Sprache: Gedankenbilder zur Literatur Gert Neumanns.' In *Die andere Sprache*, ed. Arnold, 206–14.

Habermas, Jürgen. 'The Entwinement of Myth and Enlightenment: Rereading *Dialectic of Enlightenment*.' *New German Critique* 26 (spring–summer 1982): 13–30.

———. *The Past as Future*, trans. and ed. Max Pensky. Lincoln and London: U of Nebraska P, 1994.

———. 'The Public Sphere: An Encyclopedia Article (1974).' *New German Critique* 3 (fall 1974): 49–55.

———. *The Structural Transformation of the Public Sphere: An Inquiry into a Category of Bourgeois Society*, trans. Thomas Burger with the assistance of Frederick Lawrence. Cambridge: MIT P, 1989.

———. *Vergangenheit als Zukunft*. Zürich: Pendo, 1990.

Hacks, Peter. 'Eine Neufassung, warum?' In *Die Maßgaben der Kunst*. Düsseldorf: Claasen, 1977.

———. *Das Poetische. Ansätze zu einer postrevolutionären Dramaturgie*. Frankfurt am Main: Suhrkamp, 1972.

———. 'Uber *Adam und Eva*.' In Programmheft *Adam und Eva*. Dresden: Staatstheater Dresden/Kleines Haus.

Hancock, M. Donald. 'Intellectuals and System Change.' In *The German Demo-*

275

cratic Republic: A Developed Socialist Society, ed. Lyman H. Legters. Boulder: Westview, 1978, 133–54.

Hanke, Irma. *Alltag und Politik: Zur politischen Kultur einer unpolitischen Gesellschaft.* Opladen: Westdeutscher Verlag, 1987.

Harich, Wolfgang. 'Mehr Respekt vor Lukács!' *Kultur und Gesellschaft* 11–12 (1988): 3–10.

——. 'Revision des marxistischen Nietzschebildes.' *Sinn und Form* 39, no.5 (1987): 1018–53.

Havemann, Robert. *Dialektik ohne Dogma.* Hamburg: Rowohlt, 1964.

——. '*Dialektik der Natur* – Zum Erscheinen der ersten vollständigen deutschen Ausgabe des genialen Werkes von Friedrich Engels.' *Einheit* 9 (1952): 842–55.

——. *Fragen Antworten Fragen.* München: Piper, 1973.

——. 'Meinungsstreit fördert die Wissenschaften.' Repr. in *Rückantworten an die Hauptverwaltung 'Ewige Wahrheiten.'* München: Piper, 1971.

——. Über philosophische Probleme der Physik.' *Deutsche Zeitschrift für Philosophie* 3 (1954): 681–85.

Hecht, Werner. *Brecht im Gespräch.* Frankfurt am Main: Suhrkamp, 1975.

——, ed. *Brecht 73: Dokumentation.* Berlin: Henschel, 1973.

——. 'Die Innenseite der Elefantenhaut – Wirkungsmöglichkeiten von Brecht-Stücken heute.' In *Brecht 85,* 33–44.

Heidtmann, Horst. Afterword. In *Die Verbesserung des Menschen: Märchen von Franz Fühmann, Peter Hacks, Günter Kunert, Irmtraud Morgner, Anna Seghers und vielen anderen Autoren aus der DDR,* ed. Horst Heidtmann. Darmstadt: Sammlung Luchterhand, 1982, 185–90.

——. *Utopisch-phantastische Literatur in der DDR: Untersuchungen zur Entwicklung eines literarischen Genres von 1945–1979.* München: Wilhelm Fink, 1982.

Hein, Christoph. *Öffentlich Arbeiten.* Berlin: Aufbau, 1987.

——. Discussion. In *X. Schriftstellerkongreß der Deutschen Demokratischen Republik: Arbeitsgruppen.* Berlin: Aufbau, 1988, 224–307.

Heise, Wolfgang. Forum on 'Empiricism – Theory – Perspective.' *Forum* 23 (1963).

——. 'Über die Entfremdung und ihre Überwindung.' *Deutsche Zeitschrift für Philosophie* 6 (1965): 699–702.

Helwig, Gisela. *Die DDR-Gesellschaft im Spiegel ihrer Literatur.* Köln: Wissenschaft und Politik, 1986.

Helmecke, Monika. *Lauf weg – kehr um. Klopfzeichen.* Berlin: Neues Leben, 1979.

Henrichs, Benjamin. *Die Zeit,* 7 May 1976.

Hermand, Jost. 'The "Good New" and the "Bad New": Metamorphoses in the Modernism Debate in the GDR.' *New German Critique* 3 (fall 1974): 73–92.

Herminghouse, Patricia. 'The Rediscovery of Romanticism: Revisions and Reevaluations.' In *Studies in* GDR *Culture and Society 2*, ed. Margy Gerber et al. Washington DC: UP of America, 1982, 1–18.

——. 'Whose German Literature?' GDR Literature, German Literature and the Question of National Identity.' GDR *Bulletin* 16, no.2 (1990): 6–11.

——. 'Die Wiederentdeckung der Romantik: Zur Funktion der Dichterfiguren in der neueren DDR-Literatur.' In DDR-*Roman und Literaturgesellschaft*, ed. Jos Hoogeven and Gerd Labroisse. Amsterdam: Rodopi, 1981, 217–48.

Hermlin, Stephan. 'Von älteren Tönen.' *Sinn und Form* 40, no.1 (1988): 179–83.

Hermsdorf, Klaus. *Kafka: Weltbild und Roman*. Berlin: Rütten & Löning, 1961.

Hesse, Egmont, ed. *Sprache & Antwort. Stimmen und Texte einer anderen Literatur aus der* DDR. Frankfurt am Main: Fischer, 1988.

Hewitt, Andrew. *Fascist Modernism: Aesthetics, Politics and the Avant-Garde*. Stanford, CA: Stanford UP, 1993.

Hirdina, Karen. *Pathos der Sachlichkeit: Traditionen materialistischer Ästhetik*. Berlin: Dietz, 1981.

Hohendahl, Peter U. 'Ästhetik und Sozialismus: Zur neueren Literaturtheorie der DDR.' *Literatur und Literaturtheorie in der* DDR, ed. Hohendahl and Herminghouse, 100–162.

——. *The Institution of Criticism*. Ithaca, NY: Cornell UP, 1982.

——. 'Theorie und Praxis des Erbens: Untersuchungen zum Problem der literarischen Tradition in der DDR.' In *Literatur der* DDR *in den siebziger Jahren*, ed. Hohendahl and Herminghouse, 13–52.

——. 'The Use Value of Contemporary and Future Literary Criticism.' *New German Critique* 7 (winter 1976): 3–22.

Hohendahl, Peter U., and Patricia Herminghouse, eds. *Literatur der* DDR *in den siebziger Jahren*. Frankfurt am Main: Suhrkamp, 1983.

——. *Literatur und Literaturtheorie in der* DDR. Frankfurt am Main: Suhrkamp, 1976.

Holz, Hans Heinz. 'Die Flucht aus der Geschichte: Nietzsches Wiederkehr als Alibi gegen Marx.' *Deutsche Volkszeitung* 33 (1980).

Hörnigk, Frank. '*Bau* – Stellen: Aspekte der Produktions- und Rezeptionsgeschichte eines dramatischen Entwurfs.' *Zeitschrift für Germanistik* 1 (1985): 35–52.

——. 'Erinnerungen an Revolutionen. Zu Entwicklungstendenzen in der Dramatik Heiner Müllers, Peter Hacks und Volker Brauns am Ende der siebziger Jahre.' In *Tendenzen und Beispiele. Zur* DDR-*Literatur in den siebziger Jahren*, ed. Hans Kaufmann. Leipzig: Reclam, 1981, 148–84.

Hörnigk, Therese. *Christa Wolf*. Berlin: Volk und Wissen, 1989.

Huyssen, Andreas. 'After the Wall: The Failure of German Intellectuals.' *New German Critique* 52 (winter 1991): 109–43.

Bibliography

Illes, Laszo. 'Vieilles querelles sur l'Avant-Garde.' *Littérature hongroise–Littérature européenne: Etudes de littérature comparé publiés par l'Académie des Sciences de Hongrie à l'occasion du IVe congrès de l'AILC*. Budapest, 1964, 450–73.

Immler, Hans. *Agrarpolitik in der DDR*. Köln: Wissenschaft und Politik, 1971.

Jacobeit, Wolfgang. *Bäuerliche Arbeit und Wirtschaft*. Berlin: Akademie, 1965.

Jacoby, Russell. 'Towards a Critique of Automatic Marxism: The Politics of Philosophy from Lukács to the Frankfurt School.' *Telos* 10 (winter 1971): 119–46.

Jäger, Manfred. 'Auskünfte: Heiner Müller und Christa Wolf zu Stasi-Kontakten.' *Deutschland Archiv* 26, no.2 (1993): 142–46.

———. *Sozialliteraten: Funktion und Selbstverständnis der Schriftsteller in der DDR*. Opladen: Westdeutscher Verlag, 1973.

———. *Kultur und Politik in der DDR*. Köln: Wissenschaft und Politik, 1982.

Jameson, Fredric. *The Prison-House of Language*. Princeton, NJ: Princeton UP, 1972.

Jänicke, Martin. *Der dritte Weg: Die antistalinistische Opposition gegen Ulbricht seit 1953*. Köln, 1964.

Jay, Martin. 'Once More an Inability to Mourn: Reflections on the Left Melancholy of Our Time.' *German Politics and Society* 27 (1992): 69–76.

Joho, Wolfgang. 'Das hohe Ziel der gebildeten Nation und die Steine auf dem Weg der Literatur.' *Neue Deutsche Literatur* 1 (1963): 8–18.

Joravsky, David. *Soviet Marxism and Natural Science*. New York: Columbia UP, 1961.

Kähler, Hermann. *Gegenwart auf der Bühne*. Berlin: Henschel, 1966.

Kamenetsky, Christa. 'Folklore and Ideology in the Third Reich.' *Journal of American Folklore* 90 (1977): 168–78.

Kant, Hermann. 'Unsere Worte wirken in der Klassenauseinandersetzung.' In *VII Schriftsteller Kongress der Deutschen Demokratischen Republik: Protokoll*. Berlin: Aufbau, 1974, 24–67.

Kapferer, Norbert. 'Zur Psychoanalyse-Diskussion in der DDR.' *Deutschland Archiv* 23 (February 1990): 278–80.

Karasek, Helmut. *Der Spiegel* 9 (1978): 216–17.

Kaufhold, Bernhard. 'Zur Nietzsche-Rezeption in der westdeutschen Philosophie der Nachkriegszeit.' In *Beiträge zur Kritik der gegenwärtigen bürgerlichen Geschichtsphilosophie*, ed. Robert Schulz. Berlin: Deutscher Verlag der Wissenschaften, 1958.

Klatt, Gudrun. 'Erfahrungen des 'didaktischen' Theaters der fünfziger Jahre in der DDR.' *Weimarer Beiträge* 23, no.7 (1977): 34–69.

———. 'Proletarisch-revolutionäres Erbe als Angebot. Vom Umgang mit Erfahrungen proletarisch-revolutionärer Kunst während der Übergangsperiode.' In

Literarisches Leben in der DDR, ed. Ingeborg Münz-Koenen et al. Berlin: Akademie, 1980, 244–92.

——. 'Schwierigkeiten mit der Avantgarde: Beobachtungen zum Umgang mit dem Erbe der sozialistischen Avantgarde während der Übergangsperiode in der DDR.' In *Künstlerische Avantgarde*, ed. Barck, Schlenstedt, and Thierse, 257–71.

Köhler-Hausmann, Reinhild. *Literaturbetrieb in der* DDR: *Schriftsteller und Literaturinstanzen.* Stuttgart: Metzler, 1984.

Kohlhaase, Wolfgang. *die tageszeitung,* 18 June 1990.

Kolbe, Uwe. 'Die Heimat der Dissidenten: Nachbemerkungen zum Phantom der DDR-Opposition.' In *Der deutsch-deutsche Literaturstreit,* ed. Deiritz and Krauss, 33–39.

——. *Hineingeboren.* Frankfurt am Main: Suhrkamp, 1982.

Kraft, Peter. 'Brecht auf den Bühnen der DDR 1986.' *Notate 3: Informations- und Mitteilungsblatt des Brecht-Zentrums der* DDR (1986): 5–6.

Kramer, Jane. 'Letter from Europe.' *New Yorker,* 25 May 1992, 40–64.

Kunert, Günter. Interview. *Deutschland Archiv* 23, no.2 (1990): 208–9.

——. *Der ungebetene Gast.* Berlin and Weimar: Aufbau, 1965.

——. *Diesseits des Erinnerns.* München and Wien: Hanser, 1982.

——. *Verkündigung des Wetters.* München: Hanser, 1966.

Labedz, Leopold, ed. *Revisionism – Essays on the History of Marxist Ideas.* New York: Praeger, 1962.

LaCapra, Dominick. *Rethinking Intellectual History: Texts, Contexts, Language.* Ithaca, NY: Cornell UP, 1983.

Lang, Alexander. Interview. 'Für ein komödiantisches Theater: Gespräch mit Alexander Lang.' *Theater der Zeit* 5 (1983): 21–25.

——. Interview. 'Regisseure über ihren Umgang mit Brecht.' *Theater der Zeit* 2 (1983): 15–16.

LeCourt, Dominique. *Proletarian Science? The Case of Lysenko.* London: New Left Books, 1977.

Lehmann, Günther K. 'Grundfragen einer marxistischen Soziologie der Kunst.' *Deutsche Zeitschrift für Philosophie* 13, no.8 (1965): 933–47.

——. *Phantasie und künstlerische Arbeit: Betrachtungen zur poetischen Phantasie.* Berlin: Aufbau, 1966.

Lehmann, Hans-Thies. 'Dramatische Form und Revolution in Georg Büchners *Dantons Tod* und Heiner Müllers *Der Auftrag*.' In *Georg Büchner: Dantons Tod. Die Trauerarbeit im Schönen,* ed. Direktorium Schauspielhaus Frankfurt. Frankfurt am Main, 1980.

Lehnert, Herbert. 'Fiktionalität und autobiographische Motive. Zu Christa Wolfs Erzählung *Was bleibt*.' *Weimarer Beiträge* 73, no.3 (1991): 423–43.

Bibliography

Lenin, V. I. 'One Step Forward, Two Steps Back.' In *Collected Works*, vol.7. Moscow: International, 1965.

——. 'Pages from a Diary.' In *Selected Works*, vol.3. Moscow: Progressive, 1964.

——. 'Reply to a Question from the Socialist-Revolutionaries.' In *Meeting of the All-Russia Central Executive Committee*. November 4 (17) 26: 283ff.

——. 'The Tasks of the Youth Leagues.' In *Selected Works*, vol.3. Moscow: Progressive, 1964.

Lennox, Sara. ' "Nun ja! Das nächste Leben geht aber heute an": Prosa von Frauen und Frauenbewegung in der DDR.' In *Literatur der DDR in den siebziger Jahren*, ed. Hohendahl and Herminghouse, 224–58.

Lippmann, Heinz. *Honecker and the New Politics of Europe*, trans. Helen Sebba. New York: Macmillan, 1972.

Leonhard, Wolfgang. *Am Vorabend einer neuen Revolution*. München: Bertelsmann, 1975.

Loest, Erich. *Der vierte Zensor*. Köln: Edition Deutschland Archiv, 1984.

Ludz, Peter C. *The Changing Party Elite in East Germany*. Cambridge: MIT P, 1972.

——. 'Freiheitsphilosophie oder aufgeklärter Dogmatismus? Politische Elemente im Denken Robert Havemanns.' In *Der Revisionismus*, ed. Leopold Labedz. Köln and Berlin, 1965.

——. *Mechanismen der Herrschaftssicherung: Eine sprachlich-politische Analyse gesellschaftlichen Wandels der DDR*. München: Hanser, 1980.

Lukács, Georg. *The Destruction of Reason*, trans. Peter Palmer. Atlantic Highlands, NJ: Humanities, 1981.

——. 'Franz Mehring.' In *Werke*, vol.10 Neuwied: Luchterhand, 1962.

——. 'Nietzsche als Vorläufer der faschistischen Ästhetik.' *Internationale Literatur* 8 (1935): 76–92.

Lunn, Eugene. *Marxism and Modernism: An Historical Study of Lukács, Brecht, Benjamin, and Adorno*. Berkeley: U of California P, 1982.

Malorny, Heinz. 'Friedrich Nietzsche gegen den klassischen bürgerlichen Humanismus.' In *Philosophie und Humanismus: Beiträge zum Menschenbild der deutschen Klassik*, ed. Bolko Schweinitz. Weimar: Böhlau, 1978.

——. 'Friedrich Nietzsche und der deutsche Faschismus.' In *Faschismus-Forschung*, ed. Dietrich Eichholtz and Kurt Grossweiler. Berlin: Akademie, 1980, 279–301.

——. 'Zu den gegenwärtigen Auseinandersetzungen um die Philosophie Friedrich Nietzsches.' *Deutsche Zeitschrift für Philosophie* 36, no.9 (1988): 791–96.

Mandelkow, Robert. 'Rezeptionsästhetik und marxistische Literaturtheorie.' In *Historizität in Sprach- und Literaturwissenschaft*, ed. Walter Müller-Seidel. München: Wilhelm Fink, 1974, 379–88.

Bibliography

Marcuse, Herbert. *Soviet Marxism*. New York: Random, 1961.

——. 'Repressive Tolerance' by Herbert Marcuse and Robert Paul Wolff. In *A Critique of Tolerance*. Boston: Beacon, 1965.

Maron, Monika. 'Die Schriftsteller und das Volk.' *Der Spiegel*, 4 December 1989. Repr. in *New German Critique* 52 (winter 1991): 36–40.

Martin, Biddy. 'Socialist Patriarchy and the Limits of Reform: A Reading of Irmtraud Morgner's *Life and Adventures of Troubadora Beatriz as Chronicled by Her Minstrel Laura*.' *STCL* 5, no.1 (1980): 59–74.

Marx, Karl, and Friedrich Engels. *Über Kunst und Literatur*, vol.2. Berlin: Dietz, 1968.

——. *Werke. Ergänzungsband Erster Teil*. Berlin: Dietz, 1968.

Maurer, Reinhart. 'Nietzsche und die kritische Theorie.' *Nietzsche-Studien* 10–11 (1981–82): 34–59.

Mayer, Hans. 'An Aesthetic Debate of 1951: Comment on a Text by Hanns Eisler.' *New German Critique* 2 (spring 1974): 58–62.

——. 'Stationen der deutschen Literatur. Die Schriftsteller und die Restauration, die zwei Deutschlands und die Konvergenz.' *Frankfurter Allgemeine Zeitung*, 16 June 1979.

Mayer-Burger, Bernhard. *Entwicklung und Funktion der Literaturpolitik der DDR (1945–1978)*. München: Tuduv, 1984.

Mehring, Franz. *Kapital und Presse: Ein Nachspiel zum Falle Lindau*. Berlin: Kurt Brachvogel, 1891.

——. 'Die Lessing-Legende.' In *Gesammelte Werke*, vol.9, ed. Hans Koch. Berlin: Dietz, 1975.

Mendel, Arthur P., ed. *Essential Works of Marxism*. New York: Bantam, 1961.

Middell, Eike. 'Totalität und Dekadenz: Zur Auseinandersetzung von Georg Lukács mit Friedrich Nietzsche.' *Weimarer Beiträge* 31, no.4 (1985): 558–72.

Mihan, Jörg. 'Brecht auf den Bühnen der DDR.' In *Brecht 73*, ed. Hecht, 319–25.

Mittenzwei, Werner. 'Die Brecht-Lukács Debatte.' *Sinn und Form* 19, no.1 (January 1967): 235–69.

——. *Brechts Verhältnis zur Tradition*. Berlin: Akademie, 1972.

——. 'Brecht und die Schicksale der Materialästhetik.' In *Dialog 75: Positionen und Tendenzen*. Berlin: Henschel, 1975, 9–44.

——. *Der Realismus-Streit um Brecht*. Berlin: Aufbau, 1978.

——, ed. *Theater in der Zeitenwende*, vols.1–2. Berlin: Henschel, 1972.

Mitter, A., and S. Wolle. *Ich liebe Euch doch alle! Befehle und Lageberichte des Mfs Januar–Februar 1989*. Berlin: Basis-Druck, 1990.

Mosse, George. *The Crisis of German Ideology*. New York: Grosset & Dunlap, 1964.

Müller, Heiner. *Der Auftrag. Der Auftrag Der Bau Herakles 5 Todesanzeige*. Berlin: Henschel, 1981.

——. *Cement*, trans. Helen Fehervary and Marc D. Silverman. *New German Critique* suppl. to 16 (winter 1979).

——. 'Es gilt, eine neue Dramaturgie zu entwickeln.' Interview by Ward Kässens and Michael Töteberg. In *Gesammelte Irrtümer: Interviews und Gespräche* by Heiner Müller. Frankfurt am Main: Verlag der Autoren, 1986, 50–54.

——. Interview. *Basis: Jahrbuch für Gegenwartsliteratur* 6, ed. Reinhold Grimm and Jost Hermand. Frankfurt am Main: Suhrkamp, 1976, 48–64.

——. Interview. *Der Spiegel* 31 (July 1990): 140–43.

——. Interview. *Theater Heute* 1 (January 1984): 61–62.

——. *Germania Tod in Berlin*. Berlin: Rotbuch, 1977.

——. *Geschichten aus der Produktion 1*. Berlin: Rotbuch, 1974.

——. *Geschichten aus der Produktion 2*. Berlin: Rotbuch, 1974.

——. *Hamletmachine*, ed. and trans. Carl Weber. New York: Performing Arts Journal Publications, 1984. [This volume includes *The Correction, Medeaplay, Hamletmachine, Gundling's Life Friederick of Prussia Lessing's Sleep Dream Scream, The Task, Quartet, Heartpiece, Despoiled Shore Medeamaterial Landscape with Argonauts*, and an interview with Müller.]

——. *Krieg ohne Schlacht: Leben in zwei Diktatoren*. Köln: Kiepenheuer & Witsch, 1992.

——. *Rotwelsch*. Berlin: Merve, 1982.

——. *Theater-Arbeit*. Berlin: Rotbuch, 1975.

——. *Die Umsiedlerin oder Das Leben auf dem Lande*. Berlin: Rotbuch, 1975.

Muthesius, Sibylle. *Flucht in die Wolken*. Berlin: Buchverlag der Morgen, 1981.

Mytze, Andreas W., ed. 'Über Wolf Biermann.' Special issue of *europäische ideen* (1977).

Nägele, Reiner. 'Trauer, Tropen und Phantasmen: Ver-rückte Geschichten aus der DDR.' In *Literatur der DDR in den siebziger Jahren*, ed. Hohendahl and Herminghouse, 193–223.

Neubert, Ehrhart. 'Protestantische Aufklärung: Die Bedeutung der informellen Gruppen am Rande der Kirche für die Umgestaltung in der DDR.' Unpublished ms.

Neumann, Gert. 'Geheimsprache "Klandestinität." ' In *Sprache & Antwort*, ed. Hesse, 129–44.

——. *Die Klandestinität der Kesselreiniger: Ein Versuch des Sprechens*. Frankfurt am Main: Fischer, 1989.

Neumann, Manfred, Dieter Schlenstedt, Karlheinz Barck, Dieter Kliche, and Rosemarie Lenzer. *Gesellschaft – Literatur – Lesen: Literaturrezeption in theoretischer Sicht*. Berlin: Aufbau, 1975.

New German Critique 10 (winter 1977). Special issue on Wolf Biermann.

Bibliography

Nietzsche, Friedrich. *Unzeitgemässe Betrachtungen 1.1. Sämtliche Werke: Kritische Studienausgabe,* vol.1. Berlin: de Gruyter, 1980.

——. 'Ein Tanzlied.' In *Deutsches Lesebuch von Luther bis Liebknecht,* ed. Stephan Hermlin. Leipzig: Reclam, 1976, 504–6.

IX. Kunstausstellung der DDR. Dresden: Verband bildender Künstler der DDR, 1982.

Nitsche, Bernd. 'Freuds vorsichtiges Erscheinen in der DDR.' *Die Zeit,* 1 August 1986.

Odujev, S. F. *Auf den Spuren Zarathustras: Der Einfluß Nietzsches auf die bürgerliche Philosophie.* Berlin: Akademie, 1977.

Ollman, Bertel. 'Marx's Vision of Communism.' *Critique* 8 (summer 1977): 4–42.

Ottmann, Henning. 'Anti-Lukács: Eine Kritik der Nietzsche-Kritik von Georg Lukács.' *Nietzsche-Studien* 13 (1984): 571–86.

Pepperle, Heinz. 'Revision des marxistischen Nietzsche-Bildes.' *Sinn und Form* 38, no.5 (1986): 934–69.

Pinthus, Kurt. *Menschheitsdämmerung: Ein Dokument des Expressionismus,* ed. and introduction by Werner Mittenzwei. Leipzig: Reclam, 1968 [1919].

Plessner, Helmut. *Die verspätete Nation.* Stuttgart: Kohlhammer, 1959.

Pütz, Peter. 'Nietzsche and Critical Theory.' *Telos* 50 (winter 1980): 102–14.

Rabinbach, Anson. 'Unclaimed Heritage: Ernst Bloch's *Heritage of Our Times* and the Theory of Fascism.' *New German Critique* 11 (spring 1977): 5–19.

Raddatz, Fritz J. 'Gedanken zur Nationalliteratur.' *Politik und Kultur* 7, no.5 (1980): 68–93.

——. *Traditionen und Tendenzen: Materialen zur Literatur der DDR.* Frankfurt am Main: Suhrkamp, 1972.

Rathenow, Lutz. ' "Operativer Vorgang Assistent": Stasi.' *Stern,* 9 January 1992.

Reich-Ranicki, Marcel. *Zur Literatur der DDR.* München: Piper, 1974.

——. 'Macht Verfolgung kreativ? Polemische Anmerkungen aus aktuellem Anlaß: Christa Wolf und Thomas Brasch.' *Frankfurter Allgemeine Zeitung,* 12 November 1987.

Reschke, Renate. 'Die anspornende Verachtung der Zeit: Studien zur Kulturkritik und Ästhetik Friedrich Nietzsches – Ein Beitrag zu ihrer Rezeption.' Ph.D. diss., Humboldt University, Berlin, 1983.

——. Discussion. *Nietzsche-Studien* 10–11 (1981–82): 98–100.

——. 'Kritische Aneignung und notwendige Auseinandersetzung: Zu einigen Tendenzen bürgerlicher Nietzsche-Rezeption.' *Weimarer Beiträge* 29, no.7 (1983): 1190–215.

Reso, Martin, ed. *'Der geteilte Himmel' und seine Kritiker.* Halle: Mitteldeutscher Verlag, 1965.

Richter, Hans. *Franz Kafka: Werk und Entwurf.* Berlin: Rütten & Löning, 1962.

Bibliography

Richter, Stefan. 'Spektakular und belastet.' *Sinn und Form* 1 (1988): 186–89.

Riechert, Ernst. *Daz zweite Deutschland – Ein Staat, der nicht sein darf.* Gütersloh: Sigbert Mohn, 1964.

Riewalt, Otto. 'Ein grüner Baal.' *Theater Heute* 7 (1982): 22–23.

Rohrmoser, Günther. *Nietzsche und das Ende der Emanzipation.* Freiburg: Rombach, 1971.

Rohrwasser, Michael. *Der Stalinismus und die Renegaten. Die Literatur der Exkommunisten.* Stuttgart: Metzler, 1991.

Rosellini, Jay. 'Poetry and Criticism in the GDR.' *New German Critique* 9 (fall 1976): 153–74.

——. *Wolf Biermann.* München: Beck, 1992.

Roos, Peter, ed. *Exil: Die Ausbürgerung Wolf Biermanns aus der DDR.* Köln: Kiepenheuer & Witsch, 1977.

Rosenberg, Alfred. *Der Mythos des 20. Jahrhunderts.* München: Hoheneichen, 1935.

Rosenthal, Bernice Glatzer, ed. *Nietzsche in Russia.* Princeton, NJ: Princeton UP, 1986.

Rothberg, Abraham. *The Heirs of Stalin.* Ithaca, NY: Cornell UP, 1972.

Rowe, Karen E. 'Feminism and Fairy Tales.' *Women's Studies* 6 (1979): 237–57.

Rühle, Jürgen. *Das gefesselte Theater.* Köln: Kiepenheuer & Witsch, 1957.

Rüther, Günter, ed. *Kulturbetrieb und Literatur in der DDR.* Köln: Wissenschaft und Politik, 1987.

Schädlich, Joachim. 'Tanz in Ketten.' *Frankfurter Allgemeine Zeitung,* 30 June 1990.

Schebera, Jürgen. 'Zum Beispiel *Rundköpfe* – Brecht auf dem Regietheater der 80er Jahre – Gewinn oder Verlust?' In *Brecht 85,* 24–32.

Schedlinski, Rainer. *die arroganz der ohnmacht.* Berlin: Aufbau, 1991.

——. ' "Dem Druck, immer mehr sagen zu müssen, hielt ich nicht stand." Literatur, Staatssicherheit und der Prenzlauer Berg.' *Frankfurter Allgemeine Zeitung,* 14 January 1992.

——. 'zwischen nostalgie und utopie.' *ariadnefabrik* 5 (1989).

Schirrmacher, Frank. 'Abschied von der Literatur der Bundesrepublik: Neue Pässe, neue Identitäten, neue Lebensläufe: Über die Kündigung einiger Mythen des Westdeutschen Bewußtseins.' *Frankfurter Allgemeine Zeitung,* 2 October 1990.

——. ' "Dem Druck des härteren, strengeren Lebens standhalten." Auch eine Studie über den autoritären Charakter: Christa Wolfs Aufsätze, Reden und ihre jüngste Erzählung *Was bleibt.'* *Frankfurter Allgemeine Zeitung,* 2 June 1990.

——. 'Verdacht und Verrat.' *Frankfurter Allgemeine Zeitung,* 5 November 1991.

Schiwelbusch, Wolfgang. *Sozialistisches Drama nach Brecht.* Darmstadt: Luchterhand, 1974.

Bibliography

Schlenstedt, Dieter. 'Funktion der Literatur – Relationen ihrer Bestimmung.' *Weimarer Beiträge* 20, no.8 (1974): 23–41.

——. *Wirkungsästhetische Analysen: Poetologie und Prosa in der neueren DDR-Literatur.* Berlin: Akademie-Verlag, 1979.

Schlenstedt, Silvia. 'Problem Avantgarde: Ein Diskussionsvorschlag.' *Weimarer Beiträge* 23, no.1 (1977): 126–44.

Schmidt, Alfred. 'Zur Frage der Dialektik in Nietzsches Erkenntnistheorie.' In *Zeugnisse – Theodor W. Adorno zum sechzigsten Geburtstag,* ed. Max Horkheimer. Frankfurt am Main: Suhrkamp, 1963, 115–32.

Schmitt, Hans-Jürgen, ed. *Die Expressionismusdebatte.* Frankfurt am Main: Suhrkamp, 1973.

Schneider, Peter. *The German Comedy: Scenes of Life after the Wall,* trans. Philip Boehm and Leigh Hafrey. New York: Farrar, 1991.

Schneider, Rolf. 'Das Ende der Kunst?' *die tageszeitung,* 29 July 1990.

Schnitzler, Sonja, and Manfred Walter, eds. *Die Tarnkappe.* Berlin: Eulenspiegel, 1978.

Schonauer, Franz. 'Expressionismus und Faschismus: Eine Diskussion aus dem Jahre 1938.' *Literatur und Kritik* 1 (1966): 7–8.

Schubbe, Elmir, ed. *Dokumente zur Kunst-, Literatur- und Kulturpolitik der SED.* Stuttgart: Seewald, 1972.

Schulz, Genia. *Heiner Müller.* Stuttgart: Metzler, 1980.

Schulz, Max Walter. '*Spur der Steine* – Eine Betrachtung.' In *Kritik in der Zeit,* ed. Klaus Jarmatz. Halle: Mitteldeutscher Verlag, 1969, 621–31.

Seghers, Anna. 'Das Licht auf dem Galgen.' In *Karibische Geschichten.* Berlin: Aufbau, 1962, 121–238.

Siebert, Hans. *Was sind Märchen?* Berlin: Kinderbuch, 1952.

Shtromas, A. Y. 'Dissent and Political Change in the Soviet Union.' *Studies in Comparative Communism* 12, nos.2–3 (1979): 212–44.

Sochor, Zenovia A. 'A. A. Bogdonov: In Search of Cultural Liberation.' In *Nietzsche in Russia,* ed. Rosenthal, 293–311.

Sodaro, Michael J. 'Limits to Dissent in the GDR: Fragmentation, Cooptation, and Repression.' In *Dissent in Eastern Europe,* ed. Jane Leftwich Curry. New York: Praeger, 1983, 82–116.

Solter, Friedo. Interview. 'Regisseure über ihren Umgang mit Brecht.' *Theater der Zeit* 2 (1983): 13–15.

Staritz, Dietrich. *Geschichte der DDR 1949–1985.* Frankfurt am Main: Suhrkamp, 1985.

Steinitz, Wolfgang. *Die volkskundliche Arbeit in der Deutschen Demokratischen Republik (Kleine Beiträge zur Volkskunstforschung),* vol.1. Leipzig, 1955.

Bibliography

Steinweg, Reiner. *Das Lehrstück: Brechts Theorie einer politisch-ästhetischen Erziehung*. Stuttgart: Metzler, 1972.

——. 'Das Lehrstück – Ein Modell des sozialistischen Theaters. Brechts Lehrstücktheorie.' *alternative* 78–79 (June–August 1971): 102–16.

Stern, Leo. *Der geistige und politische Standort von Jakob Grimm in der deutschen Geschichte*. Berlin: Akademie, 1963.

Stone, I. F. 'The Sakharov Campaign.' *New York Review of Books*, 8 October 1973, 8–11.

Streisand, Marianne. 'Frühe Stücke Heiner Müllers: Werkanalyse im Kontext zeitgenössischer Rezeption.' Ph.D. diss., Academy of Sciences of the GDR, 1983.

Strohbach, Hermann, Rudolf Weinhold, and Bernhard Weissel. 'Volkskundliche Forschungen in der DDR – Bilanz und Ausblick.' *Jahrbuch für Volkskunde und Kulturgeschichte* 17 (new series 2) (1974): 3–39.

Süss, Walter. 'Revolution und Öffentlichkeit in der DDR.' *Deutschland Archiv* 23, no.6 (1990): 907–20.

Sweet, Denis M. 'Friedrich Nietzsche in the GDR: A Problematic Reception.' In *Studies in GDR Culture and Society 4*, ed. Gerber, 227–43.

Tait, A. L. 'Lunacharsky: Nietzschean Marxist?' In *Nietzsche in Russia*, ed. Rosenthal, 275–92.

Teraoka, Arlene Akiko. *The Silence of Entropy or Universal Discourse: The Postmodernist Poetics of Heiner Müller*. New York: Peter Lang, 1985.

Theweleit, Klaus. *male fantasies*, vols.1–2. Minneapolis: U of Minnesota P, 1987.

Thomas, R. Hinton. *Nietzsche in German Politics and Society 1890–1920*. Manchester: Manchester UP, 1983.

Thulin, Michael. 'Sprache und Sprachkritik: Die Literatur des Prenzlauer Bergs in Berlin/DDR.' In *Die andere Sprache*, ed. Arnold, 234–43.

Tökes, Rudolph L. Introduction. *Dissent in the USSR: Politics, Ideology and People*, ed. Rudolf L. Tökes. Baltimore: Johns Hopkins UP, 1975.

Tönnies, Ferdinand. *Gemeinschaft und Gesellschaft. Grundbegriffe der reinen Soziologie*. Leipzig: R. Reisland, 1887.

Tretyakov, Sergey. *Die Arbeit des Schriftstellers*. Reinbek: Rowohlt, 1972.

Trotsky, Leon. *Literature and Revolution*. Ann Arbor: U of Michigan P, 1960.

Tümler, Edgar, Konrad Mertel, and Georg Blum. *Die Agrarpolitik in Mitteldeutschland*. Berlin: Dunker & Humblot, 1969.

Vassen, Florian. 'Der Tod des Körpers in der Geschichte. Tod, Sexualität und Arbeit bei Heiner Müller.' *Text + Kritik* 73 (January 1982): 45–57.

Vinke, Hermann, ed. *Akteneinsicht Christa Wolf: Zerrspiegel und Dialog*. Hamburg: Luchterhand, 1993.

Walther, Joachim, and Manfred Wolter, eds. *Die Rettung des Saragossa-Meeres*. Berlin: Buchverlag der Morgen, 1976.

Bibliography

Weber-Kellerman, Ingeborg. *Deutsche Volkskunde zwischen Germanistik und Sozialwissenschaften*. Stuttgart: Metzler, 1969.

Weimann, Robert. 'Kunst und Öffentlichkeit in der sozialistischen Gesellschaft.' *Sinn und Form* 31, no.2 (1979): 214–43.

——. *Phantasie und Nachahmung: Drei Studien zum Verhältnis von Dichtung, Utopie und Mythos*. Halle: Mitteldeutscher, 1976.

Weiß, Richard. *Volkskunde der Schweiz*. Zürich: F. Rentsch, 1978.

Weissel, Bernhard. 'Zum Gegenstand und zu den Aufgaben volkskundlicher Wissenschaft in der DDR.' *Jahrbuch für Volkskunde und Kulturgeschichte* 16 (new series 1) (1973): 9–44.

White, Hayden. *Metahistory: The Historical Imagination in 19th Century Europe*. Baltimore: Johns Hopkins UP, 1973.

Wichner, Herbert, and Herbert Wiesner, eds. *Ausstellungsbuch: Zensur in der DDR*. Berlin: Literaturhaus Berlin, 1991.

Wiese, Benno von. *Zwischen Utopie und Wirklichkeit. Studien zur Deutschen Literatur*. Düsseldorf: A. Bagel, 1963.

——. Discussion. 'Wo liegen unsere Maßstäbe?' *Theater der Zeit* 11 (1985): 21–24.

Woeller, Waltraut. 'Der soziale Gehalt und die soziale Funktion der deutschen Volksmärchen.' Habilitationsschrift, Humboldt University, Berlin, 1955.

Wolf, Christa. 'Eine Auskunft.' *Berliner Zeitung*, 21 January 1993.

——. *Divided Heaven*, trans. Joan Becker. New York: Adler's Foreign Books, 1981.

——. *Im Dialog*. Frankfurt am Main: Luchterhand, 1990.

——. Interview. *alternative* 143–44 (April–June 1982).

——. Interview. *Weimarer Beiträge* 20, no.6 (1974): 90–112.

——. *No Place on Earth*, trans. Jan van Heurck. New York: Farrar, Straus and Giroux, 1982.

——. *Patterns of Childhood*, trans. Ursule Molinaro and Hedwig Rappolt. New York: Farrar, Straus and Giroux, 1980.

——. *The Quest for Christa T*, trans. Christopher Middleton. New York: Farrar, Straus and Giroux, 1968.

——. *Was bleibt*. Frankfurt am Main: Luchterhand, 1990.

——. *What Remains and Other Stories*. New York: Farrar, Straus and Giroux, 1993.

Wolf, Gerhard. 'gegen sprache mit sprache / mit-sprache gegen-sprache: Thesen mit Zitaten und Notizen zu einem literarischen Prozess.' In *Die andere Sprache*, ed. Arnold, 15–25.

Woods, Roger. *Opposition in the GDR under Honecker, 1971–1985: An Introduction and Documentation*. New York: St. Martin's, 1986.

Zima, Peter V. 'Der Mythos der Monosemie: Parteilichkeit und künstlerischer Standpunkt.' In *Literaturwissenschaft und Sozialwissenschaften: Einführung in*

Bibliography

Theorie, Geschichte und Funktion der DDR *Literatur,* ed. Hans-Jürgen Schmitt. Stuttgart: Metzler, 1975, 77–108.

Zipes. Jack. *Fairy Tales and the Art of Subversion: The Classical Genre for Children and the Process of Civilization.* New York: Wildman, 1983.

——. *The Trials and Tribulations of Little Red Riding Hood: Versions of the Tale in Sociocultural Context.* New York: Bergen and Garvey, 1983.

——. *Utopian Tales from Weimar.* Edinburgh: Polygon, 1990.

INDEX

Abenteuer des Werner Holt (Noll), 18

Accident (Wolf), 55

Adorno, Theodor, 14, 48, 179, 188, 213

aesthetics, 58, 69–70, 78, 88, 89; materialist, 95–96, 105; of naturalism, 101; of production, 95–98, 100–101, 255–56 n.36

'affirmative culture,' 80

agitprop movement, 110, 111, 124, 257 n.5; and the Bitterfeld movement, 120–22; Brecht's call for, 105, 109, 160, 162, 163; and Müller, 112, 113, 114, 163

agricultural reform, 33

agrodramas, 123, 125

agroprop, 116

Alexanderplatz demonstration, 1, 243 n.1

alienation, 52, 55, 67–70, 72, 213; literature dealing with, 22, 72, 92

Alternative (Bahro), 80, 83; socialism challenged in, 57, 58, 76–78, 82, 227

amateur theater movement, 118

Anderson, Edith, 265 n.60

Anderson, Sascha, 219, 222, 237; and the Stasi, 21–22, 219, 224

anticommunism, 5–6, 9, 228

antifascism (*see also under* fascism), 64, 173; foundational narratives of, 17–18, 245 n.42, 245–46 n.43; and GDR policy, 11–15, 23, 177, 216, 230; intellectuals' relationships to, 2, 11–12, 225; and Nietzsche, 215, 216

anti-Semitism, 194, 216

anti-Stalinism, 61

Apitz, Bruno, 39

Arbeitsjournal (Brecht), 181

'Arbeitswelt' (Greiner), 257 n.6

Arendt, Erich, 71, 225–26, 247 n.1

Arendt, Hannah, 221

Arnim, Achim von, 172

Arnim, Bettina von, 187

Arnold, Heinz Ludwig, 246 n.53

art, 4, 60, 70, 95–97; time-lag between theory and, 104, 161

Artaud, Antonin, 103, 104, 106, 128, 246 n.44

artists, 24, 30–31

Arvatov, Boris, 90, 95, 96, 181

Auf den Spuren Zarathustras (Odujev), 199

Aufenthalt (Kant), 18

Auftrag (Müller), 129, 133, 144, 145–50

Aula (Kant), 39

'Author as Producer' (Benjamin), 161

avant-garde, 42, 50, 107, 152, 214; authority not respected by, 87, 94; and Brecht, 91, 151, 159–61, 163; and cultural policy, 92, 104, 127, 177, 178, 179; defined, 89, 105, 254 n.8; and folklore, 169, 175, 186; history of, 87, 105–6, 126–28, 256 n.54; and production aesthetics, 95–99, 100, 127; repression of, 87, 88, 92, 254 n.1; and socialism, 87, 98, 100, 105–7, 180, 256 n.49, 256 n.51, 256–57 n.56, 257 n.57; Soviet, 95–96, 99, 100–101, 112, 120, 126, 160, 181, 195, 215, 255 n.31, 255–56 n.36; Weimar, 99, 112, 127, 160, 183

Baal (Brecht), 93, 152–54, 155, 163, 261 n.10

Bahro, Rudolf, 77–82; arrest and exile of, 49, 57, 227; and socialism, 20, 60, 63, 76–78, 82, 227–28

Baierl, Helmut, 110, 116–19, 120, 122–23

Bakhtin, M. M., 14

Balázs, Béla, 183

Ball, Hugo, 183

Balzac, Honoré de, 88

Bammer, Angelika, 54

Barck, Karlheinz, 249 n.36, 257 n.57

Barthel, Kurt, 36

Barthes, Roland, 14, 19, 239

Bartsch, Rudolf, 35, 40
Basisgruppen, 52
Battle (Müller), 94, 103
Bau (Müller), 93, 126, 127, 136
Bauch, Paul, 123
Bauern (Müller), 94, 123–25
Bauhaus, 91, 215, 255–56 n.36
Bäumler, Alfred, 203–4
Bebel, August, 200
Becher, Johannes R., 35, 71, 78, 88, 110, 214; and the folk song movement, 178; and literature, 37, 90
Becker, Jurek, 8, 18, 51, 92, 247 n.1
Beckett, Samuel, 103, 104, 128, 148
Beethoven, Ludwig von, 79, 99
Begegnung (Keller), 118
Behler, Ernst, 265 n.16
Benjamin, Walter, 41, 91, 96, 210, 226; and the avant-garde, 95, 161; and the author as producer, 98, 161; criticism of, 101; and Nietzsche, 214; social democracy critiqued by, 200, 217; subversiveness of, 183
Benn, Gottfried, 98, 204
Berg-Schall, Barbara, 155
Berlin Wall, 1, 10, 11, 21, 59; building of, 4, 6, 71, 124, 232
Berührung ist nur eine Randerscheinung (Erb), 236–37
'Betrachtungen eines Unpolitischen' (Mann), 195
Beyer, Fred, 74
Biermann, Wolf, 5, 61, 73–76, 83, 153; compared to Bahro, 57, 58; expulsion of, 27–28, 41, 43, 49, 50, 54, 92, 226, 227, 234, 246–47 n.1; public interest in, 28, 30, 51, 71, 251 n.10; relationship with power of, 61, 82, 237
Bill-Bjelozerkowski, Vladimir, 112
Bismarck, Otto von, 53, 197, 199, 204, 215
Bitterfelder Weg. *See* Bitterfeld movement
Bitterfeld movement, 36, 120–21, 124
Blitz aus heiterem Himmel (Anderson), 265 n.60
Bloch, Ernst, 83, 161, 210; and the aesthetics of production, 98–99; and fairy tales,

169, 183, 185, 191; and fascism, 207–8, 266 n.37; Marxist-Leninism challenged by, 39, 63, 82, 217, 226; and Nietzsche, 207–10, 211, 212, 214, 217, 266 n.37
Bloom, Allan, 193–94, 217
Bogdanov, Alexander, 87, 205–6, 207
Böhme, Thomas, 195–96
Bohrer, Karl Heinz, 9
Böll, Heinrich, 8
Bolshevik Revolution, 31, 59, 130
Bolsheviks, 59, 63, 88, 90, 132, 205
bourgeois revolution (1848), 197, 201
Boxer (Becker), 18
Bracher, Karl Dietrich, 201
Brahm, Otto, 111, 200
Brandt, Sabine, 167
Brasch, Thomas, 51, 92, 244 n.17
Braun, Lily, 207
Braun, Volker, 2, 110, 128, 246–47 n.1, 254 n.8; and agitprop theater, 91–92, 160; criticism of, 3–4, 20; dissent by, 19, 55, 60, 226; and historical and self-consciousness, 41; and the individual, 122, 125; public interest in, 43, 71; relationship with power of, 20, 238
Brecht, Bertolt, 75, 124, 189, 232; adaptations by, 157, 261 n.20; and aesthetics, 69, 70, 96–97, 101, 105, 150; and agitprop, 91–92, 105, 122, 126, 160–61, 162, 163; and the avant-garde, 91, 95, 97–99, 107, 151, 159–61, 163, 254 n.8; and communism, 132, 258–59 n.5; criticism of, 101, 161; exile of, 150, 158, 260 n.33; *Lehrstück* tradition of, 114, 115, 116, 117, 118, 119, 123, 162; and Lukács, 43, 93, 94; model provided by, 71, 88, 91, 112, 128, 129, 133, 154, 230; move away from, 151–52, 158–59, 260 n.9; and Müller (*see under* Müller, Heiner); new approaches to, 157–58; and political theater, 105, 109–10, 114, 133, 154; relevance of, for the 1980s, 152, 153–54, 159–61, 163–64; reputation of, 42, 93, 94; revolutionary songs composed by, 178–79, 181–82; schematism critiqued by, 37, 110; and socialism, 152, 153, 159, 162–63, 183, 214,

Index

227–28; and Stalinism, 149–50, 260 n.33; and working-class culture, 36–37, 180, 181

Brecht im Gespräch (Hecht), 109

'Brecht-Lukács Debate' (Mittenzwei), 105, 161

Brecht Symposium, 261 n.20

'Brecht und die Schicksale der Material-ästhetik' (Mittenzwei), 161

Bredel, Willi, 18

Brentano, Clemens, 187

Breton, André, 106

Brezan, Jurij, 264 n.49

'Brief an West Deutschland' (Eisler), 179

Bronnen, Arnolt, 98

Büchner, Georg, 75, 129, 146, 148, 155

Buhr, Manfred, 68, 210–11, 215–16

Bukharin, Nikolai, 69, 143, 233, 234

Bunge, Hans, 232

Bürger, Peter, 89, 254 n.1

Calinescu, Matei, 89

Camus, Albert, 129, 130

capitalism, 3, 8, 99, 178, 204, 227; and the avant-garde, 87, 105; class struggles under, 157; and fascism, 13, 102, 174, 207, 230, 261 n.20; and freedom of speech, 243 n.10; and Lenin, 137; and Nietzsche, 197–98, 199, 200, 203, 208, 214; overthrow of, 181; and the public sphere, 46; role of writers in, 30, 35, 231; the state under, 82; struggle against, 110; and tradition, 170

Cement (Gladkov), 139, 140–41, 142–43, 144

Cement (Müller), 129, 133, 139–44, 145, 146, 259 n.13; *Mauser* in, 142, 259 n.18; Stalinism in, 149–50

censorship, 15–16, 37–38, 40–41, 127, 195; abolition of, 56, 238; condemnation of, 55–56, 250 n.50

Chamberlain, Houston Stewart, 204

church, 23, 33–34, 51–52, 61, 251 n.10

civil rights movements, 3; in the GDR, 23, 27–30, 49, 50, 52, 61, 229, 251 n.9

'Civil War in France' (Marx), 59

Clark, Katerina, 141, 245–46 n.43

Claudius, Edward, 112

cold war, 11, 132, 204, 228; and cultural policy, 177, 178; and national cultural identity, 167–68; and public life, 30, 34

collectivization, 57, 116, 117, 124

Collin (Heym), 55

comedic theater, 156

communism, 8, 22, 62–63, 67, 82

Communist Party, 38, 47, 61, 142, 202; in Brecht's *Roundheads*, 156, 157; and dissident writers, 3, 183; and Nietzsche, 197, 205, 210; Twentieth Congress of, 37, 64, 65, 110–11

Composing for the Films (Eisler and Adorno), 179

Congress of the Union of Graphic Artists, 43

Constructivism, 88, 90, 91, 101

Coriolanus (Shakespeare), 261 n.20

Correction (Müller), 93, 114, 115–16, 117

cosmopolitanism. *See* Formalism

Craig, Gordon, 201

Cremer, Fritz, 247 n.1

Critical Theory, 208, 212

critics, Western, 4, 8–10; and the literary intelligentsia, 2, 3–4, 5, 21

'Critique of the Gotha Program' (Marx), 59

cultural dissidence, 2, 4, 5–10

cultural politics, 53–55, 89; binary opposition of, 42, 174–75; and Nietzsche, 204–5, 210; Soviet, 101

culture, 24, 34, 44, 70, 101; after the Biermann expulsion, 50–56; bourgeois, 87–88, 90, 91, 95–96, 111, 180, 210–11, 212; and the contractual system, 37, 38, 41; and dissent, 41, 69; high, 88, 91, 99; and legitimation, 35–37, 42, 61–62, 83; mass, 182, and pluralism, 30, 247 n.8; popular, 179, 180–81; proletariat, 87–88; and social theory, 78; Western, 170, 182

Czechoslovakia, 28, 29, 30, 62, 80, 227; invasion of, in 1968, 4, 6, 58

Index

Dadaism, 90, 91, 106, 183, 215, 257 n.58
Dahrendorf, Ralf, 31, 201
Dali, Salvador, 106
'Dank an die Presse' (Hein), 250 n.50
Danton's Death (Büchner), 129, 130, 146, 148, 155
Darnton, Robert, 38
Day in the Life of Ivan Denisovich (Solzhenitsyn), 60
Days of the Commune (Brecht), 112
de Bruyn, Günter, 7, 8, 55
decadence (*see also* avant-garde), 87
democracy, 32, 201
Demokratischer Frauenbund Deutschlands (DFD), 33, 37
de-Nazification, 32–33
Derrida, Jacques, 205, 213
Descartes, René, 42, 194
Dessau, Paul, 91, 160
de-Stalinization, 64, 91, 110, 253 n.41; and Khrushchev, 28, 37, 67
Destruction of Reason (Lukács), 53, 174, 199
Deutscher, Isaac, 20
Deutscher Fernsehfunk, 37
Deutsche Zeitschrift für Philosophie, 60, 64, 196
DFD. *See* Demokratischer Frauenbund Deutschlands
Dialectic of the Enlightenment (Horkheimer and Adorno), 48, 179, 188, 212
Dialectics of Nature (Engels), 19, 64, 66, 67
Dialektik ohne Dogma (Havemann), 60, 64, 67, 83
Diamat (Havemann), 19
didactic theater, 109, 110–21, 160–61, 257 n.5, 257 n.9
Dilthey, Wilhelm, 174
Dimitroff theory, 156, 174
discourse, 14–17, 24, 245 n.39
'Discourse of Language' (Foucault), 13
dissent: criteria for assessment of, 63, 252 n.19; literary, 16, 22–24, 224–29
'Dissent and Political Change' (Shtromas), 252 n.19
dissident writers, 4, 10, 39–40, 229; founda-

tional narrative rewritten by, 18–20; generational differences in, 10–11, 20–21, 225, 227, 229, 236, 239–40, 244–45 n.20 (*see also* Prenzlauer Berg poets); notoriety in the West of, 8, 251 n.11; politics of, 17, 20, 42–43; publication of, 60, 251 n.11; and reform, 10, 24, 34; relationship to power of, 11–12, 13, 17, 18, 20, 30–31, 42, 43, 51, 52, 70, 219–20, 225–29, 236, 238, 241–42; sanctions against, 51, 60; status quo legitimized by, 24, 231, 241–42
Distant Lover (Hein), 55
Divided Heaven (Wolf), 39, 92, 249 n.27
Djuba, Iwan, 61
Döring, Stefan, 239
Drums in the Night (Brecht), 93, 163, 261 n.10
DSV. *See* German Writers Union
Dubček, Alexander, 28
Dubiel, Helmut, 9, 244 n.19, 244–45 n.20
Dutschke, Rudi, 73

Eastern Europe, 9, 47, 103, 227
East Germany (*see also* German Democratic Republic), 5, 6, 59; national culture claimed by, 7, 243–44 n.14; rising standard of living in, 28–29, 247 n.3
Ecce Homo (Nietzsche), 267 n.51
ecology movement, 8, 22, 23, 34, 229
Edward the Second (Brecht), 260–61 n.10
Einstein, Albert, 64, 65, 66
Eisenstein, Sergei Mikhailovich, 101
Eisler, Hanns, 91, 98–99, 161, 178–81
Emmerich, Wolfgang, 18–19
Endler, Adolf, 19, 72, 238
Engels, Friedrich, 58, 77, 170, 174; and Havemann, 19, 64, 66, 67
Enlightenment, 88, 101, 147, 150, 173, 238–39; and cultural policy, 42; and the folk tradition, 170, 172, 176, 177; and Marx, 76, 194; and Nietzsche, 194, 203, 205, 208, 209, 212–13, 214, 217; and rationality, 175; repudiation of, 183; and social oppression, 188; and the *Sonderweg* thesis, 202; viewed by Lukács, 174

Index

Entfesselte Wotan (Toller), 155
Enzensberger, Hans Magnus, 8, 101, 254 n.1
Erb, Elke, 237, 239
'Erfahrungen' (Klatt), 257 n.9
Ernst, Max, 106
Es geht seinen Gang oder Mühen in unserer Ebene (Loest), 38
exile writers, 2, 92, 110, 161, 243 n.6
existentialism, 16, 103, 132
Expressionist movement, 42, 70, 91, 98, 232; and the avant-garde, 106; fairy tales used by, 183; influence on contemporary GDR artists of, 257 n.58; and legitimate socialist heritage, 215; reassessment of, 92, 254–55 n.18; viewed by Harich, 195; viewed by Lukács, 174

'Fahrt nach Stalingrad' (Fühmann), 18, 184, 263 n.40
fairy tales, 186–88, 190–91, 264 n.49; and gender issues, 190–91, 265 n.60; Grimms', 167, 168–69, 175, 262 n.6; as political critique, 183–84
Farquhar, George, 261 n.20
fascism, 6, 53, 162, 180, 221; and the aestheticization of politics, 96; and capitalism, 13, 102, 174, 207, 230, 261 n.20; contradictory nature of life under, 31–32; defined, 261 n.20; and the Expressionist movement, 98; and folklore, 173, 186; and gender relations, 103; involvement of average citizens in, 44; Marxist theories of, 163; and Nietzsche, 42, 194, 198, 199, 203–4, 211; search for explanation for, 17, 174; and socialism, 13, 23, 196; and the *Sonderweg* thesis, 201–2, 216; struggle against, 4, 13, 16, 17, 42, 99, 102, 110, 178 (*see also* anti-fascism)
Fatzer (Brecht), 162, 163
Faust and the City (Lunacharsky), 205–6
FDGB. *See* Freier deutscher Gewerkschaftsbund
FDJ. *See* Freie deutsche Jugend
Federal Republic of West Germany, 18, 42,

59; cultural politics in, 5, 9, 244 n.15; interest in GDR literature in, 8–9, 243–44 n.14; national culture claimed by, 7, 63, 177, 243–44 n.14; standard of living in, 29, 247 n.3
Feher, Ferenc, 62
feminist movement, 8, 23, 34, 54, 229
Feststellung (Baierl), 116–19, 123
Feuerbach, Ludwig Andreas, 193, 194
Fiebach, Joachim, 158–59
Fiedler, Leslie, 254 n.1
Fischer, Ernst, 68
Five-Year Plan, 88, 111, 167–68
Flores, John, 184
folklore (*see also* fairy tales), 167, 169–71, 172, 173, 175–77, 182–84; and official cultural policy, 185
folk song movement, 170, 177, 178, 181, 182
formalism (*see also* avant-garde), 87, 89–90, 95, 120, 177–78; and Brecht, 91, 97, 132
Forum, 72, 79, 80
Foucault, Michel, 22, 205, 213, 240; and discourse, 13, 14, 15, 18–19, 229, 239, 245 n.39, 246 n.44
France Press, 246–47 n.1
Frankfurter Allgemeine Zeitung, 3
Frankfurt School, 48, 212, 217, 226
Franz Kafka: Werk und Entwurf (Richter), 254–55 n.18
Frau Flinz (Baierl), 122–23
Frederick the Great, 53, 197, 215, 233
freedom of speech, 23, 47, 228, 229, 238; and dissident writers, 11, 17, 52; and the Nietzsche debates, 195, 197; in the Soviet Union, 6, 243 n.10
Freie deutsche Jugend (FDJ), 33, 37, 55
Freier deutscher Gewerkschaftsbund (FDGB), 33, 37
French Revolution, 129, 171
Freud, Sigmund, 45, 193, 215, 237, 249 n.30
'Friedrich Nietzsche in the GDR,' (Sweet), 250 n.45
Fuchs, Jürgen, 51, 82, 92, 223, 227–28

293

Fühmann, Franz, 8, 12, 18, 28, 253 n.41; aesthetic models provided by, 71; Biermann's expulsion protested by, 246–47 n.1; fairy tales used by, 184–86; and Freud, 45, 249 n.30; relationship to the state of, 230; and socialism, 228
Funke, Christoph, 151, 157
'Für unser Land,' 2
Futurism, 10, 95–96, 195; and Lenin and Trotsky, 87, 90, 254 n.3

Garbe, Hans, 110, 112
gay movement, 17, 34, 229
GDR. *See* German Democratic Republic
'Genesis and Adventures' (Anderson), 265 n.60
German Classicism, 102, 183, 193, 203; and the Kulturpolitik, 42, 63, 91, 173
German Democratic Republic (GDR) (*see also* East Germany), 12, 29, 49–50, 201–2, 216; constitutional rights in, 32, 37; cultural legitimation in, 61–62; foundational narratives of, 16–19, 202, 245 n.39, 245 n.42, 245–46 n.43; official public communication in, 43, 248 n.26
Germania Tod in Berlin (Müller), 18, 94, 102, 103, 145
German Romanticism, 42
German Writers Union, 36
Germany (*see also* East Germany; Federal Republic of West Germany; German Democratic Republic), 16; cultural unity in, 7–8, 243–44 n.14, 244 n.15
Gesamtwerk Stalin (Groys), 255–56 n.36
Gesellschaft-Literatur-Lesen, 45
Gesellschaft und Demokratie in Deutschland (Dahrendorf), 31
Gladkov, Feodor, 139, 140–41, 142–43, 144
Goebbels, Joseph, 103
Goethe, Johann Wolfgang von, 42, 75, 171, 173, 261 n.20
Goldfarb, Jeffrey, 251 n.7
' "Good New" and "Bad New" ' (Hermand), 254 n.8
Good Woman of Sezuan (Brecht), 93, 103, 160

Gorbachev, Mikhail, 29, 223, 252 n.19
Göttinger Seven, 171
Graf, Carl Maria, 183
Gramsci, Antonio, 20, 226
Grass, Günter, 8, 243–44 n.14
Greiner, Ulrich, 4, 9, 22, 248 n.23, 257 n.6
Grimm, Reinhold, 131
Grimms, Jakob and Wilhelm (*see also* fairy tales, Grimms'), 168, 171–73, 262 n.14
Gropius, Walter, 91
Grunenberg, Antonia, 246 n.58
Guns of Carrar (Brecht), 151
Günther, Hans, 194
Gysi, Gregor, 243 n.1

Habermas, Jürgen, 14, 34, 76, 237; on the bourgeois public sphere, 46–47, 48; on the Stasi, 219, 220–21
Hacks, Peter, 110, 119, 120, 122, 125; and agitprop theater, 91–92, 160; call for a postrevolutionary dramaturgy by, 161; and the fairy tale, 264 n.49; and Müller, 232; official aesthetic doctrine challenged by, 225–26
Hagen-Stahl, Müller, 111–12, 114
Hager, Jurt, 5
Hamletmachine (Müller), 103, 145, 146, 233
Hans Garbe erzählt (Rülicke), 112
Harich, Wolfgang, 5, 60, 61, 82–83; Nietzsche viewed by, 193–95, 196, 197, 210, 214, 217
Hartmann, Eduard von, 198
Havel, Václav, 10, 227, 247 n.8
Havemann, Robert, 57, 60, 61, 100; Einstein defended by, 19, 64–66; and Engels's *Dialectics of Nature*, 64, 66, 67; incarceration by the Nazis of, 63, 245 n.42, 253 n.34; resistance by, 63–64; and socialism, 64, 69, 82–83, 227–28
Heartfield, John, 91, 256 n.49
Hecht, Werner, 109
Hegel, Georg Wilhelm Friedrich, 66, 68, 76, 103, 194, 213; and cultural policy, 20, 42, 46, 174; and Lukács, 69, 174; and the Nazis, 216; and rationalism, 174, 198, 209; and reevaluation of, 60

Index

Heidegger, Martin, 42, 204
'Heimat der Dissidenten' (Kolbe), 227
Hein, Christoph, 3–4, 155, 243 n.1, 249–50 n.40, 254 n.8; censorship condemned by, 55–56, 250 n.50; relationship with power of, 238; reputation of, 8, 42–43, 55; and socialism, 1, 238; and Surrealism, 128; viewed by Prenzlauer Berg poets, 20
Heise, Wolfgang, 61, 68–69, 124, 253 n.34
Hellpach, Willy, 207
Helmecke, Monika, 190
Herakles (Müller), 94
Herder, Johann Gottfried von, 172
Heritage of Our Times (Bloch), 207
Hermlin, Stephan, 13, 42–43, 71, 230; protest by, 196, 246–47 n.1
Hermsdorf, Klaus, 68, 254–55 n.18
Hesse, Hermann, 215
Heym, Stefan, 3–4, 5, 43, 58, 243 n.1; Biermann's expulsion protested by, 246–47 n.1; and the fairy tale, 264 n.49; relationship with power of, 61, 237, 238; reputation of, 8, 42, 55; and socialism, 2, 60, 227–28
Hineingeboren (Kolbe), 245 n.21
Hinze-Kunze-Roman (Braun), 55
Hitler, Adolf, 31, 201, 202, 244–45 n.20, 260 n.33; and fascism, 17, 44, 99, 173; in Müller's *Germania*, 103; and Nietzsche, 199, 203; studied in Brecht's *Roundheads*, 156
Hoernle, Edwin, 183
Hoffmann, E. T. A., 187
Hofmannsthal, Hugo von, 20
Hofmeister (Lenz), 261 n.20
Hohendahl, Peter, 187–88, 256–57 n.56
Holländerbraut (Strittmatter), 122
Holz, Hans Heinz, 214
Honecker, Erich, 27, 28, 29, 51, 92, 223; incarceration by the Nazis of, 245 n.42, 253 n.34
Horkheimer, Max, 48, 179, 188
Hörnigk, Frank, 126, 150
Howe, Irving, 254 n.1
Huchel, Peter, 39, 71, 225–26

humanism, 18, 203, 210
Hungary, 6, 29, 33, 62, 111

Illes, Laszlo, 105
imperialism, 199, 202, 203, 208
In diesem besseren Land (Endler and Michel), 72
individualism, 103, 201, 205
industrialization, 33, 77, 88, 173, 201, 203
industry: and civil rights, 29–30, 247 n.6
intellectuals. *See* intelligentsia
intelligentsia, 60, 64, 111, 254 n.13; and the Biermann expulsion, 27, 28, 30, 51, 246–47 n.1; contribution to reform of, 2–3, 5; criticism of, 2, 3–4, 5, 24; and cultural identity, 7–8, 63; and democratic socialism, 1–2, 3, 20; and dialogue, 233–34; dissent among, 57, 58, 61, 62, 251 n.12; political positions of, 3–4, 11–12; and the public sphere, 58–63; relationship to power of, 2, 3, 4, 5, 23–24, 219, 221; repression and mourning by, 9, 244–45 n.20; role of, 4, 22, 23–24, 30–31, 52, 53
intertextuality, 14, 19
In the Jungle of the Cities (Brecht), 158, 163, 260–61 n.10
irrationalism, 104, 175, 202, 207; and Nietzsche, 16, 42, 173–74, 198, 201, 203, 208, 215

Jacobeit, Wolfgang, 176
Jahn, Turnvater, 172
Jena group, 251 n.11
Jews, 17, 199
Johst, Hanns, 98
Joyce, James, 19, 88, 215
Jung, Franz, 91
Junge Kunst (Bahro), 78
Jünger, Ernst, 204, 232
Just (Camus), 129, 130

Kafka, Franz, 70, 88, 128, 189, 232; and alienation under socialism, 67; and legitimate socialist heritage, 215; reassessment of, 92, 254–55 n.18
Kafka Conference, 67, 68

Kafka debates, 43, 70, 92
Kafka: Weltbild und Roman (Hermsdorf), 254–55 n.18
Kähler, Hermann, 121
Kaiser, Georg, 232
'Kampf gegen den Formalismus in Kunst und Literatur,' 90, 177
Kant, Hermann, 43
Kant, Immanuel, 5, 8, 18, 39, 42, 174, 201; and the progressive tradition, 42
Kapital und Presse (Mehring), 200
Karasek, Hellmut, 151
'*Katzgraben*-Notes' (Brecht), 110
Katzgraben (Strittmatter), 110
Kaufmann, Hans, 40
Kein Ort. Nirgends (Wolf), 249 n.28
Keller, Herbert, 118
Kennedy, John F., 6
Khrushchev, Nikita, 28, 37, 67
Kierkegaard, Søren, 174
Kinderlieder (Brecht), 181, 182, 263 n.38
Kinder- und Hausmärchen (Grimms), 167, 168
Kindheitsmuster (Wolf), 18
Kipper (Braun), 125
Kipper Paul Bauch (Braun), 122, 125
Kirsch, Rainer, 71, 92, 264 n.49
Kirsch, Sarah, 19, 51, 71, 74, 92; Biermann's expulsion protested by, 246–47 n.1; and the fairy tale, 264 n.49
Klages, Ludwig, 204
Klatt, Gudrun, 118, 256 n.49, 257 n.9
Kleist, Heinrich von, 187, 215
Kliche, Dieter, 249 n.36
Kohlhasse, Wolfgang, 13
Kolbe, Uwe, 21, 227–29, 245 n.21
Kommunistische Partei Deutschlands (KPD), 63, 111, 173, 258–59 n.5
König, Hartmut, 55
Königsdorf, Helga, 3–4, 8, 54
Kosik, Karel, 68
KPD. *See* Kommunistische Partei Deutschlands
Krieg ohne Schlacht: Leben in zwei Diktaturen (Müller), 230

Kuba. *See* Barthel, Kurt
Kulturnation, 243–44 n.14
Kulturpolitik, 4, 41, 89, 91, 195, 196; call for more creative and agitational, 111–12; and censorship, 16; and folklore, 169, 173, 174; literature in, 104; and Nietzsche, 214, 215, 216; shift in conception of, 53–55
Kunert, Christian, 51
Kunert, Günter, 44, 51, 71, 74, 92; alienation in poetry of, 72; on antifascism, 11–12; criticism of, 80; and the fairy tale, 264 n.49; and poetic double entendre, 73; protest by, 225–26, 230, 246–47 n.1
Künstlerische Avantgarde, 105, 257 n.57
'Kunst und Öffentlichkeit in der sozialistischen Gesellschaft' (Weimann), 47–48
Kunze, Reiner, 51, 71
Kurella, Alfred, 5

LaCapra, Dominick, 15
laissez-faire liberalism, 48, 49
Landwirtschaftliche Produktionsgenossenshaft (LPG), 117, 118
Lang, Alexander, 155–58, 162, 163, 261 n.18, 261 n.21
Lange, Hartmut, 122
language, 44, 176; and power, 15, 24, 225, 226, 238, 242; and transformation of social order, 14, 15, 22–23, 237–38, 241
Lask, Berta, 91–92
Leben und Abenteuer der Troubadora Beatrix (Morgner), 189
Le Bon, Gustav, 206
LEF. *See* Left Front of Literature
Left Front of Literature (LEF), 88, 95, 97, 255 n.31
Left Futurists, 88
Lehmann, Günter, 45, 249 n.36
Lehmann, Hans-Thies, 147
Lehnert, Herbert, 234
Lehrstück, 118, 131, 257 n.5; and Brecht, 110, 116, 117, 150, 160, 161, 162; and Müller, 114, 115, 116, 120, 129, 133, 137, 146, 150
Leibniz, Gottfried Wilhelm, 193, 194

Lenin, V. F., 61, 80, 90, 174, 200; aesthetics of, 95–96; classical bourgeois culture emphasized by, 87–88, 254 n.3; and Nietzsche, 194, 205; and the Party, 34, 137; and the public sphere, 34, 36, 50, 58, 59; and sectarianism, 120
Leninism, 48–49, 101, 136, 137, 138
Leninist-Stalinist party, 129
Lenz, Heinrich F. E., 261 n.20
Lenzer, Rosemarie, 249 n.36
Leonhard, Wolfgang, 60–61
Lessing, Gotthold Ephraim, 42
Lessing Sleep's Dream Scream (Müller), 145
Letter to Lord Chandos (von Hofmannsthal), 20
Life of Galileo (Brecht), 93, 160
Life of Gundling (Müller), 145
Lindau, Paul, 200
literary sphere, 34, 52, 69, 70; and audience, 39, 44, 45; and authenticity, 44, 249 n.28; debates in, 43–44, 249 n.27; and legitimation, 35–37; and pluralism, 30, 54, 247 n.8; and the public sphere, 42, 44–46, 50, 54, 56; resistance to ideological positions of, 69–70; and a semiotics of culture, 14–15; state and Party control of, 35–39; status of, 42–43
literature. *See* literary sphere
Loest, Erich, 51
Lohndrücker (Müller), 93, 112–15, 116, 120–21, 136
LPG. *See* Landwirtschaftliche Produktionsgenossenshaft
Lukács, Georg, 37, 88, 110, 174, 184, 208, 226; and aesthetics, 69, 89, 105; and the avant-garde, 180; on bourgeois art, 98–99; and Brecht, 43, 93, 94; Classicism and socialist realism linked by, 173; culture divided into rational and irrational by, 174–75, 207; and the Expressionist movement, 98; Nietzsche viewed by, 174, 194, 198–99, 211, 265 n.16; and reactionary German thought, 53; Romanticism viewed by, 173–74, 198; social democracy critiqued by, 200; and the *Sonderweg* thesis, 202

Lunacharsky, Anatoly, 205–6, 207
Lusitanian Bogey (Weiss), 145
Luther, Martin, 53, 197, 215, 228–30
Luxemburg, Rosa, 83
Lyotard, Jean, 14, 213, 239
'lyric debates,' 38–39, 43, 80
Lysenko, Trofim Denisovich, 64, 65

Macbeth (Müller), 55, 94, 231
Mach, Ernst, 66
Mäde, Hans Dieter, 114, 115
male fantasies (Theweleit), 103
Malorny, Franz, 199
Malorny, Heinz, 194, 202, 210, 211
managerial revolution, 247 n.6
Mandel, Ernest, 20
Manichaeanism, 53–54
Man Is Man (Brecht), 93, 152, 158, 162
Mann, Thomas, 88, 193, 194, 195, 201
Marat/Sade (Weiss), 146, 147
Marcuse, Herbert, 39, 70, 80, 239, 243 n.10
Marlitt, Eugene, 246 n.58
Marquardt, Fritz, 126
Marski (Lange), 122
Märten, Lu, 214
Martin, Biddy, 189
Marx, Karl, 42, 77, 80, 226; and capitalism, 82, 214; on civil society, 46, 47; and Nietzsche, 205, 206, 213–14, 216, 217, 266 n.34; and the proletariat, 48–49; and the public sphere, 46, 58–59; and rationalism, 194, 198
Marxism, 3, 20, 54, 62, 67, 69; and aesthetics, 89; and the avant-garde, 105; critique of, 217; dialectics of, 62, 63, 67, 123, 175; failures of, 9, 104, 214; and the fairy tale, 185; and fascism, 12, 163; and the folk tradition, 170, 172, 182, 185; historiography of, 101, 102, 123, 188; and literature, 14, 39; and Nietzsche, 193, 194, 205, 206, 208, 209, 210, 212, 213–14, 266 n.34; and production, 98, 100; and rationality, 174, 175; and science, 19–20, 66, 70, 76; Soviet, 77, 78, 100

Marxist-Leninism, 53, 69, 72, 77, 159; discourse of, 15, 16; and fairy tales, 186, 190, 191; historiography of, 41, 177; and literary dissidence, 16, 39, 44, 60, 225; and Nietzsche, 215; and production aesthetics, 97, 100; and the public sphere, 47; and science, 64–65; and the state, 32, 92

'Marx und/oder Nietzsche' (Bathrick), 266 n.34

'master plot,' 245–46 n.43

Masur, Kurt, 247 n.8

Maurer, Georg, 71

Mauser (Müller), 133–39, 140, 144, 149–50; in *Cement*, 142, 259 n.18; the intellectual and violence in, 129, 146

Mayakovsky, Vladimir, 87, 88, 95, 101, 181, 254 n.3

Mayer, Hans, 39, 110, 179, 243–44 n.14

Measures Taken (Brecht), 130–33, 143, 146, 147, 148–49; rewritten by Müller, 129, 131, 133, 134, 135, 136, 137, 139, 140, 150

Mechanismen der Herrschaftssicherung (Ludz), 248 n.26

mechanists, 65, 101

media, 37, 105; Western, 29, 34, 61, 177, 248 n.14

media theory, 48

Medvedev, Roy, 61

Mehring, Franz, 170, 174, 208, 254 n.2; and Nietzsche, 194, 197–98, 199, 200

Menschen an unserer (Claudius), 112

Meyerhold, V. E., 91, 101

Michnik, Adam, 10

Mickel, Karl, 19, 71, 72, 74, 92

Middell, Eike, 211–12

Midsummer Night's Dream (Shakespeare), 155

Ministry of Culture, 35, 37, 38, 55, 56

Mitscherlich, Alexander and Margarethe, 244–45 n.20

Mittenzwei, Werner, 68, 254–55 n.18, 257 n.5; and the move away from Brecht, 105, 151, 161

modernism (*see also* avant-garde), 91, 106, 152, 254 n.8; aesthetics of, 99, 109; and Brecht, 159–60; cultural impact of, 18, 22, 42, 89, 104; cultural policy regarding, 90–92, 94; defined, 89, 254 n.8; and the political status quo, 19, 70; and production aesthetics, 98, 99, 127; and the universalizing of art, 255–56 n.36; viewed by Marxism and socialists, 87, 88, 92, 104

modernity, 173, 178; and fascism, 31, 201, 202; and Nietzsche, 200, 212

modernization, 22, 31, 72, 175, 220; and agricultural reform, 33; and alienation, 173; and folklore, 177; overcoming fascism through, 178; and the Romantic consciousness, 188; and social discontent, 29, 247 n.4

Monat, 167

Morgner, Irmtraud, 8, 42–43, 54, 188–89, 226

Moritz, Karl Philip, 172

Moritz Tassow (Hacks), 122, 125

Moscow Show Trials, 143, 234

Mosse, George, 173

Mother (Brecht), 91, 160

Mother Courage and Her Children (Brecht), 91, 93, 122, 160, 181–82

Müller, Adam von, 172

Müller, Heiner, 5, 74, 110, 112, 243 n.1; and aesthetics, 101–2, 120, 231–32; and agit-prop, 111–12, 114, 160; and agrodrama, 123–24; and audience, 113–14, 115–16, 124–25, 127; and the avant-garde, 55, 91, 111–12, 160, 254 n.8; and Brecht, 93, 94–95, 100, 101–2, 103, 107, 140, 151, 161–63, 230; Brecht rewritten by, 129, 131, 133, 142–43, 144; on *Cement*, 259 n.13; compared to Bahro, 58; criticism of, 3–4, 20, 43, 103, 120, and history, 18, 102–4, 137–38, 150; industrial plays of, 119, 125–26; and the *Lehrstück*, 116, 162; protest by, 60, 225–26, 246–47 n.1; relationship to the state of, 2, 11, 61, 229–34, 236, 237; reputation of, 8, 42; revolution plays of, 129, 130, 133; sanctions against, 93–94; and socialism, 117, 227–28, 238; and the Stasi, 22, 219, 223, 224, 233; and Surrealism, 128

Index

Müller, Inge, 115, 120
music, 178, 179–80, 182
Mussolini, Benito, 203
'myth of monosemia,' 16

Nachdenken über Christa T (Quest for Christa T) (Wolf), 50, 92, 244 n.17
Naked among Wolves (Apitz), 39
National Front, 247–48 n.9
nationalism, 62, 91, 199, 201; and the folk tradition, 171, 172, 175, 176
nationalization, 53
naturalism (*see also* avant-garde), 87, 101, 232, 254 n.2
Nazis, 17, 184, 216, 245 n.42
Nazism, 12–13, 30, 31–32, 202
Neo-Marxism, 212, 213
neorappism (*see also* proletkult), 97
Neue Deutsche Literatur, 38, 115
Neue Sachlichkeit, 91, 106, 215
Neues Deutschland, 38, 60, 65, 246–47 n.1
Neues ökonomisches System (NÖS), 29, 64, 139
Neumann, Gert, 238, 240–41
Neumann, Manfred, 249 n.36
Neutsch, Erik, 39, 74, 126
Nietzsche, Friedrich, 151, 153, 267 n.51; and bourgeois culture, 210–11, 212; and capitalism, 197–98, 199, 200, 203, 208, 214; and cultural identity, 193–95, 197, 201, 204–5, 210, 246 n.44; and Enlightenment thought, 194, 203, 205, 208, 209, 212–13, 214–17; and fascism, 42, 194, 198, 199, 203–4, 211; and irrationalism, 16, 42, 173–74, 198, 201, 203, 208, 215; politics of, 199–200; and the politics of identity, 209–17; and the public sphere, 195–97; reception within German socialism of, 197–200, 201, 203, 205–7; renaissance of, in the Federal Republic, 53, 204, 210, 213–14, 215; and the *Sonderweg* thesis, 201, 202, 203, 204, 216; viewed by Lukács, 174, 194, 198–99, 211, 265 n.16
Nitschke, Karl-Heinz, 251 n.9
Noll, Dieter, 18

NÖS. *See* Neues ökonomisches System
novel, 19, 22, 187, 245–46 n.43

October Revolution (1989), 1, 56, 61, 76, 112; and the avant-garde, 87, 90
Odujev, S. F., 199
Oedipus Tyrann (Müller), 94
'Öffentlich arbeiten' (Hein), 249–50 n.40
'Once More an Inability to Mourn' (Jay), 244–45 n.20
On Cultural Freedom (Goldfarb), 251 n.7
'On the German Cultural Nation' (de Bruyn), 7
Opitz, Detlev, 222
Opoyaz group, 95
opposition. *See* dissent
Opposition in the GDR (Woods), 251 n.12
Optimistic Tragedy (Vishnevsky), 129, 130
'Other Language: New GDR Literature of the 1980s' (Arnold), 246 n.53

Pannach, Gerulf, 51
Paris Commune, 59
'Pathétique' (Bahro), 79
Patrioten (Uhse), 18
Patterns of Childhood (Wolf), 41, 44
Paul, Jean, 187
peace movement, 8, 23, 34, 229, 251 n.10
Pepperle, Heinz, 194
perestroika, 29–30
Phenomenology of the Spirit (Hegel), 76
Philoktet (Müller), 94
Pietsch, Reinhardt, 176
Pinthus, Kurt, 254–55 n.18
Piscator, Erwin, 92, 111
Plekhanov, 89, 120, 205
Plenzdorf, Ulrich, 8
Plessner, Helmut, 202
poetry, 70–76
Poland, 6, 28, 33, 62, 111
Polish revolt (1956), 6
Pollatschek, Walther, 168
postmodernism, 212, 213, 222, 254 n.1
poststructuralism, 20, 212, 213, 239
Prague trials, 143

Praxis group, 68
Prenzlauer Berg poets, 219, 222, 246 n.53; and language, 20–21, 225, 237–41; older generation of dissident writers viewed by, 52, 227–28, 236–37, 239
Prenzlauer Connection, 21
Prinzip Hoffnung (Bloch), 185
'Problem Avantgarde' (Schlenstedt), 256 n.51
'Proletarisch-revolutionäres Erbe als Angebot' (Klatt), 256 n.49
Proletkult, 88, 101, 181, 205, 206, 255 n.31; and cultural policy, 97; and Müller, 94; and production, 100
Prometheus (Müller), 94
Protestant Church. *See* church
protofascism. *See* Expressionist movement
Prüfung (Bredel), 18
psychoanalytical literature, 45, 249 n.30
public sphere, 34; after the Biermann expulsion, 50–56; bourgeois, 46–47, 48; and dissent, 58–63, 82–83, 196, 240; official, 31–35; proletarian, 112, 257 n.6; socialist, 30, 45–50, 249–50 n.40; and socialist theater, 109, 110, 112
Pushkin, Alexander, 87

Raddatz, Fritz, 243–44 n.14
RAPP. *See* Russian Association of Proletarian Writers
Rathenow, Lutz, 222
rationalism, 174, 208
Realism, 19
reception theory, 45, 127, 249 n.36
Recruiting Officer (Farquhar), 261 n.20
Red Army, 13
Reed, John, 112
Reich-Ranicki, Marcel, 8, 244 n.17
Reimann, Brigitte, 54
Reinhold, Otto, 216
'repressive tolerance,' 243 n.10
Reschke, Renate, 210–11, 212, 213–14
Rettung (Walther and Wolter), 264 n.49
revisionism, 63, 64
Revue Roter Rummel (Piscator), 111

Richter, Hans Werner, 8
Richter, Helmut, 68, 254–55 n.18
Richter, Stefan, 196
'Richtung der Märchen' (Fühmann), 184–85
Rise and Fall of the Town Mahagonny (Brecht), 158
Rodchenko, Alexander, 95
Rohrmoser, Günther, 213
Romanticism, 16, 184, 202, 207, 215; and folklore, 169, 171, 173, 187; and Nietzsche, 16, 201; and official cultural policy, 185; reevaluation of, 187–88; viewed by Lukács, 173–74, 198
Rosenberg, Alfred, 199, 203
'Rotkäppchen und der Klassenkampf' (Brandt), 167
Rotwelsch (Müller), 260 n.33
Roundheads and Peakedheads (Brecht), 154, 156, 163, 261 n.18, 261 n.20
Rülicke, Käthe, 112
Russian Association of Proletarian Writers (RAPP), 255 n.31

SA. *See* Sturm Abteilung
Sailors of Cattaro (Wolf), 129, 130
Sakharov, Andrei, 7, 30, 60–61
Samizdat, 59, 61, 251 n.7
Sartre, Jean-Paul, 39, 226
Schabowski, Günter, 243 n.1
Schädlich, Hans Joachim, 51, 223
Schaff, Adam, 68
Schall, Eckehard, 246–47 n.1
Schedlinski, Reiner, 238–39, 248 n.14; and the Stasi, 21–22, 219, 222–23, 224, 237
Schelling, Frederick Wilhelm Joseph von, 16, 174, 198, 202
schematism, 110, 111
Schieff, Klaus, 153
Schiller, Johann Christoph Friedrich von, 42, 173, 254 n.2
Schirrmacher, Frank, 4, 9, 22
Schiwelbusch, Wolfgang, 120
Schlenstedt, Dieter, 249 n.36, 256 n.51
Schlesinger, Klaus, 51

Schmitt, Carl, 232
Schneider, Peter, 3
Schneider, Rolf, 8, 246–47 n.1
Schnitzler, Arthur, 264 n.49
Schönberg, Arnold, 179
Schopenhauer, Arthur, 42, 174, 193, 197, 198
Schorlemmer, Pastor Friedrich, 243 n.1
Schreyer, Wolfgang, 39
Schriftstellerverband, 249–50 n.40
Schroth, Christoph, 260–61 n.10
Schubert, Helga, 54
Schulz, Genia, 259 n.18
Schumacher, Ernst, 68, 259 n.18
Schütz, Helga, 264 n.49
SED. *See* Socialist Unity Party
Seghers, Anna, 18, 37, 110, 145, 214; and the fairy tale, 264 n.49
'Sendung' (Morgner), 188–89
Seventh Cross (Seghers), 18
Shakespeare, William, 124, 155, 261 n.20
Shklovsky, Viktor, 95, 97
sickle movement, 157
Siebert, Hans, 168, 262 n.6
Sinn und Form, 38, 39, 179, 180, 194
Sinyavsky, Andrey, 59
social Darwinism, 174, 203
Social Democratic Party, 61, 197, 200, 205
socialism, 14, 16, 31, 104, 133; and alienation, 55, 67–70, 72; and the avant-garde, 87, 98, 100, 105–7, 180, 256 n.49 n.51, 256–57 n.56, 257 n.57; contradictions under, 189; and dissent, 49, 227; and fascism, 13, 23, 196; fetishism under, 137, 138; in the GDR, 20, 28, 67, 202, 216, 254–55 n.18; and historical materialism, 76; and human rights, 196; inadequacies of, 9; and the individual, 188; leadership in, 149; and the past, 13, 42; and the public sphere, 30, 45–50, 249–50 n.40
socialist-communist movement, 12
socialist realism, 54, 122, 173, 232; and the aesthetics of production, 97, 99; and artistic endeavor, 16, 111; and the avant-garde, 255–56 n.36; and Brecht, 150, 160; and culture, 42, 69, 169; and literature,

88, 141, 246 n.58; theater of, 92, 101, 112, 127
Socialist Unity Party (SED), 17, 41, 93, 111, 137; and the avant-garde, 106; and the Biermann expulsion, 27, 28, 246–47 n.1; and the breakdown of bourgeois culture, 39; Central Committee of, 35, 36, 90, 120; culture controlled by, 35–36, 39, 42, 51, 61–63, 90, 170, 173, 224; dissent within, 6, 57, 243 n.1, 251 n.7; and the intelligentsia, 3, 110–12, 112; and production aesthetics, 101; and public life, 31, 32–33, 34, 48, 49, 50; and real democracy, 32, 247–48 n.9; social contract with citizens held by, 29, 247 n.4; and theater, 120, 124; and Western influence, 177–78; and writers, 71, 120, 225, 240
Sodaro, 251 n.13
Söhne (Bredel), 18
Solidarnösc, 28
Solter, Friedo, 154–55, 157, 159; Brecht's *Baal* directed by, 152, 153, 155, 158, 162, 163, 260–61 n.10, 260–61 n.10
Solzhenitsyn, Alexander, 60, 61
Sonderweg [special path], 201, 216
Sorgen und die Macht (Hacks), 119, 120–21
Soviet Novel: History as Ritual (Clark), 141
Soviet Union, 13, 58, 150, 178, 184; anti-Einsteinian science in, 19; cultural policy in, 89; democracy in, 7, 30; dissidence in, 6, 59–61, 227, 251 n.7; folklore studied in, 175; founding years of, 65; modern technology in, 29; and Nietzsche, 205; organization of social life in, 49; public sphere in, 31, 59, 251 n.7; socialism in, 17, 70, 89
Sozialdemokratische Partei Deutschlands (SPD), 111, 254 n.2
Sozialistische Einheitspartei Deutschlands. *See* Socialist Unity Party
Spengler, Oswald, 174, 204
Der Spiegel, 11, 151, 220
Spur der Steine (Neutsch), 39, 74–76, 126
Stalin, Joseph, 65, 71, 101, 150, 260 n.33; and writers and artists, 40, 100

Stalinism, 1, 23, 82, 221, 227, 234; and
Brecht, 132; and fascism, 6, 11; in the
GDR, 13, 193, 228; and Harich, 193, 196,
197; and Havemann, 66, 67; Marxist cri-
tiques of, 76; and Müller, 139, 143, 149;
and the Soviet avant-garde, 255–56 n.36
Stalinization, 99, 180
Stasi, 52, 220–21, 241; and the writers, 3–4,
22, 219, 221, 224–25, 229, 230, 233, 267 n.1;
and the Prenzlauer Berg poets, 239, 240
State and Revolution (Lenin), 59
Steinberg, Werner, 39
Steinitz, Wolfgang, 170, 177
Steinweg, Reiner, 131–32
Stern, Leo, 175
Stern, Victor, 64, 66
Stone, I. F., 7
Storm (Bill-Bjelozerkowski), 112
'Story of Mother Courage' (Brecht), 181
Strassburg, Gottfried von, 170
Strelch (Fühmann), 186
Strittmatter, Erwin, 110, 122
*Structural Transformation of the Public
Sphere* (Habermas), 46–47, 48
'Struggle against Formalism in Art and Lit-
erature,' 177
Sturm Abteilung (SA, Storm Troopers), 116
Sturm und Drang movements, 170–71
Surrealism, 96, 106, 128, 146, 189, 257 n.57;
and cultural policy, 90, 91, 215; influence
on contemporary GDR artists of, 257 n.58
Surrealismus in Paris (Barck), 257 n.57
Sweet, Denis, 203, 250 n.45

Tangospieler (Hein), 55
Tarnkappe (Schnitzler and Wolter),
264 n.49
Tassow, Mortiz, 123
Taylorism, 101
Teraoka, Arlene, 149
Tetzner, Gerti, 54
theater, 111, 117, 152, 158–59; comedic, 156;
epic, 122
Theater der Zeit, 260 n.9, 261 n.18
Theater in der Zeitenwende (Mittenzwei),
121, 257 n.5

Theater of the Absurd, 128
'Theorie und Praxis des Erbens' (Hohen-
dahl), 256–57 n.56
Theory of the Avant-Garde (Bürger), 254 n.1
Theweleit, Klaus, 103
Third Reich, 2, 12, 16, 63, 225; and folklore,
171, 176; and irrationalism, 174; and na-
tionalism, 62; and Nietzsche, 204; and
the public sphere, 31–32, 34
Threepenny Opera (Brecht), 93, 151, 158
Thulin, Michael, 20, 240
Tieck, Ludwig, 187
Toller, Ernst, 155
Tolstoy, Alexei, 69
Tolstoy, Leo, 88
Totale Mensch (Braun), 125
Toten bleiben jung (Seghers), 18
tractor poems, 71
Tragelehn, B. K., 124
Tretyakov, Sergey, 90, 91, 95, 101, 181
Trial of Lukullus (Brecht and Dessau), 160
Tristan (von Strassburg), 170
Trotsky, Leon, 87, 88, 200, 254 n.3
Trotz alledem (Piscator), 111
True Story of Ah Q (Hein), 155

Uhse, Bodo, 18
Ulbricht, Walter, 49–50, 64, 90, 91, 187; in
Brecht's *Roundheads*, 156; and cultural
policy regarding Formalism, 89; and Ex-
pressionism, 254–55 n.18; on German
folk songs, 178, 179; poetry written for,
71; and theater, 109, 115, 120, 121
Ulbricht group, 63
Ulrich, Wehler, Hans, 201
Umsiedlerin (Müller), 93, 94, 123–24, 232
'Unclaimed Heritage' (Rabinbach) 266 n.37
unification, 1–2, 62, 63, 177, 230
United Nations, 251 n.9
Urfaust (Goethe), 261 n.20
USSR. *See* Soviet Union

'value formation,' 50
Väter (Bredel), 18

VBK. *See* Verband bildender Künstler

Verband bildender Künstler (VBK), 1

Vergangenheit als Zukunft (Habermas), 219

Verhör des Lukullus (Dessau), 91

Vierte Zensor (Loest), 38

Vishnevsky, Vsevolod, 129, 130

Volkskammer, 32, 247–48 n.9

'*Volkstümlichkeit und Realismus*' (Brecht), 180

Vom schweren (Claudius), 112

Wagner, Richard, 99, 211, 216

Waiting for Godot (Beckett), 148

Wall. *See* Berlin Wall

Walser, Martin, 8

Was bleibt (Wolf), 3, 219, 234–36

Waschninsky, Peter, 260 n.9

Was sind Märchen? (Siebert), 262 n.6

Weber, Max, 172, 174, 220

Wegner, Bettina, 51

Weigel, Helene, 93, 122

Weimarer Beiträge, 38, 210

Weimann, Robert, 47–50

Weimar Republic, 17, 63, 95, 179, 215; avant-garde of, 91–92, 109, 112, 256 n.49; and the public sphere, 31–32; theater in, 105, 111, 154; writers of, 18, 190

'Weisheit der Märchen' (Fühmann), 184–85

Weiss, Peter, 145, 146, 147

Weltanschauung, 65, 66

West Germany. *See* Federal Republic of West Germany

White, Hayden, 17

'Whose German Literature?' (Herminghouse), 244 n.15

Wille, Bruno, 207

Winkler, Heinrich August, 201, 202

Wittfogel, August, 20

Wolf, Christa, 18, 50, 51, 54, 58; on antifascism, 12; on authenticity, 249 n.28; Biermann's expulsion protested by, 246–47 n.1; criticism of, 3–4, 9, 20, 21, 219, 234, 244 n.17, 248 n.23; and cultural policy, 61, 244 n.15; democratic socialism called for by, 1, 2, 227; dissent by, 1, 60, 224, 226, 243 n.1; and the fairy tale, 264 n.49; and German history, 18, 44; and the language of discourse, 19, 241; reputation of, 8, 39, 42, 55; relation to the system of, 3, 5, 61, 219–20, 229–30, 234–36, 237, 238; and the Romantic consciousness, 187–88; scandals surrounding publications by, 3, 43, 219, 249 n.27; on self-censorship, 40–41, 236; and socialism, 227–28, 238; and the Stasi, 3–4, 22, 219–20, 221, 223–24, 234–35; subjectivist experimentation by, 4, 92

Wolf, Friedrich, 129, 130

Wolf, Gerhard, 224, 239, 246–47 n.1

Wolf, Markus, 243 n.1

Wolff, Christian, 195

Wolter, Christine, 54, 264 n.49

women, 16, 22, 54, 188

women's movement. *See* feminist movement

workers movements, 110, 111, 174, 194, 216

workers' writing movement, 36

Wort, 98

Writers Congresses, 40, 41, 55, 110; and literary culture, 36, 37; and political theater, 109, 114

Yugoslavia, 68

Zarathustra, 205–6, 208

Zehn Tage, die die Welt erschütterten (Müller and Hagen-Stahl), 111–12, 114

Die Zeit, 3, 9, 237

Zeitschrift für Germanistik, 38

Zerreißprobe (Bartsch), 35, 40

Zhdanov, Andrey, 88

Zima, Peter, 16, 19

Zinoviev, Grigori, 143

Zuchhardt, Karl, 39

In the Modern German Culture and Literature series.

Making Bodies, Making History: Feminism and German Identity by Leslie A. Adelson

The Powers of Speech: The Politics of Culture in the GDR by David Bathrick

The Institutions of Art: Essays by Peter Bürger and Christa Bürger translated by Loren Kruger

The Past as Future by Jürgen Habermas, interviewed by Michael Haller, translated and edited by Max Pensky

The Cinema's Third Machine: Writing on Film in Germany, 1906–1933 by Sabine Hake

The Soul of Wit: Joke Theory from Grimm to Freud by Carl Hill

A History of German Literary Criticism, 1730–1980 edited by Peter Uwe Hohendahl

Prismatic Thought: Theodor W. Adorno by Peter Uwe Hohendahl

Bertolt Brecht and the Theory of Media by Roswitha Mueller

Toward a Theory of Radical Origin: Essays on Modern German Thought by John Pizer

Art and Enlightenment: Aesthetic Theory after Adorno by David Roberts